Divided

SERIES IN POLITICAL PSYCHOLOGY

Series Editor
John T. Jost

Editorial Board
Mahzarin Banaji, Gian Vittorio Caprara, Christopher Federico, Don Green, John Hibbing, Jon Krosnick, Arie Kruglanski, Kathleen McGraw, David Sears, Jim Sidanius, Phil Tetlock, Tom Tyler

Image Bite Politics: News and the Visual Framing of Elections
Maria Elizabeth Grabe and Erik Page Bucy

Social and Psychological Bases of Ideology and System Justification
John T. Jost, Aaron C. Kay, and Hulda Thorisdottir

The Political Psychology of Democratic Citizenship
Eugene Borgida, Christopher M. Federico, and John L. Sullivan

On Behalf of Others: The Psychology of Care in a Global World
Sarah Scuzzarello, Catarina Kinnvall, and Kristen R. Monroe

The Obamas and a (Post) Racial America?
Gregory S. Parks and Matthew W. Hughey

Ideology, Psychology, and Law
Jon Hanson and John Jost

The Impacts of Lasting Occupation: Lessons from Israeli Society
Daniel Bar-Tal and Izhak Schnell

Competing Motives in the Partisan Mind
Eric W. Groenendyk

Personalizing Politics and Realizing Democracy
Gian Vittorio Caprara and Michele Vecchione

Representing Red and Blue: How the Culture Wars Change the Way Citizens Speak and Politicians Listen
David C. Barker and Christopher Jan Carman

The Ambivalent Partisan: How Critical Loyalty Promotes Democracy
Howard G. Lavine, Christopher D. Johnston, and Marco R. Steenbergen

Disenchantment with Democracy: A Psychological Perspective
Janusz Reykowski

Divided: Open-Mindedness and Dogmatism in a Polarized World
Edited by Victor Ottati and Chadly Stern

Divided

Open-Mindedness and Dogmatism in a Polarized World

Edited by
Victor Ottati and Chadly Stern

OXFORD
UNIVERSITY PRESS

Oxford University Press is a department of the University of Oxford. It furthers
the University's objective of excellence in research, scholarship, and education
by publishing worldwide. Oxford is a registered trade mark of Oxford University
Press in the UK and certain other countries.

Published in the United States of America by Oxford University Press
198 Madison Avenue, New York, NY 10016, United States of America.

© Oxford University Press 2023

All rights reserved. No part of this publication may be reproduced, stored in
a retrieval system, or transmitted, in any form or by any means, without the
prior permission in writing of Oxford University Press, or as expressly permitted
by law, by license, or under terms agreed with the appropriate reproduction
rights organization. Inquiries concerning reproduction outside the scope of the
above should be sent to the Rights Department, Oxford University Press, at the
address above.

You must not circulate this work in any other form
and you must impose this same condition on any acquirer.

Library of Congress Cataloging-in-Publication Data
Names: Ottati, Victor, editor. | Stern, Chadly, editor.
Title: Divided : open-mindedness and dogmatism in a polarized world /
edited by Victor Ottati and Chadly Stern.
Description: New York, NY : Oxford University Press, [2023] |
Series: Series in political psychology |
Includes bibliographical references and index. |
Identifiers: LCCN 2023006105 (print) | LCCN 2023006106 (ebook) |
ISBN 9780197655467 (hardcover) | ISBN 9780197655481 (epub) |
ISBN 9780197655498
Subjects: LCSH: Dogmatism. | Toleration. | Polarization (Social sciences)
Classification: LCC BF698.35.D64 D58 2023 (print) | LCC BF698.35.D64 (ebook) |
DDC 148—dc23/eng/20230415
LC record available at https://lccn.loc.gov/2023006105
LC ebook record available at https://lccn.loc.gov/2023006106

DOI: 10.1093/oso/9780197655467.001.0001

Printed by Sheridan Books, Inc., United States of America

*We dedicate this book to
Karin T. O'Connell and Nigel Bosch*

Contents

Acknowledgments   *ix*
Contributors   *xi*

I DEFINING AND UNDERSTANDING OPEN-MINDEDNESS, DOGMATISM, AND POLARIZATION

1 Open-Mindedness and Dogmatism in a Polarized World: Core Concepts and Definitions   3
Victor Ottati, Chadly Stern, Whinda Yustisia, and Lori D. Bougher

2 Identity Strength Leads to Out-Group Animus and Polarization   19
Shanto Iyengar and Matthew DeBell

II OPEN- AND CLOSED-MINDED PROCESSING: ATTITUDE FORMATION AND CHANGE

3 Attitudes in a Polarized World: Sociological and Psychological Processes of Reinforcement of Social and Political Worldviews   41
Angelita Repetto and Dolores Albarracín

4 Openness and Persuasion: Multiple Processes, Meanings, and Outcomes   59
Pablo Briñol and Richard E. Petty

III INTELLECTUAL HUMILITY AND OPEN-MINDEDNESS

5 Links Between Intellectual Humility and Open-Mindedness: Does Strength of Belief Matter?   81
Elizabeth J. Krumrei-Mancuso and Everett L. Worthington, Jr.

6 Forms of Intellectual Humility and Their Associations with Features of Knowledge, Beliefs, and Opinions   101
Rick H. Hoyle and Erin K. Davisson

IV NORMATIVE STANDARDS AND OPEN-MINDEDNESS: OPEN-MINDED COGNITION AND ACTIVELY OPEN-MINDED THINKING

7 Situation-Specific Open-Minded Cognition: Scale Validation and Incremental Effects of Person and Situation 123
Victor Ottati, Chase Wilson, Devon Price, Yelyzaveta Distefano, and Fred B. Bryant

8 The Role of Group Context in Open-Minded Cognition 144
Salma Moaz, Kelsey Berryman, Jeremy R. Winget, R. Scott Tindale, and Victor Ottati

9 Actively Open-Minded Thinking and the Political Effects of Its Absence 162
Jonathan Baron, Ozan Isler, and Onurcan Yılmaz

V IDEOLOGY, AUTHORITARIANISM, AND DOGMATISM

10 Persistent Problems with the Conceptualization, Measurement, and Study of "Left-Wing Authoritarianism" 185
Benjamin A. Saunders and John T. Jost

11 New Evidence on an Enduring Question: The Role of Political Ideology and Extremism in Dogmatic Thinking 211
Chadly Stern and Benjamin C. Ruisch

VI DOGMATISM AND OPEN-MINDEDNESS: THE INTERPLAY OF AFFECT, MOTIVATION, AND COGNITION

12 Open-Mindedness and Dogmatism in a Darwinian World: The Roles of Affective Appraisals over Time and Circumstance 233
George E. Marcus

13 Feeling Open- or Closed-Minded: The Role of Affective Feelings in the Closing or Opening of the Mind 253
Akila Raoul and Jeffrey R. Huntsinger

14 Terror Management, Dogmatism, and Open-Mindedness 268
Dylan E. Horner, Alex Sielaff, Sheldon Solomon, and Jeff Greenberg

Index 287

Acknowledgments

We wish to thank Oxford University Press for publishing this book and to express our gratitude to Abby Gross (Head of Acquisitions, Social and Behavioral Sciences) and Nadina Persaud (Editor, Social Psychology & Neuropsychology). We also thank Katharine Pratt (Project Editor, Social and Behavioral Sciences) for her assistance. In addition, we wish to thank Loyola University Chicago and the University of Illinois Urbana-Champaign for providing us with a stimulating academic environment within which to perform our work.

Our ability to take on this project was, in no small part, rooted in invaluable training provided by our academic mentors and teachers. These include Robert S. Wyer, Martin Fishbein, Harry Triandis, Joseph E. McGrath, Tessa West, John Jost, and Yaacov Trope. Lastly, we also wish to acknowledge the exceptional level of guidance and support provided by our family and friends.

Contributors

Dolores Albarracín
Alexandra Heyman Nash University Professor, University of Pennsylvania, Philadelphia, PA, USA

Jonathan Baron
Professor of Psychology, University of Pennsylvania, Philadelphia, PA, USA

Kelsey Berryman
Doctoral Student, Loyola University Chicago, Chicago, IL, USA

Lori D. Bougher
Director of Research, Initiative for Data-Driven Social Science,, Princeton University, Princeton, NJ, USA

Pablo Briñol
Professor of Psychology, Universidad Autónoma de Madrid, Madrid, Spain

Fred B. Bryant
Emeritus Professor of Psychology, Loyola University Chicago, Chicago, IL, USA

Erin K. Davisson
Research Scientist, Duke University, Durham, NC, USA

Matthew DeBell
Senior Research Scholar, Stanford University, Stanford, CA, USA

Yelyzaveta Distefano
Doctoral Student, Loyola University Chicago, Chicago, IL, USA

Jeff Greenberg
Regents Professor, University of Arizona, Tucson, AZ, USA

Dylan E. Horner
Doctoral Candidate, University of Arizona, Tucson, AZ, USA

Rick H. Hoyle
Professor of Psychology and Neuroscience, Duke University, Durham, NC, USA

Jeffrey R. Huntsinger
Associate Professor, Loyola University Chicago, Chicago, IL, USA

Ozan Isler
Research Fellow, University of Queensland, St Lucia, Australia

Shanto Iyengar
Professor of Political Science and Communication, Stanford University, Stanford, CA, USA

John T. Jost
Professor of Psychology and Politics, Co-Director of the Center for Social and Political Behavior, New York University, New York, NY, USA

Elizabeth J. Krumrei-Mancuso
Professor of Psychology, Pepperdine University, Malibu, CA, USA

George E. Marcus
Professor of Political Science, Emeritus, Williams College, Williamstown, MA, USA

Salma Moaz
Doctoral Student, Loyola University Chicago, Chicago, IL, USA

Victor Ottati
Professor of Psychology, Loyola University Chicago, Chicago, IL, USA

Richard E. Petty
Distinguished University Professor of Psychology, Ohio State University, Columbus, OH, USA

Devon Price
Clinical Assistant Professor, Loyola University Chicago, Chicago, IL, USA

Akila Raoul
Doctoral Candidate, Loyola University Chicago, Chicago, IL, USA

Angelita Repetto
Doctoral Candidate, University of California, Davis, Davis, CA, USA

Benjamin C. Ruisch
Lecturer, University of Kent, Canterbury, UK

Benjamin A. Saunders
Associate Professor, Long Island University–Brooklyn, Brooklyn, NY, USA

Alex Sielaff
Doctoral Student, University of Arizona, Tucson, AZ, USA

Sheldon Solomon
Professor of Psychology, Skidmore College, Saratoga Springs, NY, USA

Chadly Stern
Associate Professor, University of Illinois Urbana-Champaign, Champaign, IL, USA

R. Scott Tindale
Professor of Psychology, Loyola University Chicago, Chicago, IL, USA

Chase Wilson
Senior Hiring Scientist, Indeed, Chicago, IL, USA

Jeremy R. Winget
Instructor of Psychology, Loyola University Chicago, Chicago, IL, USA

Everett L. Worthington, Jr.
Commonwealth Professor Emeritus, Virginia Commonwealth University, Richmond, VA, USA

Onurcan Yılmaz
Associate Professor, Kadir Has University, Istanbul, Turkey

Whinda Yustisia
Doctoral Student, Loyola University Chicago, Chicago, IL, USA

I
DEFINING AND UNDERSTANDING OPEN-MINDEDNESS, DOGMATISM, AND POLARIZATION

1
Open-Mindedness and Dogmatism in a Polarized World

Core Concepts and Definitions

Victor Ottati, Chadly Stern, Whinda Yustisia, and Lori D. Bougher

Stories suggesting that the United States and many other countries throughout the world have become more "polarized" are ubiquitous in newscasts, newspapers, magazines, and other forms of media (e.g., French, 2020; Just, 2021; "Party Polarization Hit a High Under Trump," 2021). Although some scholars have argued that assertions of increasing political polarization are exaggerated (e.g., Fiorina et al., 2011), a wealth of empirical research buffers the claims of these reports. There have been rises in the polarization of people's political views as well as the acrimonious attitudes they hold toward others who espouse views that clash with their own (e.g., Abramowitz, 2010; Iyengar et al., 2019; see Chapter 2 in this volume).

The term *political polarization* commonly evokes negative sentiment. However, it is important to note up front that political polarization is not completely undesirable. Groups that polarize toward a consensus position are more likely to actually enact policies and plans endorsed by the group (Kameda & Tindale, 2006). Moreover, the existence of political attitude differences between groups can contribute to a vibrant democratic life in which alternative solutions to social problems are fully explored (Mutz, 2006). Thus, under some conditions, polarization can promote beneficial forms of social and political action. Unfortunately, though, polarization can also produce dysfunctional outcomes when it pushes groups too far apart and groups are isolated from critical sources of information. Under such conditions, polarization can produce suboptimal decisions within groups and reduce the likelihood that groups with competing interests resolve their differences and implement compromises (Janis, 1982; Paluck, 2010). Political polarization can also decrease substantive policy reasoning, increase violence within and between states, amplify economic inequality, and impede the enactment of legislation (Ottati & Wilson, 2018). Pernicious forms of polarization are presumably exacerbated by dogmatic (or closed-minded) thinking that fails to openly consider the viability of opposing viewpoints, as well as low levels of intellectual humility in which people rarely consider the possibility that their own beliefs and opinions might be fallible.

A primary purpose of this volume is to increase the scientific comprehension of open-mindedness and dogmatism. An understanding of open-mindedness and dogmatism can illuminate the nature and causes of political polarization and provide clues regarding how one might attempt to reduce damaging aspects of polarization. Negative outcomes of polarization constitute one of the most salient challenges to be addressed in the 21st century. The promise of open-mindedness as a means to achieve greater social harmony and reduce problematic forms of polarization is timely. Indeed, it is difficult to uncover an arena of contemporary life that does not emphasize the value of open-mindedness. Open-mindedness is a prominent theme in commencement addresses at universities and constitutes a core value of many organizations (e.g., the Carnegie Endowment for International Peace, the National Council for Social Studies, the Foundation for Critical Thinking, the International Baccalaureate). Endorsement of open-mindedness is also evident in remarks from the 46th US president Joseph Biden, Pope Francis, the Dalai Lama, and many other prominent political and religious leaders.

Yet, just as polarization possesses both positive and negative outcomes, so might open-mindedness (Church & Samuelson, 2016). According to some accounts, an exclusive focus on the virtues of open-mindedness could inadvertently ignore the fact that it may not be desirable in all circumstances. Open-minded acceptance of fallacious or unrealistic claims may constitute an unhealthy form of gullibility, and open-mindedness toward unethical viewpoints may reflect an inappropriate lack of moral conviction. Indeed, some theoretical approaches suggest that the dogmatic refusal to openly consider false or immoral claims may be virtuous in some situations (Church & Samuelson, 2016). By focusing on both the descriptive and normative components of open-minded and dogmatic patterns of social thought, the present volume addresses questions that undergird the development of a more intellectually diverse and vibrant society.

The present volume collectively considers questions regarding open-mindedness, dogmatism, and polarization from multiple theoretical perspectives. Chapters focus on contemporary theory and research regarding the psychology of attitudes, intellectual humility, normative models of open-mindedness, political ideology and open-mindedness, as well as affectively driven models of open-mindedness and dogmatism. To lay the foundation for these different theoretical approaches, this introductory chapter provides definitions of core theoretical constructs that occupy an important role in the chapters that follow. We begin by focusing on core concepts identified in the title of this volume and then shift toward defining and describing related theoretical constructs that play an important part in the remaining chapters.

Defining Polarization, Dogmatism, and Open-Mindedness

We have suggested that open-mindedness and dogmatism are critical in eliciting and maintaining political polarization. But what does *polarization* mean? Iyengar conceptualizes political polarization in terms of affect and social identity. Specifically, affective polarization is defined as the tendency for "people identifying as Republicans or Democrats to view opposing partisans negatively and copartisans positively" (Iyengar & Westwood, 2015, p. 691). Iyengar and DeBell (see Chapter 2 in this volume) document substantial increases in this form of polarization during recent decades. While there are alternative approaches to defining political polarization (e.g., Fiorina et al., 2008), this affectively based definition provides a firm foundation for understanding polarization in contemporary politics, as well as its relation to dogmatism and closed-mindedness. That is, it seems likely that dogmatic (or closed-minded) patterns of thought often serve to create or maintain this form of political polarization. This leads to the next question: What is the nature of "dogmatism" and "closed-mindedness"?

Different definitions of these constructs have been proposed over the years. Rokeach (1954) provided one of the first conceptual delineations of *dogmatism*: "(a) a relatively closed cognitive organization of beliefs and disbeliefs about reality, (b) organized around a central set of beliefs about absolute authority which, in turn, (c) provides a framework for patterns of intolerance and qualified tolerance towards others" (p. 195). Both "dogmatism" and "rigidity" can produce resistance to belief change. However, Rokeach (1954) regarded dogmatism as a more general "intellectualized and abstract form than rigidity" (p. 196). Dogmatism, from this perspective, can often be construed as a general trait characteristic of the individual. Indeed, the dogmatism scale was developed as a non-ideological alternative to measures of authoritarianism, a personality dimension often found to be correlated with right-wing conservatism. Authoritarian individuals endorse submission to established authority, conventional forms of morality, and aggression toward scapegoats and deviants (Altemeyer, 1996; Feldman, 2003; see Chapter 10 in this volume). Rokeach's attempt to separate dogmatism from ideology is controversial, however, as research suggests that individual differences in "dogmatism" are sometimes correlated with right-wing conservatism (Jost, 2017).

In this volume, Stern and Ruisch (see Chapter 11) define dogmatism as a "tendency to hold one's beliefs and principles as objectively correct, without consideration of the evidence or the opinions of others". Marcus (see Chapter 12) views dogmatism as devotion to or strict reliance on a given course of action, combined with a disinterest in exploring alternative possibilities. Ottati et al. (see Chapter 7) use *dogmatic cognition* and *closed-minded cognition* interchangeably. In this case, however, these terms designate a "directionally biased cognitive style," a tendency to process information in a manner that reinforces or confirms the individual's preexisting beliefs, attitudes, opinions, or expectations. From this perspective, dogmatic or closed-minded thought is not closed to all viewpoints. On the contrary, it is "open" to messages that support the individual's preexisting opinion but is "closed" to messages that convey alternative viewpoints. This "cognitive style" possesses not only a chronic trait component but also a malleable component that varies across situations. All of these definitions of dogmatism and closed-mindedness share some common ground. However, these definitions also differ in the extent to which they involve a focus on chronic individual differences, adherence to authority, presumption of belief infallibility, or a cognitive style.

Ottati et al. (see Chapter 7 in this volume) consider "open-minded cognition" as the bipolar opposite of dogmatic or closed-minded cognition (but see Chapter 12 in this volume). *Open-minded cognition* is defined as a directionally unbiased cognitive style, a tendency to select, interpret, retrieve, and elaborate upon information in an impartial manner that is not biased by the individual's prior beliefs, attitudes, opinions, or expectations (Ottati & Wilson, 2018; Price et al., 2015; see Chapter 7 in this volume). MacKuen et al. (2010) and Marcus (see Chapter 12 in this volume) similarly view open-mindedness as a tendency to be attentive, thoughtful, and deliberative and to critically examine not only familiar and favored but also unfamiliar and opposing perspectives. In a related vein, Baron et al. (see Chapter 9 in this volume) defines *actively open-minded thinking* (AOT) as a virtuous pattern of critical thinking that involves actively seeking out new information and evidence against possibilities that already seem strong. According to Baron (2007), this form of thinking should involve a thorough information search in proportion to the importance of the question, confidence that is appropriate to the amount and quality of thinking done, and fairness to possibilities other than the one initially favored. Importantly, Hoyle and Davisson (see

Chapter 6 in this volume) emphasize the distinction between willingness to consider new ideas without prejudgment (open-mindedness) and a willingness to change one's beliefs or opinions.

A different conceptual framework is introduced by Briñol and Petty (see Chapter 4 in this volume). They define *open* or *openness* in a multifaceted and flexible manner. For example, *open* or *openness* can reflect a motivation (low resistance to being persuaded), a mindset (a willingness to change one's attitude), a characteristic of a person (a person low in resistance to persuasion), or an outcome (a treatment reduces a person's resistance). In contrast to the previously described approaches, Briñol and Petty (see Chapter 4 in this volume) regard openness to be independent of "directionally biased" versus "unbiased" processing. That is, openness may lead not only to more objective (unbiased) processing but also to more biased processing. In the former case, openness presumably increases not only favorable cognitive responses that accept strong messages but also unfavorable cognitive responses that reject weak message arguments. In the latter case, openness may primarily elicit cognitive responses that are biased in favor of one side of an issue regardless of the strength of the message arguments. From this perspective, the previously described definitions of open-mindedness and dogmatism exemplify specific forms of openness that are either objective (open-minded) or biased (dogmatism).

Many chapters in this volume emphasize that dogmatism and open-mindedness possess not only a chronic trait component but also a component that varies across specific domains, situations, topics, or issues. For example, Ottati et al. (see Chapter 7) and Marcus (see Chapter 12) both suggest that open-mindedness and dogmatism vary across messages, with some messages (e.g., tenable messages) eliciting more open-minded reactions than other messages (e.g., untenable messages). Similarly, Hoyle and Davisson (see Chapter 6) distinguish "trait" intellectual humility from "specific" levels of intellectual humility that pertain to a particular domain, topic, or issue. Hoyle and Davisson (see Chapter 6) and Ottati et al. (see Chapter 7) emphasize that open-mindedness is distinct from agreement with a communication. Unbiased open-minded consideration of a message may lead to an attitudinal shift in the direction advocated but not when the individual encounters weak arguments.

Another important feature of the various conceptualizations involves the degree to which they presume that open-mindedness entails deliberative or systematic processing. Marcus (see Chapter 12 in this volume) often emphasizes the "deliberate" nature of open-mindedness. However, following long-standing work in the area of persuasion (e.g., Petty & Cacioppo, 1986),

Ottati and Wilson (2018) assume that "directional bias in elaboration" is conceptually independent of "amount of elaboration." From this perspective, systematic or central processing can be directionally biased (closed-minded) or directionally unbiased (open-minded). This approach assumes that cognitive elaboration will often be biased when the message recipient is motivated to defend a preexisting attitude but unbiased when the message recipient is motivated to develop an accurate belief or opinion. Ottati and Wilson (2018) also argue that peripheral or heuristic processing can be directionally biased (closed-minded) or directionally unbiased (open-minded). For example, on the one hand, heuristic reliance on a gender stereotype might produce biased impressions of a female political candidate, a form of closed-mindedness that reinforces a preexisting stereotype. On the other hand, when deriving a policy preference regarding global warming, a voter might adopt the opinion of a trusted scientific expert who possesses a reputation for being reasonable, fair, and unbiased, a form of open-mindedness that does not entail a great deal of cognitive deliberation.

An important difference between the various conceptualizations of open-mindedness involves the extent to which open-mindedness is defined as inherently desirable. Many definitions of open-mindedness presume that open-mindedness is virtuous and something that people ought to work toward. From this perspective, one cannot be "excessively open-minded." In contrast, Ottati et al. (see Chapter 7 in this volume) propose that open-mindedness may be inappropriate or socially undesirable when individuals encounter blatantly fallacious or unethical viewpoints. Under such conditions, open-mindedness may reflect naive gullibility or a lack of moral conviction. According to this view, a dogmatic refusal to openly consider fallacious or unethical viewpoints can be socially desirable and normatively appropriate.

It is also important to consider constructs that are related to, yet distinct from, open-mindedness. As a construct, "intellectual humility" possesses clear linkages with open-mindedness. Indeed, some researchers regard intellectual humility as a broader concept that contains multiple components, one of which is open-mindedness. For example, Hoyle and Davisson (see Chapter 6 in this volume) suggest that an intellectually humble person accepts the potential fallibility of their views, is willing to consider new information relevant to their view (open-minded), and is willing to change their viewpoints. Relatedly, Krumrei-Mancuso and Rouse (2016) argue that intellectual humility consists of independence of intellect and ego, openness to revising one's viewpoint, respect for others' viewpoints, and lack of intellectual overconfidence. Importantly, however, research and conceptual definitions of intellectual humility and open-mindedness are continuously evolving.

Manifestations of Open- and Closed-Minded Thought

Multiple psychological processes can unfold in an unbiased or a biased manner (Ottati et al., 2002). These include exposure, attention, encoding, interpretation, retrieval, and weighting of information when deriving a judgment. The "congeniality hypothesis," for example, suggests that people attend to attitudinally agreeable information and screen out uncongenial information at multiple stages of information processing (Hart et al., 2009). Biased selective exposure to congenial information can enable individuals to maintain and reinforce their preexisting attitudes, beliefs, and opinions (Hart et al., 2009; see Chapter 3 in this volume). For example, "partisan selective exposure" enables individuals to select media outlets and social situations that reinforce their partisan predispositions (e.g., attitudes on policies, preferred political candidates) and is a critical factor that contributes to polarization (see Chapter 2 in this volume). Effects of this nature may be amplified by spatial or residential segregation of politically polarized groups (see Chapter 3 in this volume).

Biased information selection is reflected not only in selective attention biases but also in selective encoding and retrieval of political information (Ottati et al., 2002). In each instance, biased information selection can potentially serve to reinforce the individual's preexisting political beliefs and opinions and prevent an individual from openly considering political arguments in an unbiased fashion. Closed-mindedness can also arise when individuals interpret ambiguous political information in a manner that supports their preexisting predispositions. For example, a remark about racial inequality that is ambiguous in its meaning might be interpreted as "racist" when a member of an opposing party utters the statement but not when a member of one's own party does so (Ottati et al., 2002). *Selective judgment* constitutes another manifestation of closed-mindedness, wherein individuals selectively criticize messages that contradict their prior opinion (see Chapter 3 in this volume). The aforementioned biases can be compounded at the interpersonal level when individuals engage in *selective sharing* or *dissemination*, a tendency to share mostly congenial attitude information when communicating with others (Cappella et al., 2015; see Chapter 3 in this volume).

When conceptualized as a process, *resistance to persuasion* involves the use of cognitive mechanisms that enable the individual to maintain their preexisting attitude (Petty et al., 2004; see Chapter 4 in this volume). A prime example is *counterarguing*, which involves generating cognitive responses to a communication that discount its validity, accuracy, or logic. Indeed, the elaboration likelihood model argues that the effect of a communication on the message recipient's attitude is often mediated by self-generated cognitive elaborations. *Biased elaboration* can serve as an important manifestation of closed-mindedness, especially when it fails to consider the potential merits of a counter-attitudinal message. In contrast, an open-minded reaction to a strong and compelling counter-attitudinal communication will presumably include not only counterarguments but also arguments that acknowledge the merits of the message. This might result in attitude change or belief updating, whereby people revise their initial view after receiving new information that challenges that view.

Attitude Strength, Confidence, and Conviction

The political beliefs and attitudes that citizens and politicians hold can vary by strength, confidence, and conviction. Several chapters in this volume consider ways in which these characteristics of beliefs and attitudes may engender (or be engendered by) dogmatic and open-minded thinking. An understanding of these approaches rests upon establishing suitable definitions for the core concepts involved. *Attitude strength* refers to the extent to which an attitude is accessible when the individual thinks about the attitude object, as well as the extent to which the attitude is subjectively important or consequential in shaping thinking and action (Briñol et al., 2019; Petty et al., 2019).

A related, but slightly different, construct is *metacognitive confidence*. *Confidence* refers to a subjective belief about the validity of one's thoughts or judgments, or the degree to which one believes that one's own judgments, decisions, and attitudes are objectively correct (Briñol & Petty, 2009; Rucker et al., 2014; Ruish & Stern, 2021; see Chapter 11 in this volume). Baron (2007) argues that, when "good thinking" is present, confidence is proportional to the evidence available. Overconfidence arises when an individual possesses a high level of confidence that is based upon an insufficient or biased search of evidence or when people overestimate how objectively accurate their judgments and decisions are (Baron, 2007; Moore & Healy, 2008). In some situations, overconfidence can lead people to hold problematic beliefs about the world. For example, conspiracy theories are often dangerous beliefs held with great confidence despite minimal or biased thinking (Albarracin et al., 2021). Overconfidence may also be associated with *belief superiority*, a cognition that one's viewpoints are superior to alternative views (see Chapter 6 in this volume).

The distinction between attitude strength and confidence is subtle yet noteworthy. Attitude strength centers on the accessibility, importance, and consequential nature of an attitude. In contrast, confidence entails meta-cognitive appraisals about the validity or accuracy of a belief, and overconfidence concerns whether that appraisal is unjustified. Although the psychological properties underlying these constructs may often be correlated, the constructs are nevertheless distinct. A person might possess a highly accessible belief or attitude that is held with little confidence, and the accessibility of the belief does not inherently speak to whether a person's subjective appraisal about the accuracy of the belief is justified.

A construct that is closely related to attitude strength and confidence is *conviction*. According to Krumrei-Mancuso and Worthington (see Chapter 5 in this volume), *convictions* are firmly held ideas, beliefs, opinions, or attitudes. Convictions can be specific to certain belief domains. For example, *moral convictions* are convictions that pertain to morality. It is interesting to contrast *conviction* with *overconfidence*. Holding more confidence in one's views and abilities than is justified by the facts is often viewed in a socially undesirable way, and, in turn, researchers seek out ways to reduce it (e.g., Arkes et al., 1987). In contrast, moral convictions can possess socially desirable qualities. For example, moral convictions can act as a protection against obedience to potentially malevolent authorities (Skitka & Morgan, 2014). As such, in some instances, moral convictions may serve to guard against pernicious forms of authoritarianism. Moreover, when individuals encounter communications that convey blatantly false or unethical viewpoints, moral convictions may elicit a dogmatic refusal to openly consider such viewpoints. Under such conditions, the dogmatic refusal to openly consider such viewpoints may be viewed as socially desirable or normatively appropriate (see Chapter 7 in this volume).

Motivational and Normative Determinants of Open-Mindedness and Dogmatism

A variety of theoretical approaches in the present volume consider motivational and normative determinants of open-mindedness and dogmatism. We have previously noted that resistance to persuasion can be viewed as a process that occurs during persuasion (e.g., counterarguing). However, *resistance to persuasion* can also refer to a motivation. In this usage of the term, *resistance* refers to the goal of blocking attitude change or the desire to maintain one's current attitude (Petty et al., 2004). We have also suggested that this motivation might elicit a biased or one-sided pattern of elaboration, wherein the message recipient generates counterarguments that focus on the shortcomings of a counter-attitudinal communication, ignoring commendable aspects of the persuasive appeal. Resistance to persuasion might be construed as closed-minded when viewed in this manner. On the other hand, if a communication possesses few commendable qualities, the motive to resist persuasion may serve to generate relatively accurate and unbiased cognitive responses to the communication. Thus, resistance to persuasion may not be "closed-minded" in all circumstances. Moreover, as previously noted, a closed-minded response to a blatantly inaccurate or unethical idea may be socially desirable in some circumstances. In other words, the motive to resist persuasion may sometimes trigger closed-minded reactions that are merited.

Epistemic motivation reflects the degree to which people are motivated to engage in deliberative thought when forming a judgment relative to making a quick and low-effort decision (De Dreu et al., 2006; see Chapter 11 in this volume). Measures of epistemic motivation have captured this goal in various ways, such as through assessing the degree to which people value cognitive closure (Webster & Kruglanski, 1994) and structure (Neuberg & Newsom, 1993) over deliberation (Cacioppo & Petty, 1982). People who are motivated to quickly reach a judgment are more likely to engage in a heuristic processing style that rests on well-learned prior associations, whereas people who value deliberation are more likely to engage in effortful and systematic processing. Of direct relevance to constructs discussed in the present volume, the motivation to deliberate (vs. quickly reach closure) may underlie AOT, a cognitive style that is characterized by a conjunction of openness to alternative possibilities and critical deliberative thinking. However, the motivation to deliberate is distinct from open-minded cognition, in the sense that the latter also includes unbiased patterns of thought that entail low levels of deliberation (e.g., following the advice of a trusted expert who possesses a reputation for being fair and unbiased).

When focusing on intergroup relations, the distinction between motivation (intention) to cooperate and the expectation that the other group will cooperate may also be relevant to understanding polarization. Cooperation among negotiating parties should be optimized under conditions that jointly promote the intention (goal) to cooperate and the expectation that the other party will cooperate. Thus, Moaz et al. (see Chapter 8 in this volume) emphasize that open-mindedness between groups is maximized when group norms activate an intention (motive) to be open-minded and group members possess an expectation that members of the other group will reciprocate.

Three chapters in this volume suggest that social norms play an important role in motivating open- and closed-minded thinking. Ottati and colleagues (Ottati et al., 2015, 2018; see Chapter 7 in this volume) argue that individuals exposed to a message activate a prescriptive norm that identifies an appropriate or ideal level of open-mindedness (subjective norm [SNORM]). Perceptions of this normative ideal are determined by characteristics of the person and situation. This subjective norm influences intentions to be open-minded (situation-specific open-minded cognition [SOMC]), which produces downstream effects on manifestations of open-minded cognition (e.g., open-minded information selection). According to this approach, when situation specific open-mindedness is guided by intentions (SOMC), prescriptive norms regarding the "ideal" or "appropriate" response in the situation (SNORM) constitute an important and proximal determinant of open-mindedness in the situation. Moaz et al. (see Chapter 8 in this volume) emphasize that normative perceptions mediate effects on SOMC in a group context. For example, they demonstrate that social norms motivate individuals to be open-minded toward in-group members but entitle them to be more closed-minded toward out-group members. They also demonstrate that variation in open-mindedness toward out-group members is associated with group norms.

The role of normative considerations is also evident in Baron's conceptualization of AOT. AOT is consistent with prescriptive norms that encourage "good" thinking (Baron, 2019). AOT involves an information search that is in proportion to the question involved and, as such, reflects a normatively appropriate amount of information search. It also results in a level of confidence that is appropriate to the amount and quality of thinking done. All of these facets of AOT convey that it reflects a normatively appropriate or socially desirable style of thinking and an intellectual virtue that promotes good, moral character. At a conceptual level, AOT shares linkages with the SNORM assessed by Ottati and associates (see Chapter 7 in this volume).

Affect, Open-Mindedness, and Dogmatism

Open-minded and dogmatic thinking are inherently cognitive in their process but, like most cognitive activity, exist within a context of affective or emotional experience. Several chapters in this volume explore relations between affective states and open- versus closed-minded thought. Here, the term *affect* typically refers to any evaluative state. All emotions are affective, but not all affective things are emotions (Clore et al., 1994). Emotions are linked to a salient object or source (e.g., "Politician X's statement made me feel angry"), whereas moods are diffuse affective states without a salient object or source (Huntsinger et al., 2014).

Early work on authoritarianism presumed that unconscious affective forces are at play in creating an authoritarian predisposition. Rooted in psychoanalytic theory, the authoritarian personality was hypothesized to arise from early childhood. Harsh and punitive parenting presumably caused a child to feel great anger toward their parents. Due to fear of parental disapproval and punishment, this anger was suppressed or rendered unconscious, and the child in turn came to identify with and idolize authority figures. Although this psychoanalytic interpretation is only rarely emphasized in contemporary work on authoritarianism and dogmatism, recent work does suggest that affect and emotion occur in a relatively automatic or preconscious manner (see Chapters 12 and 13 in this volume).

A substantial amount of research regarding dogmatism has also been rooted in terror management theory (Greenberg et al., 1986; see Chapter 14 in this volume). According to this theoretical approach, humans are, like all life forms, built to avert death; but knowledge of their own mortality creates an ever-present potential for intense anxiety or terror. Humans manage this terror by sustaining faith in a worldview that enables them to feel that they are beings of enduring value, rather than simply being animals fated to annihilation and death. Situations that increase *mortality salience*, or conscious thought of one's own death, produce heightened cognitive accessibility of death, which in turn triggers efforts to sustain faith in one's worldview (Greenberg et al., 2014). This process can lead individuals to adopt a dogmatic and rigid cultural worldview that contains clear definitions of what is good and bad, as well as right and wrong, and that focuses on the greatness of the in-group and the need to heroically triumph over perceived evil others (Pyszczynski et al., 2003).

Contemporary research regarding the affect–cognition relation often focuses on the effect of affective states on cognitive processing style. According to the "affect as information" account, affective states provide information about the environment that adaptively tunes cognitive processing to meet situational demands (see Chapter 13 in this volume). Positive affect signals a safe and benign environment, and therefore triggers more heuristic processing. Negative affect signals the presence of a problem, and therefore triggers more systematic processing. A different "affect-as-cognitive-feedback" account suggests that positive and negative affect function like reward and punishment (Huntsinger et al., 2014; see Chapter 13 in this volume). That is, positive affect reinforces whatever cognitive style the individual is presently employing, whereas negative affect inhibits such processes and may provoke an alternative processing style. This recent approach suggests that positive affect will enhance (reinforce) open- or closed-mindedness, depending on which cognitive tendency is currently accessible. Negative affect will presumably elicit the opposite pattern (see Chapter 13 in this volume).

Closing Remarks

This introductory chapter provides a foundation for this volume by defining core theoretical constructs and identifying similarities and differences between various conceptual definitions of these constructs. The remaining chapters consider questions regarding open-mindedness, dogmatism, and political polarization from multiple vantage points. At the onset, contemporary and foundational work regarding the psychology of political polarization is presented. The remaining chapters, which focus on open-mindedness and dogmatism, are grouped into five sections. These sections focus on theory and research pertaining to attitudes and persuasion, intellectual humility, normative models of open-mindedness, political ideology and dogmatism, and affectively driven models of open-mindedness and dogmatism. We hope that this collective volume proves fruitful for readers interested in understanding the current state of scientific evidence about open-mindedness, dogmatic thinking, and polarization.

References

Abramowitz, A. I. (2010). *The disappearing center*. Yale University Press.
Albarracin, D., Albarracin, J., Chan, M. P. S., & Jamieson, K. H. (2021). *Creating conspiracy beliefs: How our thoughts are shaped*. Cambridge University Press.
Altemeyer, B. (1996). *The authoritarian specter*. Harvard University Press.
Arkes, H. R., Christensen, C., Lai, C., & Blumer, C. (1987). Two methods of reducing overconfidence. *Organizational Behavior and Human Decision Processes, 39*(1), 133–144.
Baron, J. (2007). *Thinking and deciding*. Cambridge University Press. https://doi.org/10.1017/CBO9780511840265
Baron, J. (2019). Actively open-minded thinking in politics. *Cognition, 188*, 8–18. https://doi.org/10.1016/j.cognition.2018.10.004
Briñol, P., & Petty, R. E. (2009). Persuasion: Insights from the self-validation hypothesis. In M. P. Zanna (Ed.), *Advances in experimental social psychology* (Vol. 41, pp. 69–118). Academic Press. https://doi.org/10.1016/S0065-2601(08)00402-4

Briñol, P., Petty, R. E., & Stavraki, M. (2019). Structure and function of attitudes. In M. Hogg (Ed.), *Oxford encyclopedia of social psychology*. Oxford University Press. https://doi.org/10.1093/acrefore/9780190236557.013.320

Cacioppo, J. T., & Petty, R. E. (1982). The need for cognition. *Journal of Personality and Social Psychology, 42*(1), 116–131. https://doi.org/10.1037/t04601-000

Cappella, J., Kim, H., & Albarracín, D. (2015). Selection and transmission processes for information in the emerging media environment: Psychological motives and message characteristics. *Media Psychology, 18*(3), 396–424. https://doi.org/10.1080/15213269.2014.941112

Church, I., & Samuelson, P. (2016). *Intellectual humility: An introduction to the philosophy and science*. Bloomsbury Publishing. https://doi.org/10.5040/9781474236775

Clore, G. L., Schwarz, N., & Conway, M. (1994). Affective causes and consequences of social information processing. In R. Wyer & T. Srull (Eds.), *Handbook of social cognition* (2nd ed., pp. 323–417). Erlbaum.

De Dreu, C. K., Beersma, B., Stroebe, K., & Euwema, M. C. (2006). Motivated information processing, strategic choice, and the quality of negotiated agreement. *Journal of Personality and Social Psychology, 90*(6), 927–943. https://doi.org/10.1037/0022-3514.90.6.927

Feldman, S. (2003). Enforcing social conformity: A theory of authoritarianism. *Political Psychology, 24*, 41–74. http://dx.doi.org/10.1111/0162-895X.00316

Fiorina, M. P., Abrams, S. J., & Pope, J. (2008). Polarization in the American public: Misconceptions and misreadings. *The Journal of Politics, 70*(2), 556–560. https://doi.org/10.1017/S002238160808050X

Fiorina, M. P., Abrams, S. J., & Pope, J. (2011). *Culture war? The myth of a polarized America*. Pearson Longman.

French, D. (2020, November 4). It's clear that America is deeply polarized. No election can overcome that. *Time*. https://time.com/5907318/polarization-2020-election/

Greenberg, J., Pyszczynski, T., & Solomon, S. (1986). The causes and consequences of a need for self-esteem: A terror management theory. In R. F. Baumeister (Ed.), *Public self and private self* (pp. 189–212). Springer-Verlag. https://doi.org/10.1007/978-1-4613-9564-5_10

Greenberg, J., Vail, K., & Pyszczynski, T. (2014). Terror management theory and research: How the desire for death transcendence drives our strivings for meaning and significance. *Advances in Motivation Science, 1*, 85–134. https://doi.org/10.1016/bs.adms.2014.08.003

Hart, W., Albarracín, D., Eagly, A. H., Brechan, I., Lindberg, M. J., & Merrill, L. (2009). Feeling validated versus being correct: A meta-analysis of selective exposure to information. *Psychological Bulletin, 135*(4), 555–588. https://doi.org/10.1037/a0015701

Huntsinger, J. R., Isbell, L. M., & Clore, G. L. (2014). The affective control of thought: Malleable, not fixed. *Psychological Review, 121*(4), 600–618. https://doi.org/10.1037/a0037669

Iyengar, S., Lelkes, Y., Levendusky, M., Malhotra, N., & Westwood, S. J. (2019). The origins and consequences of affective polarization in the United States. *Annual Review of Political Science, 22*, 129–146. https://doi.org/10.1146/annurev-polisci-051117-073034

Iyengar, S., & Westwood, S. J. (2015). Fear and loathing across party lines: New evidence on group polarization. *American Journal of Political Science, 59*(3), 690–707. https://doi.org/10.1111/ajps.12152

Janis, I. L. (1982). *Groupthink* (2nd ed.). Houghton Mifflin.

Jost, J. T. (2017). Ideological asymmetries and the essence of political psychology. *Political Psychology, 38*(2), 167–208. https://doi.org/10.1111/pops.12407

Just, S. (Executive Producer). (2021, April 4). *PBS newshour* [TV series episode]. WTTW.

Kameda, T., & Tindale, R. S. (2006). Groups as adaptive devices: Human docility and group aggregation mechanisms in evolutionary context. In M. Schaller, J. A. Simpson, & D. T. Kenrick (Eds.), *Evolution and social psychology* (pp. 317–342). Psychology Press.

Krumrei-Mancuso, E. J., & Rouse, S. V. (2016). The development and validation of the comprehensive intellectual humility scale. *Journal of Personality Assessment, 98*, 209–221. https://doi.org/10.1080/00223891.2015.1068174

MacKuen, M., Wolak, J., Keele, L., & Marcus, G. E. (2010). Civic engagements: Resolute partisanship or reflective deliberation. *American Journal of Political Science, 54*(2), 440–458. https://doi.org/10.1111/j.1540-5907.2010.00440.x

Moore, D. A., & Healy, P. J. (2008). The trouble with overconfidence. *Psychological Review, 115*(2), 502–517. https://doi.org/10.1037/0033-295X.115.2.502

Mutz, D. C. (2006). *Hearing the other side: Deliberative versus participatory democracy*. Cambridge University Press. https://doi.org/10.1017/CBO9780511617201

Neuberg, S. L., & Newsom, J. T. (1993). Personal need for structure: Individual differences in the desire for simpler structure. *Journal of Personality and Social Psychology, 65*(1), 113–131. https://doi.org/10.1037/0022-3514.65.1.113

Ottati, V., Price, E. D., Wilson, C., & Sumaktoyo, N. (2015). When self-perceptions of expertise increase closed-minded cognition: The earned dogmatism effect. *Journal of Experimental Social Psychology, 61*, 131–138. https://doi.org/10.1016/j.jesp.2015.08.003

Ottati, V., & Wilson, C. (2018). Open-minded cognition and political thought. In William R. Thompson (Ed.), *Oxford research encyclopedia of politics* (pp. 1–26). Oxford University Press. https://doi.org/10.1093/acrefore/9780190228637.013.143

Ottati, V., Wilson, C., Osteen, C., & Distefano, Y. (2018). Experimental demonstrations of the earned dogmatism effect using a variety of optimal manipulations: Commentary and response to Calin-Jageman (2018). *Journal of Experimental Social Psychology, 78*, 250–258. https://doi.org/10.1016/j.jesp.2018.05.010

Ottati, V., Wyer, R. S., Deiger, M., & Houston, D. (2002). The psychological determinants of candidate evaluation and voting preference. In V. Ottati, R. S. Tindale, J. Edwards, F. B. Bryant, L. Heath, D. C. O'Connell, Y. Suarez-Balcazar, & E. J. Posavac (Eds.), *The social psychology of politics* (pp. 3–28). Springer. https://doi.org/10.1007/978-1-4615-0569-3_1

Paluck, E. L. (2010). Is it better not to talk? Group polarization, extended contact, and perspective taking in eastern Democratic Republic of Congo. *Personality and Social Psychology Bulletin, 36*(9), 1170–1185. https://doi.org/10.1177/0146167210379868

Party polarization hit a high under Trump. Can Biden reel it back? (2021, January 20). *Washington Post*. washingtonpost.com/politics/2021/01/20/party-polarization-hit-high-under-trump-can-biden-reel-it-back/

Petty, R. E., Briñol, P., Fabrigar, L. R., & Wegener, D. T. (2019). Attitude structure and change. In R. F. Baumeister & E. J. Finkel (Eds.), *Advanced social psychology* (2nd ed., pp. 117–156). Oxford University Press.

Petty, R. E., & Cacioppo, J. T. (1986). The elaboration likelihood model of persuasion. In *Communication and persuasion* (pp. 1–24). Springer. https://doi.org/10.1007/978-1-4612-4964-1_1

Petty, R. E., Tormala, Z. L., & Rucker, D. D. (2004). Resisting persuasion by counterarguing: An attitude strength perspective. In J. T. Jost, M. R. Banaji, & D. A. Prentice (Eds.), *Perspectivism in social psychology: The yin and yang of scientific progress* (pp. 37–51). American Psychological Association. https://doi.org/10.1037/10750-004

Price, E., Ottati, V., Wilson, C., & Kim, S. (2015). Open-minded cognition. *Personality and Social Psychology Bulletin, 41*(11), 1488–1504. https://doi.org/10.1177/0146167215600528

Pyszczynski, T., Solomon, S., & Greenberg, J. (2003). *In the wake of 9/11: The psychology of terror*. American Psychological Association. https://doi.org/10.1037/10478-000

Rokeach, M. (1954). The nature and meaning of dogmatism. *Psychological Review, 61*(3), 194–204. https://doi.org/10.1037/h0060752

Rucker, D. D., Tormala, Z. L., Petty, R. E., & Briñol, P. (2014). Consumer conviction and commitment: An appraisal-based framework for attitude certainty. *Journal of Consumer Psychology*, *24*(1), 119–136. https://doi.org/10.1016/j.jcps.2013.07.001

Ruisch, B. C., & Stern, C. (2021). The confident conservative: Ideological differences in judgment and decision-making confidence. *Journal of Experimental Psychology: General*, *150*(3), 527–544. https://doi.org/10.1037/xge0000898

Skitka, L. J., & Morgan, G. S. (2014). The social and political implications of moral conviction. *Political Psychology*, *35*, 95–110. https://doi.org/10.1111/pops.12166

Webster, D. M., & Kruglanski, A. W. (1994). Individual differences in need for cognitive closure. *Journal of Personality and Social Psychology*, *67*(6), 1049–1062. https://doi.org/10.1037/0022-3514.67.6.1049

2
Identity Strength Leads to Out-Group Animus and Polarization

Shanto Iyengar and Matthew DeBell

Political scientists have typically defined *polarization* in terms of ideology, proposing the ideological distance between party platforms as the appropriate yardstick. By this metric, there is no doubt that political elites representing the two major American parties have indeed moved toward the ideological extremes over the past half-century (Fleisher & Bond, 2001; Hetherington, 2001; McCarty et al., 2006). However, the extent to which rank-and-file supporters of the parties are similarly polarized remains open to debate. Some scholars present data showing that most partisans remain centrist on the issues despite the movement of their leaders to the ideological extremes (Fiorina et al., 2008). Others claim that over time party members have gradually emulated the extreme views of party elites (Abramowitz & Saunders, 2008).

Disagreement over questions of public policy is but one way of defining partisan polarization. An alternative definition—rooted in social identity theory (Billig & Tajfel, 1973)—considers mass polarization as the extent to which partisans view each other as a stigmatized out-group. In the US party system, partisanship is reduced to either identifying with the "Democrat" group or the "Republican" group. Social identity theory posits that once people adopt a partisan identity, they immediately categorize the political world into an in-group (their own party) and an out-group (the opposing party). Decades of experimental research documents that any in-group versus out-group distinction, even one based on the most trivial of shared characteristics, will elicit both positive feelings for the in-group and negative evaluations of the out-group (for reviews, see Abrams & Hogg, 1990; Hogg, 2020). The more salient the sense of identity and the more competitive the relationship between the groups, the more severe these intergroup divisions (Brewer, 2001; Gaertner et al., 1993).

For Americans, partisanship is a particularly salient and powerful identity. They acquire this identity at a young age through parental influence, and it remains remarkably stable over the life cycle, notwithstanding significant shifts in personal circumstances (Jennings et al., 2009; Sears, 1975). Moreover, elections and political campaigns are occasions for meaningful competition between the parties, recur on a regular basis, and last for many months. The frequency and duration of campaigns provide powerful reminders of the high political stakes associated with the partisan divide. It is hardly surprising, therefore, that partisan identity triggers strong feelings of hostility toward political opponents, a phenomenon that political scientists now refer to as *affective polarization* (Iyengar et al., 2019).

In this chapter, we review the voluminous evidence on the rise of partisan animus. We then investigate predispositions that may explain variability in feelings toward the parties, focusing on the intensity of individuals' partisan identity and a measure of political tolerance as explanatory factors. We consider two indicators of identity intensity. The first corresponds to the American National Election Study's (ANES') measure of party identification that differentiates "strong" from "not so strong" and "leaning" identifiers.[1] Second, we include an indicator of what political scientists have termed *sorting*, meaning the degree to which individuals' partisan and ideological identities reinforce each other (see Levendusky, 2009). As anticipated, and in keeping with previous studies (Crawford & Pilanski, 2014; Toner et al., 2013; Van Proojean et al., 2015), we find that people at the two extremes of the partisan identity continuum (strong partisans) express substantially higher levels of out-group animus. Polarization is also higher among sorted partisans but only by a slight margin.

Political tolerance is a multidimensional concept (as illustrated by the chapters in this volume) and encompasses (among other things) openness to dissonant information (Hunt & Miller, 1968), acceptance of uncertainty (Van Baar et al., 2021), and willingness to grant rights and privileges to political and cultural out-groups (Golebiowska, 2014). Our measurement of the concept focuses on out-group tolerance since the ANES surveys regularly included only this question: "We should be more tolerant of people who choose to live according to their own moral standards even if they are very different from our own."

Previous research has documented a significant positive correlation between indicators of intolerance and measures of identity strength. People who identify as either strongly liberal or strongly conservative, for instance, score higher on dogmatic intolerance—the tendency to view one's political views as superior to the views of others (Brandt et al., 2014; Van Proojien & Krouwel, 2016). In a related study, strong liberals and strong conservatives both demonstrated lower support for the free speech rights of opposing political groups (Crawford & Pilanski, 2014).

While much of the evidence linking identity strength to intolerance focuses on political ideologues (e.g., strong liberals and strong conservatives), we can expect a similar result for partisanship, given the strong correlation between ideology and party identity in the United States.[2] As we noted above, Democrats in the United States increasingly identify as liberals, with Republicans having moved in the opposite direction. In one of the few studies to directly investigate the partisanship–tolerance nexus, Luttig (2017) found that people identifying as strong Republicans and strong Democrats both scored higher on a significant predictor of intolerance, namely, a standard measure of authoritarianism.[3]

Since strength of partisanship is implicated as a cause of out-party animus (see, e.g., Luttig, 2017), we anticipate that polarization should be weakened among the more tolerant. However, our results show that respondents who are relatively tolerant on the ANES measure express no less partisan animus than do their intolerant counterparts.

Affective Polarization: The Evidence

There is now ample evidence documenting the extent to which partisans treat each other as a disliked "other." The preponderance of the evidence derives from surveys but also includes behavioral indicators of discrimination and measures of implicit or subconscious partisan prejudice.

Survey Measures of Partisan Affect

Survey data tracking Americans' feelings toward the parties and their followers dates back to the 1960s. The indicator with the longest time series is the "feeling thermometer" question. Introduced into the ANES in 1964, the question asks respondents to rate the two parties, or "Democrats" and "Republicans," on a scale ranging from (0) indicating coldness to (100) indicating warmth. Since the measure targets both parties, by dividing the sample into Democrats and Republicans, it is possible to compare in-group and out-group affect over the past half-century.[4]

As widely reported in scholarly outlets (as well as in news reports), the trends in the feeling thermometer scores reveal substantially increased affective polarization. As shown in Figure 2.1, the gap between the in- and out-party thermometer scores more than doubled from around 23 degrees in 1978 to around 50 degrees in 2020. Virtually all the increase in affective

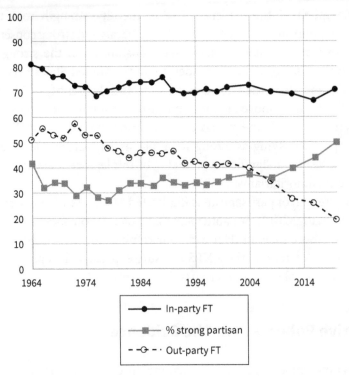

Figure 2.1 In-party and out-party thermometer scores and percentage of the electorate who are strong partisans: 1964–2020. FT = feeling thermometer.

polarization has occurred because of increased animus toward the opposing party. Warm feelings for one's own party have remained stable across the entire period.

Figure 2.1 also shows the trend in the proportions of Americans with a strong sense of partisan identity. Clearly, the increase in the number of strong partisans is associated with greater polarization. Stronger hostility for the out-party is a recent but rapidly escalating trend that began at the turn of the century. While the percentage of partisans who rated the out-party between 1 and 49 on the thermometer has increased steadily since the 1980s, the share of partisans expressing intense negativity for the out-party (ratings of 0) remained quite small until 2000. Post-2000, the size of this group has surged dramatically—from 8% in 2000 to 40% in 2020. Thus, the first two decades of the 21st century represent an acute era of polarization, in which what was only mild dislike for political opponents now appears to be a deeper form of animus (Iyengar & Krupenkin, 2018). As we will document, the recent intensification in intense negativity is attributable primarily to the growth in the number of strong partisans.

The identical pattern of increasing polarization reappears when we track respondents' feelings toward the presidential candidates. Until about 2000, partisans reported only ambivalent feelings toward the opposing party's nominee (average feeling thermometer scores of around 40). However, beginning in 2004, feelings toward the out-party candidate turn significantly colder, with average thermometer scores dropping to around 15 in 2016. As in the case of the party thermometers, partisans' feelings toward their own party nominee remain unchanged, and the strengthened polarization occurs because of increased hostility toward the opposing party nominee (see Iyengar & Krupenkin, 2018).

The feeling thermometer data show clearly the pronounced degree of affective polarization. It is important, however, to place the findings on partisan affect in some context. How does partisanship compare with other salient cleavages as a source of group polarization? Fortunately, the ANES surveys apply the feeling thermometers to multiple groups, making it possible to compare in-group versus out-group evaluations based on party, with evaluations based on race, religion, region, and other relevant groupings. These comparisons reveal that party is easily the most affectively laden group divide in the United States. Social out-groups including Muslims, atheists, Latinos, African Americans, gays, and poor people all elicit much warmer thermometer scores than the out-party (Iyengar et al., 2012).

This contrast between the party divide and sociocultural divides points to a major limitation of self-reported indicators of group affect. Survey responses on sensitive topics are highly reactive and susceptible to intentional exaggeration/suppression based on normative pressures. In the case of race, religion, gender, and other social divides, the expression of animus toward out-groups is tempered by strong social norms. Most individuals are prone to comply with applicable norms when asked sensitive questions. In the case of the party divide, however, there are no corresponding pressures to moderate disapproval of political opponents. If anything, the rhetoric and actions of political leaders suggest to their followers that hostility directed at the opposition is not only acceptable but also appropriate.

Implicit Measures

The normative pressures facing survey respondents make it difficult to establish a fair comparison of social with political divides as a basis for out-group animus. Fortunately, psychologists have developed an array of implicit or subconscious measures of group prejudice. These implicit measures provide a potentially more valid comparison of the bases for prejudice because they are harder to manipulate than explicit self-reports and therefore less susceptible to impression management or political correctness (Boysen et al., 2006).

Iyengar and Westwood (2015) developed the Party Implicit Association Test (IAT; based on the brief version of the Race IAT) to document unconscious partisan bias. Their results showed that approximately 70% of Democrats and Republicans demonstrate implicit bias in favor of their party. Interestingly, implicit bias proved less extensive than explicit bias as measured through survey questions; 91% of Republicans and 75% of Democrats in the same study explicitly evaluated their party more favorably. This is a clear reversal from the case of race or religion where social norms restrain the expression of conscious hostility toward out-groups, resulting in higher levels of implicit over explicit prejudice.

To place the results from their Party IAT in context, Iyengar and Westwood also administered the Race IAT. Surprisingly, relative to implicit racial bias, implicit partisan bias proved more widespread. The difference in the D-score—the operational indicator of implicit bias—was .50 for the party divide.[5] The corresponding difference in implicit racial bias across the racial divide was only .18. Thus, prejudice toward the partisan out-group exceeded bias directed at the racial out-group by more than 150 percent!

Indicators of Social Distance

An even more unobtrusive measure of partisan affect is the sense of *social distance*, the extent to which individuals feel comfortable interacting with out-group members in a variety of different settings. If political affiliations are meaningful, partisans should be averse to entering into close interpersonal relations with their opponents. The most striking case of increased social distance across the party divide concerns interparty marriage. In the early 1960s, the percentage of partisans expressing concern over the prospect of their son or daughter marrying someone from the opposition party was in the single digits, but some 45 years later, it had risen to more than 25% (Iyengar et al., 2012). Among Republicans, one-half expressed dismay at the prospect of their offspring marrying a Democrat. Today, the party divisions and resulting out-party animus are sufficiently strong to motivate partisans to associate with like-minded others.

More compelling evidence of politically motivated social distance comes from online dating sites and other available sources of "big data" indicating that the party cue does in fact influence the decision to enter into interpersonal relations. In one longitudinal analysis spanning 1965–2015, the authors found that spousal agreement on partisanship moved from 73% to 82%, while disagreement fell from 13% to 6% (Iyengar et al., 2018). Since the 1965 sample of spouses had been married for decades, they had many opportunities to persuade their partner, thus inflating the observed level of agreement. When the researchers limited the focus to younger couples, they found a more impressive shift in spousal agreement; among recently married couples in 1973, spousal agreement registered at 54%. For the comparable group of recently married couples in the 2014 national voter file, spousal partisan agreement reached 74%. This is an increase of 36% in partisan agreement among couples who have had little opportunity to persuade each other.

Online dating sites are a rich source of data on the politics underlying interpersonal attraction. Huber and Malhotra (2017) leveraged data from a major dating website where they gained access to both the daters' personal profiles as well as their messaging behavior. They found that ideological agreement increases the likelihood of two people exchanging messages by 10%.[6] To put that difference in perspective, the comparable difference for couples matched on socioeconomic status (using education as the indicator) was 11%. Thus, politics appears to be just as relevant as social standing in the process of selecting a romantic partner.

The fact that individuals date and marry co-partisans does not necessarily mean that politics was the basis for their choice. Agreement on partisanship may be a byproduct of spousal selection on some other attribute correlated with partisan identity, such as economic status. While some researchers argue that partisan agreement among couples is in fact "induced" or accidental, others provide evidence in favor of an active selection model in which the political affiliation of the prospective partner is the point of attraction. For instance, Iyengar et al. (2018) and Klofstad et al. (2013) showed that spousal agreement in the current era is more attributable to selection based on politics than alternative mechanisms including induced selection, the homogeneity of marriage markets, and agreement due to one spouse gradually persuading the other.

Dating and marriage both entail long-term and more intimate relationships. Does politics also impede the initiation of more casual friendships? Surveys by the Pew Research Center suggest that it does. About 64% of Democrats and 55% of Republicans say they have "just a few" or "no" close friends who are from the other political party (Pew Research Center, 2017). Thus, partisanship appears to act as a litmus test even at the level of casual social encounters.

Intergenerational Transmission of Polarized Attitudes

Further evidence of the extreme level of polarization emerges from studies of childhood socialization. For decades, the socialization literature documented the absence of party polarization among preadults. Instead, children affiliating with both parties granted political leaders uniformly high levels of support, a finding some scholars dubbed the "benevolent leader" syndrome (Greenstein, 1960; Hess and Torney, 1967; for a review of the literature, see Kinder & Sears, 1981; Sears, 1975). More recent studies, conducted after the advent of affective polarization, discovered that children no longer display blanket positivity; instead, the party divide in evaluations of political leaders and institutions closely matches adult attitudes (Mayer et al., 2022; Tyler & Iyengar, 2022). Moreover, these more recent studies show that other indicators of affective polarization—including the sense of social distance from political opponents—are just as prevalent in children as in adults.

The dominant explanation for heightened polarization in childhood is parental influence. In the 1980s, the level of parent–offspring agreement on partisanship was around 60%; by 2019, it had risen substantially to over 80% (Tyler & Iyengar, 2022). The impact of strengthened parent–child correspondence on polarization is clear. In 1980, children who adopted or rejected the parent's affiliation expressed uniform levels of trust in political leaders; but by 2019, there is a significant trust differential in favor of the in-party among offspring who report the same party affiliation as their parents. Since familial agreement is a proxy for parental influence, these results indicate that parental influence has contributed to partisan animus among children.

Behavioral Evidence of Partisan Bias

Survey measures of partisan affect are subject to several limitations since people can answer questions in ways that do not reveal their true feelings. In response, scholars have turned to behavioral manifestations of partisan animus in both lab and naturalistic settings. Iyengar and Westwood (2015) have used economic games as a platform for documenting the extent to which partisans are willing to endow or withhold financial rewards from players who either share or do not share their partisan affiliation. In the trust game, the researcher gives Player 1 an initial endowment ($10) and instructs them that they are free to give all, some, or none to Player 2 (said to be a member of a designated group). Player 1 is further informed that any amount they donate to Player 2 will be tripled by the researcher and that Player 2 is free (although under no obligation to do so) to transfer an amount back to Player 1. The dictator game is an abbreviated version of the trust game in which there is no opportunity for Player 2 to return funds to Player 1 and the researcher does not add to the funds transferred. Since there is no opportunity for Player 1 to observe the strategy of Player 2, variation in the amount Player 1 allocates to the different categories represented by Player 2 in the dictator game is attributable only to group dislike and prejudice. As Fershtman and Gneezy (2001, p. 354) put it, "any transfer distribution differences in the dictator game must be due to a taste for discrimination."

The trust and dictator games provide a consequential test of out-group bias, for they assess the extent to which participants are willing to transfer money they would otherwise receive themselves to co-partisans while simultaneously withholding money from opposing partisans. For both the trust game and the dictator game, partisan bias emerges as the difference between the amount allocated to co-partisans and opposing partisans. The results reported by Iyengar and Westwood (2015) show the expected pattern: Co-partisans consistently receive a bonus, while opposing partisans are subject to a financial penalty. As in the case of implicit bias, the effects of party affiliation on donations exceeded the effects of ethnicity. In fact, the effects of racial similarity proved negligible and not significant—co-ethnics were treated more generously (by 8 cents) in the dictator game but incurred a loss (7 cents) in the trust game. As in the case of the survey data, social norms appear to suppress racial discrimination in the trust and dictator games.

Iyengar and Westwood (2015) shed further light on the extent of affective polarization by comparing the effects of partisan and racial cues on non-political judgments. In one study, they asked participants to select one of two candidates for a college scholarship. The candidates (both high school students) had similar academic credentials but differed in their ethnicity (White or African American) or partisanship (Democrat or Republican). The results indicated little racial bias; Whites, in fact, preferred the African American applicant (55.8%). In contrast, partisan favoritism was rampant: 79.2% of Democrats picked the Democratic applicant, and 80% of Republicans picked the Republican applicant. These results held even when the out-partisan candidate had a significantly higher grade point average (4.0 vs. 3.5); in fact, the probability of a partisan selecting the more qualified out-party candidate never rose above 30%.

In an important extension to the behavioral literature, researchers have shown that partisanship can distort labor markets. Using an audit design, Gift and Gift (2015) mailed out resumés signaling job applicants' partisan affiliation in a heavily Democratic area and a heavily Republican area. They found that in the Democratic area, Democratic resumés were 2.4 percentage points more likely to receive a callback than Republican resumés; the corresponding partisan preference for Republican resumés in the Republican area was 5.6 percentage points. Whereas Gift and Gift examined employer preferences, McConnell et al. (2018) examined the other side of the labor market and how partisanship affects employee behavior. These researchers hired workers to complete an online editing task and subtly signaled the partisan identification of the employer. Unlike Gift and Gift, they mainly found evidence of in-group favoritism as opposed to out-group prejudice.

In summary, self-reported feelings toward the parties, subconscious partisan prejudice, increased social distance based on political affiliation, and multiple instances of behavioral discrimination against opposing partisans all converge on the finding of intensified party polarization in the United States. We turn next to our analysis of individual differences in affective polarization.

Using the ANES Time Series to Identify Individual-Level Variability in Polarization

Despite the extensive literature bearing on affective polarization, few studies have addressed the question of variability across individuals in partisan attitudes. Given the focus of this volume, we are especially interested in whether individuals who exhibit higher levels of political tolerance are less polarized. We also investigate the strength of partisan identity as a likely explanatory variable. In what follows, we describe our data sources, measurement strategy, and results.

In a series of public opinion surveys spanning eight decades, the ANES has polled the American people concerning their partisanship, attitudes toward candidates and social groups, and many other opinions, traits, and behaviors. The ANES has consistently used high-quality probability samples to represent the American citizen population as accurately as possible and has been conducted during every presidential election since 1948 (and after "off-year" congressional elections from 1958 through 2002).

We rely on the previously described "thermometer" questions about Democrats and Republicans to measure affective polarization by taking the difference between the in-party and out-party ratings. Larger differences indicate a more polarized populace. These questions appear in ANES surveys conducted during every presidential election since 1964 and every off-year congressional election from 1966 through 1998. We analyze these differences to answer two questions about individual variability in polarized feelings.

First, as polarization has increased over time, how has individual variability in polarized feelings changed? In other words, as the parties in the electorate became more hostile to one another on average, has the public also become more consistently polarized? Second, what characteristics help to explain the individual-level differences? As we noted earlier, these analyses are limited to partisans, excluding about a tenth of the population who neither identify with Democrats or Republicans nor "lean" toward one of these parties.

Variability in polarized feelings toward the parties is measured by the standard deviation (SD) and the relative standard deviation (RSD) of the difference between the in-party and out-party feeling thermometers. RSD, also known as the *coefficient of variation*, is the SD divided by the mean. In this case, it is the SD of the difference between the in-party and out-party feeling thermometers divided by the mean of the difference between those feeling thermometers. A higher SD or RSD indicates more variation in polarization, such as an electorate in which many partisans are highly polarized but many others are polarized only slightly or not at all. In contrast, a lower SD or RSD indicates less variation among individual partisans.

We examine individual characteristics associated with polarization by regressing several variables on the difference between in-party and out-party feeling thermometers. As in the first analysis, this analysis is limited to partisans. The predictor variables include the following:

1. Dummy variables for partisan strength (identifying strong and weak partisans, compared to leaning partisans as the reference category)
2. A dummy variable for partisan sorting (comparing sorted partisans who respond consistently to the party identification and ideology questions with partisans who respond inconsistently)
3. Tolerance, indicated by a question asking how much respondents agree or disagree with the following statement: "We should be more tolerant of people who choose to live according to their own moral standards even if they are very different from our own." We categorized respondents who agreed as tolerant. The analysis is limited to the years 1988 through 2020, when the ANES surveys included the tolerance question.
4. Dummy variables for year
5. Interaction terms for year and tolerance
6. Control variables for gender and for race (White or non-White)

We present the results showing individual variability in polarization over time in Table 2.1. In-party feeling thermometers fell slightly from a mean around 80 in the mid-1960s to values mostly in the low or mid-70s since 1972. This

Table 2.1 Individual Differences in In- versus Out-party Attitude Differences: 1964–2020

	Feeling thermometer means				
Year	In-party	Out-party	Difference	SD of Diff.	RSD
1964[a]	81	51	30	31	1.01
1966[a]	79	56	24	26	1.10
1968[a]	76	53	23	27	1.17
1970[a]	76	52	24	26	1.07
1972[a]	73	57	15	25	1.61
1974[a]	72	53	19	24	1.27
1976[a]	69	53	16	22	1.37
1978	71	48	23	25	1.09
1980[a]	72	53	19	24	1.25
1980	72	47	25	27	1.08
1982[a]	73	49	24	26	1.12
1982	74	44	30	27	0.90
1984	74	46	28	29	1.04
1986	74	46	28	28	1.02
1988	76	46	30	30	0.99
1990	71	47	24	27	1.12
1992	70	42	28	27	0.99
1994	70	42	27	27	0.98
1996	71	41	30	29	0.97
1998	70	41	29	29	0.99
2000	72	42	31	28	0.93
2002	–	–	–	–	–
2004	73	40	34	30	0.89
2006	–	–	–	–	–
2008	70	35	36	30	0.86
2010	–	–	–	–	–
2012	69	28	42	31	0.75
2014	–	–	–	–	–
2016	67	26	41	32	0.79
2018	–	–	–	–	–
2020	71	19	52	33	0.63

[a] A question asked about "Democrats" or "Republicans"; absence of an "a" indicates the question asked about "Democratic Party" or "Republican Party."

Note. Estimates are weighted using VCF0009z. *SD* = standard deviation; *RSD* = relative standard deviation (a.k.a. coefficient of variation; the *SD* divided by the mean [difference]). From ANES Cumulative Data File, version November 18, 2021.

consistency of in-party affect was described earlier. Clearly, polarization has been driven by a precipitous decline in out-party affect, as ratings declined from the neutral 50s in the 1960s and 1970s to the slightly negative 40s in the 1980s and 1990s to the low of 19 in 2000. With these declines the differences between in- and out-party thermometers increased from, for example, a low of 15 points in 1972 to a high of 52 points in 2020.

In absolute terms the variability in partisan affect has remained stable (*SD* of 28 in 2000 compared to 33 in 2020), but with the growing divide between the parties the *RSD* has narrowed from .93 to .63 over the same period. This indicates that the change over these 20 years is concentrated in the average thermometer rating of the out-party, with changes to the in-party rating and the variability of the difference between the ratings being relatively minor. The relative stability of the *SD* in partisan affect differences ("*SD* of Diff." in Table 2.1) suggests consistency over time in the mechanisms driving individuals' ratings of the two parties.

We turn next to the regression analysis of polarization over time (see Table 2.2). The results show, unsurprisingly—given the results shown in Figure 2.1—that the difference between in-party and out-party attitudes is driven strongly by partisan identity strength, such that strong partisans are expected to have a 30-point increase in feeling thermometer differences compared to the weakest (leaning) partisans, and weak partisans are expected to have a 4-point increase. Also as expected, sorted partisans have larger thermometer differences (but only by a margin of about 4 points). More unexpectedly, the model shows that tolerance of different moral standards is not a meaningful predictor of affective polarization. The estimated difference in the in-party and out-party thermometer scores between tolerant and intolerant respondents is less than 1 point.

In an attempt to replicate the results shown in Table 2.2, we carried out a parallel cross-sectional analysis of the thermometer scores by focusing on the "post-polarization" election years. We pooled the 2008, 2012, 2016, and 2020 studies and reran the earlier regression model on this data set. These results appear in Table 2.3. In this more parsimonious model, partisan strength and partisan sorting have effect sizes similar to the first model; but sorting becomes non-significant, and tolerance now surpasses the traditional threshold of statistical significance with a very small effect of −0.6 points on the thermometer difference.

Overall, the over-time and cross-sectional regressions indicate that strength of partisanship is the primary driver of affective polarization. If we consider identity strength as a continuum ranging from strong to weak

Table 2.2 Regression Model of Party Polarization: 1988–2020

Characteristic	B	SE	p
Strong partisan	29.6	0.53	.000
Weak partisan	3.9	0.52	.000
Partisan sorting	−4.1	1.48	.006
Moral tolerance	0.4	0.52	.429
Year 1988	3.7	2.22	.095
Year 1990	−0.9	2.53	.728
Year 1992	1.5	1.96	.435
Year 1994	−4.1	2.16	.059
Year 1996	−1.1	2.45	.655
Year 1998	4.2	2.36	.074
Year 2000	1.8	2.40	.448
Year 2004	6.0	2.61	.021
Year 2008	9.8	2.28	.000
Year 2012	15.6	1.92	.000
Year 2016	12.1	1.95	.000
Year 1988 × tolerance	−0.9	0.82	.262
Year 1990 × tolerance	−1.2	0.90	.195
Year 1992 × tolerance	−0.6	0.70	.381
Year 1994 × tolerance	1.4	0.78	.078
Year 1996 × tolerance	1.3	0.86	.119
Year 1998 × tolerance	−1.2	0.91	.185
Year 2000 × tolerance	0.2	0.87	.821
Year 2004 × tolerance	−0.5	0.95	.626
Year 2008 × tolerance	−1.1	0.85	.189
Year 2012 × tolerance	−1.3	0.69	.052
Year 2016 × tolerance	−0.7	0.73	.332
Race (White)	−1.8	0.53	.001
Gender (male)	−0.7	0.43	.120
Constant	17.1	1.51	.000

Note. $R^2 = .236$, $n = 21{,}709$. Sampling errors are linearized but do not account for sample clusters or strata.

leaning partisans, the mean thermometer differences show a significant drop-off in polarization among partisans who do not express a strong identity. The mean thermometer differences are 54 points for strong partisans, 25 for weak partisans, and 23 for leaners. Given recent work suggesting that dogmatism and perceptions of group threat are more likely to be expressed by conservatives than liberals (see, e.g., Jost, 2017; Jost et al., 2003), we computed the mean in-party versus out-party thermometer rating separately

Table 2.3 Regression Model of Party Polarization: 2008, 2012, 2016, 2020

Characteristic	B	SE	p
Strong partisan	32.5	0.87	.000
Weak partisan	4.1	0.95	.000
Partisan sorting	−4.5	3.07	.146
Moral tolerance	−0.6	0.31	.039
Race (White)	−3.1	0.87	.000
Gender (male)	0.1	0.74	.914
Constant	29.7	1.22	.000

Note. $R^2 = .231$, $n = 9539$. Sampling errors are linearized but do not account for sample clusters or strata.

for Republicans and Democrats. The results showed no traces of ideological asymmetry in out-party animus; the mean ratings were no different across the party divide.

Discussion

To the extent that affective polarization varies across individuals, the strength of individuals' partisan identity is clearly the paramount explanatory variable. When we treat the average thermometer difference in each election study as the outcome variable and regress it against the proportion of partisans who fall into the "strong" category (see Figure 2.2), the model achieves a very good fit, explaining 82% of the over-time variance in the thermometer difference scores. As the proportion of strong partisans has increased, so too has the difference in the thermometer ratings of the in- and out-parties.[7]

Although our results for strength of partisan identity represent a clear dispositional explanation for the increased level of affective polarization, we must acknowledge the importance of potential situational factors that may contribute to both strength of partisan identity and out-party animus. In particular, affective polarization has spread during a period of profound changes in the media environment. Changes in the media market coupled with the revolution in information technology have empowered consumers to encounter news on their own terms. The availability of 24-hour cable news channels provided partisans with their first real opportunity to obtain news from like-minded sources (Fox News first for Republicans and MSNBC later for Democrats). The subsequent development of "new media" provided a much wider range of media choices, which greatly facilitated partisans' ability to obtain political information and commentary

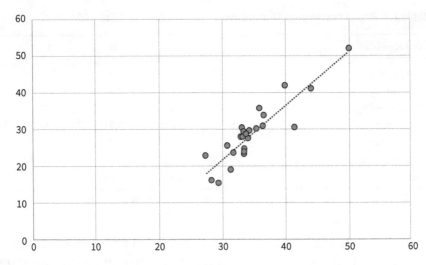

Figure 2.2 Scatter plot (with trend line) of percentage of partisans who are "strong" (*x*-axis) and in-/out-party thermometer difference (*y*-axis): 1964–2020.

consistent with their leanings. In a break with the dominant paradigm of non-partisan journalism, a growing number of outlets, motivated in part by the commercial success of the Fox News network, offered reporting in varying guises of partisan commentary. Many of these partisan outlets depict the opposing party in harsh terms (Berry & Sobieraj, 2013) and focus disproportionately on out-party scandals (real or imagined). Hundreds of politically oriented websites provide news and analysis—often vitriolic—with very little cross-party exposure (Adamic & Glance, 2005). The creation of vast online social networks permitted extensive recirculation of news reports, even to those not particularly motivated to seek out news. This technologically enhanced media environment and partisans' ability to encounter "friendly" information providers are likely agents of polarization (see, e.g., Sunstein, 2017).

There is another possible situational explanation of why partisans have increasingly become sworn enemies. It is abundantly clear that elite rhetoric and campaign messaging in America have become more shrill and hostile over time (Berry & Sobieraj, 2013). During campaigns, attack ads outnumber promotional ads by at least 4:1 in recent elections (Fowler et al., 2013). Even in non-election contexts, political elites engage in name-calling and taunting of their opponents (Grimmer & King, 2011).

The conventional persuasion paradigm posits that exposure to and acceptance of persuasive communication are the key ingredients of "persuadability" (McGuire, 1985; Zaller, 1992). Given the extreme negativity of elite discourse, we can expect that relatively attentive voters (disproportionately strong partisans) will be both exposed to and accepting of the sentiment expressed by their party leaders, thereby increasing their level of affective polarization. There is only one direct test of this explanation, a study by Sood and Iyengar (2016) documenting that out-party animus increases over the course of recent presidential campaigns and that this change is attributable specifically to exposure to negative campaign advertising.

In closing, we note that the tendency of partisans (and especially strong partisans) to treat each other as stigmatized out-groups has grave ramifications for mechanisms of electoral accountability. Politicians who violate conventional norms or engage in inappropriate behavior or whose performance in office demonstrates incompetence remain unscathed at the polls. The release of the *Access Hollywood* tape and the lurid details of Donald Trump's behavior toward women would surely have ended the candidacy of any presidential candidate. Yet the impact on Donald Trump's poll numbers was miniscule. When animus toward the opposing candidate becomes the primary motive underlying vote choice, candidates who demonstrate incompetence, dishonesty, and unethical behavior will not face sanctions. We can only hope that at some point voters will return to the logic of "reward–punish" based on candidates' credentials and performance.

Notes

1. The ANES first asks respondents to indicate whether they consider themselves as Democrats, Independents, or Republicans (or something else). Democrats and Republicans answer a follow-up question about the strength of their identification. The pair of questions results in a 7-point scale: strong Republican, weak Republican, independent leaning Republican, independent, independent leaning Democratic, weak Democrat, strong Democrat.
2. In the 2020 ANES, the simple correlation between ideology and party identity (both measured along 7-point scales) was .74.
3. Stenner (2005) provides extensive evidence of the authoritarianism–intolerance linkage.
4. By definition, in-group and out-group affect applies only to partisans. Scholars of affective polarization typically exclude independents from consideration.
5. The D-score in the IAT ranges from −2 to 2.
6. The researchers did not consider any indicator of affective polarization in their research.
7. Figure 2.2 is based on the combined ANES data, pooling across the face-to-face and online survey modes. When we limit the data to the former, the relationship between strength of partisanship and polarization falls slightly but remains highly significant.

References

Abramowitz, A. I., & Saunders, K. L. (2008). Is polarization a myth? *The Journal of Politics, 70*(2), 542–555. https://doi.org/10.1017/S0022381608080493

Abrams, D. E., & Hogg, M. A. (1990). *Social identity theory: Constructive and critical advances*. Springer-Verlag.

Adamic, L. A., & Glance, N. (2005, May 10–14). *The political blogosphere and the 2004 U.S. election: Divided they blog* [Paper presentation]. Annual Workshop on the Weblogging Ecosystem, WWW2005, Chiba, Japan.

Berry, J. M., & Sobieraj, S. (2013). *The outrage industry: Political opinion media and the new incivility*. Oxford University Press.

Billig, M., & Tajfel, H. (1973). Social categorization and similarity in intergroup behaviour. *European Journal of Social Psychology, 3*(1), 27–52. https://doi.org/10.1002/ejsp.2420030103

Brandt, M. J., Reyna, C., Chambers, J. R., Crawford, J. T., & Wetherell, G. (2014). The ideological-conflict hypothesis: Intolerance among both liberals and conservatives. *Current Directions in Psychological Science, 23*(1), 27–34. https://doi.org/10.1177/0963721413510932

Boysen, G. A., Vogel, D. L., & Madon, S. (2006). A public versus private administration of the implicit association test. *European Journal of Social Psychology, 36*(6), 845–856. https://doi.org/10.1002/ejsp.318

Brewer, M. B. (2001). Ingroup identification and intergroup conflict. In R. D. Ashmore, L. Jussim, & D. Wilder (Eds.), *Social identity, intergroup conflict, and conflict reduction* (Vol. 3, pp. 17–41). Oxford University Press.

Crawford, J. T., & Pilanski, J. M. (2014). Political intolerance, right and left. *Political Psychology, 35*, 841–851. https://doi.org/10.1111/j.1467-9221.2012.00926.x

Fershtman, C., & Gneezy, U. (2001). Discrimination in a segmented society: An experimental approach. *The Quarterly Journal of Economics, 116*(1), 351–377. https://doi.org/10.1162/003355301556338

Fiorina, M. P., Abrams, S. A., & Pope, J. C. (2008). Polarization in the American public: Misconceptions and misreadings. *The Journal of Politics, 70*(2), 556–560. https://doi.org/10.1017/S002238160808050X

Fleisher, R., & Bond, J. R. (2001). Evidence of increasing polarization among ordinary citizens. In J. E. Cohen, R. Fleischer, & P. Kantor (Eds.), *American political parties: Decline or resurgence?* (pp. 55–77). CQ Press.

Fowler, E. F., & Ridout, T. N. (2013). Negative, angry, and ubiquitous: Political advertising in 2012. *The Forum, 10*, 51–61. https://doi.org/10.1515/forum-2013-0004

Gaertner, S. L., Dovidio, J. F., Anastasio, P. A., Bachman, B. A., & Rust, M. C. (1993). The common ingroup identity model: Recategorization and the reduction of intergroup bias. *European Review of Social Psychology, 4*(1), 1–26. https://doi.org/10.1080/14792779343000004

Gift, K., & Gift, T. (2015). Does politics influence hiring? Evidence from a randomized experiment. *Political Behavior, 37*(3), 653–675. https://doi.org/10.1007/s11109-014-9286-0

Golebiowska, E. A. (2014). *The many faces of tolerance: Attitudes toward diversity in Poland*. Routledge.

Greenstein, F. I. (1960). The benevolent leader: Children's images of political authority. *American Political Science Review, 54*(4), 934–943. https://doi.org/10.2307/1952644" https://doi.org/10.2307/1952644

Grimmer, J., & King, G. (2011). General purpose computer-assisted clustering and conceptualization. *Proceedings of the National Academy of Sciences of the United States of America, 108*(7), 2643–2650. https://doi.org/10.1073/pnas.1018067108

Hess, R. D., & Torney, J. (1967). *The development of political attitudes in children*. Aldine Publishing.

Hetherington, M. J. (2001). Resurgent mass partisanship: The role of elite polarization. *American Political Science Review*, 95(3), 619–631. https://doi.org/10.1017/S000305540 1003045

Hogg, M. A. (2020). *Social identity theory*. Stanford University Press.

Huber, G. A., & Malhotra, N. (2017). Political homophily in social relationships: Evidence from online dating behavior. *The Journal of Politics*, 79(1), 269–283. https://doi.org/10.1086/687533

Hunt, M. F., Jr., & Miller, G. R. (1968). Open- and closed-mindedness, belief-discrepant communication behavior, and tolerance for cognitive inconsistency. *Journal of Personality and Social Psychology*, 8(1, Pt. 1), 35–37. https://psycnet.apa.org/doi/10.1037/h0021238Iyengar, S., Konitzer, T., & Tedin, K. (2018). The home as a political fortress: Family agreement in an era of polarization. *The Journal of Politics*, 80(4), 1326–1338. https://doi.org/10.1086/698929

Iyengar, S., & Krupenkin, M. (2018). The strengthening of partisan affect. *Political Psychology*, 39, 201–218. https://doi.org/10.1111/pops.12487

Iyengar, S., Lelkes, Y., Levendusky, M., Malhotra, N., & Westwood, S. J. (2019). The origins and consequences of affective polarization in the United States. *Annual Review of Political Science*, 22(1), 129–146. https://doi.org/10.1146/annurev-polisci-051117-073034

Iyengar, S., Sood, G., & Lelkes, Y. (2012). Affect, not ideology: A social identity perspective on polarization. *Public Opinion Quarterly*, 76(3), 405–431. https://doi.org/10.1093/poq/nfs038

Iyengar, S., & Westwood, S. J. (2015). Fear and loathing across party lines: New evidence on group polarization. *American Journal of Political Science*, 59(3), 690–707. https://doi.org/10.1111/ajps.12152

Jennings, M. K., Stoker, L., & Bowers, J. (2009). Politics across generations: Family transmission reexamined. *The Journal of Politics*, 71(3), 782–799. https://doi.org/10.1017/S002238160 9090719

Jost, J. T. (2017). Ideological asymmetries and the essence of political psychology. *Political Psychology*, 38(2), 167–208. https://doi.org/10.1111/pops.12407

Jost, J. T., Glaser, J., Kruglanski, A. W., & Sulloway, F. J. (2003). Political conservatism as motivated social cognition. *Psychological Bulletin*, 129(3), 339–375. https://psycnet.apa.org/doi/10.1037/0033-2909.129.3.339

Kinder, D. R., & Sears, D. O. (1981). Prejudice and politics: Symbolic racism versus racial threats to the good life. *Journal of Personality and Social Psychology*, 40(3), 414–431. https://psycnet.apa.org/doi/10.1037/0022-3514.40.3.414

Klofstad, C. A., McDermott, R., & Hatemi, P. K. (2013). The dating preferences of liberals and conservatives. *Political Behavior*, 35(3), 519–538. https://doi.org/10.1007/s11 109-012-9207-z

Levendusky, M. (2009). *The partisan sort: How liberals became Democrats and conservatives became Republicans*. Chicago University Press.

Luttig, M. D. (2017). Authoritarianism and affective polarization: A new view on the origins of partisan extremism. *Public Opinion Quarterly*, 81(4), 866–895. https://doi.org/10.1093/poq/nfx023

Mayer, J. D., Andolina, M. W., & McGrath, R. J. (2022). *Polarization's children: Political socialization in the age of hatred* [Unpublished manuscript]. George Mason University.

McCarty, N., Keith P., & Howard R. (2006). *Polarized America: The dance of ideology and unequal riches*. MIT Press.

McConnell, C., Margalit, Y., Malhotra, N., & Levendusky, M. (2018). The economic consequences of partisanship in a polarized era. *American Journal of Political Science*, 62(1), 5–18. https://doi.org/10.1111/ajps.12330

McGuire, W. J. (1985). Attitudes and attitude change. In G. Lindzey & E. Aronson (Eds.), *Handbook of social psychology* (3rd ed., Vol. 2, pp. 233–346). Random House.

Pew Research Center. (2017, October 5). *The partisan divide on political values grows even wider*. http://pewrsr.ch/2z0qBnt

Sears, D. O. (1975). Political socialization. In F. I. Greenstein & N. W. Polsby (Eds.), *Handbook of political science* (pp. 93–153). Addison-Wesley.

Sood, G., & Iyengar, S. (2016). *Coming to dislike your opponents: The polarizing impact of political campaigns* [Unpublished manuscript]. Stanford University. http://dx.doi.org/10.2139/ssrn.2840225" http://dx.doi.org/10.2139/ssrn.2840225

Stenner, K. (2005). *The authoritarian dynamic*. Cambridge University Press.

Sunstein, C. R. (2017). *#Republic: Divided democracy in the age of social media*. Princeton University Press.

Toner, K., Leary, M. R., Asher, M. W., & Jongman-Sereno, K. P. (2013). Feeling superior is a bipartisan issue: Extremity (not direction) of political views predicts perceived belief superiority. *Psychological Science*, *24*(12), 2454–2462. https://doi.org/10.1177%2F0956797613494848

Tyler, M., & Iyengar, S. (2022). *Learning to dislike your opponents: Political socialization in the era of polarization* [Unpublished manuscript]. Stanford University.

van Baar, J. M., Halpern, D. J., & FeldmanHall, O. (2021). Intolerance of uncertainty modulates brain-to-brain synchrony during politically polarized perception. *Proceedings of the National Academy of Sciences of the United States of America*, *118*(20), Article e2022491118. https://doi.org/10.1073/pnas.2022491118

van Prooijen, J. W., & Krouwel, A. P. (2017). Extreme political beliefs predict dogmatic intolerance. *Social Psychological and Personality Science*, *8*(3), 292–300. https://doi.org/10.1177%2F1948550616671403

van Prooijen, J. W., Krouwel, A. P., Boiten, M., & Eendebak, L. (2015). Fear among the extremes: How political ideology predicts negative emotions and outgroup derogation. *Personality and Social Psychology Bulletin*, *41*(4), 485–497. https://doi.org/10.1177%2F0146167215569706

Zaller, J. R. (1992). *The nature and origins of mass opinion*. Cambridge University Press.

II

OPEN- AND CLOSED-MINDED PROCESSING

Attitude Formation and Change

3
Attitudes in a Polarized World

Sociological and Psychological Processes of Reinforcement of Social and Political Worldviews

Angelita Repetto and Dolores Albarracín

On March 13, 2022, Google returned 55,900,000 entries associated with *political polarization*, and Google Trends showed that, in the United States, searches for this term had tripled since the creation of the application in 2004. Similarly popular has been the term *echo chamber*, which had 52,300,000 Google entries on March 13, 2022, and whose Google Trends index had doubled since 2004. Americans are polarized on such diverse topics as policing of African Americans, immigration, abortion, and the COVID-19 vaccine. For example, an analysis of the General Social Survey showed that, in 1985, 34% of Democrats and 33% of Republicans supported abortion "for any reason." In contrast, the gap widened in 1998, when 40% of Democrats and 29% of Republicans supported abortion "for any reason." By 2018, the gap had widened even more, when 62% of Democrats and 29% of Republicans supported abortion "for any reason" (see Kane, 2020; for an earlier analysis, see Dimaggio et al., 1996).

But what are the sociological and psychological processes that foster political polarization and the cultural wars that dominate American politics and other democracies in the world? This chapter concerns these issues and integrates sociological and social psychological perspectives to understand the complex interplay of de facto and self-initiated processes that allow individuals to maintain consistent, and often polarized, worldviews. Segregation and attitudinal selectivity provide a framework to consider how people develop social and political attitudes that are maintained by de facto (Sears & Freedman, 1967) selective exposure to attitudinally consistent information (Festinger, 1954; Hart et al., 2009).

A complete understanding of the processes that maintain attitudinal polarization must first address the sociological and structural determinants of the attitudes and information circulating within a group. In the case of political ideology and polarization, over time, segregation by education, socioeconomic status, as well as race and ethnicity separates the views of these demographic groups and causes ideological polarization through lifelong processes. In the United States, populations are physically segregated by education, socioeconomic status, and race/ethnicity. Thus, different groups interact primarily with others who are like them not only demographically but also in beliefs. This societal structure creates a perfect environment for psychological processes that further support attitudinal polarization in many areas but chiefly on social and political issues. For instance, in the United States, higher education is associated with being more liberal, higher socioeconomic status with being more conservative, and being a racial or ethnic minority with a Democratic affiliation and liberal ideology. Segregation that produces ideology is then aptly maintained by the media. Psychologically, selective exposure, selective attention, selective judgment, and selective dissemination are four processes that can help people to maintain their worldviews and uphold preestablished attitudes associated with segregated groups. Research has documented selective exposure to attitudinally agreeable information, as well as biased judgment and dissemination of information. These processes, which we review here, are relevant to social and political attitudes.

Figure 3.1 presents a theoretical integration of the sociological and psychological factors implicated in the maintenance of polarized attitudes. As shown, sociologically (see top part of the model), segregation among social groups (i.e., socioeconomic, educational, and racial/ethnic groups) creates attitude polarization. At the psychological level of the individual (see bottom part of model), these attitudes are thus maintained through selective exposure, selective judgment, and selective dissemination.

Sociological and Structural Processes

People are born into different zip codes and demographic groups that then instill core values aligned with ideology. They then espouse attitudes that are consistent with those values, which are also maintained through exposure to media after individuals are socialized. We begin with the processes by which segregation influences ideology and then continue with a brief analysis of the effects of the media.

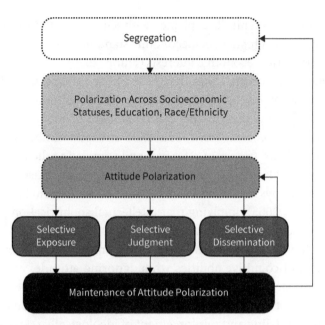

Figure 3.1 Chart visualizing the sociological and psychological processes that create attitude polarization.

Segregation by Socioeconomic Status, Education, and Race/Ethnicity

The people with whom you interact influence your attitudes and life outcomes, but in the United States, these interactions are not random (Baldassarri & Bearman, 2007). Spatial segregation by income, social class, and race/ethnicity influences with whom a person interacts and has been on the rise for decades (Massey & Denton, 1989). This increasing spatial segregation provides the sociological foundation for people interacting with similar others, even more now than in the past. In this section, we analyze how socioeconomic status and education as well as race/ethnicity drive polarization within a structural context of segregation.

Socioeconomic Status and Education

As mentioned, socioeconomic status is a demographic characteristic associated with political ideology (Argyle, 1994). Generally speaking, people with higher socioeconomic status are more likely to vote conservative (Gelman et al., 2005), to align with right-wing ideology, and to vote against programs that would increase their taxes (Barreto & Pedraza, 2009; Gelman et al., 2005).

This phenomenon is typically explained with self-interest theory, according to which people with a higher socioeconomic standing have conservative views to preserve their own economic interests (Dunn, 2011).

The general consensus about the United States is that education pushes individuals toward the liberal side of the ideological continuum (Dunn, 2011). There are two leading theories that can explain this phenomenon. According to the first, *developmental thesis*, education strengthens liberal attitudes by expanding students' frames of reference and stimulating their cognitive and personality growth (Phelan et al., 1995). However, increases in cognitive ability do not always mediate the link between education and liberal ideology (Kingston et al., 2003), implying that intellectual sophistication plays a role for some attitudes but not others.

The developmental thesis, however, has been criticized for emphasizing personality and cognitive abilities while ignoring attitudes and values. In response, the *socialization thesis* purports that education liberalizes political ideology not through cognitive development and personality growth but through modeling and reinforcement of ideologically relevant attitudes (Phelan et al., 1995). Ultimately, this theory assumes a more iterative process in which, if a society's values lean right, then education moves students toward the ideological right. In contrast, if a society's values lean left, then education moves students toward the ideological left. That is, education transmits political attitudes through the transmission of *core values* (Phelan et al., 1995). Even though, in theory, education instills values, not political identification, value priorities in the United States are such that a person's value priorities are associated with their liberal–conservative identification (Jacoby, 2006). According to Dunn (2011), core values of a country affect the direction of education's influence on political ideology. Moreover, education increases openness and cognitive flexibility, which in turn creates fertile ground for students to learn the core values instilled by the educational system (Dunn, 2011).

Regardless of the emphasis of each school of thought, it is clear that educational attainment influences political ideology. Considering the extreme educational inequality present in the United States, education is thus critical to American political polarization. In fact, according to an analysis of many nationally representative samples of American residents born between 1908 and 1995, educational inequality has increased largely as some populations continue to accumulate graduate degrees while many others cannot finish high school. These increasing educational inequalities are a potentially critical determinant of ideological polarization in the United States.

Race and Ethnicity

In the United States, the feeling of a shared fate associated with racial minorities is often stronger than party affiliation or political ideology (Kinder & Sanders, 1996). Accordingly, race and ethnicity directly influence political ideology, with members of particular racial and ethnic groups leaning toward political parties in ways that cannot be fully explained by other demographic characteristics such as education (Wolfinger, 1965). Lewis-Beck and colleagues (2008) studied ingroup identity and partisanship, verifying that African Americans vote for Democratic candidates. Nonetheless, racial and ethnic groups alone do not necessarily affect vote choice unless group membership is internalized as a collective identity (Barreto & Pedraza, 2009). Apart from members of racial and ethnic groups having similar disadvantages that influence voting interests, campaign messaging often targets voters by race and ethnicity. For example, campaign materials often appear in English and Spanish, with important Latinx officials promoting candidates and immigrant themes being present in campaign materials directed at Latinx households (De la Garza et al., 2010). Thus, campaigns remind Latinx voters of their ethnic identity in ways that strategically connect this identity to political attitudes (De la Garza et al., 2010).

The polarization associated with race appears in not only partisanship but also ideologically driven beliefs. For example, racial and ethnic identity can shape attitudes toward climate change in ways not accounted for by political ideology (Schuldt & Pearson, 2016). In a survey of US adults conducted by Schuldt and Pearson (2016), political ideology influenced White respondents' support for federal regulation of greenhouse gas emissions independently of whether or not they believed that climate change was real. In contrast, the climate change attitudes among non-White respondents were relatively unaffected by political ideology (Schuldt & Pearson, 2016). Beyond climate change, racial and ethnic identities predict support for a wide range of policy issues like education and unemployment spending (Chong & Rogers, 2005; Kinder & Winter, 2001). For example, a racial divide demarcates attitudes toward racial inequality and social services, as shown by the 1992 American National Election Study (Kinder & Winter, 2001). Furthermore, racial identification and racial consciousness affect political participation in the form of campaign activities, petitioning government officials, and participating in protests and boycotts more than they do turnout (Chong & Rogers, 2005), suggesting that specific issues energize activism among American racial and ethnic minorities.

Media Influences Once Ideology Is Established

The effects of demographic segregation on ideology go beyond socialization. In fact, in the United States, much of the news media are also separated by ideology, and partisan sites are disproportionally populated by partisan audiences (Shore et al., 2018). For example, liberals and conservatives overlap in only 51% of the accounts they follow (Eady et al., 2019). Interestingly, data collected by the Pew Research Center suggest that conservatives more frequently follow left-leaning accounts than liberals follow conservative-leaning accounts (Eady et al., 2019; Jurkowitz et al., 2020).

Online and offline media integrate a large media ecosystem (Benkler et al., 2018). Media ecosystems can maintain segregated attitudes through several mechanisms such as persuasion, cultivation, and familiarity. Persuasion entails internalization of media advocacies due to arguments that are perceived as convincing or originating from a trustworthy communicator (Albarracín, 2002, 2021; Albarracín & Shavitt, 2018; Albarracín & Vargas, 2010; Chaiken, 1980; Petty & Cacioppo, 1986). Cultivation entails the natural inclination to take an event's frequency in the media as evidence that the event is common in real life (Morgan & Shanahan, 1997; Wyer & Adaval, 2004; Wyer & Shrum, 2015). Cultivation also entails repeated presentation of an issue or statement in the media, creating perceptions that an issue is real or that a statement is accurate (De Keersmaecker et al., 2020; Hasher et al., 1977; Prentice & Miller, 1993). Thus, exposure to homogeneous realities or claims within one's segregated media can maintain social and political attitudes that were initially based on demographic segregation.

A series of studies on partisan beliefs and conspiracy beliefs analyzed associations with social influence in the United States (Albarracín et al., 2022). Media use influenced beliefs in political facts such as Obama's inaction contributing to the Syrian crisis during his presidency. For this belief, exposure to conservative media correlated with stronger endorsement of these beliefs, whereas exposure to both liberal and mainstream media correlated with weaker belief in these facts (Albarracín et al., 2022). In contrast, conspiracy beliefs were associated almost exclusively with conservative media exposure (Albarracín et al., 2022). This association was present for the belief that Obama faked his birth certificate to become president, the belief that the measles–mumps–rubella vaccine causes autism, and the belief that immigrants voting illegally swayed the 2016 popular vote from Donald J. Trump to Hillary Clinton. Informal social influence can also help to maintain attitudinal homogeneity within segregated demographic groups. For example, discussing a vaccination conspiracy theory with acquaintances and people online is correlated with these conspiracy beliefs (Albarracín et al., 2022), supporting the notion that weak ties are key sources of information (Granovetter, 1983).

Psychological Processes

Groups and their segregation within society create and maintain our social and political attitudes. But these attitudes are also sustained through social information processing mechanisms that start with the information we choose to consume and end with the information we disseminate to others. According to Albarracín (2021), having a prior attitude is among the most consequential factors in determining how external information is processed. To begin, people who have a prior attitude toward an issue have already made up their minds and may thus dismiss information that may seem redundant. Furthermore, even if they do seek out further information, the decision of what to seek and the processing of that information are largely driven by a person's attitudes. In the end, selective exposure, selective judgment, and selective dissemination can each reinforce prior attitudes, strengthening commitment to segregated worldviews and maintaining informational homogeneity within demographic groups.

Selective Exposure

Hart et al. (2009) meta-analyzed the experimental literature on selective exposure to determine the effects of preexisting attitudes, beliefs, and behaviors in a variety of contexts. The meta-analysis revealed a moderate to large and robust effect by which people chose more agreeable than disagreeable information, particularly for political and religious attitudes. Evidence regarding selective exposure is quite extensive. Therefore, we concentrate on social and political attitudes, presenting evidence about intergroup and political attitudes in turn.

Intergroup Attitudes

Intergroup attitudes and exposure to prejudice in informal and formal communication with others are intimately connected. The United States has seen a considerable shift in terms of legal equality for minority groups, and open bigotry against them has subsided. However, economic, educational, and health inequalities persist (Melican & Dixon, 2008). To begin, White Americans generally do not support public policies that would close racial gaps and continue to endorse racial stereotypes and negative intergroup attitudes (Entman & Rojecki, 2001; Sniderman & Piazza, 1993). These racial stereotypes include Whites' perception that Black people have a poor work ethic, low self-reliance, inadequate impulse control, and low levels of obedience to authority (Melican & Dixon, 2008).

Prejudice against out-groups is not due solely to race but also to immigrant status. Anti-immigrant attitudes are typically aimed at groups with high visibility as a result of dense settlements in major cities, distinct patterns of dress and religious/cultural patterns, and/or darker skin tone (Timberlake & Williams, 2012). According to Timberlake and Williams (2012), stereotyping and perceptions that immigrants pose a threat are partially derived from framing by news media. Also, political rhetoric and image-making activities of anti-immigration groups that target Mexican and other Latin American immigrants as a "problem" have effectively influenced popular opinion (Timberlake & Williams, 2012). Media focus on immigration is higher in states on the US–Mexican border, and this heightened media coverage leads residents in border states to label immigration as a "highly important" issue (Dunaway et al., 2010).

Not surprisingly, the contents of American media reflect prejudices and stereotypes in the American population (Monk-Turner et al., 2010). More or less subtle portrayals of ethnic and racial minorities and relevant policies often reinforce prejudice and stereotypes (Sears et al., 2000). Media coverage and population prejudice are an iterative process. The media increase prejudice in the population, and then members of that population seek media that confirm their media-based attitudes (Melican & Dixon, 2008).

Race has a nuanced effect on selective media exposure. Although White audiences do not necessarily avoid movies with largely Black casts, those who identify as "color-blind" are more interested in watching movies with White casts (Weaver, 2011). Because group membership and race play critical roles in a person's self-concept, social identity theory can explain these patterns of exposure (Archer et al., 2021; Hewstone et al., 1991; Tajfel, 1978; Weaver, 2011). First, because people strive to maintain a positive self-concept (Tajfel, 1978), they seek out media that paint their in-group in a positive light (Harwood, 1997; Mastro, 2003). Second, because people prefer their own groups and discriminate against out-groups, individuals are drawn to media that elevate the position of their in-group (Weaver, 2011).

Audiences can be divided into one group that intentionally seeks media because they support their discriminatory views and another that intentionally avoids the same media because they perpetuate racial and ethnic prejudices. Accordingly, the racial/ethnic group to which the audience belongs is an important predictor of media viewing (Archer et al., 2021; Rubin, 1982, 2002). Specifically, ethnic identity predicts both selection and avoidance of television for ethnic identity reasons (Abrams & Giles, 2009). Some of these choices, however, can be detrimental when the media present negative views about their social group. For example, Latinx and Black adults who are exposed to negative or oversexualized depictions of their racial group have less positive feelings toward their group (Tukachinsky et al., 2017).

Bandura's (2001) social cognitive theory has been used to suggest that people are drawn to media featuring their in-group because they seek similar behavioral models, rather than due to the need to elevate their in-group (see also Knobloch et al., 2005). Accordingly, audiences are motivated to seek contents featuring people of their same race because those models are useful for intergroup comparisons (Trepte, 2006; Weaver, 2011). Also, people are driven to create a positive social identity and elevate their in-groups. As such, they are partial to content that both references their in-group and depicts their in-group in a positive light (Trepte, 2006). Thus, the race of the actors impacts media choices among White audience members. The higher the percentage of Black actors in a film, the less likely White audiences are to be interested in watching the movie (Weaver, 2011).

Political Attitudes

Much of the work regarding political attitudes, selective exposure, and political polarization comes from survey research that assesses media exposure, political partisanship, and attitude polarization. Using methods designed to reduce self-report bias, survey research supports the idea that exposure to congenial political information increases political polarization. In a study of Israeli elections conducted by Tsfati and Chotiner (2016), three measures of media exposure, including direct report of the political leaning of the content participants encountered, showed that attitudes influenced exposure decisions. Specifically, exposure to agreeable media created the perception that more Israelis supported building new settlements in the West Bank among conservatives but did the opposite among liberals. That is, people chose attitude-consistent media and then derived social norms based on the contents of that media, which further increased the polarization of Israelis' attitudes.

Longitudinal approaches remain the strongest method when it comes to surveys because they can examine both the influence of ideology on media choices and the reciprocal influence of media on ideology. A panel study of Swedish elections conducted by Dahlgren et al. (2019) found reciprocal associations between media choices and ideology. The effect of attitudes on selection of ideologically consistent materials was more prevalent for online media than for other media. However, the degree of selective exposure was very low. Generally, people receive a variety of media, both in line with and opposite to their points of view.

One question is whether Democrats and Republicans show similar levels of selective exposure. Using an induced compliance paradigm, Vraga (2015) asked a sample of college students to write a counter-attitudinal essay and to then report their intentions to seek information about their own (vs. other) party and to discuss issues with people from their own (vs. other) party. Writing a counter-attitudinal essay should produce dissonance, but this hypothesis received no support. More generally, Republicans who wrote a counter-attitudinal essay selected more agreeable political information, suggesting that they were prone to selectively approach pro-attitudinal information. Democrats did not show this bias.

Selective exposure to partisan information does not always occur. For example, using an experimental design, Johnson et al. (2020) found selective exposure for only one issue. The phenomenon is also moderated by the probability that one's political party will win or lose. For example, in one experiment, participants made choices of articles that were presented in either print or online form (Pearson & Knobloch-Westerwick, 2019). Liberals, who were expected to win the election, chose liberal-leaning articles but only when the information appeared online rather than in print. Furthermore, conservatives, who were expected to lose the election, showed no bias in information exposure for either the online or print presentation.

Wojcieszak (2021) examined exposure to political information as a function of the ideological slant of the information, as well as the race and expertise of the source. Supporting the selective exposure notion, participants chose to read congenial information. They also chose to read information ostensibly coming from experts on gun control. However, race of the source was inconsequential. In fact, participants were as likely to seek information from same-race sources as they were to seek information from other-race sources.

Selective Judgment

Selective judgment occurs when messages aligned with people's beliefs and attitudes are easily accepted and contradictory messages are scrutinized and critiqued (Lord et al., 1979; Stroud, 2017). For example, people who believe that climate change is due to humans read congenial research less critically than they do research arguing that climate change is due to natural climatic patterns (Stroud, 2017). That is, judgments about information are biased by perceivers' attitudes (Lord et al., 1979). In fact, people often dismiss empirical evidence if it contradicts their previously held attitudes but readily accept evidence of the same quality if it supports their worldviews (Dursun & Tumer Kabadayi, 2013; Lord et al., 1979; Owenby, 2014).

An excellent illustration of the impact of prior beliefs and attitudes on intergroup judgments is the impact of the activation and application of a stereotype, which comprises the knowledge about a social group a person has stored in memory (Dijksterhuis et al., 2000; Krieglmeyer & Sherman, 2012; Kunda & Spencer, 2003). Stereotyping members of a social group can have extremely harmful effects, especially when the group is oppressed. For instance, evidence abounds that young Black men are stereotyped as aggressive, violent, dangerous, and likely to commit crimes (Trawalter et al., 2008), leading to implicit and explicit associations with threat (Cottrell & Neuberg, 2005; Payne, 2001). Due to being stereotyped as threatening, Black men have a higher likelihood of being wrongfully shot when holding regular objects than when holding weapons (Correll et al., 2006) and are often misperceived and misremembered as the aggressor in an interaction (Eberhardt et al., 2004; Essien et al., 2017).

One curious case of congenial judgment occurs when people hold conspiracy theories. People justify these beliefs due to the processes of (a) historic similarity, (b) psychological similarity (i.e., the audience's ability to understand the motives of others), and (c) normative plausibility (i.e., the audience's knowledge that others hold these beliefs) (Albarracín et al., 2022). According to Albarracín and colleagues (2022), people who believe that history has many examples of people falsifying documents to achieve power (i.e., historical plausibility) are more likely to also believe that Obama faked his birth certificate to become president. People who believe that people like them think that people fake documents to achieve power (i.e., normative plausibility) are also more likely to endorse the belief in Obama's cover-up. In fact, this form of normative plausibility correlated with conspiracy beliefs more strongly than it did with partisan but accurate beliefs, such as the belief that Obama's inaction caused the Syrian crisis or that the Tuskegee study occurred. Therefore, norms, inferred from discussions with others, are a key source of segregated information that maintains and even strengthens people's attitudes.

Another example of congenial judgment is unfalsifiability, the defining feature of conspiracy theories. Albarracín et al. (2022) measured perceived falsifiability by asking people to report whether, for example, any information could be used to determine if a belief was true or false. In the case of conspiracy beliefs, unfalsifiability was either uncorrelated or positively correlated with stronger endorsement of the beliefs. In contrast, beliefs in accurate events such the existence of the Tuskegee study were positively correlated with the possibility of falsifying the belief.

Selective Sharing

While biases in exposure and judgment can perpetuate the attitudes of an individual, selective information-sharing and activism can also promote attitude homogeneity within a group (see Figure 3.1). Of course, people who share an article on social media must first receive that article. For this reason, Weeks et al. (2017) studied incidental exposure, intentional exposure, and selective sharing in a longitudinal study. They found that incidental exposure drives partisans to seek more partisan information and to then share it with others. Thus, exposure and sharing are clearly related to each other.

Experimental research has also been able to compare patterns of information exposure with patterns of information-sharing. A study conducted in Norway (Johannesson & Knudsen, 2021) showed that, although participants were unbiased in their choices of reading materials, sharing was determined by their attitudes. The probability of sharing agreeable materials was 13% higher than the probability of reading the same material. Clearly then, selective sharing can be a vehicle to ensure agreement within one's social network.

The likelihood of both reading and sharing information was also higher when the source of the information was knowledgeable but was unaffected by the source's gender, religion, or popularity on social media (Johannesson & Knudsen, 2021). With respect to partisanship, participants are more likely to read news with which they agree and from sources within their own political party. For sharing, the political party of the source matters considerably but only when people have no knowledge of the direction of the advocacy. When the partisan position of the materials is known, it is the position of the news story, and not the source, that matters.

It is, however, reassuring that the patterns of political information-sharing do not always produce homogeneity. A study by Liang (2018) found that political messages are likely to travel across the ideological spectrum. That is, political messages can simply become viral and are widely shared regardless of ideology instead of being broadcasted in a top-down fashion. This diversity is likely to reduce the probability that networks will encounter congenial information just by virtue of homophily, which is the tendency to affiliate with like-minded others.

Closing Note

A combination of sociological and psychological processes appears to reinforce attitudes and maintain social and political polarization. For starters, social segregation creates intergroup boundaries across socioeconomic status, education, and race or ethnicity. The effects of segregation are then maintained through exposure to different media enclaves that support different worldviews in accordance with political ideology. The greater the segregation among groups, the greater the attitudinal polarization one observes; but these segregated attitudes are also maintained through the psychological processes of selective exposure, selective judgment, and selective dissemination of information.

One contribution of this chapter has been to integrate sociological and psychological determinants. This fruitful integration, however, should continue. For example, the links between physical segregation and the tendency to engage in selective information-processing has not been investigated. However, physical segregation may limit our capacity to reconcile conflicting information about the world, and this limitation may preclude some of the socialization benefits of education. Also, demographic variables interact to create intersectionality (Acker, 2006; Cole, 2009; McCall, 2005). In some cases, those intersectional identities dominate over and above race and ethnicity. For example, the ideological pathway for White gay men from religiously conservative families is not a straight line, and the impact of their different identities and the dynamic activation of these identities are yet to be ascertained.

References

Abrams, J. R., & Giles, H. (2009). Hispanic television activity: Is it related to vitality perceptions? *Communication Research Reports*, 26(3), 247–252. https://doi.org/10.1080/08824090903074456

Acker, J. (2006). Inequality regimes: Gender, class, and race in organizations. *Gender and Society*, 20(4), 441–464. https://doi.org/10.1177/0891243206289499

Albarracín, D. (2002). Cognition in persuasion: An analysis of information processing in response to persuasive communications. *Advances in Experimental Social Psychology*, 34, 61–130.

Albarracín, D. (2021). *Action and inaction in a social world: Predicting and changing attitudes and behaviors*. Cambridge University Press.

Albarracín, D., Albarracín, J., Chan, M.-p. S., & Jamieson, K. H. (2022). *Creating conspiracy beliefs: How our thoughts are shaped*. Cambridge University Press.

Albarracín, D., & Shavitt, S. (2018). Attitudes and attitude change. *Annual Review of Psychology*, 69, 299–327. https://doi.org/10.1146/annurev-psych-122216-011911

Albarracín, D., & Vargas, P. (2010). Attitudes and persuasion: From biology to social responses to persuasive intent. In S. T. Fiske, D. T. Gilbert, & G. Lindzey (Eds.), *Handbook of social psychology* (Vol. 1, pp. 394–427). Wiley. https://doi.org/10.1002/9780470561119.socpsy001011

Archer, J., Rackley, K. R., Broyles Sookram, S., Nguyen, H., & Awad, G. H. (2021). Psychological predictors for watching television: The role of racial representation. *Psychological Reports*, *125*(5), 2571–2590. https://doi.org/10.1177/00332941211025266

Argyle, M. (1994). *The psychology of social class*. Psychology Press.

Baldassarri, D., & Bearman, P. (2007). Dynamics of political polarization. *American Sociological Review*, *72*(5), 784–811. https://doi.org/10.1177/000312240707200507

Bandura, A. (2001). Social cognitive theory of mass communication. *Media Psychology*, *3*(3), 265–299. https://doi.org/10.1207/S1532785XMEP0303_03

Barreto, M. A., & Pedraza, F. I. (2009). The renewal and persistence of group identification in American politics. *Electoral Studies*, *28*(4), 595–605. https://doi.org/10.1016/J.ELECTSTUD.2009.05.017

Benkler, Y., Faris, R., & Roberts, H. (2018). *Network propaganda: Manipulation, disinformation, and radicalization in American politics*. Oxford University Press.

Chaiken, S. R. (1980). Heuristic versus systematic information processing and the use of source versus message cues in persuasion. *Journal of Personality and Social Psychology*, *39*(5), 752–766. https://doi.org/10.1037/0022-3514.39.5.752

Chong, D., & Rogers, R. (2005). Racial solidarity and political participation. *Political Behavior*, *27*(4), 347–374. https://doi.org/10.1007/S11109-005-5880-5

Cole, E. R. (2009). Intersectionality and research in psychology. *American Psychologist*, *64*(3), 170–180. https://doi.org/10.1037/a0014564

Correll, J., Urland, G. R., & Ito, T. A. (2006). Event-related potentials and the decision to shoot: The role of threat perception and cognitive control. *Journal of Experimental Social Psychology*, *42*(1), 120–128. https://doi.org/10.1016/J.JESP.2005.02.006

Cottrell, C. A., & Neuberg, S. L. (2005). Different emotional reactions to different groups: A sociofunctional threat-based approach to "prejudice." *Journal of Personality and Social Psychology*, *88*(5), 770–789. https://doi.org/10.1037/0022-3514.88.5.770

Dahlgren, P. M., Shehata, A., & Stromback, J. (2019). Reinforcing spirals at work? Mutual influences between selective news exposure and ideological leaning. *European Journal of Communication*, *34*(2), 159–174. https://doi.org/10.1177/0267323119830056

De Keersmaecker, J., Dunning, D., Pennycook, G., Rand, D. G., Sanchez, C., Unkelbach, C., & Roets, A. (2020). Investigating the robustness of the illusory truth effect across individual differences in cognitive ability, need for cognitive closure, and cognitive style. *Personality and Social Psychology Bulletin*, *46*(2), 204–215. https://doi.org/10.1177/0146167219853844

De la Garza, R. O., DeSipio, L., & Leal, D. L. (Eds.). (2010). *Beyond the barrio: Latinos in the 2004 elections*. University of Notre Dame Press.

Dijksterhuis, A., Aarts, H., Bargh, J. A., & van Knippenberg, A. (2000). On the relation between associative strength and automatic behavior. *Journal of Experimental Social Psychology*, *36*(5), 531–544. https://doi.org/10.1006/jesp.2000.1427

DiMaggio, P., Evans, J., & Bryson, B. (1996). Have Americans' social attitudes become more polarized? *American Journal of Sociology*, *102*(3), 690–755.

Dunaway, J., Branton, R. P., & Abrajano, M. A. (2010). Agenda setting, public opinion, and the issue of immigration reform. *Social Science Quarterly*, *91*(2), 359–378. https://doi.org/10.1111/J.1540-6237.2010.00697.X

Dunn, K. (2011). Left–right identification and education in Europe: A contingent relationship. *Comparative European Politics*, *9*(3), 292–316. https://doi.org/10.1057/cep.2010.17

Dursun, İ., & Tümer Kabadayi, E. (2013). Resistance to persuasion in an anti-consumption context: Biased assimilation of positive product information. *Journal of Consumer Behaviour*, *12*(2), 93–101. https://doi.org/10.1002/cb.1422

Eady, G., Nagler, J., Guess, A., Zilinsky, J., & Tucker, J. A. (2019). How many people live in political bubbles on social media? Evidence from linked survey and Twitter data. *Sage Open*, *9*(1). https://doi.org/10.1177/2158244019832705

Eberhardt, J. L., Purdie, V. J., Goff, P. A., & Davies, P. G. (2004). Seeing Black: Race, crime, and visual processing. *Journal of Personality and Social Psychology*, *87*(6), 876–893. https://doi.org/10.1037/0022-3514.87.6.876

Entman, R. M., & Rojecki, A. (2000). The Black image in the White mind: Media and race in America [Book Review]. *Journalism and Mass Communication Quarterly*, *77*(4), 921.

Essien, I., Stelter, M., Kalbe, F., Koehler, A., Mangels, J., & Meliß, S. (2017). The shooter bias: Replicating the classic effect and introducing a novel paradigm. *Journal of Experimental Social Psychology*, *70*, 41–47. https://doi.org/10.1016/j.jesp.2016.12.009

Festinger, L. (1954). A theory of social comparison processes. *Human Relations*, *7*(2), 117–140. https://doi.org/10.1177/001872675400700202

Gelman, A., Shor, B., Bafumi, J., & Park, D. (2005, November). *Rich state, poor state, red state, blue state: What's the matter with Connecticut?* SSRN. https://doi.org/10.2139/SSRN.1010426

Granovetter, M. S. (1983). The strength of weak ties: A network theory revisited. *Sociological Theory*, *1*, 201–233. https://doi.org/10.2307/202051

Hart, W., Albarracín, D., Eagly, A. H., Brechan, I., Lindberg, M. J., & Merrill, L. (2009). Feeling validated versus being correct: A meta-analysis of selective exposure to information. *Psychological Bulletin*, *135*(4), 555–588. https://doi.org/10.1037/a0015701

Harwood, J. (1997). Viewing age: Lifespan identity and television viewing choices. *Journal of Broadcasting & Electronic Media*, *41*(2), 203–213. https://doi.org/10.1080/08838159709364401

Hasher, L., Goldstein, D., & Toppino, T. (1977). Frequency and the conference of referential validity. *Journal of Verbal Learning and Verbal Behavior*, *16*(1), 107–112. https://doi.org/10.1016/S0022-5371(77)80012-1

Hewstone, M., Hantzi, A., & Johnston, L. (1991). Social categorization and person memory: The pervasiveness of race as an organizing principle. *European Journal of Social Psychology*, *21*(6), 517–528. https://doi.org/10.1002/EJSP.2420210606

Jacoby, W. G. (2006). Value choices and American public opinion. *American Journal of Political Science*, *50*(3), 706–723. https://doi.org/10.1111/j.1540-5907.2006.00211.x

Johannesson, M. P., & Knudsen, E. (2021). Disentangling the influence of recommender attributes and news-story attributes: A conjoint experiment on exposure and sharing decisions on social networking sites. *Digital Journalism*, *9*(8), 1141–1161. https://doi.org/10.1080/21670811.2020.1805780

Johnson, B. K., Neo, R. L., Heijnen, M. E. M., Smits, L., & van Veen, C. (2020). Issues, involvement, and influence: Effects of selective exposure and sharing on polarization and participation. *Computers in Human Behavior*, *104*, Article 106155. https://doi.org/10.1016/j.chb.2019.09.031

Jurkowitz, M., Mitchell, A., Shearer, E., & Walker, M. (2020, January 24). *Americans are divided by party in the sources they turn to for political news*. Pew Research Center. https://www.journalism.org/2020/01/24/americans-are-divided-by-party-in-the-sources-they-turn-to-for-political-news/

Kane, J. (2020, August 7). *The political polarization of abortion*. The Politics Doctor. http://thepoliticsdr.com/2020/08/08/the-political-polarization-of-abortion/

Kinder, D. R., & Sanders, L. M. (1996). *Divided by color: Racial politics and democratic ideals*. University of Chicago Press.

Kinder, D. R., & Winter, N. (2001). Exploring the racial divide: Blacks, Whites, and opinion on national policy. *American Journal of Political Science*, *45*(2), 439–456. https://doi.org/10.2307/2669351

Kingston, P. W., Hubbard, R., Lapp, B., Schroeder, P., & Wilson, J. (2003). Why education matters. *Sociology of Education, 76*(1), 53–70. https://doi.org/10.2307/3090261

Knobloch, S., Callison, C., Chen, L., Fritzsche, A., & Zillmann, D. (2005). Children's sex-stereotyped self-socialization through selective exposure to entertainment: Cross-cultural experiments in Germany, China, and the United States. *Journal of Communication, 55*(1), 122–138. https://doi.org/10.1111/j.1460-2466.2005.tb02662.x

Krieglmeyer, R., & Sherman, J. W. (2012). Disentangling stereotype activation and stereotype application in the stereotype misperception task. *Journal of Personality and Social Psychology, 103*(2), 205–224. https://doi.org/10.1037/A0028764

Kunda, Z., & Spencer, S. J. (2003). When do stereotypes come to mind and when do they color judgment? A goal-based theoretical framework for stereotype activation and application. *Psychological Bulletin, 129*(4), 522–544. https://doi.org/10.1037/0033-2909.129.4.522

Lewis-Beck, M. S., Norpoth, H., Jacoby, W. G., & Weisberg, H. F. (2008). *The American voter revisited*. University of Michigan Press. https://doi.org/10.3998/mpub.92266

Liang, H. (2018). Broadcast versus viral spreading: The structure of diffusion cascades and selective sharing on social media. *Journal of Communication, 68*(3), 525–546. https://doi.org/10.1093/joc/jqy006

Lord, C. G., Ross, L., & Lepper, M. R. (1979). Biased assimilation and attitude polarization: The effects of prior theories on subsequently considered evidence. *Journal of Personality and Social Psychology, 37*(11), 2098–2109. https://doi.org/10.1037/0022-3514.37.11.2098

Massey, D. S., & Denton, N. A. (1989). Hypersegregation in U.S. metropolitan areas: Black and Hispanic segregation along five dimensions. *Demography, 26*(3), 373–391. https://doi.org/10.2307/2061599

Mastro, D. E. (2003). A social identity approach to understanding the impact of television messages. *Communication Monographs, 70*(2), 98–113. https://doi.org/10.1080/0363775032000133764

McCall, L. (2005). The complexity of intersectionality. *Signs, 30*(3), 1771–1800. https://doi.org/10.1086/426800

Melican, D. B., & Dixon, T. L. (2008). News on the net: Credibility, selective exposure, and racial prejudice. *Communication Research, 35*(2), 151–168. https://doi.org/10.1177/0093650207313157

Monk-Turner, E., Heiserman, M., Johnson, C., Cotton, V., & Jackson, M. (2010). The portrayal of racial minorities on prime time television: A replication of the Mastro and Greenberg study a decade later. *Studies in Popular Culture, 32*(2), 101–114.

Morgan, M., & Shanahan, J. (1997). Two decades of cultivation research: An appraisal and meta-analysis. *Annals of the International Communication Association, 20*(1), 1–45. https://doi.org/10.1080/23808985.1997.11678937

Owenby, S. R. (2014). *Investigating the impact of general action and inaction goals on attitude polarization* [Unpublished doctoral dissertation]. Montana State University-Bozeman, College of Letters & Science.

Payne, B. K. (2001). Prejudice and perception: The role of automatic and controlled processes in misperceiving a weapon. *Journal of Personality and Social Psychology, 81*(2), 181–192. https://doi.org/10.1037/0022-3514.81.2.181

Pearson, G. D. H., & Knobloch-Westerwick, S. (2019). Is the confirmation bias bubble larger online? Pre-election confirmation bias in selective exposure to online versus print political information. *Mass Communication and Society, 22*(4), 466–486. https://doi.org/10.1080/15205436.2019.1599956

Petty, R. E., & Cacioppo, J. T. (1986). The elaboration likelihood model of persuasion. *Advances in Experimental Social Psychology, 19*, 123–205. https://doi.org/10.1016/S0065-2601(08)60214-2

Phelan, J., Link, B. G., Stueve, A., & Moore, R. E. (1995). Education, social liberalism, and economic conservatism: Attitudes toward homeless people. *American Sociological Review, 60*(1), 126–140. https://doi.org/10.2307/2096349

Prentice, D. A., & Miller, D. T. (1993). Pluralistic ignorance and alcohol use on campus. Some consequences of misperceiving the social norm. *Journal of Personality and Social Psychology, 64*(2), 243–256. https://doi.org/10.1037/0022-3514.64.2.243

Rubin, A. M. (1982). Television uses and gratifications: The interactions of viewing patterns and motivations. *Journal of Broadcasting, 27*(1), 37–51. https://doi.org/10.1080/08838158309386471

Rubin, A. M. (2002). The uses-and-gratifications perspective of media effects. In J. Bryant & D. Zillmann (Eds.), *Media effects: Advances in theory and research* (2nd ed., pp. 525–548). Lawrence Erlbaum Associates.

Schuldt, J. P., & Pearson, A. R. (2016). The role of race and ethnicity in climate change polarization: Evidence from a U.S. national survey experiment. *Climatic Change, 136*(3), 495–505. https://doi.org/10.1007/S10584-016-1631-3

Sears, D. O., & Freedman, J. L. (1967). Selective exposure to information: A critical review. *Public Opinion Quarterly, 31*(2), 194–213. https://doi.org/10.1086/267513

Sears, D. O., Sidanius, J., & Bobo, L. (2000). *Racialized politics: The debate about racism in America*. University of Chicago Press.

Shore, J., Baek, J., & Dellarocas, C. (2018). Twitter is not the echo chamber we think it is. *MIT Sloan Management Review, 60*(1), 1–5.

Sniderman, P. M., & Piazza, T. L. (1993). *The scar of race*. Harvard University Press. https://doi.org/10.4159/9780674043848

Stroud, N. J. (2017). Understanding and overcoming selective exposure and judgment when communicating about science. In K. H. Jamieson, D. M. Kahan, D. A. Scheufele (Eds.), *The Oxford handbook of the science of science communication* (pp. 376–387). Oxford University Press. https://doi.org/10.1093/oxfordhb/9780190497620.013.41

Tajfel, H. E. (1978). *Differentiation between social groups: Studies in the social psychology of intergroup relations*. Academic Press.

Timberlake, J. M., & Williams, R. H. (2012). Stereotypes of U.S. immigrants from four global regions. *Social Science Quarterly, 93*(4), 867–890. https://doi.org/10.1111/J.1540-6237.2012.00860.X

Trawalter, S., Todd, A. R., Baird, A. A., & Richeson, J. A. (2008). Attending to threat: Race-based patterns of selective attention. *Journal of Experimental Social Psychology, 44*(5), 1322–1327. https://doi.org/10.1016/J.JESP.2008.03.006

Trepte, S. (2006). Social identity theory. In J. Bryant & P. Vorderer (Eds.), *Psychology of entertainment* (pp. 255–271). Routledge.

Tsfati, Y., & Chotiner, A. (2016). Testing the selective exposure–polarization hypothesis in Israel using three indicators of ideological news exposure and testing for mediating mechanisms. *International Journal of Public Opinion Research, 28*(1), 1–24. https://doi.org/10.1093/ijpor/edv001

Tukachinsky, R., Mastro, D., & Yarchi, M. (2017). The effect of prime time television ethnic/racial stereotypes on Latino and Black Americans: A longitudinal national level study. *Journal of Broadcasting and Electronic Media, 61*(3), 538–556. https://doi.org/10.1080/08838151.2017.1344669

Vraga, E. K. (2015). How party affiliation conditions the experience of dissonance and explains polarization and selective exposure. *Social Science Quarterly, 96*(2), 487–502. https://doi.org/10.1111/ssqu.12138

Weaver, A. J. (2011). The role of actors' race in White audiences' selective exposure to movies. *Journal of Communication, 61*(2), 369–385. https://doi.org/10.1111/J.1460-2466.2011.01544.X

Weeks, B. E., Lane, D. S., Kim, D. H., Lee, S. S., & Kwak, N. (2017). Incidental exposure, selective exposure, and political information sharing: Integrating online exposure patterns and expression on social media. *Journal of Computer-Mediated Communication, 22*(6), 363–379. https://doi.org/10.1111/jcc4.12199

Wojcieszak, M. (2021). What predicts selective exposure online: Testing political attitudes, credibility, and social identity. *Communication Research, 48*(5), 687–716. https://doi.org/10.1177/0093650219844868

Wolfinger, R. E. (1965). The development and persistence of ethnic voting. *American Political Science Review, 59*(4), 896–908. https://doi.org/10.2307/1953212

Wyer, R. S., & Adaval, R. (2004). Pictures, words, and media influence: The interactive effects of verbal and nonverbal information on memory and judgments. In L. Shrum (Ed.), *The psychology of entertainment media: Blurring the lines between entertainment and persuasion* (pp. 137–159). Lawrence Erlbaum Associates.

Wyer, R. S., Jr., & Shrum, L. J. (2015). The role of comprehension processes in communication and persuasion. *Media Psychology, 18*(2), 163–195. https://doi.org/10.1080/15213269.2014.912584

4
Openness and Persuasion
Multiple Processes, Meanings, and Outcomes

Pablo Briñol and Richard E. Petty

A common treatment of the term *openness* within the persuasion literature is to refer to the readiness of a person to contemplate changing in response to a persuasive advocacy. It is sometimes called *receptiveness* (e.g., Hussein & Tormala, 2021; Minson & Chen, 2022) and is a mindset that precedes actual attitude change (cf., Norcross et al., 2011). It reflects that the message recipient is at least willing to listen to the speaker (cf., Itzchakov et al., 2018). Having an open mindset does not require that a person has an explicit intention to change or that change is the ultimate goal. Being open to some point of view simply means that change is possible and that change is more likely than if the person was not open to considering that view.

This definition of openness is the polar opposite of the term on the other side of the continuum, *resistance*. That is, resistance often refers to a mindset that reflects an unwillingness to change or being closed to it. Resistance is sometimes defined as an outcome (e.g., the treatment made the person more resistant), a psychological process (e.g., one can resist by counterarguing or by not trusting favorable thoughts in response to a proposal), a motivation (e.g., having the goal of not being persuaded), and a quality of an attitude (an attitude that is resistant to change), a situation (difficult to change in particular circumstances), or a person (the individual is generally resistant to change; see Wegener et al., 2004). Just as resistance can be understood in these multiple ways, so too can openness.

This definition of openness shares similarities and differences with other approaches. First, we propose that the motive to be open can be relatively objective or biased, whereas other constructs related to openness focus exclusively on objective processing. For example, Ottati et al. (see Chapter 7 in this volume) use the terms *open-mindedness* and *open-minded cognition* to refer to unbiased consideration of information on both sides of a position, whereas *closed-minded* or *dogmatic* cognition is associated with biased or one-sided processing. Our treatment of openness suggests that people can be open to any kind of information about any position (objective processing) or be open only to information relevant to a given position (biased processing). This *differential openness* can be contrasted with the extreme case in which people are not open to any information (even additional information on their own side). Thus, openness can be viewed as a continuum going from no openness to any information to openness to some types of information to openness to all sorts of information.

Second, we argue that openness can be treated as an outcome, as a motive, and as a process, whereas other conceptualizations tend to focus mostly on one of these three aspects, such as when openness is defined exclusively as an outcome (e.g., a treatment made the person more open). Unlike previous approaches focused only on either the person or the situation in isolation, we propose that the motive to be open can come from the attitude, the situation, and the person and that these variables can operate both in isolation and in combination.

Third, we emphasize that openness can include willingness to consider persuasive information coming from external sources as well as openness to self-generated insights. Therefore, instead of focusing exclusively on openness to the information provided by others, we include in our definition metacognitive processes revealing that people vary in openness to considering their own thoughts.

Fourth, we argue that openness can be appraised not only positively but also negatively. The research covered in this chapter will illustrate how openness can be imbued with positive meanings (e.g., growth, flexibility) but also with negative meanings (e.g., vulnerability), and these have important consequences for actual openness.

Finally, beyond being open, we also consider the importance of signaling openness to others, as well as perceiving openness in others. That is, although the chapter focuses on understanding the openness of the person who serves as the recipient of persuasion, we also acknowledge the importance of taking into account how persuasive sources signal openness to others, how people come to perceive openness in others, and how others are expected to vary in their openness.

In sum, although we treat openness mainly as a motivational factor that can affect both primary and secondary cognitive processes of attitude change, we also discuss it as an outcome that can stem from qualities of attitudes, situations, or people themselves. We begin with a discussion of how openness can affect the processes of attitude change.

Impact of Openness on Processes of Primary and Secondary Cognition

Impact on Primary Cognition

Openness (as a motive) can operate to influence judgment and action through processes of primary cognition. Primary thoughts are those that occur at a direct level of cognition and involve people's initial associations of an object with some attribute, such as "This policy is not good" or "I am an open person." Appeals that elicit primarily favorable thoughts toward a particular recommendation (e.g., "if that new vaccine protects me, I would take it") produce more persuasion than appeals that elicit mostly unfavorable thoughts (Petty et al., 1981). Beyond the direction or content of the thoughts, another key determinant of persuasion is the number of thoughts, with primary cognitions varying from zero or a few thoughts to many thoughts relevant to some proposal.

Contemporary theories of persuasion, such as the elaboration likelihood model (ELM; Petty & Cacioppo, 1986) and the heuristic-systematic model (HSM; Chaiken et al., 1989) have emphasized the importance of these two dimensions (valence and number) of thoughts. We rely on the ELM since many of the studies described in this chapter have been guided by this framework. This theory holds that the core processes of persuasion fall along an elaboration continuum. Sometimes attitudes are changed by relatively low thought mechanisms (e.g., an induction of openness serving as an acceptance cue such as when a person reasons that "since I am open-minded, I should accept this"), but at other times considerable thinking is involved (e.g., when openness leads people to generate their own arguments). The amount of thinking is important not only because it determines the process by which a variable affects attitudes but also because more thoughtful persuasion is more enduring and impactful than are changes produced by lower thought processes.

Furthermore, sometimes the thinking is relatively objective, and sometimes it is biased by various motives or abilities that are present. For example, when openness promotes objective processing, it leads to more thoughts that reflect the perceived merit of the arguments presented, being favorable when the arguments are strong but unfavorable when they are weak. When openness leads to biased processing (people are more open to one side than another) it can facilitate the generation of thoughts in the direction of the advocacy (if the person is open to accepting it), or it can lead to counterarguing in the opposite direction of the advocacy (if the person is only open to attitude-consistent information).

Impact on Meta-Cognitive Processes

In addition to generating primary thoughts about persuasive proposals (e.g., "this new vaccine seems promising"), people generate further thoughts that reflect upon the initial thoughts (e.g., "but I am not so sure the vaccine is promising"). These reflections on initial thoughts are referred to as *metacognition*, and they can influence what people do with their thoughts and whether the thoughts become consequential (e.g., Goupil & Kouider, 2019; Petty et al., 2002).

Much persuasion work on metacognitive processes has been guided by self-validation theory (SVT; Briñol & Petty, 2022). In addition to the valence and amount of thought (dimensions of primary cognition), SVT considers the perceived validity of those thoughts. The key notion of SVT is that the greater the perceived validity of one's thoughts, the more they are translated into overall judgments; and the greater the perceived validity of one's judgments, the more likely they are to guide behavior.

As was the case with primary cognition, when openness operates through metacognitive processes, it can do so in a relatively objective or biased way. That is, people can be open to validating any and all thoughts in mind or only to a selection of thoughts (e.g., those that support one's attitude). Perceiving greater validity to one's thoughts does not imply that the thoughts are actually accurate. People can perceive that accurate thoughts have low validity and perceive incorrect thoughts to be valid. However, in accord with SVT, greater perceptions of thought validity lead to more use of those thoughts in forming judgments and in those judgments producing behavior.

Attitude Variables as Sources of Openness

Attitudes can vary in a number of important ways that are relevant to openness. For example, attitudes differ in their extremity, with less extreme attitudes being more open to change (Siev et al., 2022). Attitudes can also vary in other ways that influence their *strength*—the extent to which they are durable and impactful (Petty & Krosnick, 1995). Strength matters because strong attitudes tend to be less open to change.

Perhaps the most studied indicator of strong attitudes is how certain people are that their attitude is the correct one to have (see Rucker et al., 2014). Initial conceptualizations of attitude certainty focused on how it often stemmed from variables that were structurally linked to the attitude, such as how much issue-relevant knowledge was behind the attitude (Wood et al., 1995), whether the attitude was based on direct experience (e.g., Fazio & Zanna, 1981), and to what extent the attitude resulted from high rather than low amounts of thinking (Petty & Cacioppo, 1986). Certainty can also develop in the absence of any structural differences. For example, research has demonstrated that simply leading people to believe that their attitudes are based on two-sided information (Rucker et al., 2008) or morality (Luttrell et al., 2016) or considerable thought (Barden & Petty, 2008; Moreno et al., 2021) can enhance attitude certainty and the subsequent likelihood of changing.

Strength indicators other than certainty are also relevant to openness. For example, when people feel ambivalent about their attitudes they are more open to changing that attitude (DeMarree et al., 2011). Furthermore, people with ambivalent attitudes are more open to processing relevant information to mitigate the unpleasantness associated with the felt ambivalence (Maio et al., 1996), doing so in an objective (Hohnsbehn et al., 2022) or biased (Sawicki et al., 2013) manner. Similar results occur for *implicit ambivalence*, which refers to when a person has an attitude object linked to both positivity and negativity in memory but one of these reactions is tagged as invalid (Petty et al., 2006). In this case, the person does not report being ambivalent because the person does not consider both reactions to be valid, yet the person still feels conflicted, and therefore is more open to processing information relevant to the object for which the discrepancy occurs (Johnson et al., 2017).

In sum, attitudes are more open when they are weak such as when associated with low extremity, low certainty, and ambivalence. Other attitude properties such as morality or perceived knowledge also affect openness. For example, under some conditions (e.g., epistemic mindset, accuracy motivation), feeling you know a lot about something can have a positive impact on openness to new information (Wood et al., 1995). Under other conditions (e.g., hedonic mindset, entertainment goals), one is less likely to seek out new information on that topic since one might conclude from the feeling of knowing that there is nothing else to learn (Radecki & Jaccard, 1995). Recent research has examined these possibilities and demonstrated that mindset (epistemic vs. hedonic) is a moderator of when perceived knowledge is likely to enhance or decrease information processing, respectively (Paredes et al., 2022).

Situational Variables as Sources of Openness

Just as people and their attitudes vary in openness to change, some situations foster more openness than others. One of the most studied factors is whether the source of the advocacy seems open to the recipient's point of view. Because of the social influence principle of reciprocity (e.g., Cialdini, 1993), if a speaker seems open to the recipient's position, the target of influence should reciprocate by being open to the speaker's view. In one early study demonstrating this, Cialdini and colleagues (1992) showed that message recipients were more likely to be influenced by a persuader who had previously yielded to their own persuasive message. Indeed, research shows that virtually any variable that suggests that speakers are open to changing their own positions makes recipients more open to changing their views. Thus, when speakers show non-verbal signs of receptiveness such as nodding or smiling (Guyer et al., 2019) or express some doubt in a view, it can make recipients more open to processing the speaker's message (see Hussein & Tormala, 2021, for a review). In interpersonal interactions, people who receive signs of receptiveness from others respond with greater receptiveness of their own (Minson & Chen, 2022).

In more static situations, one way in which advocates can indicate that they are receptive is by explicitly acknowledging some merit to the side the recipient holds. Some prior research has shown that simply acknowledging the target's resistance (e.g., "you may not like this") can enhance agreement (Schumpe et al., 2020), and thus it may be that giving some credence to the target's position would likewise enhance openness in that target. In a relevant series of studies, Xu and Petty (2022) argued that the pressure for a message recipient to reciprocate by being open to the advocate's view is especially powerful when a strong attitude is held. In one study they examined participants who were against mask-wearing during the COVID-19 pandemic and compared individuals whose attitudes were relatively high in their moral basis (e.g., mask-wearing impinges on the value of freedom) or relatively low. Basing attitudes on morals generally makes them less open to change (Skitka, 2010). Recipients were then presented either with a one-sided message advocating only for mask-wearing or a two-sided message that also acknowledged some merit to the anti-mask position. The two-sided message generally led recipients to be more open to the speaker's view, and this was especially the case for those who had strongly held views. That is, moral basis interacted with message-sidedness in predicting openness. In addition, the more recipients expressed openness to the speaker's view, the more they modified their attitudes in accord with the advocacy (see Figure 4.1).

Just as factors within a persuasive message can make the source seem open to the recipient's position, some research indicates that it is also possible to modify the recipient to facilitate seeing the message source as open. In a relevant study, Petty and colleagues (2008) subtly primed participants with openness or with resistance using a lexical decision task. The openness prime

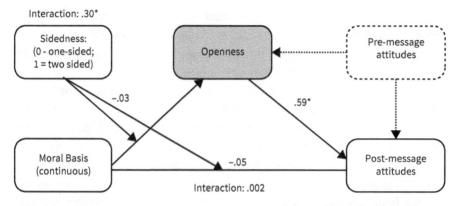

Figure 4.1 Moral basis interacts with message sidedness to impact attitudes by affecting openness. Index of moderated mediation effect = .18, 95% bootstrap confidence interval 0.10–26. (Figure adapted from Xu, M., & Petty, R. E. [2022]. Two-sided messages promote openness for morally-based attitudes. *Personality and Social Psychology Bulletin, 48,* 1151–1166. https://doi.org/10.1177/0146167220988371.)

included words related to openness (e.g., *open, accept, yield, flexible*), whereas the resistance prime included words related to resistance (e.g., *resist, oppose, rigid, reject*). Following the openness or resistance primes, participants read four ambiguous scenarios where the main characters could be viewed as being either open or resistant and were asked to rate the target with respect to openness. Participants also completed the need for cognition (NC) scale (Cacioppo & Petty, 1982). The results of this study showed that the induced primes affected the openness perceived in others and that this effect was moderated by individual differences in NC. Specifically, as NC increased, so did the assimilative effect of the openness (vs. resistance) prime on ratings of the target. Therefore, openness (in this case, how open others are perceived to be) can be facilitated by merely activating that construct via semantic priming.

Recent research in this domain reveals that inferences about the openness of others are informed by at least two antecedents: the perceptions of others' attitude bases and the perception of the position held (Teeny & Petty, 2022). First, people perceived to hold an attitude based more on affect relative to cognition were inferred to be less open. Second, targets holding a counter- (vs. pro-) attitudinal stance were inferred to be less open—an effect due to the greater affect relative to cognition presumed to underlie the attitudes of those holding counter-attitudinal positions. Finally, the perceptions of openness in others were consequential even after controlling for other variables such as perceptions of extremity and certainty. That is, the inferences of openness guided perceivers' willingness to engage in attitudinal advocacy (i.e., expressing their attitudes). Based on these findings, interventions looking to bolster dialogue between disagreeing individuals could benefit from encouraging advocates to focus on the potential cognition rather than affect that can underlie a counter-attitudinal target's position.

Another way in which situations can facilitate openness is by encouraging distanced self-reflection such as by encouraging a third- rather than a first-person perspective. Grossmann and colleagues (2021) revealed that participants induced to express their thoughts using third- (vs. first-) person pronouns were more open to new information. Affirming the self (i.e., leading people to express their important core values) is another way in which situations can facilitate openness, especially to potentially threatening information. Importantly, the effect of self-affirmation can vary depending on a number of factors, such as the content and the amount of thinking present and the time at which self-affirmation is induced (Briñol et al., 2007).

In accord with the ELM, the impact of variables affecting openness can work via multiple processes. Emotions are a prime example. For instance, consider curiosity, which is a pleasant emotion often associated with openness to new information. Although curiosity is mostly appraised positively, it is also associated with an appraisal of uncertainty (Wright et al., 2018). The effect of curiosity on openness to generating and using thoughts depends on when the emotion is induced (prior to or after message exposure). Beyond timing, the effects of curiosity also depend on which of the two appraisals is salient (pleasantness or uncertainty). When emotion was induced prior to receipt of a persuasive message, Stavraki and colleagues (2022) showed that, among participants induced to feel curiosity (vs. disgust, a negative but confident emotion), those focused on a confidence appraisal showed higher levels of information-processing. This is because when curious individuals focused on the doubt that accompanied their emotion, those feeling curious felt more uncertain about their own existing views than those feeling disgust, which increased their motivation to be open to processing new information. In contrast, individuals induced to feel curiosity (vs. disgust) who focused on the pleasantness appraisal of the induced emotion showed lower levels of processing the presented information. This is because curiosity is more pleasant than disgust, leading people to think that everything is fine and that there is little need to process information (Bless et al., 1990). In sum, curiosity, when induced before a persuasive message, not only can increase openness to considering that message carefully (compared to disgust) but also can decrease it depending on the appraisal that is considered regarding the emotion (pleasantness or uncertainty).

Importantly, when emotions occur following the message, the emotion can influence how open people are to using the thoughts previously generated. In these circumstances, when the confidence appraisal of curiosity (vs. disgust) was made salient, curiosity was found to reduce use of thoughts because of the association with uncertainty ("I feel doubt about my thoughts, so I will not use them"). In contrast, when the pleasantness appraisal of curiosity (vs. disgust) was salient, curiosity enhanced thought use because when people feel good about their thoughts they use them. The same results have been found for other emotions often associated with openness, like hope, surprise, and awe, compared to other unpleasant but certain emotions, like anger and helplessness (Briñol et al., 2018; Requero et al., 2021; Stavraki et al., 2021).

In closing this section, we note that person variables and situations relevant to openness also can be studied in combination. In particular, recipient variables can interact with source, message, and context variables to produce unique effects. For example, in one study, persuasive messages were matched to the Big 5 personality dimensions, and this matching produced an increase in persuasion. Specifically, Hirsh and colleagues (2012) found more attitude change for matching arguments to each of the Big 5 dimensions than mismatching. Most relevant to understanding openness to change, these researchers found that using words related to openness was more persuasive for those with higher scores on the Big 5 openness to experience dimension. This is an example of how a persuasive proposal can be made more appealing to people already high in "openness" simply by using the right words. It is important to note that this and other kinds of matching can influence attitudes by processes of primary cognition (e.g., by biasing thoughts when elaboration is high or by increasing the amount of thinking when it is unconstrained) and by metacognitive processes (e.g., affecting thought validation when elaboration is high and the match follows rather than precedes thought generation; see Teeny et al., 2021, for a recent review of matching effects in persuasion).

Person Variables as Sources of Openness

Some people are more open to change than others. One sign is the willingness to process the proposal and accept or reject it on its merits. Another sign is the willingness to consider the merits of one's own thoughts about the proposal. In this section, we describe three additional areas of research relevant to individual differences in openness. First, we cover general variables relevant to openness, ranging from classic work on authoritarianism to more recent research on perceived attitude stability and confidence. Second, we describe research on openness as an objective motive to consider all sorts of information. Third, we cover individual differences in biased processing.

Individual Differences in General Openness

Researchers and practitioners historically have been interested in developing and measuring a persuasibility dimension which would identify individuals who are generally open versus resistant to change in response to any persuasive treatment across topics and proposals. Early approaches assessed variables such as dogmatism (Rokeach, 1954) and authoritarianism (Altemeyer, 1996) as proxies to persuasibility. We discuss more recent approaches next.

Although the construct of openness has mostly referred to whether or not people are open to change (or at least receptive to considering an advocacy), one contributor to this is just how stable people's attitudes are over time even when not directly confronted. That is, a person whose attitude is highly stable would presumably be less open to change in response to a message than someone whose attitude bounces around naturally. Recent research by Xu and colleagues (2020) has found that people seem to be aware of their attitude stability and that measuring these perceptions can predict actual attitude stability. These individual differences can be assessed reliably with the Personal Attitude Stability Scale (PASS), which includes items such as "It is hard for me to change my ideas." Across several studies and distinct topics, Xu and colleagues showed that the PASS predicts attitude stability following a delay period of about 2 weeks. One question of particular interest to openness would be to what extent the predictive ability of the PASS depends on individuals not receiving any new information in the intervening period (i.e., no persuasive attacks on their original attitudes). In the Xu et al. work it was possible that there were some attempts to influence people's attitudes during the period (e.g., through advertisements or political campaigns). That is, it may have been the case that despite having their attitudes challenged, some people resisted influence more than others, leading to more stable attitudes. If the latter is the case, then the PASS might be useful in predicting persuasibility in addition to stability.

In addition to variations in the beliefs regarding one's own attitude stability, people differ in their perception of attitude stability in others (Petrocelli et al., 2010). Furthermore, it is also possible to measure perceptions about the extent to which people see their personality as stable (entity theorists) or as changeable (incremental theorists). For example, Ehrlinger and colleagues (2016) showed that teaching people growth mindsets led to more openness to difficult information (process of primary cognition) and to being less overconfident in their judgments (a metacognitive process).

There are also individual differences in attitude confidence, which, as noted previously, is linked to openness to change (Rucker et al., 2014). Earlier, we described how attitude confidence could vary with particular issues, but recent research has shown that people can vary in how certain they are about all of their attitudes, therefore making them generally less open to change. To assess dispositional differences in attitude confidence, DeMarree et al. (2020) had participants report their attitudes toward a variety of objects (e.g., taxes, political candidates) and report their certainty in each evaluation. Confidence in attitudes toward one issue was predictive of confidence in attitudes toward other unrelated issues, even a completely novel one. This dispositional tendency to be confident in one's opinions across multiple topics is important because it allows making predictions about whose attitudes will be stronger and more resistant to change and therefore about who is more likely to be open to new information.

Individual Differences in Openness as an Objective Motive

The motivation to be open can be conceptualized as a general individual difference to seek and process information in a relatively objective mindset in which people are willing to consider the merits of all information from others (Riggs, 2010). Some variables have been associated with a person being open to process virtually all contents, such as individual differences in curiosity (Kashdan et al., 2018), openness to experience (Stumm, 2018), NC (Cacioppo & Petty, 1982), need for closure (Webster & Kruglanski, 1994), open-minded cognition (Price et al. 2015), and humility (Porter & Schumann, 2018). In addition to these, other scales have focused more specifically on the motivation to be open to considering both sides of an issue such as the receptiveness to opposing views scale (Minson et al., 2020) and measures of holistic and dialectical thinking capable of predicting how open people are to contradictory information (Santos et al., 2021), mixed information (Luttrell et al., 2022), and two-sided persuasive messages (Ein-Gar et al., 2012).

Individual Differences in Openness as a Biased Motive

A third category of individual differences considers being primarily open to information in a particular direction (i.e., biased processing). For example, variables relevant to self-enhancement (e.g., narcissism; Raskin & Terry, 1988) are associated with being open to just some information about the self (e.g., positive, pleasant, rewarding), with still other variables being associated with openness to information that verifies any previous self-views, even if those views are negative, such as preference for consistency (Cialdini et al., 1995).

As a final example of how people can vary in what kind of specific information they are open to, consider recent research on the need to evaluate (NE). Whereas the original NE scale focused on classifying people according to their tendency to possess attitudes (Jarvis & Petty, 1996), research by Xu and colleagues (2021) introduced two additional NE scales focused on the tendencies to learn and express attitudes. Those who are motivated to learn evaluations are particularly open to advocacies presented by others, especially if they employ evaluative language. In contrast, those who are motivated to express evaluations are particularly open to persuasive messages that they generate themselves.

The Meaning of Openness

People are likely to vary in their naive theories about the extent to which openness to persuasion (and openness more generally) is something good or bad. That is, the meaning associated with openness can vary across individuals, situations, and cultures. For example, feeling that one is open-minded often has a clear positive association (e.g., growth, improving, advancing). However, the experience of openness can sometimes include appraisals of negative valence (e.g., openness is bad when it is associated with perceived vulnerability, oscillation, and flip-flopping), uncertainty (e.g., openness is sometimes wrong due to unpredictability of what a new message can deliver and how the resulting change might feel), and an avoidance orientation (e.g., openness can paralyze when perceived as uncontrollable or when it is associated with ambivalence and conflict during decision-making).

Although the effects of people's naive theories about openness on actual openness have not been studied explicitly, the meaning of related constructs like being open to persuasion have received some empirical attention. For example, Briñol and colleagues (2015) manipulated participants' views of persuasion to establish an initial causal claim about the relationship between the meaning of persuasion and the amount of message processing. In the *persuasion good* condition, participants were given the target word *persuasion* and asked to choose the five best words to define persuasion from a list that was only positive (e.g., *communication, dialogue, negotiation*). In the *persuasion bad* condition, participants were given the same task but had to choose from a list of only negative words (e.g., *brainwashing, manipulation,* and *propaganda*). After this manipulation, participants received an argument quality manipulation about a new foster care program and reported their attitudes toward the proposal. Those who were induced to have salient negative associations about persuasion scrutinized the information presented in a message more carefully. A second experiment by Briñol and colleagues (2015) replicated these findings by showing that individuals who naturally held more negative views of persuasion scrutinized the message more carefully than individuals who naturally held more positive views of persuasion. The studies are consistent with other persuasion work demonstrating that people are more likely to attend to the quality of persuasive messages when they have some skepticism, such as when a message source is seen as untrustworthy (e.g., Priester & Petty, 2003).

Summary and Future Directions

Throughout this chapter, openness has been treated as an outcome, as a motive, and as a process. The motive to be open can be relatively objective or biased, and it can affect processes of both primary and secondary cognition. Understanding these processes is critical for predicting when variables like curiosity, ambivalence, and morality relate to openness and for predicting long-term consequences associated with openness to change.

As noted, the motivation to be open can come from people's particular attitudes, with weaker attitudes (e.g., those held with doubt and ambivalence) being associated with greater openness to all relevant information and with moral attitudes being associated with greater openness to some information (e.g., moral messages, two-sided messages) more than others (practical messages, one-sided messages). Situations can also prime openness directly (by making openness salient) or indirectly (e.g., by presenting two-sided messages and by showing that the source is open to the recipient's view). The motivation to be open can also come from the person, with some individuals being particularly open to all information and thoughts (e.g., those high in curiosity, intellectual humility, NC, open-minded cognition) but others primarily being open to particular kinds of information (e.g., NE-learning is especially open to external information, while NE-expressing is more open to self-generated thoughts). Indeed, we noted that many of the processes discussed would apply both to openness to persuasive information coming from external sources as well as to openness to self-generated insights.

Furthermore, we illustrated how openness and other related constructs can be imbued with positive (e.g., growth) but also with negative (e.g., vulnerability) meanings, with potential consequences for actual openness. Finally, although the chapter focused on understanding the openness of the person who serves as the recipient of persuasion, we also acknowledged the importance of taking into account how potential advocates signal openness to others (Hussein & Tormala, 2021; Xu & Petty, 2022), how people come to perceive openness in others (e.g., Petty et al., 2008; Teeny & Petty, 2022), and how others are expected (Bohns, 2016) and perceived to be responding (Itzchakov et al., 2018) to their persuasive attempts.

Although this chapter focused on two key processes of persuasion based on primary and secondary cognition, there are other relevant mechanisms. For example, openness can operate by serving as a simple cue of acceptance, acquiescence, and agreeability (e.g., a process that is more likely to occur when motivation to process is low), and openness can also serve as a persuasive argument itself (e.g., when it is informative about the merits of the proposal, such as when screening patients for psychotherapy). According to the ELM, inductions of openness could serve these multiple roles depending on the circumstances (acting as a cue when elaboration is low, affecting processing when elaboration is unconstrained, biasing the generation and subsequent use of thoughts under high thinking conditions, etc.). Furthermore, people can perceive their openness as an unwanted bias and try to correct for it, and people can be open by correcting for particular biases or all biases (Wegener & Petty, 1997).

One might conclude from this chapter that variables like *doubt* are inherently beneficial for being open-minded since uncertainty can motivate people to seek information relevant to the object for which the doubt exits. But it is important to clarify that the impact of doubt can vary as a function of the meaning of doubt and what the doubt is about. If the person has doubt about the validity of their previous attitudes, then doubt will trigger openness by facilitating processing of relevant information (Gur et al., 2021; Vitriol et al., 2019). However, if the thoughts invalidated by doubt were going to trigger openness, then doubt in those thoughts would reduce openness (Shoots-Reinhard et al., 2015). Therefore, doubt can increase or decrease openness depending on what mental constructs are invalidated by that doubt (e.g., prior views vs. initial motivation to process).

Finally, we end with an important question for future research. That is, can people deliberatively use the techniques described throughout this chapter to try to be more open? We know that openness in a person can be primed externally (e.g., by presenting two-sided messages, by inducing curiosity) and that it can be communicated to others intentionally, but can people choose to deliberatively generate doubtful memories to invalidate their own thoughts and be more open to other points of view? Or can people decide to be more humble and use it strategically to facilitate openness to exchanging opinions? The response to these questions awaits further research.

References

Altemeyer, B. (1996). *The authoritarian specter*. Harvard University Press.
Barden, J., & Petty, R. E. (2008). The mere perception of elaboration creates attitude certainty: Exploring the thoughtfulness heuristic. *Journal of Personality and Social Psychology*, 95(3), 489–509. https://doi.org/10.1037/a0012559
Bless, H., Bohner, G., Schwarz, N., & Strack, F. (1990). Mood and persuasion: A cognitive response analysis. *Personality and Social Psychology Bulletin*, 16(2), 331–345. https://doi.org/10.1177/0146167290162013
Bohns, V. K. (2016). (Mis)Understanding our influence over others: A review of the underestimation-of-compliance effect. *Current Directions in Psychological Science*, 25(2), 119–123. https://doi.org/10.1177/0963721415628011
Briñol, P., & Petty, R. E. (2022). Self-validation theory: An integrative framework for understanding when thoughts become consequential. *Psychological Review*, 129(2), 340–367. https://doi.org/10.1037/rev0000340
Briñol, P., Petty, R. E., Gallardo, I., & DeMarree, K. G. (2007). The effect of self-affirmation in nonthreatening persuasion domains: Timing affects the process. *Personality and Social Psychology Bulletin*, 33, 1533–1546. https://doi.org/10.1177/0146167207306282
Briñol, P., Petty, R. E., Stavraki, M., Lamprinakos, G., Wagner, B., & Díaz, D. (2018). Affective and cognitive validation of thoughts: An appraisal perspective on anger, disgust, surprise, and awe. *Journal of Personality and Social Psychology*, 114(5), 693–718. https://doi.org/10.1037/pspa0000118
Briñol, P., Rucker, D. D., & Petty, R. E. (2015). Naïve theories about persuasion: Implication for information processing and consumer attitude change. *International Journal of Advertising*, 34, 85–106. https://doi.org/10.1080/02650487.2014.997080
Cacioppo, J. T., & Petty, R. E. (1982). The need for cognition. *Journal of Personality and Social Psychology*, 42(1), 116–131. https://doi.org/10.1037/0022-3514.42.1.116
Chaiken, S., Liberman, A., & Eagly, A. H. (1989). Heuristic and systematic processing within and beyond the persuasion context. In J. S. Uleman & J. A. Bargh (Eds.), *Unintended thought* (pp. 212–252). Guilford Press.
Cialdini, R. B. (1993). *Influence: The psychology of persuasion*. Morrow.
Cialdini, R. B., Green, B. L., & Rusch, A. J. (1992). When tactical pronouncements of change become real change: The case of reciprocal persuasion. *Journal of Personality and Social Psychology*, 63(1), 30–40. https://doi.org/10.1037/0022-3514.63.1.30
Cialdini, R. B., Trost, M. R., & Newsom, J. T. (1995). Preference for consistency: The development of a valid measure and the discovery of surprising behavioral implications. *Journal of Personality and Social Psychology*, 69(2), 318–328. https://doi.org/10.1037/0022-3514.69.2.318

DeMarree, K. G., Morrison, K. R., Wheeler, S. C., & Petty, R. E. (2011). Self-ambivalence and resistance to subtle self-change attempts. *Personality and Social Psychology Bulletin, 37,* 674–686. https://doi.org/10.1177/0146167211400097

DeMarree, K. G., Petty, R. E., Briñol, P., & Xia, J. (2020). Documenting individual differences in the propensity to hold attitudes with certainty. *Journal of Personality and Social Psychology, 119*(6), 1239–1265. https://doi.org/10.1037/pspa0000241

Ehrlinger, J., Mitchum, A. L., & Dweck, C. S. (2016). Understanding overconfidence: Theories of intelligence, preferential attention, and distorted self-assessment. *Journal of Experimental Social Psychology, 63,* 94–100. https://doi.org/10.1016/j.jesp.2015.11.001

Ein-Gar, D., Shiv, B., & Tormala, Z. L. (2012). When blemishing leads to blossoming: The positive effect of negative information. *Journal of Consumer Research, 38*(5), 846–859. https://doi.org/10.1086/660807

Fazio, R. H., & Zanna, M. P. (1981). Direct experience and attitude–behavior consistency. *Advances in Experimental Social Psychology, 14*(1), 161–202. https://doi.org/10.1016/S0065-2601(08)60372-X

Goupil, L., & Kouider, S. (2019). Developing a reflective mind: From core meta-cognition to explicit self-reflection. *Current Directions in Psychological Science, 28*(4), 403–408. https://doi.org/10.1177/0963721419848672

Grossmann, I., Dorfman, A., Oakes, H., Santos, H. C., Vohs, K. D., & Scholer, A. A. (2021). Training for wisdom: The distanced self-reflection diary method. *Psychological Science, 32*(3), 381–394. https://doi.org/10.1177/0956797620969170

Gur, T., Ayal, S., & Halperin, E. (2021). A bright side of sadness: The depolarizing role of sadness in intergroup conflicts. *European Journal of Social Psychology, 51*(1), 68–83. https://doi.org/10.1002/ejsp.2715

Guyer, J. J., Briñol, P., Petty, R. E., & Horcajo, J. (2019). Nonverbal behavior of persuasive sources: A multiple process analysis. *Journal of Nonverbal Behavior, 43,* 203–231. https://doi.org/10.1007/s10919-018-00291-x

Hirsh, J. B., Kang, S. K., & Bodenhausen, G. V. (2012). Personalized persuasion: Tailoring persuasive appeals to recipients' personality traits. *Psychological Science, 23,* 578–581. https://doi.org/10.1177/0956797611436349

Hohnsbehn, J., Urschler, D., & Schneider, I. K. (2022). Torn but balanced: Trait ambivalence is negatively related to confirmation. *Personality and Individual Differences, 196,* Article 111736. https://doi.org/10.1016/j.paid.2022.111736

Hussein, M. A., & Tormala, Z. L. (2021). Undermining your case to enhance your impact: A framework for understanding the effects of acts of receptiveness in persuasion. *Personality and Social Psychology Review, 25*(3), 229–250. https://doi.org/10.1177/10888683211001269

Itzchakov, G., DeMarree, K. G., Kluger, A. N., & Turjeman-Levi, Y. (2018). The listener sets the tone: High-quality listening increases attitude clarity and behavior-intention consequences. *Personality and Social Psychology Bulletin, 4*(5), 762–778. https://doi.org/10.1177/0146167217747874

Jarvis, W. B. G., & Petty, R. E. (1996). The need to evaluate. *Journal of Personality and Social Psychology, 70,* 172–194. https://doi.org/10.1037/0022-3514.70.1.172

Johnson, I. R., Petty, R. E., Briñol, P., & See, Y. H. M. (2017). Persuasive message scrutiny as a function of implicit–explicit discrepancies in racial attitudes. *Journal of Experimental Social Psychology, 70,* 222–234. https://doi.org/10.1016/j.jesp.2016.11.007

Kashdan, T. B., Stiksma, M. C., Disabato, D. J., McKnight, P. E., Bekier, J., Kaji, J., & Lazarus, R. (2018). The five-dimensional curiosity scale: Capturing the bandwidth of curiosity and identifying four unique subgroups of curious people. *Journal of Research in Personality, 73,* 130–149. https://doi.org/10.1016/j.jrp.2017.11.011

Luttrell, A., Petty, R. E., Briñol, P., & Wagner, B. C. (2016). Making it moral: Merely labeling an attitude as moral increases its strength. *Journal of Experimental Social Psychology, 65*(1), 82–93. https://doi.org/10.1016/j.jesp.2016.04.003

Luttrell, A., Petty, R. E., Chang, J. H., & Togans, L. J. (2022). The role of dialecticism in objective and subjective attitudinal ambivalence. *British Journal of Social Psychology, 61*(3), 826–841. https://doi.org/10.1111/bjso.12504

Maio, G. R., Bell, D. W., & Esses, V. M. (1996). Ambivalence and persuasion: The processing of messages about immigrant groups. *Journal of Experimental Social Psychology, 32*(6), 513–536. https://doi.org/10.1006/jesp.1996.0023

Minson, J. A., & Chen, F. S. (2022). Receptiveness to opposing views: Conceptualization and integrative review. *Personality and Social Psychology Review, 26*(2), 93–111. https://doi.org/10.1177/10888683211061037

Minson, J. A., Chen, F. S., & Tinsley, C. H. (2020). Why won't you listen to me? Measuring receptiveness to opposing views. *Management Science, 66*(7), 3069–3094. https://doi.org/10.1287/mnsc.2019.3362

Moreno, L., Requero, B., Santos, D., Paredes, B., Briñol, P., & Petty, R. E. (2021). Attitudes and attitude certainty guiding pro-social behavior as a function of perceived elaboration. *European Journal of Social Psychology, 51*(6), 990–1006. https://doi.org/10.1002/ejsp.2798

Norcross, J. C., Krebs, P. M., & Prochaska, J. O. (2011). Stages of change. *Journal of Clinical Psychology, 67*(2), 143–154. https://doi.org/10.1002/jclp.20758

Paredes, B., Santos, D., Briñol, P., Guyer, J. J., Moreno, L., & Petty, R. E. (2022). *The influence of perceived knowledge on hiring decisions of job candidates* [Manuscript submitted for publication]. Department of Psychology, Universidad Autónoma de Madrid.

Petrocelli, J. V., Clarkson, J. J., Tormala, Z. L., & Hendrix, K. S. (2010). Perceiving stability as a means to attitude certainty: The role of implicit theories of attitudes. *Journal of Experimental Social Psychology, 46*(6), 874–883. https://doi.org/10.1016/j.jesp.2010.07.012

Petty, R. E., Briñol, P., & Tormala, Z. L. (2002). Thought confidence as a determinant of persuasion: The self-validation hypothesis. *Journal of Personality and Social Psychology, 82*(5), 722–741. https://doi.org/10.1037/0022-3514.82.5.722

Petty, R. E., & Cacioppo, J. T. (1986). The elaboration likelihood model of persuasion. In L. Berkowitz (Ed.), *Advances in experimental social psychology* (Vol. 19, pp. 123–205). Academic Press. https://doi.org/10.1016/S0065-2601(08)60214-2

Petty, R. E., DeMarree, K. G., Briñol, P., Horcajo, J., & Strathman, A. J. (2008). Need for cognition can magnify or attenuate priming effects in social judgment. *Personality and Social Psychology Bulletin, 34*, 900–912. https://doi.org/10.1177/0146167208316692

Petty, R. E., & Krosnick, J. A. (Eds.). (1995). *Attitude strength: Antecedents and consequences.* Lawrence Erlbaum.

Petty, R. E., Ostrom, T. M., & Brock, T. C. (1981). Historical foundations of the cognitive response approach to attitudes and persuasion. In R. Petty, T. Ostrom, & T. Brock (Eds.), *Cognitive responses in persuasion* (pp. 5–29). Erlbaum.

Petty, R. E., Tormala, Z. L., Briñol, P., & Jarvis, W. B. G. (2006). Implicit ambivalence from attitude change: An exploration of the PAST model. *Journal of Personality and Social Psychology, 90*(1), 21–41. https://doi.org/10.1037/0022-3514.90.1.21

Porter, T., & Schumann, K. (2018). Intellectual humility and openness to the opposing view. *Self and Identity, 17*(2), 139–162. https://doi.org/10.1080/15298868.2017.1361861

Priester, J. R., & Petty, R. E. (2003). The influence of spokesperson trustworthiness on message elaboration, attitude strength, and advertising effectiveness. *Journal of Consumer Psychology, 13*(4), 408–421. https://doi.org/10.1207/S15327663JCP1304_08

Price, E., Ottati, V., Wilson, C., & Kim, S. (2015). Open-minded cognition. *Personality and Social Psychology Bulletin, 41*(11), 1488–1504. https://doi.org/10.1177/0146167215600528

Radecki, C. M., & Jaccard, J. (1995). Perceptions of knowledge, actual knowledge, and information search behavior. *Journal of Experimental Social Psychology, 31*(2), 107–138. https://doi.org/10.1006/jesp.1995.1006

Raskin, R., & Terry, H. (1988). A principal-components analysis of the Narcissistic Personality Inventory and further evidence of its construct validity. *Journal of Personality and Social Psychology, 54*, 890–902.

Requero, B., Briñol, P., & Petty, R. (2021). The impact of hope and helplessness on evaluation: A meta-cognitive approach. *European Journal of Social Psychology, 51*(2), 222–238. https://doi.org/10.1002/ejsp.2726

Riggs, W. (2010). Open-mindedness. *Metaphilosophy, 41*, 172–188. https://doi.org/10.1111/j.1467-9973.2009.01625.x

Rokeach, M. (1954). The nature and meaning of dogmatism. *Psychological Review, 61*(3), 194–204. https://doi.org/10.1037/h0060752

Rucker, D. D., Petty, R. E., & Briñol, P. (2008). What's in a frame anyway? A meta-cognitive analysis of the impact of one versus two-sided message framing on attitude certainty. *Journal of Consumer Psychology, 18*(2), 137–149. https://doi.org/10.1016/j.jcps.2008.01.008

Rucker, D. D., Tormala, Z. L., Petty, R. E., & Briñol, P. (2014). Consumer conviction and commitment: An appraisal-based framework for attitude certainty. *Journal of Consumer Psychology, 24*(1), 119–136. https://doi.org/10.1016/j.jcps.2013.07.001

Santos, D., Requero, B., & Martín-Fernández, M. (2021). Individual differences in thinking style and dealing with contradiction: The mediating role of mixed emotions. *PLoS One, 16*(9), Article e0257864. https://doi.org/10.1371/journal.pone.0257864

Sawicki, V., Wegener, D. T., Clark, J. K., Fabrigar, L. R., Smith, S. M., & Durso, G. R. O. (2013). Feeling conflicted and seeking information: When ambivalence enhances and diminishes selective exposure to attitude-consistent information. *Personality and Social Psychology Bulletin, 39*(6), 735–747. https://doi.org/10.1177/0146167213481388

Schumpe, B. M., Bélanger, J. J., & Nisa, C. F. (2020). The reactance decoy effect: How including an appeal before a target message increases persuasion. *Journal of Personality and Social Psychology, 119*(2), 272–292. https://doi.org/10.1037/pspa0000192

Shoots-Reinhard, B., Petty, R. E., DeMarree, K. G., & Rucker, D. D. (2015). Personality certainty and politics: Increasing the predictive utility of individual difference inventories. *Political Psychology, 36*(4), 415–430. https://doi.org/10.1111/pops.12104

Siev, J. J., Petty, R. E., & Briñol, P. (2022). Attitudinal extremism. In A. W. Kruglanski, C. Kopetz, & E. Szumowska (Eds.), *The psychology of extremism: A motivational perspective* (pp. 34–65). Routledge. https://doi.org/10.4324/9781003030898-4

Skitka, L. J. (2010). The psychology of moral conviction. *Social and Personality Psychology Compass, 4*(4), 267–281. https://doi.org/10.1111/j.1751-9004.2010.00254.x

Stavraki, M., Briñol, P., Petty, R. E., & Díaz, D. (2022). *Curiosity can increase but also decrease information processing: A differential appraisals perspective* [Manuscript in preparation]. Department of Psychology, University of Castilla-La Mancha.

Stavraki, M., Lamprinakos, G., Briñol, P., Petty, R. E., Karantinou, K., & Díaz, D. (2021). The influence of emotions on information processing and persuasion: A differential appraisals perspective. *Journal of Experimental Social Psychology, 93*, Article 104085. https://doi.org/10.1016/j.jesp.2020.104085

Stumm, S. (2018). Better open than intellectual: The benefits of investment personality traits for learning. *Personality and Social Psychology Bulletin, 44*(4), 562–573. https://doi.org/10.1177/0146167217744526

Teeny, J. D., & Petty, R. E. (2022). Attributions of emotion and reduced openness prevent people from engaging others with opposing views. *Journal of Experimental Social Psychology, 102*, Article 104373. https://doi.org/10.1016/j.jesp.2022.104373

Teeny, J. D., Siev, J. J., Briñol, P., & Petty, R. E. (2021). A review and conceptual framework for understanding personalized matching effects in persuasion. *Journal of Consumer Psychology*, *31*(2), 382–414. https://doi.org/10.1002/jcpy.1198

Vitriol, J. A., Tagar, M. R., Federico, C. M., & Sawicki, V. (2019). Ideological uncertainty and investment of the self in politics. *Journal of Experimental Social Psychology*, *82*(1), 85–97. https://doi.org/10.1016/j.jesp.2019.01.005

Webster, D. M., & Kruglanski, A. W. (1994). Individual differences in need for cognitive closure. *Journal of Personality and Social Psychology*, *67*(6), 1049–1062. https://doi.org/10.1037/0022-3514.67.6.1049

Wegener, D. T., & Petty, R. E. (1997). The flexible correction model: The role of naive theories of bias in bias correction. In M. P. Zanna (Ed.), *Advances in experimental social psychology* (Vol., 29, pp. 141–208). Academic Press. https://doi.org/10.1016/S0065-2601(08)60017-9

Wegener, D. T., Petty, R. E., Dove, N. L., & Fabrigar, L. R. (2004). Multiple routes to resisting attitude change. In E. S. Knowles & J. A. Linn (Eds.), *Resistance and persuasion* (pp. 13–38). Erlbaum. https://doi.org/10.4324/9781410609816

Wood, W., Rhodes, N., & Biek, M. (1995). Working knowledge and attitude strength: An information processing analysis. In R. E. Petty & J. A. Krosnick (Eds.), *Attitude strength: Antecedents and consequences* (pp. 283–313). Erlbaum.

Wright, S. A., Clarkson, J. J., & Kardes, F. R. (2018). Circumventing resistance to novel information: Piquing curiosity through strategic information revelation. *Journal of Experimental Social Psychology*, *76*, 81–87. https://doi.org/10.1016/j.jesp.2017.12.010

Xu, M., Briñol, P., Gretton, J. D., Tormala, Z. L., Rucker, D. D., & Petty, R. E. (2020). Individual differences in attitude consistency over time: The Personal Attitude Stability Scale. *Personality and Social Psychology Bulletin*, *46*, 1507–1519. https://doi.org/10.1177/0146167220908995

Xu, M., & Petty, R. E. (2022). Two-sided messages promote openness for morally-based attitudes. *Personality and Social Psychology Bulletin*, *48*, 1151–1166. https://doi.org/10.1177/0146167220988371

Xu, M., Petty, R. E., Wright, N., & Briñol, P. (2021). Individual differences in three aspects of evaluation: The motives to have, learn, and express attitudes. *Journal of Personality and Social Psychology*, *121*(2), 257–284. https://doi.org/10.1037/pspa0000279

III
INTELLECTUAL HUMILITY AND OPEN-MINDEDNESS

5
Links Between Intellectual Humility and Open-Mindedness

Does Strength of Belief Matter?

Elizabeth J. Krumrei-Mancuso and Everett L. Worthington, Jr.

> Scrooge crept towards it, trembling as he went; and, following the finger, read upon the stone of the neglected grave his own name—EBENEZER SCROOGE. . . . "Am I that man who lay upon the bed? No, Spirit! O no, no! Spirit! hear me! I am not the man I was. I will not be the man I must have been but for this intercourse. Why show me this, if I am past all hope? Assure me that I yet may change these shadows you have shown me by an altered life."
> —**Charles Dickens (*A Christmas Carol*, 1843/1986, pp. 77–78)**

What does it take for us to change our minds? When is changing our minds an indication of fickleness versus an indication that we are dedicated to accurate belief? When evidence against our beliefs mounts, so might uncertainty. Uncertainty can feel threatening. Therefore, holding convictions defensively or seeking evidence to bolster existing beliefs and values comforts us. Yet, critical self-examination of our thoughts, emotions, motivations, and values can help us discover blind spots, gain greater self-awareness, and act courageously to say with Scrooge, "I am not the [person] I was!"

Convictions and open-mindedness are often in tension. In this chapter, we explore the interplay among intellectual humility, convictions, and open-mindedness. We pay particular attention to the strength of people's beliefs (i.e., convictions) and how strength of convictions conditions the relationship between intellectual humility and open-mindedness.

The Value of Conviction and Closed-Mindedness

Two common approaches to conceptualizing the strength of a person's attitudes are (1) how central the attitude is to the person (i.e., importance of the attitude or relevance to one's sense of self or values) and (2) how committed the person is to the attitude (i.e., how certain a person is about the attitude or how likely the person is to change the attitude). There is some evidence for the independence of these aspects of attitude strength. For example, when making an experimentally induced attitude more salient by having a person express the attitude repeatedly, this strengthens the person's commitment to the attitude, but not the importance of the attitude to the person (Holland et al., 2003). Therefore, let's think of strength of belief along the lines of both how central a belief is to a person and how committed a person is to a belief, which can involve closed-mindedness to alternative options.

Convictions—firmly held ideas, principles, beliefs, opinions, and attitudes—have advantages. Being closed-minded to alternative viewpoints and perspectives can help protect a person's convictions and can preserve their mental resources for investment in their chosen ideologies. We all take certain assumptions for granted; that's how our minds are wired. When going to sleep at night, we don't wonder whether gravity will exist in the morning. As Worthington (2018) observed, we also live by core psychological beliefs, values, and practices. As he put it, constantly considering alternatives to one's core beliefs would result in cognitive anarchy. As such, holding convictions is a characteristic of maturing into adulthood (Erikson, 1956). Convictions are central to ideological commitments. They have been studied in many life domains such as religion, politics, occupation, family, sexuality, and relationships. Having convictions gives stability to a person's sense of self, belief structure, and feelings of belonging with those who share convictions. Thus, convictions benefit functioning, by enhancing emotional regulation, self-esteem, and social identity and reducing impulsivity, compulsivity, and neuroticism (for a review, see Ellison et al., 2021). Because people invest in the social, moral, and behavioral ideals promoted by their convictions, convictions help organize and define a consistent and stable sense of self for individuals.

The clinical literature has examined individuals with a weak or fragile sense of self. These individuals do not know what they think, what their opinions are, or what ideological commitments they should make (Flury & Ickes, 2007). They tend to display situation-based identities, taking on the feelings, opinions, and values of whomever they are with at the time. Such individuals who lack clarity and confidence in their concepts of self tend to experience worse psychological adjustment (Campbell et al., 1996). Forming convictions and associated ideological commitments can minimize existential anxiety and offer hope, positive affect, and happiness (Burrow & Hill, 2011). Furthermore, convictions motivate consistent decisions and actions (Kraus, 1995; Skitka et al., 2021). James Marcia's (1966) identity formation work, although not without its criticisms, suggests a healthy, mature identity is based not only on a commitment to a certain set of convictions but also on a commitment to a certain set of convictions in light of active exploration of one's viewpoints and beliefs. This emphasizes the relevance of open-mindedness in formulating and maintaining convictions.

The Value of Open-Mindedness

Of course, there is also a potential downside to harboring strong convictions. A side effect of holding convictions—and beliefs in general—is that people exhibit *confirmation bias*, whereby they seek out information that supports and maintains their perspectives and overlook or minimize the importance of disconfirming information (Hart et al., 2009). Open-mindedness is the ability and willingness to consider an issue from multiple perspectives (Baehr, 2011). Open-mindedness represents one antidote to confirmation bias by fairly considering ideas that intellectually compete with one's convictions. Thus, open-mindedness offers opportunities to correct false beliefs and attain more accurate knowledge and beliefs. Open-mindedness is considered central to critical thinking, good judgment, and effective decision-making. To use an analogy, scientific knowledge exists because falsifiable claims have withstood attempts to prove them wrong. Similarly, open-minded thinking provides individuals with opportunities in everyday life to form opinions and beliefs after making serious efforts to consider reasons why their conclusions might be incorrect. Open-mindedness may also help combat some of the interpersonal consequences of strongly held convictions, such as intolerance for differing viewpoints and less willingness to compromise with others (Skitka et al., 2021). Our defense of open-mindedness is brief in this context, given that it is a highly valued ideal of democratic societies (Wilson et al., 2017).

Intellectual Humility and Its Relation to Open-Mindedness

Let us consider intellectual humility and its value for promoting open-mindedness, with consideration for the role of conviction. A recent systematic review by Porter and colleagues (2022) indicated that there is no clear consensus about a precise definition of *intellectual humility*. Yet most philosophers view intellectual humility as an orientation toward one's intellectual limitations that accepts one's intellectual fallibility and ignorance. Similarly, the most common definitional feature of intellectual humility among psychologists involves acceptance of one's intellectual limitations. Given that the current chapter is concerned with beliefs, values, and opinions more so than knowledge, we might emphasize that intellectual humility involves an awareness of the limitations of one's evidentiary basis for one's perspectives (Hoyle et al., 2016) as well as the ability to recognize that beliefs, values, and opinions do not constitute facts.

Philosophers have pointed out the need to distinguish intellectual humility from the close but distinct construct of open-mindedness. Intellectual humility involves attentiveness to one's intellectual limitations, whereas open-mindedness emphasizes caring about alternative perspectives (Whitcomb et al., 2017). As such, intellectual humility and open-mindedness are complementary cognitive tendencies. If intellectual humility involves an awareness of one's intellectual fallibility, a likely response is a willingness to consider additional information and perspectives (i.e., open-mindedness) in an effort to improve one's perspectives.

Although intellectual humility and open-mindedness are distinct, the line between them is not consistently drawn, complicating the study of how intellectual humility and open-mindedness relate to one another. Some scholars have conceptualized intellectual humility in ways similar to open-mindedness, such as the tendency to remain cognitively open to counterarguments and information that may conflict with one's personal views (Jarvinen & Paulus, 2017; Reis et al., 2018). Intellectual humility has also been considered the opposite of closed-mindedness (Hazlett, 2012) and dogmatism (e.g., Kidd, 2016). Others have considered open-mindedness to be a component of intellectual humility (e.g., Wilson et al., 2017).

To explore how the conceptual links between intellectual humility and open-mindedness manifest in measurement strategies, in Table 5.1, we provide an overview of quantitative measures of intellectual humility that have undergone psychometric assessment. We highlight how researchers conceptualized open-mindedness in relation to intellectual humility and whether intellectual humility items reflect content overlapping with open-mindedness. The table illustrates that most measures of intellectual humility use open-mindedness as an indicator of intellectual humility. Therefore, open-mindedness is often considered a manifestation of intellectual humility.

Table 5.1 Conceptualizations of Open-Mindedness in the Measurement of Intellectual Humility

Definition of intellectual humility	How open-mindedness fits into the conceptualization of intellectual humility	Assessment of any open-mindedness content in intellectual humility scale?
Alfano et al. (2017): Multidimensional Intellectual Humility Scale		
A multidimensional construct marked by four core dimensions: open-mindedness, intellectual modesty, corrigibility, and engagement	Open-mindedness is one of four core dimensions of intellectual humility. Here, open-mindedness is defined more uniquely as an acknowledgment of the limitations of one's knowledge but includes a desire to gain knowledge.	Yes; open-mindedness subscale (assesses mostly limits of knowledge). Sample item: "I think that paying attention to people who disagree with me is a waste of time" (reverse-coded).
Brienza et al. (2018): Intellectual Humility subscale of the Situated Wise Reasoning Scale		
Recognition of the limits of one's knowledge	Not specified	No
Haggard et al. (2018): Limitations Owning Intellectual Humility Scale		
Owning one's intellectual limitations	Open-mindedness is considered distinct from intellectual humility and is thought to be correlated with intellectual humility.	No
Hook et al. (2015): Cultural Humility Scale, Adapted (religious beliefs and values)		
A subdomain of general humility involving an accurate view of one's intellectual strengths and weaknesses and the ability to negotiate different ideas in a respectful manner	Open-mindedness is considered a characteristic of an intellectually humble person.	Yes; sample item: "Regarding different types of religious beliefs and values, the clergy/minister is open to seeing things from other perspectives."
Hoyle et al. (2016): Specific Intellectual Humility Scale		
An inclination to recognize one's opinions, beliefs, and positions are subject to further consideration. Specific intellectual humility is the recognition that a particular personal view may be fallible, accompanied by an appropriate attentiveness to limitations in the evidentiary basis of that view and to one's own limitations in obtaining and evaluating information relevant to it.	Openness to actions, ideas, and values (NEO Personality Inventory-Revised) is considered a covariate of intellectual humility that is empirically distinct.	Yes; sample item: "I am open to new information in the area of _____ that might change my view."

(continued)

Table 5.1 Continued

Definition of intellectual humility	How open-mindedness fits into the conceptualization of intellectual humility	Assessment of any open-mindedness content in intellectual humility scale?
Krumrei-Mancuso and Rouse (2016): Comprehensive Intellectual Humility Scale		
A non-threatening awareness of one's intellectual fallibility	Open-mindedness is considered a direct outgrowth of being aware of one's intellectual fallibility; open-mindedness is used as an indicator of intellectual humility.	Yes; openness to revising one's viewpoint subscale. Sample item: "I am open to revising my important beliefs in the face of new information."
Leary et al. (2017): Intellectual Humility Scale		
Recognizing a particular personal belief may be fallible, accompanied by an appropriate attentiveness to limitations in the evidentiary basis of that belief and to one's own limitations in obtaining and evaluating relevant information	Open-mindedness is understood as a manifestation of intellectual humility. Open-mindedness is described as necessary but not sufficient for intellectual humility.	Yes; sample item: "In the face of conflicting evidence, I am open to changing my opinions."
McElroy et al. (2014): Intellectual Humility Scale		
Insight about the limits of one's knowledge (marked by openness to new ideas) and regulating arrogance (marked by the ability to present one's ideas in a non-offensive manner and receive contrary ideas without taking offense)	Openness to new ideas is a defining feature of intellectual humility (as an indicator of insight into the limits of one's knowledge).	Yes; intellectual openness subscale. Sample item: "Seeks out alternative viewpoints."
Porter and Schumann (2018): Intellectual Humility Scale		
A willingness to recognize the limits of one's knowledge and appreciate others' intellectual strengths	Open-mindedness is described as an outcome of intellectual humility.	Very limited; closest sample item: "I actively seek feedback on my ideas, even if it is critical."
Zachry et al. (2018): State-Trait Intellectual Humility Scale		
A disposition to be alert to and to own cognitive limitations and mistakes	Awareness and openness to new information that differs from one's existing opinion or belief are central to the conceptualization of intellectual humility.	Yes; sample item: "Even when I am certain about my opinion, I will research information supporting the opposing viewpoint."

In some instances, open-mindedness is even considered a core feature of intellectual humility that is necessary but not sufficient for defining intellectual humility.

With the important caveat that there is some conceptual and measurement overlap between intellectual humility and open-mindedness, we review themes from the empirical literature about how intellectual humility relates to open-mindedness. These include correlational links between intellectual humility and open-mindedness, links between intellectual humility and seeking information, and links between intellectual humility and belief or opinion change.

Correlational Links Between Intellectual Humility and Open-Mindedness

Correlational data show that scores on self-report measures of intellectual humility are associated with more open-mindedness and open-minded thinking (Krumrei-Mancuso & Rouse, 2016; Leary et al., 2017; Zachry et al., 2018). In addition, intellectual humility is associated with less closed-mindedness and dogmatism (Haggard et al., 2018; Hoyle et al., 2016; Leary et al., 2017; Zachry et al., 2018). The correlations between intellectual humility and open-mindedness (or its inverse) tend to be substantial, often with an absolute value around .50. This is not surprising given the conceptual links already discussed and the fact that many scales use items related to open-mindedness to operationalize intellectual humility.

Links Between Intellectual Humility and Information-Seeking

There is a growing body of literature that suggests intellectual humility is associated with people engaging with a greater amount and variety of information. When presented with hypothetical disagreements, people who rate themselves higher in intellectual humility report being more open to learning about the perspective of a person they disagree with (Porter & Schuman, 2018). This was supported behaviorally: Those reporting higher levels of intellectual humility spent more time reading about viewpoints that opposed their own perspectives (Porter & Schuman, 2018).

Other research has suggested intellectual humility relates to more interest in searching for information in general, not necessarily an interest in contradictory opinions, at least when it comes to how people use information while they are learning or practicing a new skill (Gorichanaz, 2022). This work highlights that, consistent with an intellectual humility–open-mindedness link, people higher in intellectual humility report searching in more places for information (though not relying on a greater number of types of information sources). However, contrary to expectations, people with more intellectual humility preferred easily accessible sources of information.

Intellectual Humility and Change in Beliefs or Opinions

Beyond a willingness to engage with multiple perspectives, belief revision has been considered a component of open-minded thinking because belief revision indicates how people condition their beliefs when presented with new evidence (Stanovich & Toplak, 2019). For some individuals, intellectual humility is associated with viewing belief revision more favorably. One study presented a hypothetical political candidate who changed his position after learning more about a political issue (Leary et al., 2017). Participants higher in intellectual humility regarded the political candidate as more ethical. They did not consider the change in views to represent flip-flopping to get elected. They also expressed greater willingness to vote for the candidate. However, these links were observed only among Republicans, not among Democrats or Independents.

Research examining how intellectual humility relates to people revising their own beliefs or attitudes indicates that intellectual humility is associated with small shifts in beliefs in some cases but not across the board. A few studies have examined belief revision after exposing people to information or another person's opinion, without interpersonal interaction (Krumrei-Mancuso & Newman, 2020, 2021; Porter & Schumann, 2018). In one such study, intellectual humility was associated with spending a greater proportion of one's time reading about opposing views compared to congenial views; however, this exposure to opposing viewpoints did not result in changes in participants' attitude strength (Porter & Schumann, 2018).

In another study, intellectual humility was associated with people changing the strength of their opinions on the basis of another person's argument, but only in the direction of strengthening preexisting beliefs (Krumrei-Mancuso & Newman, 2021). In fact, when people were exposed to an argument that conflicted with their preexisting beliefs, being more intellectually humble was associated with being less persuaded by the argument. This may be because individuals high in intellectual humility are more attuned to the strength of persuasive arguments (Leary et al., 2017) and may not have found one person's opinion sufficiently strong to persuade change. Findings reported by Porter and Schumann (2018) and Krumrei-Mancuso and Newman (2021) suggest that genuinely considering an alternative perspective does not necessarily mean adopting that perspective, especially during a brief research study. Being open to belief revision does not mean overturning, within a few minutes, perspectives that have developed over years of living.

Research has started exploring under what conditions intellectual humility is more likely to result in belief revision. Intellectual humility seems to be associated with opinion change on the basis of reading factual information when people are put in a position to defend their own perspectives but not when people are explicitly asked to consider both sides of an issue (Krumrei-Mancuso & Newman, 2020). It makes sense that dispositional levels of intellectual humility may not provide as much added value when people are in situations that require them to consider both sides of an issue compared to when people are in situations that encourage them to defend their own views. This suggests intellectual humility may particularly benefit open-mindedness when people are motivated by their circumstances to defend their own positions.

In addition, asking individuals high in dispositional intellectual humility to rate the possibility that their viewpoints on a particular topic may be uninformed or misinformed has been associated with more opinion change when individuals read factual information (Krumrei-Mancuso & Newman, 2020). The same was not the case for individuals low in dispositional intellectual humility. This suggests that making the fallibility of people's knowledge salient to them may activate preexisting intellectual humility, thereby resulting in more open-mindedness.

Notably, these studies on belief and attitude revision asked participants to read viewpoints, opinions, or factual information. This research may simulate what people experience when they are exposed to information via blogs, articles, books, television newscasts, webinars, or social media posts.

However, this research has not captured the real-time interpersonal interactions that so often form the backdrop for whether intellectual humility will result in belief revision. A remarkable exception is a study that paired people who disagreed on contentious religious issues to engage in a discussion (Rodriguez et al., 2019). People changed their viewpoints after these discussions only when they were high in intellectual humility and they perceived their discussion partners as high in intellectual humility. This suggests open-mindedness may be enacted only when both discussion partners show signs of intellectual humility, such as give and take in discussions, rather than when someone perceives a discussion partner as inflexible. An implication is that intellectual humility not only affords a person the opportunity to reconsider personal viewpoints but also increases the likelihood that others will seriously consider and be persuaded by one's viewpoints. Research pairing people in actual interactions is rare but valuable because it moves beyond an examination of individuals' dispositions to be intellectually humble and open-minded and examines how these dispositions are enacted in genuine interactions. It seems that if both discussion partners are high in intellectual humility, this results in a mutual exchange of ideas that is more likely to cause opinion change.

Intellectual Humility, Open-Mindedness, and the Strength of Beliefs

We have examined several ways that intellectual humility and open-mindedness relate to one another. Next, we consider whether the strength of beliefs or their importance to a person matters for the relationship between intellectual humility and open-mindedness. One thing is clear: Intellectual humility and open-mindedness are challenging to achieve when it comes to highly important beliefs. People express lower levels of intellectual humility about viewpoints they find important and hold strongly (e.g., Hoyle et al., 2016). In addition, people are more likely to seek out information that is congenial relative to uncongenial to them when it comes to beliefs they hold with conviction (Hart et al., 2009). Thus, people tend to become increasingly entrenched precisely in their most cherished viewpoints.

Even though intellectual humility is particularly challenging to views that are conferred with special status, intellectual humility and open-mindedness are particularly important to these views. One position is that intellectual humility is most relevant and pressing in contexts in which it is most challenged (McElroy et al., 2014). Those situations include convictions related to identity, moral emotions, religious and political viewpoints, power struggles over ideas, and any other topics a person is highly invested in (Church, 2018; Worthington, 2018).

Some say intellectual humility is only relevant to viewpoints that reach a certain level of importance to a person. Importance can be conceptualized similarly to belief strength, involving (1) how central the belief is as an organizing force for the person's sense of self, values, and behaviors and (2) the person's level of commitment to the belief over time. Circa 2013, I (E. J. K.-M.) had a conversation with philosopher Jason Baehr about intellectual humility.

He gave an example of disagreeing about whether there is milk in the fridge. What I took away from the conversation is that it is easy to give in to an intellectual disagreement if being out of milk is of little consequence to you. Being open-minded about milk may not be the result of intellectual humility but rather the result of apathy or lack of concern. One solution to the potential conflation of intellectual humility and open-mindedness around matters people find trivial would be to conceptualize intellectual humility as a domain of humility that involves how people hold and negotiate "cherished" beliefs (McElroy et al., 2014, p. 27). Others have assessed intellectual humility in contexts that are likely to challenge intellectual humility, such as interpersonal conflicts (Brienza et al., 2018). Still others have centered assessments of intellectual humility on viewpoints that people consider to be important (Krumrei-Mancuso & Rouse, 2016).

Next, we take a closer look at three content areas in which it can be particularly challenging for people to acknowledge that their views might be wrong and to be willing to engage with alternative perspectives: religious/spiritual convictions, moral convictions, and areas of expertise.

Religious, Spiritual, and Moral Convictions

Many have acknowledged that religious and spiritual convictions make intellectual humility difficult to practice (Church, 2018; Dormandy, 2018; Hook et al., 2015). People can view virtually any aspect of life as sacred. Furthermore, people go to extraordinary lengths to preserve and protect that which they view as sacred (Pargament et al., 2017). When people perceive others as threatening something they hold sacred, this evokes a strong desire for retaliation (Pargament et al., 2017). Religious beliefs help people answer questions about life and death, so stakes are high when it comes to considering being wrong about these ultimate questions. In addition, some religious teachings emphasize being certain of what one believes, which may pose challenges to intellectual humility about these beliefs (Hook et al., 2015).

Empirical research supports this theorizing. People with higher levels of intellectual humility express less certainty about religious beliefs and place less importance on religious beliefs in their lives (Krumrei-Mancuso, 2018; Leary et al., 2017). The literature on actively open-minded thinking suggests that the negative link between intellectual humility and religiosity is the result of an emphasis on open-mindedness, specifically belief-revision items. When survey items ask participants whether they are willing to revise their beliefs, religious participants are prone to interpret the word *belief* as referring to religious belief and therefore respond to defend a protected value. For non-religious participants, the word *belief* is less likely to cue thinking about a particularly protected or valued belief (Stanovich & Toplak, 2019). Stanovich and Toplak (2019) have recommended using items that assess belief revision with regard to specific, non-religious topics rather than belief revision with regard to beliefs generically in order to assess religious and non-religious individuals more comparably. This would allow for an assessment of topic-specific intellectual humility but not general intellectual humility. Another option would be to encourage both religious and non-religious participants to think about beliefs that are important to them (e.g., see the Comprehensive Intellectual Humility Scale; Krumrei-Mancuso & Rouse, 2016), which might minimize some of the discrepancy in responding between religious and non-religious people. When assessing intellectual humility among monotheistic individuals, an additional solution would be to use a measure of theistic intellectual humility that is appropriate for those who hold religious beliefs (Hill et al., 2021).

Religious and spiritual convictions have been of particular interest in the intellectual humility literature. However, viewpoints need not be imbued with religious or spiritual significance to evoke extraordinary allegiance. Moral convictions, that is, attitudes based on beliefs about right and wrong, are also highly valued. People tend to believe that their moral convictions are universally and objectively true (Skitka et al., 2021). As a result, people do not allow their moral perspectives to be influenced by expert or peer perspectives, and people tend to avoid and marginalize those with different moral perspectives (Skitka et al., 2021).

Perceptions of Expertise

People may feel strongly about viewpoints because they have carefully contemplated and researched them. Hoyle et al. (2016) found that people who have done research and sought out information on a viewpoint tend to be less intellectually humble about that viewpoint. Because they feel like they have developed expertise, they are less inclined to view their knowledge as fallible. The question is whether this is functional for people.

Expertise should be associated with a lower likelihood of being incorrect in basic facts and inferences, and thus more certainty of one's beliefs. However, deep expertise in a topic often reveals fundamental uncertainties around concepts, doubts over the adequacy of some evidence, and knowledge of different perspectives and counterarguments to one's positions. Thus, deep expertise might result in less certainty for some beliefs and assumptions. An inverted-U curve might accurately represent the relationship between degree of expertise and certainty of one's position, especially on controversial topics.

For the layperson, self-perception of some level of expertise can increase closed-minded thinking because they view dogmatism as more warranted for experts than for novices, and they apply this standard to themselves (Ottati et al., 2015). Most laypeople will not understand the deep nuances of knowledge in the area in which they have shallow expertise. Yet, for both experts and laypeople, losing sight of the possibility of being wrong poses dangers when it comes to epistemic gains (Fisher & Keil, 2016). Therefore, this tendency to be less intellectually humble about strongly held views can pose risks to individuals and their knowledge.

Strength of Beliefs as a Moderator Between Intellectual Humility and Open-Mindedness

The literature suggests that, at least to some degree, the relationship between intellectual humility and open-mindedness is able to transcend the challenges posed by holding viewpoints strongly. That is, some research demonstrating links between intellectual humility and open-mindedness has focused on social and political issues that are explicitly very important to participants (Porter & Schumann, 2018; Rodriguez et al., 2019). In addition, the relationship between intellectual humility and open-mindedness persists even when controlling the importance of a topic to participants or participants' attitude strength (e.g., Krumrei-Mancuso & Newman, 2020, 2021; Porter & Schumann, 2018).

However, the literature also suggests that the importance of viewpoints might be a moderator between intellectual humility and open-mindedness. That is, intellectual humility may function differently when it comes to beliefs that are central to a person's identity and beliefs that are more peripheral in importance (Hook et al., 2015). People who are generally intellectually humble and who report that they are generally open-minded about their viewpoints may still be closed-minded about certain views that are most important to them (Hoyle et al., 2016). That is, when it comes to belief revision, intellectual humility seems to be expressed differently depending on the centrality of a given belief (see also Chapter 6 in this volume).

Worthington (2018) has suggested the substance of intellectual humility shifts depending on the importance of viewpoints. Specifically, when beliefs are more peripheral in importance to oneself, intellectual humility is more closely related to open-mindedness, and people will tend to revise those beliefs more easily. However, when it comes to core beliefs, Worthington shifts the emphasis of intellectual humility from strictly intrapersonal considerations to interpersonal considerations. People who are high in intellectual humility, regardless of level of open-mindedness, will act with *convicted civility* in their interactions with others around their differences. Recall from our earlier review that interpersonal discussions can influence shifts in belief if both people act in ways that convey they are open to change (see Rodriguez et al., 2019). Thus, intellectual humility, through convicted civility, signals that an interactant is willing to meaningfully discuss issues about which both parties hold convictions.

It would be helpful to continue to parse out people's awareness of their intellectual limitations from their openness to alternative perspectives and their willingness to revise their viewpoints. That is, does the extent to which people view particular beliefs as important moderate the extent to which an awareness of the fallibility of those beliefs produces genuine openness to engage with alternative perspectives and a willingness to revise beliefs when presented with relevant evidence?

Theory and research suggest that core beliefs tend to remain stable, and thus even people high in intellectual humility might not be open to revising core beliefs—at least not easily. Church (2018) has argued, when it comes to beliefs that are of utmost centrality and importance, it may be justifiable or even virtuous to be dogmatic and inflexible with regard to belief revision. This suggests holding justified beliefs dogmatically is not in conflict with intellectual humility. However, the idea that intellectual humility need not result in open-mindedness for strongly held beliefs opens the possibility for people to carve out what they view as their immutable beliefs and then intellectually justify shielding those topics from open-mindedness. This may be akin to attitude justification of open-mindedness, where individuals make judgments about when open-mindedness is and is not desirable so that they can protect their personal convictions (Wilson et al., 2017). Ironically, perceptions of the appropriateness of open-mindedness can take the form of a confirmation bias: People inflate the normative appropriateness of open-mindedness when open-mindedness reinforces their convictions but devalue the normative appropriateness of open-mindedness when open-mindedness contradicts their convictions.

The possibility that the intellectual humility–open-mindedness connection breaks down for closely held viewpoints seemingly conflicts with the idea that intellectual humility is most useful when it comes to viewpoints and contexts that most strain intellectual humility. If individuals can exempt their most cherished beliefs from intellectual humility, then the benefits intellectual humility has to offer in terms of open-mindedness may stop short of the issues that are most critically important to individuals and society. A few lines of thinking suggest intellectual humility can be compatible with open-mindedness even when it comes to important and strongly held viewpoints.

First, core beliefs do not need to be shielded from intellectual humility or open-mindedness in order to be preserved. Research suggests we need not worry that intellectual humility makes people gullible to unreasonable viewpoints. For example, intellectual humility in the political domain is not associated with believing in undersupported political claims (Krumrei-Mancuso & Newman, 2020). Furthermore, as reviewed earlier in this chapter, intellectual humility can be associated with open-mindedness in terms of seeking out information, learning about opposing views, and being interested in more perspectives without belief or attitude revision. Intellectual humility only leads to belief or attitude change when this seems warranted to people on the basis of the evidence they gain through their open-minded approach to new information (Krumrei-Mancuso & Newman, 2020, 2021; Porter & Schumann, 2018; Rodriguez et al., 2019). Meanwhile, the characteristics of open-mindedness such as learning about opposing views and being interested in alternative perspectives can promote civil interpersonal interactions and fruitful dialogues.

Second, even in situations where a person's beliefs are correct (objectively speaking), realizing that one might be wrong (i.e., intellectual humility) can benefit the person's thinking through open-mindedness. When people contemplate their convictions and explore alternatives, they can increase their evidence and confidence for their position and come to a richer understanding of what they believe. Dormandy (2018) illustrated this in the case of religious beliefs, suggesting that, although intellectual humility about one's most sacred beliefs poses some epistemic risks, these risks are outweighed by the epistemic benefits of experiencing opportunities to build more complex cognitive schemas and explore one's belief systems in greater depth.

The Interplay Among Intellectual Humility, Open-Mindedness, and Conviction

We live in a world in which the answers to big, existential questions are offered plausibly by a plethora of philosophies, religions, and worldviews. Being willing to hold strong convictions in the midst of such uncertainty is risky. However, the risk has psychological payoffs like reduced anxiety and increased self-esteem (Lillevoll et al., 2013; Ryeng et al., 2013). Perhaps intellectual humility can be thought of as acknowledging the risks necessitated by committing to and investing in particular beliefs.

In our view, intellectual humility, though challenged and conditioned by convictions, is compatible with people's most important beliefs. We suggest intellectual humility is a mental posture that can balance convictions with open-mindedness. Research suggests that realizing one's beliefs might be wrong is associated with being more willing to (a) engage with alternative perspectives and (b) consider revising one's beliefs. But importantly, willingness to revise one's beliefs is not the same as a decision to revise one's beliefs in response to new evidence.

Those higher in intellectual humility tend to be attuned to the strength of arguments, particularly on topics that matter to them (Leary et al., 2017). Therefore, people high in intellectual humility are not likely to revise their important beliefs without a compelling reason. Thus, core beliefs tend to remain stable. Being intellectually humble does not require indefinitely suspending beliefs, avoiding decisions, or eschewing convictions. These behaviors are more akin to *troubled confusion* in the identity literature, involving fear of committing to the wrong kinds of convictions while being anxious about one's indecision (Newman & Newman, 2020).

Intellectual humility does not involve an overconcern with one's intellectual limitations. Some have taken the approach of conceptualizing intellectual humility as a golden mean between intellectual servility and intellectual arrogance (e.g., Haggard et al., 2018). Similarly, the limitations-owning conceptualization of intellectual humility emphasizes having appropriate, reasonable levels of discomfort with one's intellectual limitations (Whitcomb et al., 2017). As such, it seems possible to hold beliefs and values strongly—to invest emotionally, behaviorally, and socially in one's views—while also remaining open to the possibility they could be wrong and, therefore, open to compelling evidence one encounters.

In essence, most of us do this every day. Awareness of our cognitive biases can help us realize that, despite our levels of confidence in the moment about what we think, our views may still be wrong, incomplete, or limited. Even when we don't feel like we're wrong, we can embrace an openness to engage with other interpretations of our circumstances by acknowledging the reality that our cognitive faculties are limited and error-prone. Although such intellectual humility is particularly challenging when it comes to core convictions, intellectual humility can benefit individuals by enriching their most cherished perspectives through the exploration and reflection offered by open-mindedness. Intellectual humility also benefits individuals interpersonally when it helps them signal to others that they will fairly consider the content of what is being discussed. This benefits relationships and society by helping people engage meaningfully with each other despite weighty ideological differences.

Where to Go from Here?

We have suggested that intellectual humility benefits individuals, relationships, and society, in part through open-mindedness. Intellectual humility, the realization that our understanding may be wrong or limited, can spur meaningful journeys of exploration through open-mindedness. Examining contrary perspectives fairly can strengthen a person's convictions by uncovering additional support for preexisting perspectives. Examining contrary perspectives fairly can also weaken convictions that were held only because they were unexamined, unopposed, or founded on faulty information. Worthington (2018) discussed the reality that people are unlikely to change core beliefs, even when provided with new evidence. But he also acknowledged that at times people's core beliefs can be disrupted, opening space for dramatic belief revision. The impetus for this can be situational: surprising new information, open discussions with a person committed to civility, emotional turmoil that challenges one's worldview, or trauma. More research is needed to examine conditions that break down the barriers to core-belief revision. Those barrier-busters may be rare in a person's life. Specifically, it would be valuable to continue to evaluate whether a person's level of awareness about the fallibility of their thinking (intellectual humility) stimulates an openness to revising beliefs as a manifestation of open-mindedness. To pursue this exploration, we must gain greater clarity about whether open-mindedness is a component of intellectual humility or an outcome of intellectual humility.

Conceptual advances that clarify the connections among intellectual humility, open-mindedness, and conviction are also needed. In particular, more work can be done to examine how the strength and importance of viewpoints may moderate the relationship between intellectual humility and open-mindedness. Furthermore, as research on the intersection of intellectual humility, conviction, and open-mindedness progresses, we must attend to the substance of beliefs that are being examined, and we must assess intellectual humility in ways that are compatible with the worldviews of the people being assessed (Hill et al., 2021).

In this chapter, we focused primarily on beliefs, opinions, and attitudes rather than knowledge. It would be useful to consider how the relationship between intellectual humility and open-mindedness might look different concerning knowledge rather than convictions and how the intellectual humility–open-mindedness relationship may continue to be shaped by the centrality of some knowledge to a person and the person's level of commitment to the knowledge.

In our global village, we constantly encounter new ideas, theories, and values. Intellectual humility, or the realization that one's current beliefs might be wrong, can be a starting point that motivates a variety of intellectual virtues that help us gain more accurate understanding. Open-mindedness can help us explore a full range of ideas, and intellectual caution can help us evaluate whether belief revision is warranted. This illustrates how intellectual humility does not operate in a vacuum. It is interconnected not only with open-mindedness but also with many cognitive traits and intellectual virtues (for more on intellectual virtues, see Baehr, 2011). People must constantly discern which intellectual virtues are most appropriate for their situation. Some contexts may call for intellectual humility and associated open-mindedness. Others may call for intellectual firmness, caution, courage, or dependability. Additional research can elucidate how these intellectual qualities relate to each other and how people select which to use in particular situations.

References

Alfano, M., Iurino, K., Stey, P., Robinson, B., Christen, M., Yu, F., & Lapsley, D. (2017). Development and validation of a multi-dimensional measure of intellectual humility. *PloS One, 12*(8), e0182950. https://doi.org/10.1371/journal.pone.0182950

Baehr, J. (2011). The structure of open-mindedness. *Canadian Journal of Philosophy, 41*, 191–213. https://doi.org/10.1353/cjp.2011.0010

Brienza, J. P., Kung, F. Y. H., Santos, H. C., Bobocel, D. R., & Grossmann, I. (2018). Wisdom, bias, and balance: Toward a process-sensitive measurement of wisdom-related cognition. *Journal of Personality and Social Psychology, 115*, 1093–1126. https://doi.org/10.1037/pspp0000171

Burrow, A. L., & Hill, P. L. (2011). Purpose as a form of identity capital for positive youth adjustment. *Developmental Psychology, 47*, 1196–1206. https://doi.org/10.1037/a0023818

Campbell, J. D., Trapnell, P. D., Heine, S. J., Katz, I. M., Lavallee, L. F., & Lehman, D. R. (1996). Self-concept clarity: Measurement, personality correlates, and cultural boundaries. *Journal of Personality and Social Psychology, 70*, 141–156.

Church, I. M. (2018). Intellectual humility and religious belief. *Journal of Psychology and Theology, 46*, 219–242. https://doi.org/10.1177/0091647118807188

Dickens, C. (1986). *A Christmas carol*. Bantam Books. (Original work published 1843)

Dormandy, K. (2018). Does epistemic humility threaten religious beliefs? *Journal of Psychology and Theology, 46*, 292–304. https://doi.org/10.1177/0091647118807186

Ellison, W. D., Yun, J., Lupo, M. I., Lucas-Marinelli, A. K., Marshall, V. B., Matic, A. F. R., & Trahan, A. C. (2021). Development and initial validation of a scale to measure momentary self-concept clarity. *Self and Identity, 21*, 1–20. https://doi.org/10.1080/15298868.2021.2010796

Erikson, E. H. (1956). The problem of ego identity. *Journal of the American Psychoanalytic Association, 4*, 56–121. https://doi.org/10.1177/000306515600400104

Fisher, M., & Keil, F. C. (2016). The curse of expertise: When more knowledge leads to miscalibrated explanatory insight. *Cognitive Science, 40*, 1251–1269. https://doi.org/10.1111/cogs.12280

Flury, J., & Ickes, W. (2007). Having a weak versus strong sense of self: The Sense of Self Scale (SOSS). *Self and Identity, 6*, 281–303. https://doi.org/10.1080/15298860601033208

Gorichanaz, T. (2022). Relating information seeking and use to intellectual humility. *Journal of the Association for Information Science and Technology, 73*, 643–654. https://doi.org/10.1002/asi.24567

Haggard, M., Rowatt, W. C., Leman, J. C., Meagher, B., Moore, C., Fergus, T., Whitcomb, D., Battaly, H., Baehr, J., & Howard-Snyder, D. (2018). Finding middle ground between intellectual arrogance and intellectual servility: Development and assessment of the limitations-owning intellectual humility scale. *Personality and Individual Differences, 124*, 184–193. https://doi.org/10.1016/j.paid.2017.12.014

Hart, W., Albarracín, D., Eagly, A. H., Brechan, I., Lindberg, M. J., & Merrill, L. (2009). Feeling validated versus being correct: A meta-analysis of selective exposure to information. *Psychological Bulletin, 135*, 555–588. https://doi.org/10.1037/a0015701

Hazlett, A. (2012). Higher-order epistemic attitudes and intellectual humility. *Episteme, 9*, 205–223. https://doi.org/10.1017/epi.2012.11

Hill, P. C., Lewis Hall, M. E., Wang, D., & Decker, L. A. (2021). Theistic intellectual humility and well-being: Does ideological context matter? *The Journal of Positive Psychology, 16*, 155–167. https://doi.org/10.1080/17439760.2019.1689424

Holland, R. W., Verplanken, B., & van Knippenberg, A. (2003). From repetition to conviction: Attitude accessibility as a determinant of attitude certainty. *Journal of Experimental Social Psychology, 39*, 594–601. https://doi.org/10.1016/S0022-1031(03)00038-6

Hook, J. N., Davis, D. E., Van Tongeren, D. R., Hill, P. C., Worthington, E. L., Jr., Farrell, J. E., & Dieke, P. (2015). Intellectual humility and forgiveness of religious leaders. *The Journal of Positive Psychology, 10*, 499–506. https://doi.org/10.1080/17439760.2015.1004554

Hoyle, R. H., Davisson, E. K., Diebels, K. J., & Leary, M. R. (2016). Holding specific views with humility: Conceptualization and measurement of specific intellectual humility. *Personality and Individual Differences, 97*, 165–172. https://doi.org/10.1016/j.paid.2016.03.043

Jarvinen, M. J., & Paulus, T. B. (2017). Attachment and cognitive openness: Emotional underpinnings of intellectual humility. *The Journal of Positive Psychology, 12*(1), 74–86. https://doi.org/gf4twq

Kidd, I. J. (2016). Intellectual humility, confidence, and argumentation. *Topoi, 35*, 395–402. https://doi.org/10.1007/s11245-015-9324-5

Kraus, S. J. (1995). Attitudes and the prediction of behavior: A meta-analysis of the empirical literature. *Personality and Social Psychology Bulletin, 21*, 58–75. https://doi.org/cmdxwt

Krumrei-Mancuso, E. J. (2018). Intellectual humility's links to religion and spirituality and the role of authoritarianism. *Personality and Individual Differences, 130*, 65–75. https://doi.org/hd9n

Krumrei-Mancuso, E. J., & Newman, B. (2020). Intellectual humility in the sociopolitical domain. *Self and Identity, 19*, 989–1016. https://doi.org/10.1080/15298868.2020.1714711

Krumrei-Mancuso, E. J., & Newman, B. (2021). Sociopolitical intellectual humility as a predictor of political attitudes and behavioral intentions. *Journal of Social and Political Psychology, 9*, 52–68. https://doi.org/10.5964/jspp.5553

Krumrei-Mancuso, E. J., & Rouse, S. V. (2016). The development and validation of the Comprehensive Intellectual Humility Scale. *Journal of Personality Assessment, 98*, 209–221. https://doi.org/10.1080/00223891.2015.1068174

Leary, M. R., Diebels, K. J., Davisson, E. K., Jongman-Sereno, K. P., Isherwood, J. C., Raimi, K. T., Deffler, S. A., & Hoyle, R. H. (2017). Cognitive and interpersonal features of intellectual humility. *Personality and Social Psychology Bulletin, 43*, 793–813. https://doi.org/f96wsf

Lillevoll, K. R., Kroger, J., & Martinussen, M. (2013). Identity status and anxiety: A meta-analysis. *Identity, 13*, 214–227. https://doi.org/10.1080/15283488.2013.799432

Marcia, J. E. (1966). Development and validation of ego-identity status. *Journal of Personality and Social Psychology, 3*, 551–558. https://doi.org/10.1037/h0023281

McElroy, S. E., Rice, K. G., Davis, D. E., Hook, J. N., Hill, P. C., Worthington, E. L., Jr., & Van Tongeren, D. R. (2014). Intellectual humility: Scale development and theoretical elaborations in the context of religious leadership. *Journal of Psychology and Theology, 42*, 19–30. https://doi.org/10.1177/009164711404200103

Newman, B. M., & Newman, P. R. (2020). *Theories of adolescent development*. Elsevier Academic Press.

Ottati, V., Price, E. D., Wilson, C., & Sumaktoyo, N. (2015). When self-perceptions of expertise increase closed-minded cognition: The earned dogmatism effect. *Journal of Experimental Social Psychology, 61*, 131–138. https://doi.org/10.1016/j.jesp.2015.08.003

Pargament, K. I., Oman, D., Pomerleau, J., & Mahoney, A. (2017). Some contributions of a psychological approach to the study of the sacred. *Religion, 47*, 718–744. https://doi.org/hd9j

Porter, T., Baldwin, C. R., Warren, M. T., Murray, E. D., Cotton Bronk, K., Forgeard, M. J., Snow, N. E., & Jayawickreme, E. (2022). Clarifying the content of intellectual humility: A systematic review and integrative framework. *Journal of Personality Assessment, 104*, 573–585. https://doi.org/hd9h

Porter, T., & Schumann, K. (2018). Intellectual humility and openness to the opposing view. *Self and Identity, 17*, 139–162. https://doi.org/10.1080/15298868.2017.1361861

Reis, H. T., Lee, K. Y., O'Keefe, S. D., & Clark, M. S. (2018). Perceived partner responsiveness promotes intellectual humility. *Journal of Experimental Social Psychology, 79*, 21–33. https://doi.org/10.1016/j.jesp.2018.05.006

Rodriguez, D., Hook, J. N., Farrell, J. E., Mosher, D. K., Zhang, H., Van Tongeren, D. R., Davis, D. E., Aten, J. D., & Hill, P. C. (2019). Religious intellectual humility, attitude change, and closeness following religious disagreement. *The Journal of Positive Psychology, 14*, 133–140. https://doi.org/10.1080/17439760.2017.1388429

Ryeng, M. S., Kroger, J., & Martinussen, M. (2013). Identity status and self-esteem: A meta-analysis. *Identity, 13*, 201–213. https://doi.org/10.1080/15283488.2013.799431

Skitka, L. J., Hanson, B. E., Morgan, G. S., & Wisneski, D. C. (2021). The psychology of moral conviction. *Annual Review of Psychology, 72*, 347–366. https://doi.org/gk3zdd

Stanovich, K. E., & Toplak, M. E. (2019). The need for intellectual diversity in psychological science: Our own studies of actively open-minded thinking as a case study. *Cognition, 187*, 156–166. https://doi.org/10.1016/j.cognition.2019.03.006

Whitcomb, D., Battaly, H., Baehr, J., & Howard-Snyder, D. (2017). Intellectual humility: Owning our limitations. *Philosophy and Phenomenological Research, 94*, 509–539. https://doi.org/10.1111/phpr.12228

Wilson, C., Ottati, V., & Price, E. (2017) Open-minded cognition: The attitude justification effect. *The Journal of Positive Psychology, 12*, 47–58. https://doi.org/10.1080/17439760.2016.1167941

Worthington, E. L., Jr. (2018). Fine-tuning the relationship between religion and intellectual humility. *Journal of Psychology and Theology, 46*, 305–314. https://doi.org/gk5pn5

Zachry, C. E., Phan, L. V., Blackie, L. E. R., & Jayawickreme, E. (2018). Situation-based contingencies underlying wisdom-content manifestations: Examining intellectual humility in daily life. *The Journals of Gerontology: Series B, 73*, 1404–1415. https://doi.org/hd9g

6
Forms of Intellectual Humility and Their Associations with Features of Knowledge, Beliefs, and Opinions

Rick H. Hoyle and Erin K. Davisson

In virtually all domains—politics included—few, if any, beliefs, opinions, and assumptions that people hold to be true or right can be verified beyond doubt. Even factual knowledge that could unequivocally be proven right or wrong often can be verified firsthand by only a small number of experts (e.g., the nuclear capability of different countries, the likelihood of sexual ambiguity at birth). The fact that people are unable to personally verify their beliefs, opinions, assumptions, and understanding suggests that they should always harbor some doubt about whether what they hold to be true is accurate or could, with at least reasonable confidence, be justified given critical thinking about relevant evidence from credible sources.

The fact that people are unable to personally verify most of what they hold to be right and true does not prevent them from expressing confidence in their knowledge and beliefs (Moore & Schatz, 2017). Overconfidence can manifest as *overplacement*, the belief that one's views are simply better than alternative views. This belief is rarely based on superior knowledge or experience compared to others. In fact, the degree to which people view their own beliefs to be superior to alternative beliefs held by others, though related to self-perceived knowledge (Raimi & Leary, 2014), is unrelated to actual knowledge (Hall & Raimi, 2018). It may also present as *overprecision*, the belief that one's views are almost certainly accurate as reflected in narrow subjective confidence intervals that often do not include the correct view when it is known (Alpert & Raiffa, 1982). In other words, people often are highly confident in their views even when they are wrong. Overprecision and other forms of overconfidence are particularly puzzling for beliefs, opinions, and other views about which truth or accuracy cannot be determined.

Widespread consumption of online content has strengthened people's confidence in the truth or accuracy of their views and, in so doing, deepened the divide between people who hold different views on a topic or issue (Friedkin et al., 2016). Automated personalization of online content produces *filter bubbles*, which contribute to digital isolation and expose users primarily to content that is consistent with their personal preferences and views (Milan & Agosti, 2019). In addition, people seek out online content biased toward confirming their understanding and views (Flaxman et al., 2016). This is especially true for political and news content—increasingly consumed online and via social media—resulting in distinct news streams that often fall along party lines and serve to reinforce people's existing political views (Peterson et al., 2021; see Chapter 2 in this volume). The digital connections that emerge from social aspects of online content consumption give rise to *echo chambers*, in which the accuracy or truth of people's views is verified to their satisfaction socially, typically without analysis or consideration of alternative views. As a result, opinions and beliefs are unlikely to be challenged, revised, or updated.

These realities suggest that people generally are unlikely to believe that their views are inaccurate or untrue and, as a result, revise or abandon them when justified. Yet, growing evidence suggests that some people—and perhaps all people at least some of the time—are willing to entertain the possibility that they could be wrong and, importantly, that others could be right. Specifically, people dispositionally high in *intellectual humility* recognize and are comfortable with their intellectual limitations (Whitcomb et al., 2017), understanding that their views could be ill-informed or wrong (Leary et al., 2017) and, as a result, are willing to consider, even seek out, new information and alternative views (for a review, see Porter et al., 2022). Yet, even people who are generally intellectually humble are hesitant to reconsider and potentially change their position on certain topics and issues (Hoyle et al., 2016). Thus, intellectual humility can be understood in both dispositional and position-specific terms.

We begin with a brief overview of the intellectual humility construct as it has transitioned from a topic of interest to philosophers and theologians to a topic of empirical inquiry led primarily by psychological scientists. Next, we elaborate on the conceptualization of intellectual humility with specific reference to its overlap with and differences from open-mindedness and low dogmatism and its connections with political cognition. Building on this conceptualization of the general intellectual humility construct, we present a model of specific intellectual humility, emphasizing its similarity to and differences from general intellectual humility. We present previously unpublished results from analyses of data sets in which we assessed specific intellectual humility with respect to a range of topics and issues. We close with a discussion of intellectual humility as a potential target of intervention.

The Intellectual Humility Construct

Intellectual humility has been aptly described as a "a concept in progress" (Johnson et al., 2017). Despite a long history of interest in humility in many religious and philosophical traditions, humility has only received attention from social and behavioral scientists since (about) 2005, and attention from empirically oriented political scientists has only emerged more recently. Empirical inquiry on the broader construct of humility was stimulated by an influential review pointing out that the humility construct had largely been neglected by psychological scientists (Tangney, 2000). The author concluded that a fundamental concern to be addressed if humility was to become a topic of empirical inquiry was theoretically informed measures, noting that psychological scientists were best positioned to develop measurement instruments and strategies. In response to the review and call for action, numerous measures of humility have been developed, and dozens of reports of empirical work on humility are now published each year (for a review, see Hoyle & Krumrei-Mancuso, 2021).

About a decade later, an interdisciplinary group of scholars reached a similar conclusion about the related concept of intellectual humility (Davis et al., 2019). In a meeting convened by the John Templeton Foundation, philosophers, theologians, and psychological scientists discussed the value of investing in systematic, empirical inquiry into intellectual humility. Consistent with conclusions based on the earlier review of general humility, it was the opinion of the group that significant attention should be devoted to defining the intellectual humility construct in such a way that it could be measured and then studied using empirical methods. With funds provided by the foundation, teams of philosophers and psychologists began measurement work in 2012, and the first reports of empirical research on intellectual humility began to appear 2 years later (e.g., Gregg & Mahadevan, 2014; Hopkin et al., 2014; McElroy et al., 2014)[1] Building on these early efforts, published empirical work on intellectual humility has increased dramatically, resulting in a growing empirical literature on the construct (Porter et al., 2022). Focusing on papers with *intellectual humility* in the title as indexed in the American Psychological Association's PsycInfo database, the number of papers published annually increased from 0 in 2013 to 11 or more each year from 2017 to 2021. Although early papers focused primarily on conceptualization and measurement of the construct, recent papers have examined intellectual humility regarding a range of politically charged opinions and beliefs, including affective polarization (Bowes et al., 2020; Krumrei-Mancuso & Newman, 2020), use of nuclear energy to address the climate crisis (Vaupotič et al., 2022), and vaccination against COVID-19 (Huynh & Senger, 2021). The increasing interest in intellectual humility in relation to politics, religion, and social issues is consistent with our argument, developed in the next section, that considering the intellectual humility with which specific views are held is conceptually and methodologically useful.

As a concept in progress, the defining features of intellectual humility are still a matter of fruitful discussion among philosophers and psychologists interested in the construct. Yet, at a broad level, several of its features are widely accepted. These might be viewed as core features of the construct as currently conceptualized and measured. Foremost among these is the assumption that the intellectually humble person recognizes and accepts the potential fallibility of their views. That is to say, they generally are not prone to dogmatism. A recent review found that all current measures of intellectual humility capture this feature of the construct (Porter et al., 2022). Another core feature that is evident in most definitions and measures overlaps with the open-mindedness construct. Intellectually humble people are willing to consider new information relevant for their views, information that comes from other people or that they seek out from credible sources (e.g., Leary et al., 2017). Some conceptualizations suggest that people who are intellectually humble, recognizing the limits of their knowledge and positions and realizing the availability of information that would strengthen them, are willing to update their knowledge and potentially change their views (e.g., Leary et al., 2017). It should be recognized that humility with respect to knowledge in particular does not imply modesty (Krumrei-Mancuso & Rouse, 2016). Some views of intellectual humility suggest that it includes an accurate assessment of personal knowledge (e.g., Hook et al., 2015). As such, a highly knowledgeable person, particularly with respect to specific topics or issues, is not evidencing low intellectual humility in claiming or feeling comfortable with their expertise. For example, a climate scientist who points out errors in projections or claims reflected in proposed climate change policy or legislation is not demonstrating intellectual arrogance. They are making the reasonable assumption that their expertise exceeds that of policymakers and politicians responsible for such proposals. Additional characteristics are evident in the many published reflections on and studies of the construct (for a review, see Porter et al., 2022); however, our own work has embraced these features that we view as core to the construct.

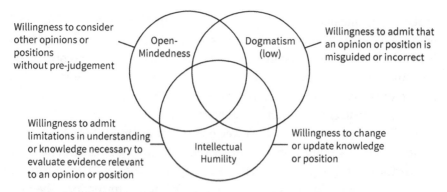

Figure 6.1 Intellectual humility shares some conceptual features with open-mindedness and dogmatism but includes additional core features.

Our working conceptualization and its relation to open-mindedness and dogmatism is depicted in Figure 6.1. Looking first to the upper right portion of the figure, intellectual humility shares with low dogmatism the acknowledgment that one's understanding, positions, or beliefs could be wrong or misguided. Empirically, the association between scores on measures of intellectual humility and measures of dogmatism ranges from moderate to strong. In unpublished data from an online sample of adults, we observed a correlation of $-.60$ ($N = 391$) between scores on the General Intellectual Humility Scale (Leary et al., 2017) and the Dogmatism (DOG) Scale (Altemeyer, 2002). In published work (Leary et al., 2017), we reported correlations of $-.49$ between the same scales but $-.20$ between the General Intellectual Humility Scale and the Rokeach Dogmatism Scale (Rokeach, 1960). Scores on the two dogmatism scales were modestly correlated for two measures of the same construct ($r = .55$), likely owing to the focus on closed-mindedness in the Altemeyer DOG Scale versus the focus on unjustified belief certainty in the Rokeach Dogmatism Scale. Each conceptualization shares features of intellectual humility, with the Altemeyer conceptualization, especially as typically measured, showing significant overlap with a core feature of the construct.

Looking now to the upper left portion of the figure, intellectual humility shares with open-mindedness a willingness to thoughtfully consider alternative views. We are aware of no published work to date examining the empirical link between open-mindedness and intellectual humility (see Chapter 5 in this volume for an in-depth consideration of the link). Using unpublished data from a 4-year study of college students ($N = 534$), we can offer an initial estimate of the association. In addition to the General Intellectual Humility Scale, students completed a three-item measure of endorsement of the universalism value as assessed by the Portrait Values Questionnaire (Schwartz et al., 2001). One item reads, "It is important to this person to listen to people who are different from him/her. Even when this person disagrees with them, he/she still wants to understand them." The correlation between scores on this item and the General Intellectual Humility Scale was .43, providing initial evidence of the conceptual overlap between features of open-mindedness and features of intellectual humility as we have conceptualized it.[2]

Finally, as can be seen in the lower portion of Figure 6.1, intellectual humility comprises other features not shared with low dogmatism and open-mindedness. One, described earlier, is a willingness to update positions or beliefs and correct knowledge as warranted by new information. The other is an acknowledgment that the basis for the views one holds to be true might itself be inadequate or untrustworthy. As such, even if one's understanding is correct or position is justified given the evidence, the confidence with which it is held may be weak and in need of strengthening by relevant information from credible sources. Consistent with this feature, we have shown that people high in intellectual humility prefer information from experts when their knowledge about or opinion on a matter is not confidently held (Leary et al., 2017).

Despite considerable, ongoing attention from philosophers and psychological scientists to define intellectual humility, relatively little attention has been devoted to its presumed nature. Although there is clear agreement that intellectual humility is a characteristic that varies between people, there is little agreement about, or even consideration of, what sort of characteristic it is. We view this consideration as critical because it offers clues about whether people's characteristic level of intellectual humility could be changed and, if so, how. What are the possibilities? Is it, for example, an attitude that, with age and experience, becomes increasingly resistant to change? If so, then clues to its conceptual structure and how it might be changed could be found in the voluminous literature on attitude change. Alternatively, intellectual humility might be viewed as a mindset, a trait, or a meta-belief.[3] Mindsets, as understood by psychological scientists, are beliefs about the nature of the world and one's place in it (e.g., whether personality can change, whether stress undermines performance). Importantly with respect to intellectual humility, mindsets are amenable to at least temporary change (e.g., Crum et al., 2020). *Meta-beliefs*, that is, beliefs about one's beliefs (e.g., Pennycook et al., 2020), may similarly be amenable to change through intervention, though no strategy for changing meta-beliefs has been empirically validated. Traits are, by definition, stable characteristics. Although a number of definitions of intellectual humility refer to it as a trait (e.g., Whitcomb et al., 2017), none has justified that designation.

Two lines of evidence, one conceptual and one empirical, offer some insight into the nature of intellectual humility as an individual difference. Spiegel (2012) argues persuasively that intellectual humility is a second-order, or meta-, attitude that people take toward themselves as believers and knowers. Relevant for our depiction of relations between intellectual humility, open-mindedness, and low dogmatism in Figure 6.1, Spiegel argues that open-mindedness is a first-order attitude toward one's beliefs. In this characterization, intellectual humility is, in part, a meta-belief about the degree to which one is open-minded in one's knowledge and beliefs. Empirical evidence from our own work (Hoyle et al., 2021) suggests that intellectual humility as we have measured it is trait-like. We assessed general intellectual humility early in the first year and about a month before the end of the fourth year of college in a sample of 538 students. An examination of change accounting for unreliability of measurement showed that, for 74% of the sample, intellectual humility did not change across this 3.5-year period, during which they were confronted with an abundance of new knowledge and exposed to an array of opinions and beliefs. Among the remainder, intellectual humility declined for 15% and increased for 11%. This level of stability across time despite changes in relevant inputs is consistent with the view that general intellectual humility is a trait. A clearer understanding of the nature of intellectual humility will require longitudinal research, with a particular focus on childhood and adolescence.

Specific Intellectual Humility

As conceptualized by most scholars and reflected in frequently used measures, individual differences in intellectual humility reflect a set of beliefs about oneself as knower and believer that applies to one's views across all domains, topics, and issues. Evidence to date suggests that intellectual humility conceptualized in this way is relevant for understanding why some people generally are more inclined than others to accept the limits of their knowledge and beliefs and be open to new information about and potential change in their views. Importantly, however, some evidence shows that intellectually humble people are not equally inclined to hold all views in this way. Here, we review published research and present new findings showing that (1) intellectually humble people are not intellectually humble with respect to their knowledge of or beliefs about all topics and issues and (2) there is substantial variability in the degree of intellectual humility evident in how people view their knowledge and beliefs across domains, topics, and issues (see Ottati &

Wilson, 2018; see Chapter 7 in this volume for a similar conceptualization when assessing open-minded cognition).

Specific intellectual humility refers to people's beliefs about their knowledge of or position on a particular domain, topic, or issue (Hoyle et al., 2016). The content of those beliefs mirrors the content for general intellectual humility presented earlier. Specific intellectual humility is evident in people's beliefs that what they view as true or right with respect to a particular domain, topic, or issue could be wrong, accompanied by a willingness to consider relevant and credible new information and a willingness to update or change their knowledge or position if warranted. Given the parallel conceptualizations of general and specific intellectual humility, we would expect a positive correlation between them. People who generally are intellectually humble should, on average, be more intellectually humble with respect to specific domains, topics, and issues. Yet specific intellectual humility is more than an expression of general intellectual humility. As we argue below, people's intellectual humility with respect to a specific domain, topic, or issue is a reflection of their general intellectual humility plus characteristics of their knowledge or position on the matter. For that reason, specific intellectual humility is more complex and variable than dispositional intellectual humility.

The "specific" qualifier can refer to at least three categories of knowledge, beliefs, or opinions that vary in breadth.[4] The broadest is *domain*, which refers to a broad category of knowledge or experience such as politics, religion, education, and finances. Domains are higher-order categories that encompass a potentially large number of specific concerns about which people's knowledge or opinions may vary. For example, the domain of politics includes many concerns of political significance on which opinions vary widely between people and over time. Within, and sometimes across, domains are *topics*, which are more narrow categories of knowledge or opinion that encompass a smaller, relatively homogeneous set of specific concerns. Within the political domain, examples of topics are states' rights, tax policy, and immigration. Immigration is an example of a topic that, for some people, spans domains; some people see immigration policy as a reflection of religious beliefs about hospitality and inclusiveness. At the lowest level of specificity are *issues*. Issues often fit within topics, although sometimes they span two or more topics. Examples in the political domain are legalization of marijuana, teaching critical race theory, and vaccine mandates. Vaccine mandates may, for some people, span the states' rights, religious liberty, and individual freedom topics. Moving from domain to topic to issue, the degree to which general intellectual humility fully captures people's willingness to admit they are wrong, thoughtfully consider alternative views, and change their view if warranted declines.

Specific intellectual humility with respect to a particular domain, topic, or issue reflects people's general level of intellectual humility as well as characteristics of their view about what is true or right and the basis for it.

Specific intellectual humility is a useful complement to the general intellectual humility construct for at least three reasons. First, it conceptualizes the construct as more than a general tendency, similar in nature and influence to personality traits. It allows for the possibility that intellectual humility with respect to specific, personal, and important matters may change without a noticeable change in the general tendency to engage with knowledge and ideas with or without humility. Second, it allows for specificity matching in research designed to evaluate the relations between people's views and the degree to which they hold them with humility (Hoyle & Leary, 2009). As noted earlier, intellectual humility research is increasingly focused on understanding people's views on important social issues. Attempting to understand the role of intellectual humility in the adoption, maintenance, and change of people's knowledge about or position on specific issues using general intellectual humility is to risk underestimating, even failing to detect, the relation.[5] A conceptualization of and approach to measuring intellectual humility at a level of specificity equivalent to that of views at the domain, topic, and issue level increase the likelihood of detecting and estimating the strength of relations between them. In this respect, research on intellectual humility and characteristics of people's views is not unlike research on the prediction of behavior from attitudes. In the same way that general attitudes only weakly predict specific behaviors compared to specific attitudes (Ajzen & Fishbein, 1977), correlations of general intellectual humility with expressions of humility on specific topics or issues will underestimate the role of intellectual humility in those expressions. Following from these justifications is the possibility that intellectual humility with respect to a specific topic or issue might be changed, leading to change in, or at least thoughtful consideration of, one's position. We suggest potential strategies for increasing specific intellectual humility in the last section of the chapter.

Contributors to Variability in Specific Intellectual Humility

We have proposed a conceptual model of specific intellectual humility that characterizes it as the product of general intellectual humility and a set of attributes of the position one holds (Hoyle et al., 2016). By *conceptual*, we mean that the model proposes potential influences without commitment to formal expressions of the strength, direction, or shape of the relations. For a subset of the influences, we have completed analysis that led us to more formal and specific statements about their contribution to specific intellectual humility. The model in conceptual form is expressed as follows:

$$IH_S = f(IH_G, \text{extremity of } S, \text{basis for } S)$$

Subscripts G and S denote general and specific intellectual humility, respectively, with S referring to a particular domain, topic, or issue. The use of f reflects our view that, although the factors in parentheses together give rise to levels of specific intellectual humility, the shape of the relations and the potential interactions between them are not specified. The inclusion of extremity of a specific position proposes that, beyond the particular position people hold with respect to domains, topics, and issues, the extremity of their position is a factor in their willingness to admit it could be wrong or merits further consideration. The last term encompasses a set of factors that explain, to some extent, why people hold the specific position they hold. Examples include the sources that informed their position and the psychological function served by their position. We now have extensive data on the relations of general intellectual humility and extremity of position on specific intellectual humility. At this time, our data on the basis of people's position as it affects specific intellectual humility are more preliminary.

We have collected data on specific intellectual humility with respect to a wide range of domains, topics, and issues using self-report questionnaire items (e.g., "My views about [domain/topic/issue] today may someday turn out to be wrong," "It is quite likely that there are gaps in my understanding of [domain/topic/issue]," "My views about [domain/topic/issue] may change with additional evidence or information"). Initial psychometric evaluation of the measure indicated that it is reliable and, importantly, measures the same construct regardless of domain, topic, or issue (Hoyle et al., 2016). That is to say, a person's intellectual humility scores will differ from one domain, topic, or issue to the next; but in every case their score reflects the same form of intellectual humility. As a result, comparisons and correlations between specific intellectual humility scores across targets are meaningful. Typically, in addition to reporting on their specific intellectual humility for one or more domains, topics, and issues, participants report their general intellectual humility and their position with respect to specific targets of interest. In some cases, we have information about other features of people's views such as relevant information sources, certainty, and function served by the view.

Specific intellectual humility is not just the general tendency toward intellectual humility limited to a particular topic or issue. We now have considerable evidence that the correlation between general intellectual humility and specific intellectual humility is typically weak to moderate. Moreover, the correlations between specific intellectual humility for different views are often weak. Relevant correlation coefficients from analyses of five data sets are presented in Table 6.1. The samples include university students, community members, and online participant samples and span the adult age range. The more than two dozen specific views are wide-ranging and represent each of the three levels of specificity. The table shows correlations between specific intellectual humility measured using items like those above and the General Intellectual Humility Scale (Leary et al., 2017). In the bottom two rows is a summary of correlations between specific intellectual humility scores for the data sets that includes ratings for more than one domain, topic, or issue.

Several characteristics of the set of correlations are noteworthy. Perhaps most striking is their magnitude, which, in absolute terms, is not large and, given that the associations are between two forms of the same construct, surprisingly small. Yet, all suggest at least some overlap between the two forms of intellectual humility but, consistent with our model, indicating that specific intellectual humility is more than a focused form of the general tendency toward intellectual humility. Another notable characteristic of the pattern is more subtle. The list of domains, topics, and issues is generally ordered from broad to narrow. Our hypothesis has been that the more specific the view about which specific intellectual humility is expressed, the weaker its association with general intellectual humility should be. Viewed differently, we expected stronger effects of how and why people hold specific views as they move toward positions on specific issues such as K–12 curriculum and legalization of marijuana. Although the observed pattern sometimes departs from this expected pattern, especially when moving from topics to issues, there is scattered evidence consistent with our hypothesis. Specifically, the *r*s for domains such as politics, religion, and health and fitness are generally the highest in a column. The *r*s for issues such as abortion and background checks for gun ownership are noticeably lower. One significant departure from this pattern, and one that we anticipated, concerns topics about which people have little personal involvement. In one study, we included the topic of intelligent life on other planets to evaluate this expectation. The *r* of .48 is among the highest in the table, suggesting that it reflects general, more than specific, intellectual humility. Information in the last two rows of the table makes clear that the correlations between ratings of specific intellectual humility for different views are often modest. The level of these correlations suggests that,

Table 6.1 Correlations Between General Intellectual Humility and Specific Intellectual Humility for Different Domains, Topics, and Issues

Domain/topic/issue	Young adults (N = 156)	First-year college students (N = 534)	Online adult sample (n ≈ 200)[a]	Online adult sample (N = 391)	Middle-aged adults (N = 410)
Politics	.36		.51	.55	
Religion			.35	.32	
Morality	.20				
Education	.23				
Health/fitness			.41		.33
Parenting	.16				.18
Abortion	.14		.30	.20	
Manners			.40		
Gun control				.33	
Climate change			.28		
Vaccination				.28	.12
Voter ID requirement			.41		
Trustworthiness of political news		.28			
Background checks for gun purchase				.26	
Baby care	.19				
Breastfeeding vs. formula	.19				
Medical ethics	.22				
Physician-assisted suicide	.26				
K–12 curriculum	.22				
Common Core standards	.14				
Surveillance	.09				
Use of drones in warfare	.22				
Legalization of same-sex marriage	.14				
Legalization of marijuana	.17				
Intelligent life on other planets			.48		
Correlations between intellectual humility for specific domains, topics, and issues					
Mean	.38	–	.44	.46	.30
Range	.16–.63	–	.12–.80[c]	.32–.72[b]	.23–.42

[a]The total sample size was 804, but subsamples of approximately 200 provided ratings for each domain or topic; actual Ns ranged from 195 to 207.

[b]The highest r was between the gun control topic and the background checks for gun purchases issue. The next highest r was .57.

[c]The highest r was between the politics domain and the voter identification topic. The next highest r was .61.

in addition to the common thread of intellectual humility that runs through them, specific intellectual humility ratings reflect additional features of people's specific positions such as those highlighted in our model.

In our earliest work on specific intellectual humility, which focused exclusively on intellectual humility in the religion domain, we found an inverted-U pattern of association between position and scores on an ad hoc measure of intellectual humility with respect to religion. Specifically, we found equivalently low levels of specific intellectual humility for the highly atheistic and the highly religious (Hopkin et al., 2014, Figure 5). We have repeatedly observed this pattern when correlating position and specific intellectual humility, whereby intellectual humility is relatively low among people with extreme positions on issues and relatively high among those with more moderate views (see Hoyle et al., 2016, Figure 1, for examples). In our initial work with the Specific Intellectual Humility Scale, we found forms of this relationship between specific intellectual humility and extremity of position for five of the six diverse areas considered, including formula versus breastfeeding, physician-assisted suicide, drone use, and the Common Core learning standards (Hoyle et al., 2016, Figure 1). When we fail to observe this pattern, it has often been attributable to the failure of the measure of position to capture the full range of positions. For example, in the original study showing this pattern, the measure of people's position on key religious beliefs ranged from strongly atheistic to strongly religious. Measures of position on a topic or issue often allow for extremity only in one direction. The curvilinear pattern emerges only when expression of both extreme positions is permitted. For example, on the politically charged topic of government use of drones for surveillance, people who strongly oppose or favor their use score equivalently lower on intellectual humility than people with a more moderate position (Hoyle et al., 2016).

Our research on the final set of characteristics in the model is in the early stages. In this work, we ask whether the degree of humility with which people hold a specific belief or position is a function of the origins of the view, the certainty with which they hold the view, the psychological functions their view serves, and other underlying characteristics. At this time, we can offer several hypotheses based on our understanding of the nature of intellectual humility and beliefs or opinions along with some preliminary findings. The source of people's information about a topic or issue should be relevant for understanding their willingness to entertain the possibility they could be wrong or should seek out additional information. Results of initial analyses suggest that higher scores on specific intellectual humility items such as those shown in Table 6.1 are associated with a lower likelihood of engaging in personal research and careful reasoning (*r*s between –.24 and –.31). Some insight into the meaning of this result can be gleaned from associations with certainty and the need for consensus with respect to one's position. For most topics and issues, specific intellectual humility is negatively correlated with certainty (*r*s between –.25 and –.44) and the need for consensus on the topic or issue (*r*s between –.25 and –.35). People who score higher on specific intellectual humility express less certainty about their position and greater comfort with people holding positions on the topic or issue that differ from their own. In terms of function, only the association with an item designed to capture the ego-defensive function (Herek, 1987) produces reliable results across topics and issue. People who score higher on specific intellectual humility are more likely to indicate a reluctance to think about the topic or issue (*r*s between .20 and .25). These preliminary findings suggest that people who evidence intellectual humility with respect to a specific topic or issue have spent relatively little effort thinking critically about their position, are less certain about it, yet are comfortable with others not sharing their view. Additional research is needed to shed light on this pattern with particular focus on reconciling it with features of the general intellectual humility construct such as a tendency to seek out credible information relevant to one's views.

Intellectual Humility as a Potential Target of Intervention

The willingness to admit that one could be wrong accompanied by a willingness to consider credible information that might lead to improved knowledge or better judgment is an adaptive attribute. Yet, evidence abounds that many people are unwilling to admit that their knowledge, beliefs, or opinions could be incorrect and, relatedly, unwilling to consider credible information representing alternative views or perspectives. The overconfidence that accompanies the assumptions that one's views are right and true, even when those views are based on substantial expertise (Ottati et al., 2015), thwarts learning and encourages the denigration of alternative views. For these reasons, consideration of ways to increase intellectual humility is warranted.

A significant challenge for attempts to increase intellectual humility is the nature of the construct. We have argued and presented initial findings that suggest general intellectual humility is best understood as a higher-order trait that reflects meta-beliefs about the acquisition, maintenance, and change of personal knowledge, beliefs, and opinions. A full three-quarters of our sample of college students became neither more nor less intellectually humble across

3.5 years of coursework, extracurricular activities, and social interactions with people representing different views across domains. Of the remainder, more than half became less intellectually humble despite these potential challenges to their views. Follow-up analyses revealed no specific factor (e.g., major, grades, demographic characteristics) that predicted stability or change. Although our study provides only one data point, as one of the only studies available on change in intellectual humility over time, it suggests that attempts to change general intellectual humility are not likely to be successful.

Although changing intellectual humility at the topic and issue levels is less efficient, it may be the most promising avenue for increasing it. Moreover, the benefits of intellectual humility often are most needed with respect to important and divisive social issues such as gun control, immigration policy, voting rights, and vaccination. As we have suggested, the humility with which people reach and maintain a position on these matters is affected by more than their general tendency toward intellectual humility. Among the factors we have identified are specific features such as extremity and function, about which substantial research literatures are available. As such, the potential targets of interventions that aim to increase intellectual humility with respect to a specific topic or issue are more numerous, better understood, and more likely to change than features of general intellectual humility that interventions might target (e.g., admitting that, in general, what one holds to be right and true could be wrong). For example, topic- or issue-focused interventions might focus on reducing position extremity, promoting consideration of alternative sources of information, or proposing alternative means of satisfying the function served by the position.

A critical concern, one that has not yet been addressed empirically, is the nature of the association between intellectual humility, features of positions, and the judgments or behaviors they inform. Although our own work has, for some features, examined the magnitude, direction, and shape (when nonlinear) of those associations, we have not examined causality. Thus, for instance, we cannot determine whether low specific intellectual humility with respect to an issue follows from or leads to the adoption of an extreme position on the issue. Similarly, we cannot state whether judgments of people whose position on an issue is different from one's own fuels or is itself a product of low specific intellectual humility with respect to the issue. In short, although additional research is needed to more fully document the associations between intellectual humility, features of the positions one holds, and how one relates to others as a function of those positions, research using methods and designs that support causal inferences with respect to those associations is critical. Should such research find support for causal connections, programs and practices that take into account intellectual humility may help to improve understanding, decision-making, and interpersonal relations required for solutions to complex, pressing, and contentious social issues.

Acknowledgments

We thank Elizabeth Krumrei-Mancuso for helpful comments on a draft of this chapter. The data on which results presented in this chapter are based were collected with support from the John Templeton Foundation (Grant 29630). Opinions are those of the authors and do not necessarily reflect the views of the foundation. Address correspondence to Rick Hoyle, rhoyle@duke.edu.

Notes

1. An earlier empirical project not associated with the Templeton-funded effort coded expressions of intellectual humility as partial evidence of wise reasoning in college students' reasoning about "the current economic situation" (Kross & Grossman, 2012). Coding instructions referenced definitions from the literature on wisdom.
2. Correlations between intellectual humility and the other two items, which assessed equality and justice for all and care for nature and the environment, were .26 and .24, respectively.
3. Although intellectual humility is frequently referred to, especially by philosophers, as a virtue, the implications of that label for understanding the nature of the constructs are not clear. Virtues have not been considered by psychological scientists as a category or type of construct.
4. For this reason, we do not use the common term *domain-specific* as a descriptor for this form of intellectual humility. Although it might refer to domains (e.g., Krumrei-Mancuso & Newman, 2021), it might also refer to narrower, more specific forms within domains.
5. The generally small correlation between personality and behavior pointed out in Mischel's (1968) critique of research on the personality–behavior link was resolved, in part, by a recognition of the need to measure predictor and outcome at the same level of specificity (e.g., Ajzen & Fishbein, 1977).

References

Ajzen, I., & Fishbein, M. (1977). Attitude–behavior relations: A theoretical analysis and review of empirical research. *Psychological Bulletin, 84*(5), 888–918. https://content.apa.org/doi/10.1037/0033-2909.84.5.888

Alpert, M., & Raiffa, H. (1982). A progress report on the training of probability assessors. In D. Kahneman, P. Slovic, & A. Tversky (Eds.), *Judgment under uncertainty: Heuristics and biases* (pp. 294–305). Cambridge University Press.

Altemeyer, B. (2002). Dogmatic behavior among students: Testing a new measure of dogmatism. *Journal of Social Psychology, 142*(6), 713–721. https://doi.org/10.1080/00224540209603931

Bowes, S. M., Blanchard, M. C., Costello, T. H., Abramowitz, A. I., & Lilienfeld, S. O. (2020). Intellectual humility and between-party animus: Implications for affective polarization in two community samples. *Journal of Research in Personality, 88*, Article 103992. https://doi.org/10.1016/j.jrp.2020.103992

Crum, A. J., Handley-Miner, I. J., & Smith, E. N. (2020). The stress mindset intervention. In G. M. Walton & A. J. Crum (Eds.), *Handbook of wise interventions: How social-psychological insights can help solve problems* (pp. 217–238). Guilford Press.

Davis, D. E., Hook, J. N., & Hill, P. C. (2019). Seven challenges of an interdisciplinary project to measure intellectual humility. *Journal of Psychology and Christianity, 38*(3), 148–156.

Flaxman, S., Goel, S., & Rao, J. M. (2016). Filter bubbles, echo chambers, and online news consumption. *Public Opinion Quarterly, 80*(S1), 298–320. https://doi.org/10.1093/poq/nfw006

Friedkin, N. E., Proskurnikov, A. V., Tempo, R., & Parsegov, S. E. (2016). Network science on belief system dynamics under logic constraints. *Science, 354*(6310), 321–326. https://doi.org/10.1126/science.aag2624

Gregg, A. P., & Mahadevan, N. (2014). Intellectual arrogance and intellectual humility: An evolutionary-epistemological account. *Journal of Psychology and Theology, 42*(1), 7–18. https://doi.org/10.1177%2F009164711404200102

Hall, M. P., & Raimi, K. T. (2018). Is belief superiority justified by superior knowledge? *Journal of Experimental Social Psychology, 76*, 290–306. https://doi.org/10.1016/j.jesp.2018.03.001

Herek, G. M. (1987). Can functions be measured? A new perspective on the functional approach to attitudes. *Social Psychology Quarterly, 50*(4), 285–303. https://doi.org/10.2307/2786814

Hook, J. N., Davis, D. E., Van Tongeren, D. R., Hill, P. C., Worthington, E. L., Jr., Farrell, J. E., & Dieke, P. (2015). Intellectual humility and forgiveness of religious leaders. *Journal of Positive Psychology, 10*(6), 499–506. https://doi.org/10.1080/17439760.2015.1004554

Hopkin, C. R., Hoyle, R. H., & Toner, K. (2014). Intellectual humility and reactions to opinions about religious beliefs. *Journal of Psychology and Theology, 42*(1), 50–61. https://doi.org/10.1177%2F009164711404200106

Hoyle, R. H., Davisson, E. K., Diebels, K. J., & Leary, M. R. (2016). Holding specific views with humility: Conceptualization and measurement of specific intellectual humility. *Personality and Individual Differences, 97*, 165–172. https://doi.org/10.1016/j.paid.2016.03.043

Hoyle, R. H., & Krumrei-Mancuso, E. J. (2021). Psychological measurement of humility. In M. Alfano, M. P. Lynch, & A. Tanesini (Eds.), *Routledge handbook on the philosophy of humility* (pp. 387–400). Routledge.

Hoyle, R. H., & Leary, M. R. (2009). Methods for the study of individual differences in social behavior. In M. R. Leary & R. H. Hoyle (Eds.), *Handbook of individual differences in social behavior* (pp. 12–23). Guilford Press.

Hoyle, R. H., Weeks, M. S., & Student Resilience and Well-Being Project Research Group. (2021). The Student Resilience and Well-Being Project: Opportunities, challenges, and lessons learned. *International Journal of Community Well-Being, 4*, 669–690. https://doi.org/10.1007/s42413-021-00138-2

Huynh, H. P., & Senger, A. R. (2021). A little shot of humility: Intellectual humility predicts vaccination attitudes and intention to vaccinate against COVID-19. *Journal of Applied Social Psychology, 51*(4), 449–460. https://doi.org/10.1111/jasp.12747

Johnson, C. R., Lynch, M., Gunn, H., & Sheff, N. (2017). *Intellectual humility*. Oxford Bibliographies Online. https://www.oxfordbibliographies.com/view/document/obo-9780195396577/obo-9780195396577-0347.xml

Kross, E., & Grossman, I. (2012). Boosting wisdom: Distance from the self enhances wise reasoning, attitudes, and behavior. *Journal of Experimental Psychology: General, 141*(1), 43–48. https://doi.org/10.1037/a0024158

Krumrei-Mancuso, E. J., & Newman, B. (2020) Intellectual humility in the sociopolitical domain. *Self and Identity*, *19*(8), 989–1016. https://doi.org/10.1080/15298868.2020.1714711

Krumrei-Mancuso, E. J., & Newman, B. (2021). Sociopolitical intellectual humility as a predictor of political attitudes and behavioral intentions. *Journal of Social and Political Psychology*, *9*(1), 52–68. https://doi.org/10.5964/jspp.5553

Krumrei-Mancuso, E. J., & Rouse, S. V. (2016). The development and validation of the Comprehensive Intellectual Humility Scale. *Journal of Personality Assessment*, *98*(2), 209–221. https://doi.org/10.1080/00223891.2015.1068174

Leary, M. R., Diebels, K. J., Davisson, E. K., Jongman-Sereno, K. P., Isherwood, J. C., Raimi, K. T., Deffler, S. A., & Hoyle, R. H. (2017). Cognitive and interpersonal features of intellectual humility. *Personality and Social Psychology Bulletin*, *43*(6), 793–813. https://doi.org/10.1177/0146167217697695

McElroy, S. E., Rice, K. G., Davis, D. E., Hook, J. N., Hill, P. C., Worthington, E. L., Jr., & Van Tongeren, D. R. (2014). Intellectual humility: Scale development and theoretical elaborations in the context of religious leadership. *Journal of Psychology and Theology*, *42*(1), 19–30. http://dx.doi.org/10.1177/009164711404200103

Milan, S., & Agosti, C. (2019). *Personalisation algorithms and elections: Breaking free of the filter bubble*. Internet Policy Review. https://policyreview.info/articles/news/personalisation-algorithms-and-elections-breaking-free-filter-bubble/1385

Mischel, W. (1968). *Personality and assessment*. Wiley.

Moore, D. A., & Schatz, D. (2017). The three faces of overconfidence. *Social and Personality Psychology Compass*, *11*(8), Article e12331. https://doi.org/10.1111/spc3.12331

Ottati, V., Price, E. D., Wilson, C., & Sumaktoyo, N. (2015). When self-perceptions of expertise increase close-minded cognition: The earned dogmatism effect. *Journal of Experimental Social Psychology*, *61*, 131–138. https://doi.org/10.1016/j.jesp.2015.08.003

Ottati, V., & Wilson, C. (2018). Open-minded cognition and political thought. In *Oxford Research Encyclopedia of Politics*. Retrieved June 8, 2022, from https://oxfordre.com/politics/view/10.1093/acrefore/9780190228637.001.0001/acrefore-9780190228637-e-143

Pennycook, G., Cheyne, J. A., Koehler, D. J., & Fugelsang, J. A. (2020). On the belief that beliefs should change according to evidence: Implications for conspiratorial, moral, paranormal, political, religious, and science beliefs. *Judgment and Decision Making*, *15*(4), 476–498. http://dx.doi.org/10.31234/osf.io/a7k96

Peterson, E., Goel, S., & Iyengar, S. (2021). Partisan selective exposure in online news consumption: Evidence from the 2016 presidential campaign. *Political Science Research and Methods*, *9*(2), 242–258. https://doi.org/10.1017/psrm.2019.55

Porter, T., Baldwin, C. R., Warren, M. T., Murray, E. D., Bronk, K. C., Forgeard, M. J. C., Snow, N. E., & Jayawickreme, E. (2022). Clarifying the content of intellectual humility: A systematic review and integrative framework. *Journal of Personality Assessment*, *104*(5), 573–585. https://doi.org/10.1080/00223891.2021.1975725

Raimi, K. T., & Leary, M. R. (2014). Belief superiority in the environmental domain: Attitude extremity and reactions to fracking. *Journal of Environmental Psychology*, *40*, 76–85. https://doi.org/10.1016/j.jenvp.2014.05.005

Rokeach, M. (1960). *The open and closed mind*. Basic Books.

Schwartz, S. H., Melech, G., Lehmann, A., Burgess, S., Harris, M., & Owens, V. (2001). Extending the cross-cultural validity of the theory of basic human values with a different method of measurement. *Journal of Cross-Cultural Psychology*, *32*(5), 519–542. https://doi.org/10.1177%2F0022022101032005001

Spiegel, J. S. (2012). Open-mindedness and intellectual humility. *Theory and Research in Education*, *10*(1), 27–38. https://doi.org/10.1177%2F1477878512437472

Tangney, J. P. (2000). Humility: Theoretical perspectives, empirical findings and directions for future research. *Journal of Social and Clinical Psychology, 19*(1), 70–82. http://dx.doi.org/10.1521/jscp.2000.19.1.70

Vaupotič, N., Kienhues, D., & Juck, R. (2022). Taking a stance on the role of nuclear energy to combat the climate crisis: How communication task and expert's personal stance impact individuals' intellectual humility and strategies for dealing with a complex topic. *Educational and Developmental Psychologist, 39*(1), 70–84. https://doi.org/10.1080/20590776.2021.2018916

Whitcomb, D., Battaly, H., Baehr, J., & Howard-Snyder, D. (2017). Intellectual humility: Owning our limitations. *Philosophy and Phenomenological Research, 94*(3), 509–539. https://doi.org/10.1111/phpr.12228

IV
NORMATIVE STANDARDS AND OPEN-MINDEDNESS

Open-Minded Cognition and Actively Open-Minded Thinking

7
Situation-Specific Open-Minded Cognition

Scale Validation and Incremental Effects of Person and Situation

Victor Ottati, Chase Wilson, Devon Price, Yelyzaveta Distefano, and Fred B. Bryant

> [Lincoln] was a patient, attentive listener, rather looking for the opinion of others, than hazarding his own.
> —**Doster (1915, p. 17)**

> How, in God's name, do you let such paragraphs into the Tribune?
> —**Abraham Lincoln; June 27, 1858; Letter to Chicago Tribune editor (Johnson, 2019)**

Introduction

By most biographical accounts, Lincoln was an attentive listener who openly considered the opinions and viewpoints of others (e.g., Doster, 1915). However, this general description provides only a partial understanding of Abraham Lincoln. Lincoln was open-minded in many situations but sometimes demonstrated an adamant refusal to openly consider unethical or fallacious claims that appeared in the newspaper. Importantly, his refusal to openly consider such fallacious claims was quite intentional, presumably driven by the normative belief that such claims should not be published, much less openly considered. This normative belief was prescriptive in nature. This is because open-minded acceptance of unethical or fallacious claims violates normative ideals regarding truth, honesty, and humanitarianism. Thus, it is important to consider not only an individual's general level of open-mindedness but also situation-specific levels of open-mindedness influenced by prescriptive norms and intentions (Ottati et al., 2015; Ottati et al., 2018).

Individual differences in trait open-mindedness shape human cognition and behavior (e.g., Adorno et al., 1950; Jost, 2017; Price et al., 2015; Rokeach, 1954). However, just as open- and closed-minded people exist, there may also exist situations that elicit an open- or closed-minded response (Ottati et al, 2015; Ottati et al., 2018; Samuelson & Church, 2021). The first objective of this chapter is to validate situation-specific measures of open-minded cognition (SOMC) and normative beliefs (subjective norm [SNORM]). The second objective of this chapter is to demonstrate that situation specific open-minded cognition (SOMC) is jointly determined by general (trait) open-minded cognition (GOMC) and the situation.

General Open-Minded Cognition (GOMC): A Focus on Directional Bias

In this chapter, *open-mindedness* is defined as open-minded cognition. *Open-minded cognition* is a directionally unbiased cognitive style; a tendency to select, interpret, retrieve, and elaborate upon information in an impartial manner that is not biased by the individual's prior opinion or expectation. *Closed-minded* or *dogmatic cognition* is directionally biased, a tendency to process information in a manner that reinforces the individual's prior opinion or expectation. General Open-Minded Cognition (GOMC; Price et al., 2015) assesses "trait" open-minded cognition (e.g., "I often tune out messages I disagree with," "When thinking about an issue, I consider as many different opinions as possible"). Most information-processing entails comprehension processes that require activation of previously acquired concepts and knowledge. The distinction between open- and closed-minded cognition occurs for cognitive processing that goes beyond mere comprehension, cognitive processes that potentially bias the individual to reach a particular judgmental conclusion (e.g., selective attention, interpretation). When cognition is open-minded, these processes are driven by a motive to derive an accurate or unbiased understanding of events and issues. When cognition is closed-minded, these processes are driven by a motive to reinforce or maintain the individual's preexisting opinions or expectations (e.g., motive to maintain a partisan attitude).

The focus on assessing directional bias distinguishes open-minded cognition from other self-report measures (see Price et al., 2015, for discriminant validation). Thus, open-minded cognition is distinct from need for cognition

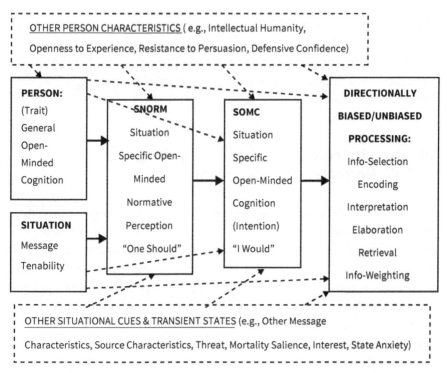

Figure 7.1 The core theoretical model (boldface) and possible relations to other constructs (dotted).

because *biased* elaboration is distinct from *amount of* elaboration (Petty & Cacioppo, 2012; Price et al., 2015). Open-minded cognition can also be distinguished from scales that assess potential determinants of directionally biased processing (see Figure 7.1, dotted boxes). These include intellectual humility and openness to experience measures that assess awareness of intellectual limitation, willingness to learn, curiosity, or willingness to revise one's viewpoint (e.g., Alfano et al., 2017; Haggard et al., 2018; Krumrei-Mancuso & Rouse, 2016; Leary et al., 2017; McCrae & Costa, 1987; Porter & Schuman, 2018). These measures assess important predispositions that predict open-minded cognition but do not exclusively focus on directional bias in cognitive processing. Important predictors of open-minded cognition may also include resistance to persuasion (Briñol et al., 2004) and defensive confidence (Albarracín & Mitchell, 2004).

Open-minded cognition can also be distinguished from measures intended to assess a broader construct that includes open-minded cognition, but also traits that determine open-minded cognition (Alfano et al., 2017; Leary et al., 2017; Webster & Kruglanski, 1994). These traits include emotional orientations, cognitive complexity, willingness to learn, awareness of intellectual fallibility, and so on. These broader measures can produce effects similar to open-minded cognition. However, because open-minded cognition is more focused, it can yield distinct effects and is not always strongly correlated with these measures (Price et al, 2015).

Situation Specific Open-Minded Cognition (SOMC): Normative Beliefs and Intention

GOMC reflects "trait" open-mindedness. However, "state" open-mindedness should vary across situations (see also Chapter 6 in this volume). Indeed, although often perceived as socially desirable, open-mindedness may not be viewed as admirable or appropriate in all situations. There are situational limits to open-minded cognition. For example, an open-minded reaction may be considered appropriate when contemplating a reasonable economic proposal (a "tenable" viewpoint). However, prescriptive norms may dictate that one should refuse to openly consider the claim that sexual promiscuity caused Hurricane Katrina (an "untenable" viewpoint). In the former, *tenable* message condition, individuals encounter realistic viewpoints that do not directly contradict mainstream social values (e.g., "exercise increases longevity"). These viewpoints presumably activate prescriptive normative beliefs that indicate one "should" (ideally) be open-minded toward the viewpoints. In the *untenable* message condition, however, individuals encounter viewpoints that are fallacious or that contradict mainstream values (e.g., "petty theft merits the death penalty"). These viewpoints presumably activate prescriptive normative beliefs that exhort people to be more closed-minded (e.g., "One should not listen to this outlandish viewpoint!"). Valid measures of situation-specific norms and open-minded cognition should capture this glaring and obvious difference.

To validate a "state" measure, it is useful to demonstrate that it varies when manipulating an obvious situational determinant of the state. For example, to validate a state hope measure, Snyder et al. (1996) demonstrated that it is strongly influenced by a situational manipulation of success versus failure. In a similar fashion, we demonstrate that a situational manipulation of "message tenability" activates situation-specific normative beliefs that influence SOMC. This approach is inspired by related work that examines the normative determinants of behavior intentions (Fishbein & Ajzen, 1975; Huesmann & Guerra, 1997). As is the case with intentional behavior, we assume the situation (e.g., message tenability) activates subjective norms (SNORM) that influence intentions to be open-minded in the situation (SOMC; Figure 7.1, bold boxes). This should be true regardless of whether these normative beliefs accurately reflect socially prescribed norms (Huesmann & Guerra, 1997). Importantly, we assume open- and closed-mindedness are, in part, intentional. When Lincoln read a fallacious and untenable claim in the newspaper, his refusal to openly consider the untenable claim was intentional and presumably rooted in the normative belief that such claims should not be published or openly considered.

Scale Validation and the Incremental Person–Situation Effect

Situation-specific measures of norms and open-minded cognition have yet to be validated. To validate the SNORM and SOMC scales, we begin by establishing factorial and discriminant validity (Bryant & Cvengros, 2004). Then, consistent with prior work that validates "state" measures (e.g., Snyder et al., 1996), we employ an experimental validation procedure. Finally, consistent with previous work that suggests psychological states possess both a chronic and a temporary component (Schwarz & Bless, 2007; Snyder et al., 1996), we propose that a valid measure of SOMC should be jointly determined by chronic characteristics of the person and temporary situational conditions. According to this *person–situation incremental validity* hypothesis, GOMC and situation tenability will produce unique and incremental effects when predicting situation-specific measures of normative perception (SNORM) and situation-specific measures of open-minded cognition (SOMC; Figure 7.1, bold boxes).

Overview

When exposed to a message, we propose that individuals activate a prescriptive norm that identifies an appropriate or ideal level of open-mindedness (SNORM). Perceptions of this normative ideal are determined by characteristic of the person (GOMC) and situation (e.g., message tenability). This subjective norm, in turn, influences intention to be open-minded (SOMC). This model does not rule out alternative determinants of open-mindedness or dogmatism (e.g., threat, mortality salience, anxiety) that may be mediated by automatic or uncontrollable forces (Figure 7.1, dotted boxes). We simply propose that, when situation-specific open-mindedness is guided by conscious intention (SOMC), prescriptive norms regarding the most appropriate response in the situation (SNORM) constitute an important determinant of open-mindedness (Figure 7.1, bold).

Study 1 provides factorial and discriminant validation of the two scales. Study 2 assesses their validity using an experimental manipulation of situation tenability and demonstrates normative beliefs (SNORM) mediate the effect of situation tenability on situation specific open-minded cognition (SOMC). Study 3 confirms that GOMC and situation tenability produce incremental effects on SOMC that are mediated by normative beliefs (SNORM; Figure 7.1, bold boxes).

Methodology, Sample, Power

All studies employed MTurk convenience samples of US adults 18 or older. We often used pretests to guide sample size selection (see Bell et al., 2018) and employed experimental manipulations that elicit large effect sizes (yielding adequate power when budget constraints precluded large sample sizes). Data collection was terminated before analysis. For Studies 1–3, all materials, supplemental tables, demographics, data files, and analytic code are available on Open Science Framework (OSF) (https://osf.io/9efmb/).

Study 1: Factorial and Discriminant Validation of the Situation-Specific Scales

Our goal was to validate situation specific open-minded cognition (SOMC) and situation specific normative perception (SNORM) measures that (a) focus on directional bias; (b) contain items that mirror the general open-minded cognition items (GOMC); (c) replicate the single, bipolar factor structure of GOMC; (d) control for acquiescence; and (e) are factorially distinct. SNORM items ask participants how one ideally "should" respond. SOMC items ask participants how they actually "would" respond to the same situation. Confirmatory factor analysis (CFA) assessed the structure and distinctiveness of the scales. A target sample ≥300 provides more than 10 participants for each of 26 estimated parameters in our largest CFA model (Kline, 2016). Thus, 338 participants were recruited (six had missing data, final $N = 332$). The sample was 48% female, 26% non-White, 40 years old (average), with 63% having completed college.

Method

We created 24 situational scenarios: (a) eight "untenable" scenarios containing viewpoints that are unrealistic or strongly contradict mainstream values (e.g., "acceptance of gays in America caused Hurricane Katrina"), (b) eight "moderate tenability" scenarios (e.g., "to honor one's religion, one should try to live as people lived when religion was founded"), and (c) eight "highly tenable" scenarios containing realistic viewpoints that do not strongly contradict mainstream values (e.g., "all US citizens should be permitted to vote"). Each "untenable" scenario corresponded to a topic contained in a "moderate" and "highly tenable" scenario (example scenarios G7, P11, and R12 in Table 7.1). Participants read an untenable, moderately tenable, or tenable scenario, then completed the SNORM, SOMC, and demographic items (for complete scenarios, see Supplementary Materials in OSF repository).

Table 7.2 provides the scale items. SOMC assesses intention to be open-minded (e.g., "In this situation, *I would* be open to considering these viewpoints," 1 = strongly disagree to 7 = strongly agree). SNORM assesses normative beliefs (e.g., "In this situation, *one should* be open to considering these viewpoints"; see Johnston & White, 2003). Each scale contained three items worded in the "open" direction and three in the "closed" direction.

Results and Discussion

We used CFA via LISREL 8 (Jöreskog & Sörbom, 2001) to test hypotheses. Robust maximum-likelihood estimation was used to adjust goodness-of-fit chi-square values and standard errors of parameter estimates for non-normality, and scaled difference chi-square ($\Delta\chi^2$) testing (Bryant & Satorra, 2012) was used to compare the fit of nested CFA models in order to test hypotheses about factorial and discriminant validity.

Acquiescent individuals agree with all items. Low-acquiescence individuals disagree with all items. This inflates positive correlations for open–open and closed–closed item pairs but reduces negative correlations for closed–open item pairs. To control for this problem, a one- (substantive) factor solution was imposed on each six-item scale (with all factor loadings freely estimated), along with a second acquiescence method factor where all items were forced to load with an unstandardized value of 1.0 (see Billiet & McClendon, 2000). Acquiescent participants score high, whereas low-acquiescence participants score low on the acquiescence method factor. The correlation between the two factors was fixed at zero, ensuring that the substantive factor was not

Table 7.1 Situational Scenario Abbreviated Examples (Only Study 1 Includes "Moderate" Tenability)

Highly tenable condition	Moderate tenability	Untenable condition
General life situations		
Gay issues (G7$_T$): Imagine you see... panelists predict that by 2025 gay marriage will be fully legalized in the United States and all of Europe.	Gay issues (G7$_M$): Imagine you see... panelists argue religions should be permitted to exclude gay people from being ministers, priests, clergy (Study 1).	Gay issues (G7$_U$): Imagine you see... panelists argue acceptance of gays in America has caused Hurricane Katrina and other natural disasters.
Internet restriction (G16$_T$): Imagine you observe... school board members propose school computers should block pornographic sites and terrorist message(s).		Internet restriction (G16$_U$): Imagine you watch... panelists argue that info about guns, sex, alternate lifestyles, etc. should be blocked from internet to prevent moral degradation.
Political situations		
Search/seizure (P11$_T$): You see panelists [who] expect airline searches will increase... creating long delays.	Search/seizure (P11$_M$): Panelists argue... the law should make it easier for police to obtain warrant. (Study 1)	Search/seizure (P11$_U$): Panelists argue... federal government should have right to search any home without warrant.
Voting (P2$_T$): You listen to panelists who say all US citizens should be permitted to vote. They cite Constitution.		Voting (P2$_U$): You listen to panelists who argue ethnic minorities should be denied the right to vote.
Religious situations		
Tradition (R12$_T$): You listen to panel... [that] claims anyone can have religious experience. A variety of spiritual experiences are considered, prayer, inspired by nature, meditation	Tradition (R12$_M$): You listen to panelists [who] argue one should try to live as people lived when religion was founded. Other panelists agree with return to traditional lifestyle. (Study 1)	Tradition (R12$_U$): You listen to panelists argue one must live as when religion was founded, with no technology, continuing customs such as public stoning, polygamy, and animal sacrifices.
Spiritual insight (R9$_T$): Imagine you read online bloggers [who] suggest ways to cultivate spiritual experience... introspect, read spiritual books, attend services.		Spiritual insight (R9$_U$): Imagine you read online bloggers who agree spiritual insight can only be obtained by taking psychedelic drugs.

Note. Study 1: G1, G7, P8, P11, P17, R3, R12, R15. Study 2 Pretest: P2. Study 2: all scenarios. Study 3 Pretest: G16. Study 3: G16, P11, R9 (for complete scenarios, see Supplementary Materials in OSF repository).

Table 7.2 Study 1: Results for the Three-Factor Confirmatory Factor Analysis Model of Situation-Specific Open-Minded Cognition (SOMC) and Situation-Specific Open-Minded Normative Perception (SNORM) Items

Items	SOMC λ_U (SE)	SOMC λ_{CS}	SNORM λ_U (SE)	SNORM λ_{CS}	Acquiescence λ_U (SE)	Acquiescence λ_{CS}	R^2
SOMC							
1. In this situation, I would be open to considering these viewpoints.	1.65 (.07)	.78	0.0	—	1.0	.20	.65
2. In this situation, I would "tune out" messages I disagree with.	−1.43 (.10)	−.73	0.0	—	1.0	.21	.58
3. I believe it would be a waste of time to pay attention to some of these ideas.	−1.74 (.07)	−.83	0.0	—	1.0	.20	.72
4. I would try to reserve judgment until I had a chance to hear all of these arguments.	1.64 (.08)	.84	0.0	—	1.0	.21	.75
5. In this situation, I would have no patience for arguments I disagree with.	−1.72 (.08)	−.86	0.0	—	1.0	.21	.79
6. When thinking about this issue, I would seriously consider all of these opinions.	1.81 (.06)	.91	0.0	—	1.0	.21	.87
SNORM							
1. In this situation, one should be open to considering these viewpoints.	0.0	—	1.76 (.07)	.89	1.0	.21	.84
2. In this situation, one should "tune out" messages one disagrees with.	0.0	—	−1.59 (.10)	−.83	1.0	.21	.73
3. People should believe it would be a waste of time to pay attention to some of these ideas.	0.0	—	−1.85 (.07)	−.86	1.0	.19	.78
4. People should try to reserve judgment until they have a chance to hear all of these arguments.	0.0	—	1.74 (.08)	.91	1.0	.21	.87
5. In this situation, people should not have patience for arguments they disagree with.	0.0	—	−1.55 (.10)	−.77	1.0	.21	.63
6. When thinking about this issue, one should seriously consider all of these opinions.	0.0	—	1.76 (.08)	.91	1.0	.21	.88

Note. Results are from a robust maximum-likelihood confirmatory factor analysis, $\chi^2(53, N = 332) = 160.62$, root mean square error of approximation = .080, standardized root mean square residual = .037, comparative fit index = .987, non-normed fit index = .984. λ_U = unstandardized factor loading; SE = standard error; λ_{CS} = completely standardized factor loading; R^2 = squared multiple correlation (i.e., proportion of explained variance) for each item. Loadings of the SNORM items on the SOMC factor, and SOMC items on the SNORM factor, were fixed at zero. All item loadings on acquiescence factor were fixed at 1.0 in the unstandardized confirmatory factor analysis model.

confounded with acquiescence (Billiet & McClendon, 2000). This CFA model produced better fit than a one-factor model that omitted the acquiescence factor—for both SOMC items, $\Delta\chi^2$ (1, N = 332) = 10.93, $p < .001$, and SNORM items, $\Delta\chi^2$ (1, N = 332) = 14.66, $p < .001$.

The two-factor model (with uncorrelated substantive and acquiescence factors) provided a reasonable measurement model for both SOMC ($\alpha = .93$), χ^2 (8, N = 332) = 16.18, root mean square error of approximation (RMSEA) = .059, standardized root mean square residual (SRMR) = .022, comparative fit index (CFI) = .996, non-normed fit index (NNFI) = .992, and SNORM ($\alpha = .94$), χ^2 (8, N = 332) = 16.79, RMSEA = .052, SRMR = .013, CFI = .997, NNFI = .995. Each factor was bipolar, with all items possessing sufficiently high squared multiple correlations (SOMC > .54, SNORM >.65) and standardized loadings (SOMC $|\lambda s|$ > .71, SNORM $|\lambda s|$ > .78). To assess discriminant validity of the six-item SOMC and SNORM scales, we imposed two competing models on responses to both scales in a combined 12-item data set: (1) a two-factor model in which all 12 items freely loaded on a substantive factor and had fixed values of 1.0 on an orthogonal acquiescence factor and (2) a three-factor CFA model in which the six SOMC items freely loaded on a substantive SOMC factor, the six SNORM items freely loaded on a separate but correlated substantive SNORM factor, and all 12 items had fixed values of 1.0 on an orthogonal acquiescence factor (see Table 7.2). A priori power analysis adapting parameter specifications from Jöreskog and Sörbom (2001) indicated that 300 participants provide >99% power to detect a significant difference ($p < .05$) in chi-square values (difference in degrees of freedom = 1) when comparing goodness-of-fit of the two models.

Supporting discriminant validity, the three-factor model (separate SOMC and SNORM factors) fit the 12-item data set better than the two-factor model (a single, combined SOMC–SNORM factor), scaled $\Delta\chi^2$ (1, N = 332) = 62.45, $p < .001$. Also, the three-factor model provided an acceptable measurement model, χ^2 (52, N = 332) = 160.62, RMSEA = .080, SRMR = .037, CFI = .987, NNFI = .984, whereas the two-factor model did not, χ^2 (53, N = 332) = 488.16, RMSEA = .200, SRMR = .084, CFI = .919, NNFI = .899. The SOMC–SNORM correlation in the three-factor model was 0.782 ($p < .001$). Thus, 38.2% of the variance in each scale is unrelated to the other (i.e., 61.2% shared variance).[1] In sum, Study 1 confirms that the SOMC and SNORM scales possess factorial validity and assess correlated yet distinct constructs.

Study 2: Experimental Validation of the Situation-Specific Scales

Study 2 employs an experimental validation procedure (see Snyder et al., 1996). It involves strongly manipulating an obvious and proximal determinant of the state and demonstrating that the manipulation produces the predicted effect on the measured state (much like validating a new thermometer by demonstrating that it produces higher readings at the equator than at the North Pole). The intent is not to test a provocative or non-obvious hypothesis. On the contrary, scale validity is established using a manipulation that "must" produce an effect on the measured construct if the measure actually assesses the intended construct. In the *high-tenability* condition, participants are exposed to viewpoints that do not contradict mainstream values or views of reality (e.g., "all US citizens should be permitted to vote"). In the *low-tenability* condition, participants are exposed to viewpoints that strongly contradict mainstream values or views of reality ("minorities should be denied the right to vote"). If our measures are valid, this manipulation should produce higher levels of open-mindedness in the tenable than the untenable condition.

Participants

In a pretest, participants read an extremely tenable or untenable version of a voting rights scenario (Table 7.1, voting P2). This manipulation produced very large effects on SNORM ($d = 1.21$) and SOMC ($d = 1.38$) that achieved significance with a small sample ($p < .001$, $N = 53$). We therefore used similar subsample sizes in the main study. In the main study, subsamples responded to six general scenario pairs (non-political and non-religious, $N = 58$), six political scenario pairs ($N = 63$), or six religious scenario pairs ($N = 55$). Sensitivity and supplementary power analyses were performed after collecting the main study data. Sensitivity analyses revealed that the actual effect sizes exceeded the minimal detectable effect (MDE) size in 34 of 36 analyses (Tables 7.3–7.5; MDE sensitivity power analysis). Thus, Study 2 was adequately powered.[2] In total, 184 MTurk participants were recruited. Eight were excluded (failed attention check, incomplete data, final $N = 176$, divided into subsamples).[3] The final sample was 64% female and 44% Democratic (24% Republican), with 53% completing college.

Materials and Procedure

Eighteen tenable versus untenable scenario pairs were created. Six pairs pertained to general life topics, six pertained to religion, and six pertained to politics (included pretest scenario; Table 7.1 provides examples, complete scenarios in OSF repository). Participants read six scenarios. After each scenario, they completed the SOMC and SNORM scales. Participants were randomly assigned to one of six groups. In the "General Topic" subsample, Group 1a ($N = 36$) read the tenable version of three general topic pairs and the untenable version of the three remaining general topic pairs. Group 1b ($N = 22$) read the opposite general topic versions (untenable version first three, tenable version second three). For each topic pair, the effect of tenability is the group (1a vs. 1b) effect. An analogous system was used for the six political pairs (Group 2a, $N = 29$; Group 2b, $N = 34$) and six religious pairs (Group 3a, $N = 28$; Group 3b, $N = 27$). For some pairs, the untenable scenario reflected a conservative policy taken to an untenable extreme (e.g., "we should return to racial segregation"). For other pairs, the untenable scenario reflected a liberal policy taken to an untenable extreme (e.g., "people who practice religion are mentally ill"). The tenability effect emerged in both cases.

Results and Discussion

Tenability produced robust effects on SOMC mediated by SNORM (Tables 7.3–7.5; General, political, religious scenarios). For 17 of 18 scenario pairs, SNORM was higher in the tenable than untenable message condition (Tables 7.3–7.5; $p < .001$ all cases). For all 18 pairs, SOMC was higher in the tenable than untenable situation (Tables 7.3–7.5, $p < .001$ all cases). Hayes' bootstrapping technique confirmed that SNORM mediated the tenability effect on SOMC for 17 of 18 pairs (Tables 7.3–7.5; MEDIATE). These findings validate both measures and support our mediational model (Figure 7.1, bold). To obtain more stable point estimates, we encourage further replications using larger samples.

Exploratory analyses revealed that, for 15 of 18 scenario pairs, participants perceived one "should" strive for an ideal level of open-mindedness (SNORM) that exceeds the open-mindedness they "would" actually display (SOMC, $p < .05$ all cases). In seven cases, this was especially true in the untenable condition ("tenability × scale," $p < .01$). These findings suggest that SOMC ("I would" ratings) and SNORM ("One should" ratings) tap distinct constructs.

Table 7.3 Study 2 General Scenarios: Tenability Effect on SNORM and SOMC, with Means (SD), Mean Differences with ± 95% Confidence Interval (CI), Cohen's d (d_{T-U}), Minimal Detectable Effect (MDE = .77), and Hayes' Mediation CI (MEDIATE) for Six General Scenario Pairs (Tenability IV → Should MV → Would DV)

General Scenario $N_{TEN/UNTEN}$	Should rating (SNORM)					Would rating (SOMC)					MEDIATE .95 CI
	Tenable M(SD)	Untenable M(SD)	T − U Mdiff		d_{T-U}	Tenable M(SD)	Untenable M(SD)	T − U Mdiff	d_{T-U} (MDE = .77)	
G1 $N_{36/22}$	6.12 (1.30)	4.31 (1.53)	1.81*** ± .75		1.29	5.97 (.95)	3.83 (1.52)	2.14*** ± .65	1.78	.41/1.59
G4 $N_{36/22}$	6.11 (.85)	4.71 (1.83)	1.40*** ± .71		1.07	5.75 (1.09)	4.13 (1.83)	1.62*** ± .77	1.15	.55/1.95
G7 $N_{36/22}$	5.58 (1.42)	3.39 (1.86)	2.19*** ± .87		1.37	4.96 (1.73)	2.72 (1.87)	2.24*** ± .99	1.26	.86/2.83
G10 $N_{22/36}$	5.92 (1.04)	4.27 (1.70)	1.65*** ± .86		1.11	5.71 (1.12)	3.41 (1.60)	2.30*** ± .78	1.60	.70/1.90
G13 $N_{22/36}$	5.86 (.90)	4.35 (1.95)	1.50*** ± .89		.92	5.89 (.98)	3.69 (1.95)	2.20*** ± .90	1.33	.66/1.94
G16 $N_{22/36}$	5.94 (1.22)	4.24 (1.93)	1.70*** ± .92		1.00	5.89 (1.28)	3.60 (1.82)	2.28*** ± .88	1.39	.79/2.15

Note. Minimum detectable effect size (MDE = .77) from GPOWER Sensitivity Analysis pertains to both "Should" and "Would" rating analyses ($p < .05$, power = .80); *** $p < .001$. Scenario topics are G1, harassment; G4, e-cigarettes; G7, gay issues; G10, recycling; G13, flu shot; G16, internet restriction/censorship. IV is independent variable, MV is mediating variable, and DV is dependent variable.

Table 7.4 Study 2 Political Scenarios: Tenability Effect on SNORM and SOMC, with Means (SD), Mean Differences with ±95% Confidence Interval (CI), Cohen's d (d_{T-U}), Minimal Detectable Effect (MDE = .72), and Hayes' Mediation CI (MEDIATE) for Six Political Scenario Pairs (Tenability IV → Should MV → Would DV)

Political Scenario $N_{TEN/UNTEN}$	Should rating (SNORM)					Would rating (SOMC)				MEDIATE .95 CI
	Tenable M(SD)	Untenable M(SD)	T − U Mdiff	d_{T-U}	Tenable M(SD)	Untenable M(SD)	T − U Mdiff	d_{T-U} (MDE = .72)		
P2 $N_{29/34}$	6.05 (1.13)	2.58 (1.59)	3.47*** ±.71	2.48	6.00 (.90)	2.25 (1.29)	3.75*** ±.57	3.32	1.37/3.14
P5 $N_{29/34}$	5.96 (1.12)	2.61 (1.68)	3.35*** ±.73	2.31	5.78 (1.25)	2.41 (1.51)	3.36*** ±.71	2.40	1.70/3.36
P8 $N_{29/34}$	6.11 (1.02)	4.48 (1.82)	1.63*** ±.76	1.10	5.76 (1.03)	4.06 (1.67)	1.71*** ±.71	1.21	.68/1.85
P11 $N_{34/29}$	5.49 (1.36)	4.44 (1.87)	1.05*** ±.82	.65	5.40 (1.22)	3.88 (2.06)	1.52*** ±.84	.92	.19/1.59
P14 $N_{34/29}$	6.24 (.91)	4.16 (1.70)	2.09*** ±.67	1.57	6.21 (.98)	3.33 (1.76)	2.88*** ±.70	2.06	.96/2.38
P17 $N_{34/29}$	5.31 (1.57)	4.67 (1.63)	.64ⁿˢ ±.80	.40	5.38 (1.30)	3.99 (1.71)	1.39*** ±.76	.92	−.10/1.02

Note. Minimum detectable effect size (MDE = .72) from GPOWER Sensitivity Analysis pertains to both "Should" and "Would" rating analyses ($p < .05$, power = .80); *** $p < .001$. Scenario topics are P2, minority vote; P5, racial equality; P8, President A; P11, privacy; P14, voting rule; P17, President B. IV is independent variable, MV is mediating variable, and DV is dependent variable.

Table 7.5 Study 2 Religious Scenarios: Tenability Effect on SNORM and SOMC, with Means (SD), Mean Differences with ±95% Confidence Interval (CI), Cohen's d (d_{T-U}), Minimal Detectable Effect (MDE = .77), and Hayes' Mediation CI (MEDIATE) for Six Religious Scenario Pairs (Tenability IV → Should MV → Would DV)

Religious Scenario $N_{TEN/UNTEN}$	Should rating (SNORM)					Would rating (SOMC)					MEDIATE .95 CI
	Tenable M(SD)	Untenable M(SD)	T − U Mdiff		d_{T-U}	Tenable M(SD)	Untenable M(SD)	T − U Mdiff	d_{T-U} (MDE = .77)	
R3 $N_{28/27}$	5.83 (1.09)	3.01 (1.45)	2.83*** ±.69		2.22	5.53 (1.32)	2.35 (1.21)	3.18*** ±.69	2.51	.91/2.49
R6 $N_{28/27}$	6.21 (.77)	4.56 (1.43)	1.66*** ±.62		1.46	6.18 (.87)	3.60 (1.59)	2.58*** ±.69	2.02	.79/1.83
R9 $N_{28/27}$	5.83 (1.15)	3.48 (1.38)	2.35*** ±.69		1.85	5.63 (1.29)	2.85 (1.32)	2.79*** ±.71	2.13	1.30/2.45
R12 $N_{27/28}$	5.75 (1.07)	3.45 (1.68)	2.30*** ±.77		1.62	5.72 (1.03)	2.75 (1.63)	2.97*** ±.74	2.16	1.22/2.30
R15 $N_{27/28}$	5.43 (1.29)	3.40 (1.67)	2.02*** ±.81		1.35	5.17 (1.67)	2.80 (1.51)	2.36*** ±.86	1.49	1.06/2.35
R18 $N_{27/28}$	5.65 (1.03)	3.11 (1.86)	2.54*** ±.82		1.68	5.48 (1.36)	2.65 (1.76)	2.83*** ±.85	1.79	1.59/2.93

Note. Minimum detectable effect size (MDE = .77) from GPOWER Sensitivity Analysis pertains to both "Should" and "Would" rating analyses ($p < .05$, power = .80); *** $p < .001$. Scenario topics are R3, belonging; R6, school prayer; R9, religious insight; R12, tradition; R15, blasphemy; R18, belief in God. IV is independent variable, MV is mediating variable, and DV is dependent variable.

Study 3: Incremental Person and Situation Effects

Chronic individual differences and temporary situational conditions often produce unique effects when predicting malleable states (Sherman et al., 2015). We predicted this would occur when predicting SNORM and SOMC. Specifically, we predicted that (a) GOMC and (state) SOMC would be distinct (see Chapter 6 in this volume); (b) GOMC (trait) and situation tenability would produce unique, incremental effects when predicting the situation specific measures of SNORM and SOMC (Sherman et al., 2015); and (c) effects of GOMC and situation tenability on SOMC would be mediated by normative beliefs (SNORM; Figure 7.1, bold boxes).

Participants completed the GOMC measure. Then they read an extremely tenable or untenable scenario and completed the SNORM and SOMC scales. When predicting malleable states, chronic traits (person) and situational manipulations often produce additive effects in experiments (e.g., Schwarz & Bless, 2007), and additive effects predominate when tracking human responses in real situations (Sherman et al., 2015). Thus, our primary intent was to focus on additive effects.

Method

Using the internet restriction scenario, a pretest ($N = 81$) replicated the "very large" significant effect of tenability on SNORM and SOMC ($p < .001$ both cases) and yielded a "medium to large" (unique) GOMC effect that was significant when predicting SNORM ($\eta^2 = .16, f^2 = .19, p < .001$) and SOMC ($\eta^2 = .18, f^2 = .22, p < .001$). We therefore collected data on a similar sample size in the main study ($N = 86$). Sensitivity and supplementary power analyses were performed after collecting the main study data. Sensitivity analyses revealed that actual effect sizes in the main study exceeded the minimal detectable effect (MDE) sizes (Table 7.6). Thus, Study 3 was adequately powered.[4] The incremental validity hypothesis was tested using the internet restriction, search and seizure, and spiritual insight scenarios in the main study (Table 7.1; G16, P11, R9; see OSF repository for complete scenarios). Eighty-six MTurkers were recruited (three failed attention checks, two had missing data, final $N = 81$). The sample was 38% female, 27% non-White, and 35% Democratic (31% Republican), with 40% having completed college.

After completing the GOMC scale, Group A ($N = 44$) read the tenable versions of the internet restriction and spiritual insight scenarios and the untenable version of the search and seizure scenario (random order). Group B

Table 7.6 Study 3: Effect of general open-minded cognition (GOMC; Person) and Tenability (Situation) on Situation-Specific Open-Minded Cognition (SOMC) for Three Scenario Pairs, with Unstandardized Regression Coefficients (SE), Effect Size (Minimal Detectable Effect Size [MDE]), and Hayes' Mediation Confidence Interval (MEDIATE; Person/Situation IV → Should MV → Would DV)

	General (G16) Internet censorship			Political (P10) Search and seizure			Religious (R9) Spiritual insight		
	Predicting SOMC		IV→MV→DV	Predicting SOMC		IV→MV→DV	Predicting SOMC		IV→MV→DV
	b (SE)	Effect size (MDE)	MEDIATE .95 CI	b (SE)	Effect size (MDE)	MEDIATE .95 CI	b (SE)	Effect size (MDE)	MEDIATE .95 CI
GOMC (person)	.53*** (.14)	$f^2 = .14$ ($f^2 = .10$)	.07/.50	.66*** (.14)	$f^2 = .19$ ($f^2 = .10$)	.27/.76	.70*** (.14)	$f^2 = .22$ ($f^2 = .10$)	.15/.51
Tenability (situation)	1.40*** (.27)	$f^2 = .27$ ($f^2 = .10$)	.20/1.16	1.63*** (.29)	$f^2 = .33$ ($f^2 = .10$)	.34/1.37	1.77*** (.27)	$f^2 = .33$ ($f^2 = .10$)	.71/1.71

Note. b = unstandardized regression coefficient; *SE* = standard error. Tenability coded −.5 in untenable condition and +.5 in tenable condition. GOMC was normalized. Minimum detectable effect size (MDE) from GPOWER Sensitivity Analysis ($p < .05$, power = .80); ***$p < .001$. G16 ($N_{TEN} = 44$, $N_{UNTEN} = 37$), P10 ($N_{TEN} = 37$, $N_{UNTEN} = 44$), R9 ($N_{TEN} = 44$, $N_{UNTEN} = 37$). IV is independent variable, MV is mediating variable, and DV is dependent variable.

($N = 37$) read the opposite versions ("group" is tenability effect). After each scenario, participants completed the SNORM and SOMC scales.

Results and Discussion

As anticipated, GOMC and SOMC were correlated yet distinct (internet censorship, $r = .36, p = .001$; search and seizure, $r = .39, p < .001$; spiritual insight, $r = .43, p < .001$). Also, GOMC was higher than SOMC for all three issues ($p < .05$), especially in the untenable condition ($p < .001$). Table 7.6 reveals that GOMC and situation tenability uniquely predicted SOMC for all scenario pairs. In all cases, situation tenability produced a large and significant effect when predicting SOMC, and GOMC produced a positive incremental effect on SOMC. In all cases, the bootstrapped indirect effects were significant (MEDIATE, Table 7.6). In sum, GOMC and SOMC were distinct. Person (GOMC) and situation (tenability) produced incremental effects on SOMC, and both effects were mediated by SNORM. These effects replicated across three scenarios using a modest yet adequately powered sample. To obtain more stable point estimates, we encourage further replications using larger samples.

General Discussion and Conclusion

This chapter validates situation-specific measures of open-mindedness and demonstrates that characteristics of the person (GOMC) and situation (tenability) produce incremental effects on situation-specific open-mindedness (SNORM, SOMC). Using CFA, which controls for acquiescence (Billiet & McClendon, 2000), Study 1 confirmed the single, bipolar dimensional structure of SNORM and SOMC and demonstrated that these scales assess distinct constructs (Bryant & Cvengros, 2004). Study 2 validated these measures by strongly manipulating an obvious and proximal determinant of SNORM and SOMC and demonstrating that the predicted effects emerge (Snyder et al., 1996). Specifically, situation tenability influenced SOMC, with SNORM mediating this effect. In accordance with the person–situation incremental validity hypothesis, Study 3 revealed that SOMC is jointly determined by characteristics of the person and situation (Sherman et al., 2015), with both of these effects mediated by SNORM.

The SNORM and SOMC scales provide valid and reliable measures of situational open-mindedness that illuminate the intentional component of situation-specific open-mindedness. To return to our historical example, Abraham Lincoln generally possessed a reputation for being an open-minded listener. However, in situations where he encountered blatantly untenable claims, he was clearly less open-minded. His refusal to openly consider such claims was presumably intentional and rooted in the normative belief that such claims should not be publicized, much less openly considered. This chapter suggests that a person's general predisposition combines with specific characteristics of the situation to jointly influence normative beliefs regarding the appropriateness of open-mindedness in the situation (SNORM). These normative beliefs, in turn, shape situation-specific intentions to be open-minded (SOMC).

Acknowledgments

This research was made possible through the support of a grant from the Fuller Theological Seminary/Thrive Center with the John Templeton Foundation (IH-111, 513560). The opinions expressed in this publication are those of the authors and do not necessarily reflect the views of the Fuller Thrive Center or the John Templeton Foundation. Address correspondence to Victor Ottati, Dept. of Psychology, Loyola University Chicago, 1032 W. Sheridan Rd., Chicago, IL, 60660, vottati@luc.edu

Notes

1. The six-item SOMC and SNORM scales possessed correspondent items, SOMC assessing "I would" and SNORM assessing "one should" ratings. Thus, we also imposed on the 12-item data set a three-factor CFA model that included an autocorrelated error term for each of the correspondent item pairs. This produced a 0.771 SOMC–SNORM factor correlation (59.4% shared variance vs. 61.2% in the original model). Thus, parallel wording in these scales accounts for only 1.8% of the variance the scales share.
2. Supplementary correlational analyses involving the independent variable (IV), mediating variable (MV), and dependent variable (DV) indicated that each subsample was more than double the sample size needed to obtain significance for the effects found in the pretest ($N = 20$) and more than double the sample size needed to test mediation (Schoemann et al., 2017; Monte Carlo, $r_{IV,MV} = .52$; $r_{IV,DV} = .57$; $r_{MV,DV} = .81$; $p < .05$, 80% power, required $N = 26$).
3. Two additional cases in the OSF data file were not participants but were researchers previewing the survey and testing the data collection program. These were excluded.
4. When inputting the smaller of the two GOMC effects obtained in the pretest ($f^2 = .19$ on SNORM), power analysis revealed that $N = 44$ participants were required to achieve 80% power ($p < .05$, GPower). Even fewer participants ($N = 26$) were required to test mediation (Schoemann et al., 2017; Monte Carlo; $r_{IV,MV} = .40$; $r_{IV,DV} = .42$; $r_{MV,DV} = .90$).

References

Adorno, T. W., Frenkel-Brunswik, E., Levinson, D. J., & Sanford, R. N. (1950). *The authoritarian personality*. Harper and Row.

Albarracín, D., & Mitchell, A. L. (2004). The role of defensive confidence in preference for proattitudinal information: How believing that one is strong can sometimes be a defensive weakness. *Personality and Social Psychology Bulletin, 30*(12), 1565–1584. https://doi.org/10.1177/0146167204271180

Alfano, M., Iurino, K., Stey, P., Robinson, B., Christen, M., Yu, F., & Lapsley, D. (2017). Development and validation of a multi-dimensional measure of intellectual humility. *PLoS One, 12*(8), Article e0182950. https://doi.org/10.1371/journal.pone.0182950

Bell, M. L., Whitehead, A. L., & Julious, S. A. (2018). Guidance for using pilot studies to inform the design of intervention trials with continuous outcomes. *Clinical Epidemiology, 10*, 153–157. https://doi.org/10.2147/CLEP.S146397

Billiet, J. B., & McClendon, M. J. (2000). Modeling acquiescence in measurement models for two balanced sets of items. *Structural Equation Modeling, 7*(4), 608–628. https://doi.org/10.1207/s15328007sem0704_5

Briñol, P., Rucker, D. D., Tormala, Z. L., & Petty, R. E. (2004). Individual differences in resistance to persuasion: The role of beliefs and meta-beliefs. In E. S. Knowles & J. A. Linn (Eds.), *Resistance and persuasion* (pp. 183–104). Erlbaum.

Bryant, F. B., & Cvengros, J. A. (2004). Distinguishing hope and optimism: Two sides of a coin, or two separate coins? *Journal of Social and Clinical Psychology, 23*(2), 273–302. https://doi.org/10.1521/jscp.23.2.273.31018

Bryant, F. B., & Satorra, A. (2012). Principles and practice of scaled difference chi-square testing. *Structural Equation Modeling, 19*(3), 372–398. https://doi.org/10.1080/10705511.2012.687671

Doster, W. E. (1915). *Lincoln and episodes of the Civil War*. G. P. Putnam's Sons.

Fishbein, M., & Ajzen, I. (1975). *Belief, attitude, intention and behavior: An introduction to theory and research*. Addison-Wesley.

Haggard, M., Rowatt, W. C., Leman, J. C., Meagher, B., Moore, C., Fergus, T., Whitcomb, D., Battaly, H., Baehr, J., & Howard-Snyder, D. (2018). Finding middle ground between intellectual arrogance and intellectual servility: Development and assessment of the limitations-owning intellectual humility scale. *Personality and Individual Differences, 124*, 184–193. https://doi.org/10.1016/j.paid.2017.12.014

Huesmann, L. R., & Guerra, N. G. (1997). Children's normative beliefs about aggression and aggressive behavior. *Journal of Personality and Social Psychology, 72*(2), 408–419.

Johnson, C. J. (2019, June 5). 'Poisonous Thorns': The times Abraham Lincoln got mad- like, really mad –at the Chicago Tribune. https://www.scribd.com/article/412456592/poisonous-Thorns-The-Times-Abraham-Lincoln-Got-Mad-Like-Really-Mad-At-The-Chicago-Tribune

Johnston, K. L., & White, K. M. (2003). Binge drinking: A test of the role of group norms in the theory of planned behavior. *Psychology and Health, 18*, 63–77. https://doi.org/10.1080/0887044021000037835

Jöreskog, K. G., & Sörbom, D. (2001). *LISREL 8 user's reference guide*. Scientific Software International.

Jost, J. T. (2017). Ideological asymmetries and the essence of political psychology. *Political Psychology, 38*, 167–208. https://doi.org/10.1111/pops.12407

Kline, R. B. (2016). *Principles and practice of structural equation modeling*. Guilford Press.

Krumrei-Mancuso, E. J., & Rouse, S. V. (2016). The development and validation of the comprehensive intellectual humility scale. *Journal of Personality Assessment, 98*(2), 209–221. https://doi.org/10.1080/00223891.2015.1068174

Leary, M. R., Diebels, K. J., Davisson, E. K., Jongman-Sereno, K. P., Isherwood, J. C., Raimi, K. T., Deffler, S. A., & Hoyle, R. H. (2017). Cognitive and interpersonal features of intellectual humility. *Personality and Social Psychology Bulletin, 43*(6), 793–813. https://doi.org/10.1177/0146167217697695

McCrae, R. R., & Costa, P. T. (1987). Validation of the five-factor model of personality across instruments and observers. *Journal of Personality and Social Psychology, 52*(1), 81–90. https://doi.org/10.1037/0022-3514.52.1.81

Ottati, V., Price, E. D., Wilson, C., & Sumaktoyo, N. (2015). When self-perceptions of expertise increase closed-minded cognition: The earned dogmatism effect. *Journal of Experimental Social Psychology, 61*, 131–138. https://dx.doi.org/10.1016/j.jesp.2015.08.003

Ottati, V., Wilson, C., Osteen, C., & Distefano, Y. (2018). Experimental demonstrations of the earned dogmatism effect using a variety of optimal manipulations: Commentary and response to Calin-Jageman (2018). *Journal of Experimental Social Psychology, 78*, 250–258. https://doi.org/10.1016/j.jesp.2018.05.010

Petty, R. E., & Cacioppo, J. T. (2012). *Communication and persuasion: Central and peripheral routes to attitude change*. Springer Science & Business Media.

Porter, T., & Schumann, K. (2018). Intellectual humility and openness to the opposing view. *Self and Identity, 17*(2), 139–162. https://doi.org/10.1080/15298868.2017.1361861

Price, E., Ottati, V., Wilson, C., & Kim, S. (2015). Open-minded cognition. *Personality and Social Psychology Bulletin, 41*(11), 1488–1504. https://doi.org/10.1177/0146167215600528

Rokeach, M. (1954). The nature and meaning of dogmatism. *Psychological Review, 61*, 194–204. https://doi.org/10.1037/h0060752

Samuelson, P., & Church, I. M. (2021). Humility in personality and positive psychology. In M. Alfano, M. P. Lynch, & A. Tanesini (Eds.), *The Routledge handbook of philosophy of humility* (pp. 375–385). Routledge.

Schoemann, A. M., Boulton, A. J., & Short, S. D. (2017). Determining power and sample size for simple and complex mediation models. *Social Psychological and Personality Science, 8*(4), 379–386. https://doi.org/10.1177/1948550617715068

Schwarz, N., & Bless, H. (2007). Mental construal processes: The inclusion/exclusion model. In D. A. Stapel & J. Suls (Eds.), *Assimilation and contrast in social psychology* (pp. 119–141). Psychology Press.

Sherman, R. A., Rauthmann, J. F., Brown, N. A., Serfass, D. G., & Jones, A. B. (2015). The independent effects of personality and situations on real-time expressions of behavior and emotion. *Journal of Personality and Social Psychology, 109*(5), 872–888. https://doi.org/10.1037/pspp0000036

Snyder, C. R., Sympson, S. C., Ybasco, F. C., Borders, T. F., Babyak, M. A., & Higgins, R. L. (1996). Development and validation of the State Hope Scale. *Journal of Personality and Social Psychology, 70*(2), 321–335.

Webster, D. M., & Kruglanski, A. W. (1994). Individual differences in need for cognitive closure. *Journal of Personality and Social Psychology, 67*(6), 1049–1062. https://doi.org/10.1037/0022-3514.67.6.1049

8
The Role of Group Context in Open-Minded Cognition

Salma Moaz, Kelsey Berryman, Jeremy R. Winget, R. Scott Tindale, and Victor Ottati

Many, if not most, of our experiences involve some type of group context. We grow up in families, work in organizations, and live in communities, all of which help to define who we are and influence how we behave. Many different aspects of behavior have been studied as a function of group context. People often conform to group norms (Sherif, 1936), treat in-group members differently than out-group members (Hogg & Abrams, 1988), and work differentially hard depending on their position in groups (Kerr & Park, 2001). Recent research has also shown that some of our most basic cognitive processes, such as memory and information search, are influenced by group context (Harkins, 2006; Tindale et al., 2004). Often, people are well aware of how groups influence their behavior. They look to others in their environment to see how they should respond to a given situation (Festinger, 1954) and alter their behavior in order to fit in (Levine & Moreland, 1994). However, other group context effects are more subtle and influence behavior outside of awareness (Harkins, 2006; Latané & Bourgeois, 2001).

A group phenomenon that has received substantial research attention is *group polarization* (Iyengar et al., 2019; Myers & Lamm, 1976)—the tendency for group members to become more extreme on an issue after social interaction or information exchange. There are a number of social and psychological processes that lead to polarization, including social comparison (Sanders & Baron, 1977), information exchange (Stasser & Titus, 2003; Vinocur & Burnstein, 1974), conformity, and social identity (Hogg, 2001). In intragroup settings, polarization can be beneficial (e.g., greater consensus and commitment to a chosen position; Kameda & Tindale, 2006). However, in intergroup settings, polarization tends to be detrimental to intergroup relations (Dovidio & Gaertner, 2010; Hogg & Abrams, 1988). Polarization also tends to be more extreme in intergroup settings because in-group members try to present

Salma Moaz, Kelsey Berryman, Jeremy R. Winget, R. Scott Tindale, and Victor Ottati, *The Role of Group Context in Open-Minded Cognition* In: *Divided*. Edited by: Victor Ottati and Chadly Stern, Oxford University Press. © Oxford University Press 2023. DOI: 10.1093/oso/9780197655467.003.0008 themselves as maximally different from members of the out-group (Hogg, 2001). This can lead to out-group derogation and greater intergroup hostilities (Dovidio et al., 2010; Iyengar et al., 2019).

Group polarization can also produce closed-mindedness (Winget et al., 2019). Research has shown that people are rarely influenced by out-group sources espousing counter-attitudinal positions (Crano & Alvaro, 1998; Martin & Hewstone, 2010). In addition, in-group members become more influential as they espouse ideas in direct contrast to ideas espoused by out-group members (Hogg, 2007). Research also shows that members working in a group, as opposed to working individually, are less likely to be influenced by advice from others (Minson & Mueller, 2012). Moreover, research on group decision-making and problem-solving has shown that open-mindedness is an important aspect of making accurate judgments and finding correct or optimal solutions (Gürçay et al., 2015; Janis, 1982; Winget, 2021). Thus, group polarization, or salient group membership alone, can interfere with finding good solutions to social problems. However, it is unclear whether group membership always leads to polarization and closed-mindedness. Recent research indicates that, under some circumstances, groups are more likely than individuals to use outside advice (Larson et al., 2020). Thus, furthering our understanding of how group contexts might influence open-mindedness should prove useful for many societal domains.

This chapter will describe some early research in an attempt to better understand how group contexts influence open-mindedness. The research follows from previous research on open-minded cognition by Ottati and colleagues (Ottati & Wilson, 2018; Price et al., 2015). Cognition involves several stages of information processing such as attention, encoding, comprehension, interpretation, elaboration, and integration. Open-minded cognition assesses a cognitive style that ranges from dogmatism (closed-minded) to open-minded cognition (Price et al., 2015). *Open-minded cognition* occurs when people select, interpret, and elaborate upon information in a directionally unbiased manner (e.g., openly considering strong arguments on both sides of an issue). *Closed-minded cognition*, on the other hand, refers to a directionally biased information processing style (e.g., selectively attending to and elaborating on strong arguments that support a policy, while ignoring strong arguments that oppose the same policy). Open-minded cognition is driven by a motive to derive an accurate or unbiased policy opinion. Closed-minded (dogmatic) cognition is driven by a motive to reinforce or maintain the individual's pre-existing opinion.

According to the flexible merit standard model (Ottati & Wilson, 2018), internalized norms are an important determinant of intentions to be open-minded (open-minded cognition). This model builds upon classic theories regarding the determinants of behavior, such as the theory of planned behavior (Ajzen, 1991), which identify perceived social norms as an important determinant of intentional behavior. While not a behavior, per se, open-minded cognition reflects a conscious or controlled component of open-mindedness. According to the flexible merit standard model, this intentional component of open-mindedness is influenced by what one perceives to be the appropriate orientation in a given situation. When individuals encounter a message pertaining to a social issue, they activate a prescriptive normative standard (see Chapter 7 in this volume). That is, they consider the degree to which a closed- versus open-minded orientation is appropriate or merited in the situation. This injunctive norm influences the individual's intent to openly consider the message (situation-specific open-minded cognition). That is, situation-specific intentions to be open-minded are determined, in part, by perceived normative prescriptions (see Chapter 7 in this volume). Moreover, internalized norms regarding open-mindedness vary across individuals, domains (e.g., politics vs. religion), and specific situations (Ottati & Wilson, 2018; Price et al., 2015). Our research explores how group norms influence group members' intentions to be open-minded.

Our research is also guided by work on motivated group cognition (De Dreu et al., 2008) and earlier research on cooperation in negotiation (De Dreu & Carnevale, 2003; Pruitt, 1982). Pruitt (1982) obtained evidence for the "goal/expectation" hypothesis of cooperation. According to this hypothesis, cooperation among negotiation parties requires both an intention (goal) to cooperate from the parties and an expectation that the other parties will also cooperate. Without both conditions, cooperation will be drastically reduced. We conceptualize open-mindedness in a similar fashion. Open-mindedness will be present to the degree that a group member thinks their group norm is to be open-minded, and they expect others in the situation will also be open-minded. We explore aspects of the group context where such conditions are present versus absent. We consider three different dimensions of group context: open-mindedness toward in-group versus out-group members, group norms supporting open- versus closed-mindedness, and how being in a majority versus minority faction influences open-mindedness.

The In-group–Out-group Hypothesis

Social identity theory (Hornsey, 2008; Tajfel & Turner, 1979) argues that people define themselves according to their group memberships. Identification with a group can happen even when membership in the group is temporary (i.e., for the duration of a lab experiment) and entirely arbitrary (Tajfel, 1970). Social identity not only influences interactions between groups but also influences individuals' cognitive processes, especially when group membership is salient (Xiao et al., 2016). Humans are not objective information processors. Cognition is colored by our motives, biases, and group identities (Dunning, 1999; Kunda, 1990). This is particularly true in the domain of political ideology (Jost & Amodio; 2012; Van Bavel & Pereira; 2018). Therefore, being open-minded to other people's ideas can sometimes be beneficial since others might have perspectives that you have not considered.

Indeed, research has shown that group composition, specifically the racial composition of a group, can significantly influence group processes and outcomes (Gaither et al., 2018; Sommers, 2006). For example, members of racially diverse groups conformed less and made superior decisions than members of racially homogenous groups (Gaither et al., 2018). Racially diverse juries deliberated longer, made fewer mistakes, and discussed a wider range of information than all-White juries (Sommers, 2006). Interestingly, these effects were primarily driven by the White jury members, suggesting that the mere presence of out-group members (i.e., Black jury members) prompted them to think more systematically about the case. Other forms of diversity (e.g., ideological diversity) may produce similar results. For example, groups of both liberals and conservatives discussing policy might discuss the issue longer, come up with more comprehensive policy solutions, and be less polarized than ideologically homogeneous groups.

However, this may not always be the case. For one thing, the effects observed in studies of racial diversity on group decision-making are partially driven by a motivation to avoid prejudice; without this motivation people may not be open-minded toward out-group members. Also, racial and ideological identity differ in a key way. Ideological identity is chosen, while racial identity is not; there exists a cultural norm to avoid racial prejudice in the United States, but there is not necessarily a strong cultural norm to openly consider the opinions of ideological out-group members. Thus, having ideologically diverse groups may lead to worse, not better, group processes and outcomes, especially since groups perform worse than individuals under some circumstances (Kerr & Tindale, 2004; Tindale et al., 2012). Thus, it is important to examine the conditions in which groups may be more or less open-minded toward in-group and out-group members.

Research on group decision-making demonstrates how groups can fail to reach their potential because of intragroup information processing loss. One example of this comes from the hidden profile paradigm, which finds that groups tend to discuss shared information more so than unique information that is not accessible to every member of the group (Stasser & Titus, 2003). In this paradigm, group members are given several pieces of information in order to make a decision. There is some overlap such that all group members share some pieces of information. However, there are also some pieces of information that are unshared; that is, they are only available to some group members but not others. When pooling all the shared and unshared information, it becomes clear that one choice is superior to the others. However, when utilizing only the shared information, the inferior choice appears to be the better option (Stasser & Titus, 2003). Even though sharing unique information leads to the best possible decision, research finds that group members who discuss shared information are viewed more positively than group members who discuss unshared information (Wittenbaum et al., 1999). As a result, shared information tends to be discussed more so than unshared information, leading groups to make inferior decisions (Stasser & Titus, 2003).

This research presents an example of how intragroup information processing skews toward dogmatism by reinforcing preexisting ideas. This issue is exacerbated in intergroup contexts where groups may have competing motives. Groups are often governed by a norm of in-group favoritism (Platow & Van Knippenberg, 2001; Tajfel, 1970), which encourages group members to behave in ways that benefit their in-group. This norm can, on its own, lead to discriminatory behavior without any malice toward out-groups (Brewer, 1999; Greenwald & Pettigrew, 2014). Indeed, this in-group favoritism norm leads to a discontinuity effect, whereby intergroup interactions tend to be more competitive than interindividual interactions in prisoner's dilemma games (Wildschut et al., 2003). Prisoner's dilemma games describe situations where there are two sides in an interaction who can choose to cooperate or compete. The outcome of the game is determined by their combined choices. Each side can optimize its outcome by choosing to compete; however, if both sides choose to compete, they receive the worst possible outcome. Thus, cooperation tends to be the more favorable strategy. Research finds that individuals are more likely to cooperate than groups who play against each other (Wildschut & Insko, 2007). This trend of increasing competitiveness does not appear to be a linear function of group size, suggesting that the mere experience of being in a group exacerbates competitive tendencies (McGlynn et al., 2009; Winquist & Larson, 2004).

It follows, then, that such competitive tendencies would also be activated during information processing, leading people to be more closed-minded toward out-groups in order to advance their own group's ideas. Indeed, previous research has found evidence of an *intergroup sensitivity effect*, whereby individuals are more receptive to criticism of their group when it comes from an in-group, rather than out-group, member (Hornsey & Imani, 2004). The authors attributed this effect to the perceived constructiveness of the criticism. Namely, in-group members who critique the group are assumed to be well intentioned and do so constructively, whereas out-group members who critique the in-group are assumed to be less well intentioned. Common group membership facilitates trust and cooperation (Platow et al., 2011). This suggests that people are more open-minded toward in-group members than out-group members due to an in-group favoritism norm and increased trust of in-group members.

We found evidence for this in-group–out-group effect in two studies (Winget et al., 2022). The first study was conducted with college students at a Midwestern university. Students were asked to imagine attending an event where a speaker was giving a presentation that suggested students at the university were falling short of their eco-friendly values. The speaker in question was either a fellow student at the same university (in-group source), a student from a rival university (out-group source), or a neutral student from another regional university (control condition). Results showed that students were significantly more open-minded to the speaker when they were a member of their own in-group than when they were a member of a rival out-group or a neutral out-group. Furthermore, this effect was mediated by normative perceptions, or how open-minded students thought they should be toward the speaker, lending support to the flexible (situational) merit standard model (Ottati & Wilson, 2018). This suggests that open-minded cognition is influenced by the in-group favoritism norm.

A second study replicated these findings among political groups. Liberal Democrat and conservative Republican survey respondents were asked to imagine engaging in a conversation with a group of people about education policy in the United States (liberal Republicans and conservative Democrats were excluded to disambiguate group membership). Survey respondents imagined that the people they were talking to were either members of the same political party or members of the opposing party. They were then asked to imagine that, during this conversation, their discussion partners mentioned that the participant's party had a poor track record of advancing effective education policies. Participants were then asked how open-minded they should and would be toward those speakers. As predicted, participants were significantly more open-minded when they imagined this criticism being levied by fellow party members than out-group party members. Again, this effect was mediated by normative perceptions.

The aforementioned studies suggest that the in-group favoritism norm leads one to be more open-minded toward in-group members than out-group members. Moreover, this effect appears to be driven by in-group favoritism rather than out-group hostility (Brewer, 1999; Greenwald & Pettigrew, 2014) since the rival out-group did not significantly differ from the neutral out-group. This is interesting given that recent research suggests political polarization is driven by animosity toward the out-group rather than warmth toward the in-group (Abramowitz & Webster, 2018; Rathje et al., 2021; but see Lelkes & Westwood, 2017). However, the initial in-group–out-group study was conducted among college students in a non-political context, and the second study with Democrats and Republicans did not include a neutral control out-group. So, while open-mindedness may have been driven primarily by in-group favoritism in the first study, it may have been driven by out-group animosity in a political context. In fact, a group norm directly advocating closed-mindedness toward the out-group would be compatible with the theoretical claim that, in some circumstances, dogmatism may be viewed as more normatively appropriate than open-minded cognition (Ottati & Wilson, 2018).

The Variable Group Norm Hypothesis

Since norms impact people's situation-specific open-minded cognition (Wilson et al., 2017), it follows that the manipulation of in-group norms should alter people's level of open-minded cognition. In a second set of studies (Winget et al., 2022), we manipulated the in-group norm regarding open-mindedness toward out-group members and then measured open-minded cognition and normative open-mindedness toward the out-group. In order to activate an injunctive group norm regarding open-mindedness, Democrats and Republicans read a fictitious news article describing their party leaders urging members to be either open- or closed-minded toward opposing party members. After reading the article, they were asked how open-minded they would and should be when discussing politics with people who hold opposing political viewpoints. This initial study found no significant effects. The group norm manipulation did not influence perceived normative open-mindedness or open-minded cognition toward opposing party members. There was also no difference between Democrats and Republicans in terms of open-mindedness and no interaction between the norm manipulation and party membership.

The results of the first study suggest that the fictitious statements from party leaders in the news article failed to actually influence participants' subjective perceptions of normative appropriateness. This may have occurred because participants questioned the veracity of the article in the open-minded condition. Here, the suggestion that party leaders endorsed open-mindedness was clearly incompatible with real-world news reports that documented extreme polarization and dogmatism in congressional communications across party lines. Under such conditions, party leader endorsement of open-mindedness toward the opposing party may have been viewed as extremely implausible, rendering the manipulation ineffective.

A follow-up study addressed shortcomings associated with the initial study (Winget et al., 2022). The group norm manipulation was altered in subtle yet important ways. In the open-minded norm condition, the article suggested that "party members" advocated open-mindedness toward others who harbor "different viewpoints" or who "have differing political leanings." This prescriptive normative information was accompanied by descriptive normative information. Specifically, in the open-minded norm condition, the article suggested that a large percentage of the participant's in-group party was now "open to listening to opposing ideas." This revised manipulation should be more effective for several reasons. First, the addition of the descriptive normative information produces a "double-barreled" norm manipulation that might be more powerful. Second, the normative information pertained to "party members" (not "party leaders") who endorsed an open- (vs. closed-) minded approach to others with "different viewpoints." It was reasoned that this approach would be less likely to arouse the previously described plausibility concerns associated with the first study. Moreover, the salience of the out-group was minimized in the second study. That is, the open-minded condition promoted open-mindedness toward others possessing "different viewpoints," not others who were explicitly labeled or identified as members of an opposing party or ideological group. By minimizing the salience of out-group identity, this manipulation should be less likely to elicit the closed-minded response to out-group members that emerged in our in-group–out-group studies, a closed-minded response that could cancel the effectiveness of the norm manipulation.

With these changes incorporated, the results of the second study did indeed support our hypotheses. Democrats and Republicans in the open norm condition reported more open-minded cognition toward opposing party members compared to their counterparts in the closed norm condition. As predicted, this effect was mediated by normative perceptions. Interestingly, there were no difference between Democrats and Republicans, suggesting that the two groups are equally susceptible to group norms. Thus, this second study found support for the hypothesis that group norms regarding open-mindedness can vary and that open-minded cognition toward out-group members varies in accordance with those norms. This suggests that intergroup polarization can be reduced if group members actively endorse open-minded social norms.

Majority–Minority Status and Open-Minded Cognition

Open-mindedness is likely to be impacted not only by one's status as an in-group versus out-group member but also by one's status within the in-group. In any given group, there are likely to be factions that disagree with one another. These differences could be as large as some members endorsing police reform whereas others endorse the abolition of policing. In order for groups to move forward, they often need to resolve such differences between factions. Resolving such differences quite often depends on members of both factions being open-minded to the other faction's ideas. Recent research has shown that having members who are open-minded leads to better group performance (Gürçay et al., 2015; Winget, 2021).

Although occasionally intragroup factions can be of equal size, quite often one faction will outnumber another, creating a majority faction and a minority faction. Although there is a vast research literature on how majority versus minority factions influence other group members (see Martin & Hewstone, 2010, for a review), research on how faction membership affects open-mindedness is fairly scarce (Crano & Chen, 1998; Gruenfeld, 1995). However, theory and research on majority and minority influence point to some possible hypotheses.

Research suggests that positions held by majorities are more likely to be correct or closer to optimal than minority positions (Hastie & Kameda, 2005; Sorkin et al., 1998). This tends to make majority positions more likely to prevail when groups make decisions (Tindale et al., 2013). Majority opinion holders also possess a greater amount of social support for their viewpoints. Merely knowing that someone else agrees with us can elicit greater confidence in that opinion (Koriat et al., 2016). With many others endorsing the same opinion, those in the majority tend to be more confident in their beliefs and are quicker to express their opinion (Koriat et al., 2016). Some research has also shown that, in social influence situations, people react similarly to arguments presented by experts and arguments presented by majorities (Bohner et al., 2008).

This led us to develop the *dogmatic majority hypothesis*—individuals harboring the majority opinion on an issue are more likely to perceive themselves as possessing an accurate opinion because their opinion has been socially validated. This increases confidence in their preexisting opinion and engenders self-perceptions of competence or expertise regarding the issue. Self-perceptions of expertise can increase dogmatic or closed-minded thinking because social norms entitle experts to be more dogmatic (Ottati et al., 2015, 2018). Thus, the dogmatic majority hypothesis predicts that, all else being equal, members of the majority will be more closed-minded than members of the minority. Minority members receive less validation and may therefore be less likely to perceive themselves as possessing high expertise pertaining to the issue. Consequently, minority members should feel less entitled to be dogmatic when interacting with majority members.

However, there are also reasons to expect the exact opposite pattern. First, Moscovici and Lage (1976) have argued that, for minority factions to have influence, they must remain highly confident and vigilantly consistent. Thus, minorities with firmly held beliefs may become quite dogmatic to increase their ability to be influential. In addition, Nemeth (1986) has argued that the presence of a minority faction can lead majority members to think more divergently about a specific topic to better understand the minority position. This may lead to greater open-mindedness among the majority members. Moreover, when minority members are also considered in-group members, politeness dictates that the majority should listen to the minority perspective, even if the majority members do not change their positions (Crano & Chen, 1998). Also, Gruenfeld (1995) analyzed both majority and minority written opinions from US Supreme Court cases. She found that the opinions written by the majority were higher on integrative complexity and appeared to take a more even-handed approach to the issues than the opinions written by the minority. Although integrative complexity is not identical to open-mindedness, these results are consistent with other perspectives where majorities, due to greater social support and a greater likelihood of success, can afford to be more open-minded, while minorities tend to be more defensive given their less powerful status (Matz & Wood, 2005; Thorisdottir & Jost, 2011). With these caveats in mind, the studies described below were designed to test the dogmatic majority hypothesis.

Before we examined majority/minority status within a group setting, we set out to test the dogmatic majority hypothesis at the individual level (Tindale et al., 2022). Does the status of being in the majority versus the minority impact open-mindedness toward members with opposing viewpoints? Participants were asked to recall times that they were in the majority and in the minority opinion within a group. Those who had an opinion held by the majority of the group expressed less open-mindedness for engaging with others of the group than those in the minority, lending support to the dogmatic majority hypothesis. A limitation of this study was that it relied on participants' memories, which may be fallible and subject to change (Loftus, 2005).

Our second experiment aimed to rectify this critique by manipulating majority status. Participants were asked their opinion on whether Puerto Rico should become a US state or not (an issue that split equally among students in the sampling pool). After stating their opinion, participants were informed that either 71% of other citizens shared their opinion (majority condition) or only 29% shared their position (minority condition). Once informed, participants were asked to imagine that they were to discuss this issue with a person who disagreed with the majority (in the minority condition) or minority (in the majority condition) of the national population. Those in the majority condition reported lower open-mindedness than those in the minority condition. Those who believed that the majority of the nation agreed with their opinion felt they could interact more dogmatically with those they disagreed with than those who believed they were in the minority opinion. This study provides further support for the dogmatic majority hypothesis. Using a real political issue, one's status as a minority versus majority member impacts one's open-mindedness toward those with opposing viewpoints.

Summary and Conclusions

Our preliminary findings suggest that group context is a key component in understanding when and to what degree people will be open-minded. People are more likely to be open-minded toward in-group members than out-group members. This in-group–out-group hypothesis was supported by our studies as well as by previous research (Hornsey & Imani, 2004). This preference for open-mindedness toward in-group members over out-group members can be adaptive for groups as it serves as a means of group preservation (Kurzban & Leary, 2001), reinforces in-group favoritism (Tajfel, 1970), and fosters within-group cooperation and cohesion (Johnson et al., 2012; Tjosvold & Poon, 1998). However, dogmatic orientations toward out-groups may inhibit reaching consensus across political groups and increase polarization within societies.

The default response to out-group members is a dogmatic approach. However, this response is not immune to collective group norms. Both injunctive and descriptive norms can signal whether open-mindedness is appropriate. As group norms inform members of how they should behave in a given situation (Abrams et al., 1990), normative open-mindedness should increase open-minded cognition among its members. Indeed, we found that when both descriptive and injunctive norms from one's political party advocate for open-mindedness, individuals were more willing to listen to and engage with opposing party members. We found this effect for both Democrats and Republicans. These findings suggest that group norms regarding open-mindedness can vary and that open-mindedness toward out-group members varies along with those norms.

The possibility of enhancing open-mindedness through group norms provides a promising approach to reducing polarization. Individuals contesting the dogmatic norms of their group and encouraging open-mindedness toward out-group members could change how their political party thinks and interacts with the opposing party. Norms are subject to change and rely on in-group members to enforce them (Abrams et al., 1990). Therefore, it is possible to change the current norms of disunity and dogmatism.

Groups are not homogeneous, and differences in opinions are likely to occur (Levine, 2017). Our studies show support for a dogmatic majority hypothesis where, within groups, majority members are more dogmatic than their minority member counterparts (Tindale et al., 2022). A dogmatic majority may not be the most advantageous in the long term. Majority members' unwillingness to engage with opposing ideas can lead to conformity pressure. While conforming to the majority does indeed result in smoother group decisions, it is not without consequence. A dogmatic majority can lead to polarization and suboptimal group solutions (Tindale, 1993). Majority members may benefit from being open-minded toward their minority group members. Minority members have been responsible for advancing social change and encouraging divergent thinking (Levine, 2017; Rios, 2012). Their participation can sway national opinions and change the status quo (Centola et al., 2018), from climate control to women's suffrage (Robson, 2019). However, the norm within groups seems to facilitate a dogmatic majority and a more open-minded minority.

The research described here only scratches the surface of how group context affects open-minded cognition. It has shown that intergroup situations lead to less open-mindedness in general but that in-group norms can increase open-mindedness. We have also shown that factions within groups can influence open-mindedness. But more research is needed to examine how intentions to be open-minded influence group cognition and interaction. We have begun collecting data that seek to answer some additional questions. For example, in an ongoing study we ask groups of four students to discuss whether Puerto Rico should become a US state and to try to reach a consensus decision. Since the student population was evenly divided on this issue, most of the groups should show one of three preference distributions: 3 for and 1 against, 2 for and 2 against, and 1 for and 3 against (there will also be some 4–0 and 0–4 groups). Half of the groups are asked to share their initial positions with the other members prior to discussion, while the other half are not asked to do so. After sharing their initial positions and prior to the group discussion, we ask participants how open-minded they will be during the upcoming discussion. This will allow us to compare majority and minority members (as well as compare them to groups where no majority exists, 2 for and 2 against). We can also compare majority and minority members who knew they were in a majority/minority with those members who were unaware of their faction size. The dogmatic majority hypothesis predicts that members of three-person majorities should show less open-mindedness than minority members but only when they are aware of their status before discussion. We encourage further research that seeks to understand the conditions in which group norms may facilitate or impede open-minded interactions between polarized groups.

References

Abramowitz, A. I., & Webster, S. W. (2018). Negative partisanship: Why Americans dislike parties but behave like rabid partisans. *Political Psychology, 39*(1), 119–135. https://doi.org/10.1111/pops.12479" https://doi.org/10.1111/pops.12479

Abrams, D., Wetherell, M., Cochrane, S., Hogg, M. A., & Turner, J. C. (1990). Knowing what to think by knowing who you are: Self-categorization and the nature of norm formation, conformity, and group polarization. *British Journal of Social Psychology, 29*, 97–119. https://doi.org/10.1111/j.2044-8309.1990.tb00892.x

Ajzen, I. (1991). The theory of planned behavior. *Organizational Behavior and Human Decision Processes, 50*(2), 179–211. https://doi.org/10.1016/0749-5978(91)90020-T" https://doi.org/10.1016/0749-5978(91)90020-T

Bohner, G., Dykema-Engblade, A., Tindale, R. S., & Meisenhelder, H. (2008). Framing of majority and minority source information in persuasion: When and how "consensus implies correctness." *Social Psychology, 39*, 108–116. https://doi.org/10.1027/1864-9335.39.2.108" https://doi.org/10.1027/1864-9335.39.2.108

Brewer, M. B. (1999). The psychology of prejudice: Ingroup love and outgroup hate? *Journal of Social Issues, 55*, 429–444. https://doi.org/10.1111/0022-4537.00126" https://doi.org/10.1111/0022-4537.00126

Centola, D., Becker, J., Brackbill, D., & Baronchelli, A. (2018). Experimental evidence for tipping points in social convention. *Science, 360*(6393), 1116–1119. https://www.science.org/doi/abs/10.1126/science.aas8827" https://www.science.org/doi/abs/10.1126/science.aas8827

Crano, W. D., & Alvaro, E. M. (1998). Indirect minority influence: The leniency contract revisited. *Group Processes & Intergroup Relations, 1*(2), 99–115. https://doi.org/10.1177/1368430298012001" https://doi.org/10.1177/1368430298012001

Crano, W. D., & Chen, X. (1998). The leniency contract and persistence of majority and minority influence. *Journal of Personality and Social Psychology, 74*(6), 1437–1450. https://doi.org/10.1037/0022-3514.74.6.1437" https://doi.org/10.1037/0022-3514.74.6.1437

De Dreu, C. K. W., & Carnevale, P. J. (2003). Motivational bases of information processing and strategy in conflict and negotiation. In M. P. Zanna (Ed.), *Advances in experimental social psychology* (Vol. 35, pp. 235–291). Elsevier Academic Press. https://doi.org/10.1016/S0065-2601(03)01004-9" https://doi.org/10.1016/S0065-2601(03)01004-9

De Dreu, C. K. W., Nijstad, B. A., & van Knippenberg, D. (2008). Motivated information processing in group judgment and decision making. *Personality and Social Psychology Review, 12*(1), 22–49. https://doi.org/10.1177/1088868307304092" https://doi.org/10.1177/1088868307304092

Dovidio, J. F., & Gaertner, S. L. (2010). Intergroup bias. In S. T. Fiske, D. T. Gilbert, & G. Lindzey (Eds.), *Handbook of social psychology* (pp. 1084–1121). John Wiley & Sons. https://doi.org/10.1002/9780470561119.socpsy002029" https://doi.org/10.1002/9780470561119.socpsy002029

Dovidio, J. F., Hewstone, M., Glick, P., & Esses, V. M. (Eds.). (2010). *The SAGE handbook of prejudice, stereotyping and discrimination*. SAGE. http://digital.casalini.it/9781446248386" http://digital.casalini.it/9781446248386

Dunning, D. (1999). A newer look: Motivated social cognition and the schematic representation of social concepts. *Psychological Inquiry, 10*(1), 1–11. https://doi.org/10.1207/s15327965pli1001_1

Festinger, L. (1954). A theory of social comparison processes. *Human Relations, 7*(2), 117–140. https://doi.org/10.1177/001872675400700202

Gaither, S. E., Apfelbaum, E. P., Birnbaum, H. J., Babbitt, L. G., & Sommers, S. R. (2018). Mere membership in racially diverse groups reduces conformity. *Social Psychological and Personality Science, 9*(4), 402–410. https://doi.org/10.1177/1948550617708013

Greenwald, A. G., & Pettigrew, T. F. (2014). With malice toward none and charity for some: Ingroup favoritism enables discrimination. *American Psychologist, 69*(7), 669–684. https://doi.org/10.1037/a0036056

Gruenfeld, D. H. (1995). Status, ideology, and integrative complexity on the U.S. Supreme Court: Rethinking the politics of political decision making. *Journal of Personality and Social Psychology, 68*(1), 5–20. https://doi.org/10.1037/0022-3514.68.1.5

Gürçay, B., Mellers, B. A., & Baron, J. (2015). The power of social influence on estimation accuracy. *Journal of Behavioral Decision Making, 28*(3), 250–261. https://doi.org/10.1002/bdm.1843

Harkins, S. (2006). Mere effort as the mediator of the evaluation–performance relationship. *Journal of Personality and Social Psychology, 91*, 436–455. https://psycnet.apa.org/doi/10.1037/0022-3514.91.3.436

Hastie, R., & Kameda, T. (2005). The robust beauty of majority rules in group decisions. *Psychological Review, 112*(2), 494–508. https://doi.org/10.1037/0033-295X.112.2.494

Hogg, M. A. (2001). A social identity theory of leadership. *Personality and Social Psychology Review, 5*(3), 184–200. https://doi.org/10.1207/S15327957PSPR0503_1

Hogg, M. A. (2007). Uncertainty–identity theory. In M. P. Zanna (Ed.), *Advances in experimental social psychology* (Vol. 39, pp. 69–126). Elsevier Academic Press. https://doi.org/10.1016/S0065-2601(06)39002-8

Hogg, M. A., & Abrams, D. (1988). *Social identifications: A social psychology of intergroup relations and group processes*. Taylor & Frances/Routledge. https://doi.org/10.4324/9780203135457

Hornsey, M. J. (2008). Social identity theory and self-categorization theory: A historical review. *Social and Personality Psychology Compass, 2*(1), 204–222. https://doi.org/10.1111/j.1751-9004.2007.00066.x

Hornsey, M. J., & Imani, A. (2004). Criticizing groups from the inside and the outside: An identity perspective on the intergroup sensitivity effect. *Personality and Social Psychology Bulletin, 30*(3), 365–383. https://doi.org/10.1177/0146167203261295

Iyengar, S., Lelkes, Y., Levendusky, M., Malhotra, N., & Westwood, S. J. (2019). The origins and consequences of affective polarization in the United States. *Annual Review of Political Science, 22*(1), 129–146. https://doi.org/10.1146/annurev-polisci-051117-073034

Janis, I. L. (1982). *Groupthink: Psychological studies of policy decisions and fiascoes*. Houghton Mifflin.

Johnson, D. W., Johnson, R. T., & Tjosvold, D. (2012). Effective cooperation, the foundation of sustainable peace. In P. T. Coleman & M. Deutsch (Eds.), *Psychological components of sustainable peace* (pp. 15–53). Springer Science+Business Media. https://doi.org/10.1007/978-1-4614-3555-6_2

Jost, J. T., & Amodio, D. M. (2012). Political ideology as motivated social cognition: Behavioral and neuroscientific evidence. *Motivation and Emotion, 36*(1), 55–64. https://doi.org/10.1007/s11031-011-9260-7

Kameda, T., & Tindale, R. S. (2006). Groups as adaptive devices: Human docility and group aggregation mechanisms in evolutionary context. In M. Schaller, J. A. Simpson, & D. T. Kenrick (Eds.), *Evolution and social psychology* (pp. 317–342). Psychosocial Press.

Kerr, N. L., & Park, E. S. (2001). Group performance in collaborative and social dilemma tasks: Progress and prospects. In M. A. Hogg & S. Tindale (Eds.), *Blackwell handbook of social psychology: Group processes* (pp. 107–138). Blackwell Publishers. https://doi.org/10.1002/9780470998458.ch5

Kerr, N. L., & Tindale, R. S. (2004). Group performance and decision making. *Annual Review of Psychology, 55*(1), 623–655. https://doi.org/10.1146/annurev.psych.55.090902.142009

Koriat, A., Adiv, S., & Schwarz, N. (2016). Views that are shared with others are expressed with greater confidence and greater fluency independent of any social influence. *Personality and Social Psychology Review, 20*(2), 176–193. https://doi.org/10.1177/1088868315585269

Kunda, Z. (1990). The case for motivated reasoning. *Psychological Bulletin, 108*(3), 480–498. https://doi.org/10.1037/0033-2909.108.3.480

Kurzban, R., & Leary, M. R. (2001). Evolutionary origins of stigmatization: The functions of social exclusion. *Psychological Bulletin, 127*(2), 187–208. https://doi.org/10.1037//0033-2909.127.2.187

Larson, J. R., Tindale, R. S., & Yoon, Y.-J. (2020). Advice taking by groups: The effects of consensus seeking and member opinion differences. *Group Processes & Intergroup Relations, 23*(7), 921–942. https://doi.org/10.1177/1368430219871349

Latané, B., & Bourgeois, M. J. (2001). Dynamic social impact and the consolidation, clustering, correlation, and continuing diversity of culture. In M. A. Hogg & R. S. Tindale (Eds.), *Blackwell handbook of social psychology: Group processes* (pp. 235–258). Blackwell Publishers.

Lelkes, Y., & Westwood, S. J. (2017). The limits of partisan prejudice. *The Journal of Politics, 79*(2), 485–501. https://doi.org/10.1086/688223

Levine, J. M. (2017). Factional conflict in groups: How majorities and minorities relate to one another. *Group Processes & Intergroup Relations, 20*(5), 644–657. https://doi.org/10.1177/1368430217702726

Levine, J. M., & Moreland, R. L. (1994). Group socialization: Theory and research. *European Review of Social Psychology, 5*(1), 305–336. https://doi.org/10.1080/14792779543000093

Loftus, E. F. (2005). Planting misinformation in the human mind: A 30-year investigation of the malleability of memory. *Learning and Memory, 12*, 361–366. https://doi.org/10.1101/lm.94705

Martin, R., & Hewstone, M. (2010). *Minority influence and innovation: Antecedents, processes, and consequences*. Psychology Press.

Matz, D. C., & Wood, W. (2005). Cognitive dissonance in groups: The consequences of disagreement. *Journal of Personality and Social Psychology*, *88*(1), 22–37. https://psycnet.apa.org/doi/10.1037/0022-3514.88.1.22

McGlynn, R. P., Harding, D. J., & Cottle, J. L. (2009). Individual–group discontinuity in group–individual interactions: Does size matter? *Group Processes & Intergroup Relations*, *12*(1), 129–143. https://doi.org/10.1177/1368430208098781

Minson, J. A., & Mueller, J. S. (2012). The cost of collaboration: Why joint decision making exacerbates rejection of outside information. *Psychological Science*, *23*(3), 219–224. https://doi.org/10.1177/0956797611429132

Moscovici, S., & Lage, E. (1976). Studies in social influence III: Majority versus minority influence in a group. *European Journal of Social Psychology*, *6*(2), 149–174. https://doi.org/10.1002/ejsp.2420060202

Myers, D. G., & Lamm, H. (1976). The group polarization phenomenon. *Psychological Bulletin*, *83*(4), 602–627. https://doi.org/10.1037/0033-2909.83.4.602

Nemeth, C. J. (1986). Differential contributions of majority and minority influence. *Psychological Review*, *93*(1), 23–32. https://doi.org/10.1037/0033-295X.93.1.23

Ottati, V., Price, E. D., Wilson, C., & Sumaktoyo, N. (2015). When self-perceptions of expertise increase closed-minded cognition: The earned dogmatism effect. *Journal of Experimental Social Psychology*, *61*, 131–138. https://doi.org/10.1016/j.jesp.2015.08.003

Ottati, V., & Wilson, C. (2018). Open-minded cognition and political thought. In W. R. Thompson & T. Capelos (Eds.), *Oxford research encyclopedias: Politics*. Oxford University Press. https://doi.org/10.1093/acrefore/9780190228637.013.143

Ottati, V., Wilson, C., Osteen, C., & Distefano, Y. (2018). Experimental demonstrations of the earned dogmatism effect using a variety of optimal manipulations: Commentary and response to Calin-Jageman (2018). *Journal of Experimental Social Psychology*, *78*, 250–258. https://doi.org/10.1016/j.jesp.2018.05.010

Platow, M. J., Foddy, M., Yamagishi, T., Lim, L., & Chow, A. (2011). Two experimental tests of trust in in-group strangers: The moderating role of common knowledge of group membership. *European Journal of Social Psychology*, *42*(1), 30–35. https://doi.org/10.1002/ejsp.852

Platow, M. J., & van Knippenberg, D. (2001). A social identity analysis of leadership endorsement: The effects of leader ingroup prototypicality and distributive intergroup fairness. *Personality and Social Psychology Bulletin*, *27*(11), 1508–1519. https://doi.org/10.1177/01461672012711011 Price, E., Ottati, V., Wilson, C., & Kim, S. (2015). Open-minded cognition. *Personality and Social Psychology Bulletin*, *41*(11), 1488–1504. doi.org/10.1177/0146167215600528

Pruitt, D. G. (1982). *Negotiation behavior*. Elsevier.

Rathje, S., Van Bavel, J. J., & van der Linden, S. (2021). Out-group animosity drives engagement on social media. *Proceedings of the National Academy of Sciences of the United States of America*, *118*(26), Article e2024292118. https://doi.org/10.1073/pnas.2024292118

Rios, K. (2012). Minority opinions: Antecedents and benefits of expression. *Social and Personality Psychology Compass*, *6*(5), 392–401. https://doi.org/10.1111/j.1751-9004.2012.00431.x

Robson, D. (2019, May 13). The "3.5% rule": How a small minority can change the world. BBC Future. https://www.bbc.com/future/article/20190513-it-only-takes-35-of-people-to-change-the-world

Sanders, G. S., & Baron, R. S. (1977). Is social comparison irrelevant for producing choice shifts? *Journal of Experimental Social Psychology*, *13*(4), 303–314. https://doi.org/10.1016/0022-1031(77)90001-4

Sherif, M. (1936). *The psychology of social norms*. Harper.

Sommers, S. R. (2006). On racial diversity and group decision making: Identifying multiple effects of racial composition on jury deliberations. *Journal of Personality and Social Psychology, 90*(4), 597–612. https://doi.org/10.1037/0022-3514.90.4.597

Sorkin, R. D., West, R., & Robinson, D. E. (1998). Group performance depends on the majority rule. *Psychological Science, 9*(6), 456–463. https://doi.org/10.1111/1467-9280.00085

Stasser, G., & Titus, W. (2003). Hidden profiles: A brief history. *Psychological Inquiry, 14*(3–4), 304–313. https://doi.org/10.1080/1047840X.2003.9682897

Tajfel, H. (1970). Experiments in intergroup discrimination. *Scientific American, 223*, 96–102. http://dx.doi.org/10.1038/scientificamerican1170-96

Tajfel, H., & Turner, J. (1979). An integrative theory of intergroup conflict. In W. G. Austin & S. Worchel (Eds.), *The social psychology of intergroup relations* (pp. 33–47). Brooks/Cole.

Thórisdóttir, H., & Jost, J. T. (2011). Motivated closed-mindedness mediates the effect of threat on political conservatism. *Political Psychology, 32*(5), 785–811. https://doi.org/10.1111/j.1467-9221.2011.00840.x

Tindale, R. S. (1993). Decision errors made by individuals and groups. In N. J. Castellan (Ed.), *Individual and group decision making: Current issues* (pp. 109–124). Lawrence Erlbaum Associates.

Tindale, R. S., Meisenhelder, H. M., Dykema-Engblade, A. A., & Hogg, M. A. (2004). Shared cognition in small groups. In M. B. Brewer & M. Hewstone (Eds.), *Social cognition* (pp. 268–297). Blackwell Publishing.

Tindale, R. S., Smith, C. M., Dykema-Engblade, A., & Kluwe, K. (2012). Good and bad group performance: Same process—different outcomes. *Group Processes & Intergroup Relations, 15*(5), 603–618. https://doi.org/10.1177/1368430212454928

Tindale, R. S., Talbot, M., & Martinez, R. (2013). Group decision making. In J. M. Levine (Ed.), *Group processes* (pp. 165–194). Psychology Press.

Tindale, R. S., Winget, J., Berryman, K., Moaz, S., & Ottati, V. C. (2022, April 21–23). *Groups, norms, and open-minded cognition* [Paper presentation]. Midwestern Psychological Association Annual Meeting, Chicago, IL.

Tjosvold, D., & Poon, M. (1998). Dealing with scarce resources: Open-minded interaction for resolving budget conflicts. *Group & Organization Management, 23*(3), 237–255. https://doi.org/10.1177/1059601198233003

Van Bavel, J. J., & Pereira, A. (2018). The partisan brain: An identity-based model of political belief. *Trends in Cognitive Sciences, 22*(3), 213–224. https://doi.org/10.1016/j.tics.2018.01.004

Vinokur, A., & Burnstein, E. (1978). Novel argumentation and attitude change: The case of polarization following group discussion. *European Journal of Social Psychology, 8*(3), 335–348. https://doi.org/10.1002/ejsp.2420080306

Wildschut, T., & Insko, C. A. (2007). Explanations of interindividual–intergroup discontinuity: A review of the evidence. *European Review of Social Psychology, 18*(1), 175–211. https://doi.org/10.1080/10463280701676543

Wildschut, T., Pinter, B., Vevea, J. L., Insko, C. A., & Schopler, J. (2003). Beyond the group mind: A quantitative review of the interindividual–intergroup discontinuity effect. *Psychological Bulletin, 129*(5), 698–722. https://doi.org/10.1037/0033-2909.129.5.698

Wilson, C., Ottati, V., & Price, E. (2017). Open-minded cognition: The attitude justification effect. *The Journal of Positive Psychology, 12*(1), 47–58. https://doi.org/10.1080/17439760.2016.1167941

Winget, J. R. (2021). *Motivated information exchange: An initial demonstration of open-minded group cognition* [Unpublished doctoral dissertation]. Loyola University Chicago.

Winget, J. R., Berryman, K., Moaz, S., Tindale, R. S., & Ottati, V. (2022). *Normative openness: The influence of group norms on open-minded cognition* [Unpublished manuscript]. Department of Psychology, Loyola University Chicago.

Winget, J. R., Ottati, V. C., & Tindale, R. S. (2019, April 11–13). *Open-minded group cognition* [Paper presentation]. Midwestern Psychological Association Annual Meeting, Chicago, IL.

Winquist, J. R., & Larson, J. R., Jr. (2004). Sources of the discontinuity effect: Playing against a group versus being in a group. *Journal of Experimental Social Psychology, 40*(5), 675–682. https://doi.org/10.1016/j.jesp.2004.01.002

Wittenbaum, G. M., Hubbell, A. P., & Zuckerman, C. (1999). Mutual enhancement: Toward an understanding of the collective preference for shared information. *Journal of Personality and Social Psychology, 77*(5), 967–978. https://doi.org/10.1037/0022-3514.77.5.967

Xiao, Y. J., Coppin, G., & Van Bavel, J. J. (2016). Perceiving the world through group-colored glasses: A perceptual model of intergroup relations. *Psychological Inquiry, 27*(4), 255–274. https://doi.org/10.1080/1047840X.2016.1199221

9
Actively Open-Minded Thinking and the Political Effects of Its Absence

Jonathan Baron, Ozan Isler, and Onurcan Yılmaz

Introduction: What Is Actively Open-Minded Thinking?

The term *actively open-minded thinking* (henceforth AOT) was introduced in the first edition of *Thinking and Deciding* (Baron, 1988) by the copy editor Christie Lerch, who wanted a term for an idea running throughout the book.[1] AOT now has a literature of its own, partly due to the extensive work of Keith Stanovich and his collaborators Maggie Toplak and Richard West. But the idea originated, nameless, in Baron (1985). Lerch's name tells the story. AOT is a recommendation, a norm or standard, for how to think well so that errors are avoided and goals are achieved. In this regard it resembles other concepts discussed in this book, although these are often stated as types of thinking to avoid, such as dogmatism. But the idea of distinguishing good and bad thinking is much the same.

This chapter begins with a discussion of how AOT differs from similar ideas. In particular, it describes how AOT arises from a general theory of optimal thinking and proceeds from that to list two common departures from optimality: myside bias and overconfidence. Because AOT is a standard, it is endorsed (or opposed) to various degrees by ordinary people; and people generally try, with considerable success, to follow their own standards when they think. We can measure these standards with simple questionnaires, and it turns out that they predict a variety of politically relevant beliefs and practices. These concern not only our own thinking but also, importantly, whom we trust when we "outsource" our thinking to others, as we often do in political matters. We trust those who signal that they agree with our own standards of how to think. Here, we review some of this (rapidly expanding) literature. We suggest that individuals tend to differ systematically in their political and metacognitive beliefs, thus yielding a dimension of individual differences that we call *cognitive liberalism*. Finally, we report a study concerned with the roles of cultural background and individual thought in causing cognitive liberalism. Although cognitive liberalism is correlated with cultural background, people see the influence of background as largely opposing cognitive liberalism; and they attribute their own liberalism, insofar as it exists, to their own thought and the influences of others.

The absence of cognitive liberalism, including frequent failure to think in a way that is actively open-minded, may account in part, perhaps in large part, for political polarization, as well as other forms of extremism and populism around the world. Note that all it takes is one side. If the forces of unreason are large enough to gain some political power, it is natural for the other side to resent them, to want their children not to marry them, and so on; but this does not mean that both sides are equally irrational. Extremism has existed on both sides of the political spectrum throughout the history of all democratic nations, but recent extremist and populist movements showing some success have come largely from the political right.

A Formal Approach to Thinking

Thinking is the effort to resolve doubt about what to do or what to believe. It necessarily involves some search, maybe only a little. We search our own minds for memories and newly constructed ideas, and we often search the external world over minutes or even years for a single episode of thought. We search for three different kinds of objects:

Possibilities are possible answers to the question that inspired thinking. These are "options" in the case of decisions or "propositions" in the case of thinking about beliefs. Each possibility has a "strength."

Evidence (arguments) consists of propositions that can affect the strength of different possibilities.

Goals (criteria, objectives, values) affect how the evidence affects the strength of each possibility.

If the single goal is to get a drink of water, evidence that the drinking fountain is out of order will weaken that possible option. Sometimes the only goal is to determine what is true, but decisions usually involve more than one goal, hence possible conflict. Goals can be matters of degree, like the goal of making money.

Inference is the process of using the evidence and goals. It can be simple and automatic, but it can also involve the use of various principles, such as the rules of logic. This general outline is called the *search–inference framework*.

These processes of search and inference are not ordered. In an extended episode of thinking they operate in cycles. A possibility may emerge. The search for goals may yield a goal that it subverts. This may lead to a search for a second possibility. Goals may elicit search for other goals, as when we ask "What is the real purpose of what we are trying to do here?" We can, however, think of all these processes as filling in a table like the following, where the rows are possibilities, the columns are goals, and the cells are arguments, each of which may fall into several cells. And each cell has a value, positive or negative, for the effect of that evidence on a given possibility achieving a given goal. Each goal may have a strength as well, so the strength of the possibilities may be computed from this table by weighing the cell entries by the column weights and then adding up the cells in each row (after this adjustment). But nobody needs to do the math; it is just a way of making the search–inference framework concrete conceptually.

This process is governed by the setting of two parameters: direction and confidence. The *direction* of search and inference may favor or oppose the current strongest possibility. The optimal setting of this parameter is neutrality so that it is fair to the current possibility and the alternatives. The most common departure from optimality is *myside bias* (Perkins, 2019), that is, search and inference that favor the strongest possibility and thus tend to close off thinking prematurely by neglecting alternatives. (If people always favored the alternative, they could cycle forever and rarely reach a conclusion; they would probably notice that they do this and change the way they think, although a few "obsessive" people may not.) Note that myside bias is unlikely to lead to correction of erroneous conclusions. But *neutrality* does not imply neglect of evidence previously obtained: I need not throw away everything I know about Hitler in the face of new evidence that he was once kind to a Jew.

Confidence in the currently favored possibility is a function of the strengths of the possibilities under consideration. It is high when the favored possibility is strong and the next best alternative is weak. Thinking should continue to the extent to which confidence is low and the expected benefit of further thinking by oneself, another form of confidence, is high. Thinking often has a cost, at least in time that could be spent on other things; and when the cost exceeds the expected benefit, thinking should stop. In this regard, the theory of optimal thinking differs from theories that simply assume that more thinking is better. In the case of politics, the expected benefit of further thinking on one's own may be lower than the benefit of outsourcing to trusted others. Although I have some understanding of macroeconomics, I know that others I can easily consult have a much better understanding than I do. In politics, people may think too much on their own and reach erroneous conclusions (just as they may trust the wrong sources).

The most common error is overconfidence in the favored possibility, that is, high confidence that is not warranted by the thinking done so far. This is exacerbated by myside bias, which can lead directly to such unwarranted high confidence in the favored possibility by failing to uncover evidence against it (or for an alternative). Thus, overconfidence and myside bias tend to correlate, but they are not the same.

When we evaluate the thinking and conclusions of others, in view of the importance of confidence being warranted, we can be tolerant of their expressions of uncertainty. Indeed, a source's expressions of uncertainty indicate that the same source's expressions of certainty are warranted and that the source is more trustworthy than one that never seems uncertain. AOT must thus be defined in terms of two virtues: fairness to possibilities and willingness to accept low confidence or uncertainty when that is warranted. Warranted low confidence implies openness to further thought, which need not be done immediately.

Individual Differences in Cognitive Style

AOT provides a somewhat different account of individual differences in cognitive style from what seem to be the two other major current approaches: dual-process theory and the idea of "reflection."

Dual-Process Theory and Cognitive Reflection

A long tradition in psychology has distinguished between responses that are automatic, requiring very little effort and thus possibly occurring even when they are incorrect, and responses that require effort (Bryan & Harter, 1899; Evans & Stanovich, 2013; Kahneman, 2011; Shiffrin & Schneider, 1977). A recent version of this idea is corrective dual-process theory, which holds that, in many tasks, the automatic response (System 1) occurs and is then sometimes recognized as suspect so that a second step is to revisit the problem using System 2, which is reflective and requires some effort. A simple way to assess this effect is the two-response method (Bago & De Neys, 2017), in which the subject is instructed to provide an immediate intuitive response followed by a final response.

Corrective dual-process theory has been usefully applied to several areas, including memory tasks, logic, and trick problems (e.g., Ackerman & Thompson, 2017; Thompson et al., 2011). Importantly, the switch from System 1 to System 2 does not always occur and depends on the strength of confidence in the System 1 output (also called *feeling of rightness* in the literature), as well as individual differences (e.g., Galotti et al., 1986). An example of a commonly used trick problem is part of the original Cognitive Reflection Test (CRT; Frederick, 2005, p. 27): "If it takes 5 machines 5 minutes to make 5 widgets, how long would it take 100 machines to make 100 widgets?" System 1 would produce an answer of 100 minutes, by simple analogy. Many people give that answer. Others may worry that something might be wrong with it (or they never think of it), and they proceed to solve the problem more systematically (perhaps by imagining 20 groups of five machines working all at once).

Performance on the CRT correlates with a large variety of other tasks and judgments, including some that involve politics. In general, the CRT correlates negatively with social conservatism and with measures associated with it (e.g., Fuhrer & Cova, 2020; Pennycook et al., 2020; Ross et al., 2021) but not so much with economic conservatism, when these two types of beliefs are distinguished (e.g., Deppe et al., 2015; Yilmaz & Saribay, 2017).

Ackerman and Thompson (2017) present a version of dual-system theory that is much like the search–inference framework described above. In particular, like the search–inference framework, it allows cycling, in which an extended thought process can take many steps, each of which leads to a representation of confidence (or feeling of rightness), which then affects whether further thinking occurs. It does not (and is not meant to) specify optimal parameters, as the general model behind AOT does.

Reflection/Impulsivity

Baron et al. (2015) suggested that the predictive power of the CRT arose largely because it measures a different dimension of cognitive style, namely, reflection/impulsivity (R/I).

This idea arose initially in the study of children, who could be assessed as reflective or impulsive on the basis of their performance in problem-solving tasks that did not require particular knowledge (Kagan et al., 1964). These tasks, like most cognitive tasks, show a speed–accuracy trade-off. People (including children) can solve problems quickly (impulsively), at the expense of lower accuracy, or they could (reflectively) take more time to avoid errors. A useful and general measure of R/I, applicable to many problem-solving tasks, is the z score of accuracy plus the z score of (log) response time (Baron et al., 1986). R/I correlates with a great variety of measures of success, not just in problem-solving but also in schoolwork and self-control (Messer, 1976; Baron et al., 1986). Log response time is often as good a predictor as accuracy alone (Baron et al., 2015).

Note that the R/I dimension implicitly assumes that more thought is always better. By contrast, AOT implies that some amount of thought is optimal for each situation. (People may think too much when they think they know more than other sources whom they could easily consult.) The fact that R/I predicts so many measures of good performance suggests that most people, in the tasks that yield these measures, are thinking less than the optimum. But R/I differs from AOT in other ways. For example, myside bias can occur even in extensive thinking, as when thinking is used to justify an incorrect conclusion (Wason & Evans, 1975).

Measures of AOT

System 2 and R/I can be assessed through performance on test items, those with correct and incorrect answers, and other tasks. Several measures like these are sensitive to myside bias and overconfidence. But measures like these are also affected by other factors aside from cognitive style. For example, the CRT is affected by knowledge specific to mathematics.

Here are some examples of performance measures of myside bias:

1. In a *direct measure of myside bias*, Perkins (2019, based on a 1986 report) asked students simply to write down arguments about "vexed" issues, such as "Would a nuclear freeze agreement signed between the U.S. and the U.S.S.R. significantly reduce the possibility of world war?" (p. 628). Students listed more myside arguments than otherside arguments, but when they were asked to write more arguments on both sides they wrote more additional otherside arguments, thus showing that they could have written them initially but did not. Baron (1995) used a similar task to assess individual differences and found that myside bias in the task was correlated with myside bias in judgments of the quality of other people's lists.
2. In *predecisional distortion*, the experimenter creates a bias toward one option in a choice task (e.g., by presenting positive evidence for that option first), which then makes the subject more likely to choose that item because the subject gives more weight to evidence favoring that option over others, even if the others would be chosen more often if the information were presented in a random order (e.g., Russo et al., 2006; see Brownstein, 2003, for a review).

3. In *belief overkill* (Jervis, 1976), people distort arguments so that all arguments favor a preferred option, even though it would be perfectly reasonable to acknowledge that the option should be chosen despite some negatives because these were outweighed by the positives. Baron (2009) found striking individual differences in this effect, with some subjects showing no apparent bias at all.
4. *Probability distortion* is, like belief overkill, a distortion of one of the arguments concerning an action with some risk, in which the judged probability of favorable outcomes increases and the probability of unfavorable outcomes decreases (DeKay et al., 2009).
5. *Polarization* occurs when the presentation of arguments that are on the whole neutral, because they conflict in which side they favor, increases the judged strength of the side initially favored. Although some effects of this sort (e.g., that of Lord et al., 1979) can be explained in terms of rational use of prior beliefs in sources of evidence (Jern et al., 2014), other evidence for polarization is more difficult to explain this way because all the evidence comes from the same source (e.g., Meszaros et al., 1996).
6. *Selective exposure* is biased search for external information that is known in advance to support favored possibilities. Female coffee drinkers don't want to read articles about how coffee causes breast cancer. This effect varies in magnitude (Hart et al., 2009) and is sometimes difficult to demonstrate because people sometimes seek out otherside arguments in order to rebut them, especially if they think that the arguments will be easy to rebut.

But AOT is most often assessed through self-report tests concerning norms for what good thinking is. As noted, people generally try to follow their own standards, so these correlate with performance measures. Here are some items in current use (not in original order; "(–)" indicates reverse scoring):

Myside Bias Items (Reverse Scoring Indicated)

1. People should take into consideration evidence that goes against conclusions they favor.
2. People should revise their conclusions in response to relevant new information.
3. Changing your mind is a sign of weakness. (–)
4. People should search actively for reasons why they might be wrong.
5. It is OK to ignore evidence against your established beliefs. (–)

6. It is important to be loyal to your beliefs even when evidence is brought to bear against them. (–)
7. When faced with a puzzling question, we should try to consider more than one possible answer before reaching a conclusion.

Overconfidence Items
1. True experts are willing to admit to themselves and others that they are uncertain or that they don't know the answer.
2. Being undecided or unsure is the result of muddled thinking. (–)
3. There is nothing wrong with being undecided about many issues.
4. It is best to be confident in a conclusion even when we have good reasons to question it. (–)

A scale consisting of these items (in a different order) had a reliability coefficient (α) of .86, with no apparent separation of the two item groups, in a sample of adults used in the study we report below. But many findings suggest that a variety of scales of this sort, with somewhat different sets of items, are equally reliable and equally useful at predicting other measures.

Scales like this one are correlated with a variety of measures of cognitive bias, such as base-rate neglect, gambler's fallacy, conjunction effect, denominator neglect, Wason's four-card task, and outcome bias. Toplak et al. (2014) present some of these results and cite earlier papers by Toplak, Stanovich, and West.

Political Correlates of AOT: Cognitive Liberalism and Its Enemies

AOT measures correlate not only with cognitive tasks but also with various measures of political attitudes and various other scales that have been used to assess the relation between cognitive style and political attitudes. We might even think that there is a general trait of "cognitive liberalism," which encompasses cognitive style and political liberalism of a certain sort. We could think of this as somewhat analogous to the g factor in intelligence. All the components correlate with each other to some degree, as if there were some single underlying trait affecting everything. Such a trait may not exist, yet the question of what accounts for these correlations is worth pursuing, as we discuss later. Specifically, the following correlations of AOT have been observed:

1. Cosmopolitanism, in the sense of caring about the world and opposing parochialism and nationalism (e.g., favoring immigration).
2. Opposing social conservatism, that is, political views based on tradition that has been handed down for generations.
3. Opposition to authoritarian religion, especially *divine command theory*, the belief that we must accept the commands of God because we are incapable of reasoning ourselves.
4. Utilitarian moral reasoning (based on consequences for all affected), as opposed to deontology (morality based on rules, rights, and duties).
5. Acceptance of AOT as a standard.
6. Trust in (good) science.

Data for the British Election Survey (wave 8, 2016; Fieldhouse et al., 2018), which included a version of the AOT scale, illustrate the connection with cosmopolitanism. To begin, some items seemed to capture parochialism (the opposite of cosmopolitanism), and we put them into a scale:

1. The UK should help other EU members in times of crisis
2. Should EU citizens be able to claim child-benefit for children not in the UK
3. Good or bad for Britain: Allowing the free movement of workers within Europe
4. Allow more asylum seekers to come to UK
5. Britain should allow more workers from other EU countries
6. Britain should allow more workers from outside the EU
7. Allow more student to come to UK
8. Allow more families of people who already live here to come to UK
9. Self: Allow more or fewer immigrants
10. EU Referendum vote intention

Of primary interest, the correlation of AOT with this scale was −.38. (For other results, see Figure 1 of the online supplement.[1])

Another informative set of correlations comes from a study of susceptibility to fake news (Bronstein et al., 2019). Subjects saw 12 fake and 12 real headlines with pictures and rated their accuracy (e.g., "Mike Pence: Gay Conversion Therapy Saved My Marriage. Vice President-elect claims that a 1983 conversion therapy saved him"). AOT correlated −.32 with rated accuracy of fake news but .14 (positively) with rated accuracy of real news. (Other results are in Figure 2 of the online supplement.)

Others have observed positive correlations of AOT with utilitarian responding (Baron et al., 2015) and negative correlations with superstitious belief (Svedholm-Häkkinen & Lindeman, 2017), supernatural religious belief (Pennycook et al., 2014), paranormal belief (.43; Sirota & Juanchich, 2018, public data), and belief in divine command theory (Baron et al., 2015), the belief that humans are incapable of understanding the moral commandments from God and thus should not question them (Piazza & Landy, 2013). Note that these sorts of religious and supernatural beliefs are the sources of political disputes, where the more conservative religious beliefs tend to be associated with social conservatism.

Importantly, AOT standards also correlate with measures of trust in sources, when the sources signal whether or not they follow those standards (Baron, 2019; Baron & High, 2019). For example, Baron and High asked subjects how much they would trust the judgment of the person who made each of two types of statements. In one study, the statements differed in indications of myside bias:

Type1 It would be flat out irresponsible to oppose tuition-free access to community or technical college programs—it will create a wave of new workers prepared for the 21st century economy.

Type2 Tuition-free access to community or technical college programs will create a wave of new workers prepared for the 21st century economy. Yes, it is expensive, but it is worth the price.

In a second study, they differed in indications of overconfidence, e.g.:

1. "Those tremors don't mean anything. An earthquake won't happen. (scientist)"
2. "Those tremors probably don't mean anything. An earthquake is unlikely. (scientist)"

For both types of items, the difference in ratings of the two sources correlated with the score on an AOT scale. Thus, people who themselves oppose AOT standards are more likely to trust those who indicated absence of those standards.

Where Does Cognitive Liberalism Come From?

What can account for the correlations just described? In particular, AOT standards correlate both with actual cognitive processes and with measures of politically relevant beliefs.

One explanation that we can largely dismiss is that the correlations result from differences in the thinking that subjects do in psychology experiments themselves. For example, correlations of the CRT with various tasks could result from R/I as manifest in the tasks themselves. This sort of effect might explain some correlations: Impulsive processing of news headlines might lead to more judgments that they are real, and impulsive responses to moral dilemmas might favor simple deontological principles. But it is clear that such within-experiment effects cannot explain the whole pattern of results. The major individual differences seem likely to result from differences in what subjects bring to experiments. For example, subjects who make more deontological responses have probably accepted deontological approaches in their real-world judgments outside of the laboratory. Two other explanations seem more plausible.

Cultural Diversity

Pre-Enlightenment and post-Enlightenment cultures may exist in the same population. Older, traditional beliefs and values associated with (but not limited to) religion versus modern liberalism (tolerance, respect for science, etc.) may thrive in some regions, usually rural ones with limited opportunities for higher education. Residents of cities, by contrast, tend to have more education and more exposure to people speaking different languages and from different regions. Respect for their fellow citizens may spill over into greater willingness to consider the "other side" even when the other side does not come from other people.

In sum, cognitive liberalism is an attribute of cultural groups. Most studies of individual differences do not restrict themselves to one cultural group, which would be difficult given the fact that membership in most cultural groups is a matter of degree. The sample is usually national, and it need not be nationally representative in order to include considerable cultural variation. Cultural variation itself could arise from environmental effects (e.g., isolation) on individual development. Once it exists, it could be maintained by mechanisms that create cultural stability across generations (Cavalli-Sforza et al., 1982). Further investigation of cultural history, including both written history and language itself, may be useful.

Development of Thinking Standards

People are surely influenced by the cultural background they come from, but many people depart from it. Without such departures, it is hard to see how cultural change could happen. And it has happened extensively throughout history. The cultures that produced Socrates, Confucius, and many other ancient sages seem unlikely to have existed before the development of writing (even when what we know of the early sages comes mostly from the writings of their students), although we cannot know for sure. The Enlightenment that took place in Europe and, more generally, the Renaissance surely involved cultural change. Hallpike (2004) provides an account of the cultural evolution of morality and how it was influenced by such economic factors as the development of cities.

Thus, another determinant of thinking standards may be people's own development over their lives, perhaps especially in adolescence. Much evidence for this sort of development occurs in the literature in developmental psychology (Kohlberg, 1969; Kuhn, 1989; Marcia, 1980; Perry, 1971). Education seems to play a major role, although it is difficult to separate education itself from the cultural differences that cause people to get more or less of it. Whatever the cause, development of thinking continues at least into early adulthood, in ways that would seem to increase AOT in some people. For example, in Kohlberg's (1969) identified transition from "conventional" to "post-conventional" moral reasoning, the former is the identification of morality with what is socially prescribed, such as law or convention, while the latter allows criticism of conventional morality from a more general perspective, such as the sort of moral theory that philosophers discuss.

AOT standards themselves could arise from reflection on conflict of alternative views, which would be more likely in contexts of cultural diversity. People with different beliefs may start asking questions such as "How do I know that my beliefs are more correct than hers? Where do accurate beliefs come from?" Such questions could result in the idea that beliefs are more likely to be correct if they have withstood challenges. AOT standards could also arise from institutional efforts to reduce cultural conflict. Schools in the United States teach their students to respect others and listen to them, and it is in these terms that students themselves describe their open-mindedness (Metz et al., 2020).

More generally, we can view AOT as a form of *metacognition*, that is, thinking about thinking. People evaluate their own thinking, and that of others, according to certain standards; and they try to use these standards to control the way they think themselves (e.g., Baron, 1991, 1995). Historically, the standards of AOT may have arisen from people reflecting on what they are doing. Other forms of metacognition arise in childhood (Flavell, 1979).

Cultural and Individual Determinants: Preliminary Studies

Ideally, we could test the roles of cultural transmission and individual development with about 10 years of longitudinal data. Lacking both time and money, we asked 232 people from a panel Baron has used for other studies to engage retrospect on their own development.[2]

We presented five short scales measuring different aspects of cognitive liberalism. The utilitarianism (abbreviates as *Uscale* in figures) scale was homemade, focusing on two features of utilitarianism that distinguish it (and other consequentialist views) from other moral systems: making decisions according to consequences rather than rules and favoring harmful actions when they prevent greater harm. Three items from Piazza and Landy (2013) measured belief in divine command theory (*DivineCT*). Three other homemade items assessed religion (*Relig*), two concerned with belief in God but one just asking about religiosity. Six homemade items assessed general political views (*Liberal*); four defined conservatism as adherence to traditional views and reluctance to move away from them, a feature that could apply to most cultures around the world regardless of current defining issues; and the remaining two items simply asked about "right" versus "left." Nine items assessed AOT. For each of the 27 items, we asked subjects their current views, the views they started with, and the views of their family background. We could thus assess changes over time, as seen by each subject.

Method

The introduction to "Time travel" (the name we used for all these studies) read as follows:

> This is a study of how people's attitudes change over their lives. Unfortunately, we do not yet have a time-travel machine that will take you back to the time when you were 12 years old. So we are asking you to do your best to reflect on how you came to hold your current attitudes on a number of abstract issues.
>
> There are various influences that can cause people to change their views. Sometimes they have an effect and sometimes they do not. But we want to know about each influence that occurred and could have affected your views, whether it had an effect or not. For example, someone may have tried to persuade you of a different view, and failed. Or you may have considered a different view, on your own, but ultimately decided that your original view was best.

The main part of the study presented 27 items, making up five scales. Each question was answered on a 1–5 scale labeled "Completely disagree" at one end and "Completely agree" at the other. The scales were as follows:

Uscale (Utilitarianism)

1. When a moral rule leads to outcomes that are worse than those from breaking the rule, we should **follow** the rule. (R)
2. When a moral rule leads to outcomes that are worse than those from breaking the rule, we should **break** the rule.
3. When two options harm other people in the same ways, we should choose the option that harms fewer people.
4. When some action causes harm to some people but prevents the same harm to many more people, we should act.
5. It is morally wrong to harm some people in order to prevent the same harm to more people. (R)
6. Sometimes we should follow moral rules that prevent us from doing what is best on the whole. (R)

DivineCT (Divine Command and Religion Items)

1. The truth about morality is revealed only by God.
2. Acts that are immoral are immoral because God forbids them.
3. We don't need to try to figure out what is right and wrong, the answers have already been given to us by God.

Relig

1. There is a god that truly exists.
2. God, and gods, do not exist, despite what people believe.
3. I consider myself a religious person.

Liberal (Political Liberalism)

1. I am reluctant to make any large-scale changes to the social order. (R)
2. I favor stability in society, even if there seem to be problems with the current system. (R)
3. Society should be quicker to throw out old ideas and traditions and to adopt new thinking and customs.
4. Traditional values, customs, and morality have a lot wrong with them.

5. On SOCIAL matters, my political orientation is on the right (conservative) as opposed to left. (Here, 'agree' means that you are right wing, and 'disagree' means that you are left wing.) (R)
6. On ECONOMIC matters, my political orientation is on the right (conservative) as opposed to left. (R)

The AOT scale was essentially identical to the items listed above.

After each item, we asked the following questions:

Past. How would you have answered this question earlier in your life, when you first might have been able to understand the question as you do now?
Upbring. How would those who brought you up have wanted you to answer this question?
Please indicate how each the following influenced your views.[3]
I thought about things like this myself.
[Strongly toward 'disagree' ... Strongly toward 'agree']
People involved in my upbringing.
Other people I met later.
My formal education (e.g., school, college).
Specific life experiences that I had.

Results

Detailed results are described in the online supplement. All the scales correlated with each other, as expected (Figure 3 of the supplement). Figure 9.1 shows the means (in the direction of cognitive liberalism) for these scales for the three questions: present, past ("earlier in your life"), and upbringing ("those who brought you up"). In retrospect, on average, the subjects thought that they had become more cognitively liberal in every domain except politics ("Liberal"). But the subjects saw themselves as more liberal politically than their background, even when they were young.

Upbringing does, however, appear to affect current beliefs. Upbringing ratings for each scale were correlated with present beliefs on that scale (Figure 8 of the online supplement). Almost all of these correlations were specific to the scale. For example, upbringing in AOT did not correlate with current political liberalism, and upbringing in liberalism did not affect current AOT.

As noted above, we also asked questions about the direction of influence received from five sources: *thought* (own thinking), *upbringing*, *others*,

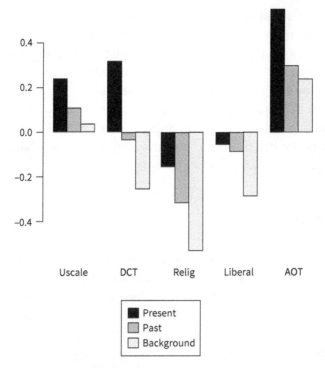

Figure 9.1 Mean responses to each scale, coded so that positive is more cognitively liberal and 0 represents the midpoint (neutrality) of the 5-point response scale. AOT = actively open-minded thinking; DCT = divine command theory.

education, and *experience*. These questions were not mutually exclusive, so we could examine their correlations with each other. For subject means of each measure, *thought, others, education,* and *experience* correlated highly with each other. This high correlation makes sense if we think that people's own thinking is inspired by inputs from others and from experiences, and thinking may also lead people to seek different sorts of people, education, and experiences. Upbringing did not correlate at all with items in this group.

In general, these influence measures all correlated with current ratings (Figure 9 in the supplement). The highest correlations were with *thought* and *experience*, and the lowest were with *upbringing*. Correlations with the change from past to current (Figures 10–12 in the supplement) told a different story: Most correlations were positive, but the correlation of change with *upbringing* was negative. That is, subjects thought that their upbringing made them less cognitively liberal. In sum, subjects thought that their change over time was influenced in a more liberal direction by their own thinking, and other influences, but in the opposite direction by their upbringing.

We could also ask whether AOT was particularly important in bringing about change from the past by looking at the correlation between the average of each scale for both times and change from past to present for each scale. Averaged AOT did not correlate substantially with any changes in other scales (highest was .11 for *Liberal*), and neither did any other scale (except that *DivineCT* and *Relig* affected each other). In summary, no particular trait that we assessed seemed to cause broad changes in the others. When subjects said that changes resulted from their own thought, they seem to have meant that they thought about each issue.

Conclusion

There is a positive manifold among measures of deontology, social conservatism, parochialism, religious "fundamentalism," and non-acceptance of AOT. This positive manifold may occur (as it does for cognitive abilities) for a variety of reasons. Some traits may affect others. AOT could lead to cosmopolitanism, rejection of moralistic values (personal values imposed on others), and utilitarianism. Utilitarianism can lead to cosmopolitanism. Belief in divine command theory can make people resist AOT.

Similar forces may work within cultures, and acculturation may affect individual thinking and beliefs. It is difficult to account for the full pattern of results without considering effects of culture. For example, divine command theory does not seem like a view that people are likely to hold as a result of their own thinking. Cultural beliefs and values may be maintained because they set up institutions to maintain themselves over generations (Cavalli-Sforza et al., 1982).

Yet some people become more cognitively liberal over their lives. Some of this is the effect of "thought about it myself." Such thought seems to be affected by other influences aside from the sort of upbringing we asked about, such as teachers, friends, or experiences with strangers. But it does not seem to be simply the transmission of culture as that would not explain the apparent movement toward cognitive liberalism.

Rather, it seems possible that AOT itself is something that people discover for themselves. The starting point may be the simple recognition that people make mistakes and that one way to prevent such mistakes is to look for possible causes, including reasons why some conclusion of the moment might turn out to be wrong. People can of course learn to do this sort of search without recognizing what they are doing, but it should not be difficult to take the next step to a metacognitive principle, which then becomes an explicit standard. Thus, we have expressions in common language that arise from this sort of metacognition, for example, *pig-headed*, *narrow-minded*, and *open-minded*. The next step after this is the realization that overconfidence can shut down search prematurely: "It ain't what you don't know that gets you into trouble. It's what you know for sure that just ain't so."[4]

AOT is important for politics. It would be nice if everyone adopted this sort of standard and used it as a basis of argument, in legislatures and their committees, in news sources, in public statements, as well as between individuals when they discuss politics, if they ever "discuss" it in this sense anymore. AOT is thus a moral virtue as well as a personal one.

For individuals, this standard can serve as a basis for evaluating sources. Much of what seems to be belief in partisan conspiracy theories may result from listening to sources who would not be trustworthy by the standards of AOT.

The concept of AOT has some advantages not shared by other concepts of cognitive style. It is more generally useful than measures based on the idea that more thinking is always better. It is not better when it serves simply to bolster an initial judgment by looking only for supporting reasons. The standards of AOT are consistent with the argument that it is sometimes better not to make judgments on one's own without help from trustworthy sources, who may reduce the amount of thinking that an individual needs to do in order to reach valid conclusions.

Politically, AOT is at least on its face more neutral than some other trait measures, such as measures of dogmatism or authoritarianism, which often contain what amounts to disputed political content. Such content may result from good or bad thinking, but it is not descriptive of thinking itself.

Despite the apparent political neutrality of AOT, it is still part of the "culture wars" playing out around the world. Explicit teaching of AOT in schools would surely be opposed by those with strong traditional values, who could see AOT as a back door to challenging values that ought to be accepted without question. Those who favor AOT should thus be prepared for battle in these wars.

Notes

1. Many details not described here are included in an online supplement, which was an earlier draft of this chapter: https://psyarxiv.com/g5jhp. We refer to this in the text.
2. Two other subjects were omitted for nonsense responses.

3. These questions were added after 102 subjects had answered all the other questions without them, leaving 130.
4. Attributed to Mark Twain but not found in any of his writings.

References

Ackerman, R., & Thompson, V. A. (2017). Meta-reasoning: Monitoring and control of thinking and reasoning. *Trends in Cognitive Sciences, 21*(8), 607–617. https://doi.org/10.1016/j.tics.2017.05.004

Bago, B., & De Neys, W. (2017). Fast logic?: Examining the time course assumption of dual process theory. *Cognition, 158*, 90–109. https://doi.org/10.1016/j.cognition.2016.10.014

Baron, J. (1985). *Rationality and intelligence*. Cambridge University Press.

Baron, J. (1991). Beliefs about thinking. In J. F. Voss, D. N. Perkins, & J. W. Segal (Eds.), *Informal reasoning and education* (pp. 169–186). Erlbaum.

Baron, J. (1995). Myside bias in thinking about abortion. *Thinking and Reasoning, 1*, 221–235. https://doi.org/10.1080/13546789508256909

Baron, J. (1988). *Thinking and deciding*. Cambridge University Press.

Baron, J. (2009). Belief-overkill in political judgments. *Informal Logic, 29*, 368–378. https://doi.org/10.22329/il.v29i4.2904

Baron, J. (2019). Actively open-minded thinking in politics. *Cognition, 188*, 8–18. https://doi.org/10.1016/j.cognition.2018.10.004

Baron, J., Badgio, P., & Gaskins, I. W. (1986). Cognitive style and its improvement: A normative approach. In R. J. Sternberg (Ed.), *Advances in the psychology of human intelligence* (Vol. 3, pp. 173–220). Erlbaum.

Baron, J., & High, D., II. (2019, November 15–18). *People who endorse actively open-minded thinking (AOT) are sensitive to cues indicating AOT of sources* [Poster presentation]. Society for Judgment and Decision Making, Montreal, Canada. http://www.sjdm.org/presentations/2019-Poster-Baron-Jonathan-endorse-AOT-cues.pdf

Baron, J., Scott, S., Fincher, K., & Metz, S. E. (2015). Why does the Cognitive Reflection Test (sometimes) predict utilitarian moral judgment (and other things)? *Journal of Applied Research in Memory and Cognition, 4*(3), 265–284. https://doi.org/10.1016/j.jarmac.2014.09.003

Bronstein, M. V., Pennycook, G., Bear, A., Rand, D. G., & Cannon, T. D. (2019). Belief in fake news is associated with delusionality, dogmatism, religious fundamentalism, and reduced analytic thinking. *Journal of Applied Research in Memory and Cognition, 8*(1), 108–117. https://doi.org/10.1016/j.jarmac.2018.09.005

Brownstein, A. (2003). Biased predecision processing. *Psychological Bulletin, 129*, 545–568. https://psycnet.apa.org/doi/10.1037/0033-2909.129.4.545

Bryan, W. L., & Harter, N. (1899). Studies on the telegraphic language: The acquisition of a hierarchy of habits. *Psychological Review, 6*, 345–375. https://psycnet.apa.org/doi/10.1037/h0073117

Cavalli-Sforza, L. L., Feldman, M. W., Chen, K. H., & Dornbusch, S. M. (1982). Theory and observation in cultural transmission. *Science, 218*(4567), 19–27. https://doi.org/10.1126/science.7123211

DeKay, M. L., Patino-Echeverri, D., & Fischbeck, P. S. (2009). Distortion of probability and outcome information in risky decisions. *Organizational Behavior and Human Decision Processes, 109*(1), 79–92. https://doi.org/10.1016/j.obhdp.2008.12.001

Deppe, K. D., Gonzalez, F. J., Neiman, J. L., Jacobs, C., Pahlke, J., Smith, K. B., & Hibbing, J. R. (2015). Reflective liberals and intuitive conservatives: A look at the Cognitive Reflection Test and ideology. *Judgment and Decision Making, 10*, 314–331.

Evans, J. S. B., & Stanovich, K. E. (2013). Dual-process theories of higher cognition: Advancing the debate. *Perspectives on Psychological Science, 8*(3), 223–241. https://doi.org/10.1177%2F1745691612460685

Fieldhouse, E., Green, J., Evans, G., Schmitt H., van der Eijk, C., Mellon, J., & Prosser, C. (2018). *British election study internet panel wave 14*. https://www.britishelectionstudy.com/data-object/wave-14-of-the-2014-2018-british-election-study-internet-panel/

Flavell, J. H. (1979). Metacognition and cognitive monitoring: A new area of cognitive-developmental inquiry. *American Psychologist, 34*(10), 906–911. https://psycnet.apa.org/doi/10.1037/0003-066X.34.10.906

Frederick, S. (2005). Cognitive reflection and decision making. *Journal of Economic Perspectives, 19*, 24–42. https://doi.org/10.1257/089533005775196732

Fuhrer, J., & Cova, F. (2020). "Quick and dirty": Intuitive cognitive style predicts trust in Didier Raoult and his hydroxychloroquine-based treatment against COVID-19. *Judgment and Decision Making, 15*, 889–908.

Galotti, K. M., Baron, J., & Sabini, J. (1986). Individual differences in syllogistic reasoning: Deduction rules or mental models. *Journal of Experimental Psychology: General, 115*, 16–25. https://psycnet.apa.org/doi/10.1037/0096-3445.115.1.16

Hallpike, C. R. (2004). *The evolution of moral understanding*. Prometheus Research Group.

Hart, W., Albarracín, D., Eagly, A. H., Brechan, I., Lindberg, M. J., & Merrill, L. (2009). Feeling validated versus being correct: A meta-analysis of selective exposure to information. *Psychological Bulletin, 135*, 555–588. https://psycnet.apa.org/doi/10.1037/a0015701

Jern, A., Chang, K. K., & Kemp, C. (2014). Belief polarization is not always irrational. *Psychological Review, 121*, 206–224. https://psycnet.apa.org/doi/10.1037/a0035941

Jervis, R. (1976). *Perception and misperception in international politics*. Princeton University Press.

Kagan, J., Rosman, B. L., Day, D., Albert, J., & Phillips, W. (1964). Information processing in the child: Significance of analytic and reflective attitudes. *Psychological Monographs, 78*(1), 1–37. https://psycnet.apa.org/doi/10.1037/h0093830

Kahneman, D. (2011). *Thinking, fast and slow*. Farrar, Strauss and Giroux.

Kohlberg, L. (1969). Stage and sequence: The cognitive developmental approach to socialization. In D. Goslin (Ed.), *Handbook of socialization theory and research* (pp. 347–480). Rand McNally & Company.

Kuhn, D. (1989). Children and adults as intuitive scientists. *Psychological Review, 96*, 674–689. https://psycnet.apa.org/doi/10.1037/0033-295X.96.4.674

Lord, C. G., Ross, L., & Lepper, M. R. (1979). Biased assimilation and attitude polarization: The effects of prior theories on subsequently considered evidence. *Journal of Personality and Social Psychology, 37*, 2098–2109. https://psycnet.apa.org/doi/10.1037/0022-3514.37.11.2098

Marcia, J. E. (1980). Identity in adolescence. In J. Adelson (Ed.), *Handbook of adolescent psychology* (pp. 159–187). Wiley.

Messer, S. B. (1976). Reflection-impulsivity: A review. *Psychological Bulletin, 83*(6), 1026–1052. https://psycnet.apa.org/doi/10.1037/0033-2909.83.6.1026

Meszaros, J. R., Asch, D. A., Baron, J., Hershey, J. C., Kunreuther, H., & Schwartz-Buzaglo, J. (1996). Cognitive processes and the decisions of some parents to forego pertussis vaccination for their children. *Journal of Clinical Epidemiology, 49*, 697–703. https://doi.org/10.1016/0895-4356(96)00007-8

Metz, S. E., Baelen, R. N., & Yu, A. (2020). Actively open-minded thinking in American adolescents. *Review of Education, 8*, 768–799. https://doi.org/10.1002/rev3.3232Pennycook,

G., Cheyne, J. A., Barr, N., Koehler, D. J., & Fugelsang, J. A. (2014). Cognitive style and religiosity: The role of conflict detection. *Memory & Cognition, 42*(1), 1–10. https://doi.org/10.3758/s13421-013-0340-7

Pennycook, G., Cheyne, J. A., Koehler, D. J., & Fugelsang, J. A. (2020). On the belief that beliefs should change according to evidence: Implications for conspiratorial, moral, paranormal, political, religious, and science beliefs. *Judgment and Decision Making, 15,* 476–498.

Perkins, D. (2019). Learning to reason: The influence of instruction, prompts and scaffolding, metacognitive knowledge, and general intelligence on informal reasoning about everyday social and political issues. *Judgment and Decision Making, 14*(6), 624–643.

Perry, W. G., Jr. (1971). *Forms of intellectual and ethical development in the college years: A scheme.* Holt, Rinehart & Winston.

Piazza, J., & Landy, J. F. (2013). "Lean not on your own understanding": Belief that morality is founded on divine authority and non-utilitarian moral judgments. *Judgment and Decision Making, 8,* 639–661.

Ross, R. M., Rand, D. G., & Pennycook, G. (2021). Beyond "fake news": Analytic thinking and the detection of false and hyperpartisan news headlines. *Judgment and Decision Making, 16,* 484–504.

Russo, J. E., Carlson, K. A., & Meloy, M. G. (2006). Choosing an inferior alternative. *Psychological Science, 17*(10), 899–904. https://doi.org/10.1111%2Fj.1467-9280.2006.01800.x

Shiffrin, R. M., & Schneider, W. (1977). Controlled and automatic human information processing: II. Perceptual learning, automatic attending and a general theory. *Psychological Review, 84*(2), 127–190. https://psycnet.apa.org/doi/10.1037/0033-295X.84.2.127

Sirota, M., & Juanchich, M. (2018). Effect of response format on cognitive reflection: Validating a two-and four-option multiple choice question version of the Cognitive Reflection Test. *Behavior Research Methods, 50*(6), 2511–2522. https://doi.org/10.3758/s13428-018-1029-4

Svedholm-Häkkinen, A. M., & Lindeman, M. (2017). Actively open-minded thinking: Development of a shortened scale and disentangling attitudes toward knowledge and people. *Thinking and Reasoning, 24*(1), 21–40. https://doi.org/10.1080/13546783.2017.1378723

Thompson, V. A., Prowse Turner, J. A., & Pennycook, G. (2011). Intuition, reason, and metacognition. *Cognitive Psychology, 63*(3), 107–140. https://doi.org/10.1016/j.cogpsych.2011.06.001

Toplak, M. E., West, R. F., & Stanovich, K. E. (2014). Rational thinking and cognitive sophistication: Development, cognitive abilities, and thinking dispositions. *Developmental Psychology, 50*(4), 1037–1048. https://doi.org/10.1037/a0034910

Wason, P. C., & Evans, J. St. B. T. (1975). Dual processes in reasoning? *Cognition, 3,* 141–154. https://doi.org/10.1016/0010-0277(74)90017-1

Yilmaz, O., & Saribay, S. A. (2017). The relationship between cognitive style and political orientation depends on the measures used. *Judgment and Decision Making, 12,* 140–147.

V
IDEOLOGY, AUTHORITARIANISM, AND DOGMATISM

10
Persistent Problems with the Conceptualization, Measurement, and Study of "Left-Wing Authoritarianism"

Benjamin A. Saunders and John T. Jost

> Communists in countries such as Canada and the United States will be very *un*submissive to the established authorities; they will favor free speech, the right to dissent, and so on, and thus they will be 'democrats.' In places such as the Soviet Union and Poland, however, Communists will be opposed to these things and so be highly authoritarian.
>
> —Altemeyer (1988, p. 260, emphasis in original)

One of the most influential—and notorious—books in the history of social science is *The Authoritarian Personality* by T. W. Adorno, Else Frenkel-Brunswik, Daniel Levinson, and R. Nevitt Sanford (1950). In nearly a thousand pages, the authors wielded psychodynamic theory and questionnaire and interview methods to explain why in the middle of the last century certain individuals in Western societies concurrently embraced political–economic conservatism (albeit selectively and hypocritically) and ethnocentric prejudice and, in so doing, rendered themselves susceptible to right-wing, authoritarian demagoguery. Their aim was to use social and personality psychology to explain the lure of fascism, Nazism, and other strains of right-wing extremism that took over the European continent and parts of Asia in the 20th century (Brown, 1965). Almost immediately, Edward Shils (1954) and Hans Eysenck (1954/1999) accused Adorno and colleagues of turning a blind eye to authoritarianism on the left. Ever since then, as Bob Altemeyer (1996, p. 216) noted, "everyone goes looking for left-wing authoritarians," but "no one can find them" (see also Brown, 1965; Stone & Smith, 1993). Altemeyer wondered if the authoritarian on the left was like the Loch Ness monster: "an occasional shadow, but no monster" (p. 216).

Altemeyer (1988, 1996) observed that in Western societies the authoritarian syndrome—originally defined in terms of nine characteristics that were eventually boiled down to three—was far more prevalent on the right than the left. The three characteristics were submission to powerful authorities, aggression against deviants and convenient scapegoats, and uncritical acceptance of conventional moral values. Because rightists are more accepting of hierarchical social orders and long-standing cultural and religious traditions—in comparison with leftists, who are more invested in egalitarian forms of social change (see Jost, 2021)—there is an "elective affinity" between authoritarian attitudes, as conceptualized by Adorno, Altemeyer, and others, and ideologies of the right. As Stone and Smith (1993) put it, "There may be some similarities between the extremes, but surely there are vast differences between individuals drawn to an ideology that stresses equality above all (communism) and one that stresses hierarchy and the superiority of a master race (fascism)" (p. 145).

However, this does not mean that conservative-rightists, who value tradition and hierarchy, are authoritarian by definition. It only means that certain excesses of conservative and right-wing zealotry often take authoritarian forms. This is why Adorno and colleagues (1950) distinguished between "true" conservatives who value individualism, equality of opportunity, meritocracy, patriotism, and economic competition and "pseudo-conservatives" who "support the concentration of economic power in big business" and "numerous forms of discrimination that put severe limitations on the mobility of large sections of the population" (p. 182).

Research carried out over the past few decades supports Altemeyer's (1988, 1996) observations about the link between authoritarianism and conservatism, even when the former is measured in terms of non-political principles such as childrearing values pertaining to obedience and discipline (Nilsson & Jost, 2020). Positive correlations between authoritarian psychological dispositions and conservative-rightist (as opposed to liberal-leftist) ideological preferences have been consistently observed in at least a dozen European countries (e.g., see Nilsson & Jost, 2020, p. 149). Altemeyer (1988) summarized numerous studies of citizens and politicians in Canada linking right-wing authoritarianism (RWA) to preferences that were conservative (and rightist) rather than liberal (and leftist). In the United States, authoritarianism—measured in a variety of ways, including Altemeyer's (1996) RWA scale—predicted support for every Republican presidential candidate from 1964 to 2020 (see Nilsson & Jost, 2020, p. 149).

Despite the strength and consistency of the above results, the search for the Loch Ness monster in the West goes on, seemingly unabated (Conway et al., 2018; Conway & McFarland, 2019; Costello et al., 2022; Eysenck, 1981; Rokeach, 1960; Van Hiel et al., 2006). Some even claim to have found definitive evidence that the beast exists—and in the United States, no less (Conway et al., 2018; Costello et al., 2022). The most perplexing aspect of their argument is that left-wing authoritarianism (LWA) is readily observable not merely in left-wing extremists—such as communists (or those who are nostalgic about communism in eastern Europe; see De Regt et al., 2011; Todosijević & Enyedi, 2008), which exist only in trifling numbers in the United States—but among liberals, who purport to endorse democratic ideals such as freedom, tolerance, and openness to diverse opinions (see also Alto et al., 2022; Feldman et al., 2021; Todosijević & Enyedi, 2008). Thus, one persistent problem is that researchers hunting for left-wing authoritarians have been strikingly inattentive to the kinds of societal–contextual factors that Altemeyer (1988) emphasized in the passage we have chosen for the epigram of this chapter.

For example, Conway and colleagues (2021, p. 423) ask, "Are political liberals sometimes subject to reliance on simple authority, psychological rigidity, and aggressive defense of the status quo in the same way as political conservatives?" Decades of research clearly indicate that the answer to this question is no (see Altemeyer, 1988, 1996; Jost, 2021, for extensive reviews). Nevertheless, these and other authors imply that liberals in the United States—and not just left-wing extremists in other regions of the world—are as prone to authoritarianism as are conservative-rightists. Their claims, which we dispute in this chapter, have reached a large audience, having been publicized in, among other places, *The Atlantic*, an ostensibly liberal magazine with nearly a million paid subscribers (Satel, 2021). Perhaps the most grotesque extension of this general line of reasoning is to be found in a book by Jonah Goldberg (2009) that preposterously equates liberalism—as exemplified by Franklin and Theodore Roosevelt, Woodrow Wilson, and Hillary Clinton, among others—with fascism.

In the remainder of this chapter, we discuss other persistent problems plaguing the conceptualization, measurement, and empirical investigation of LWA. In so doing, we focus on shortcomings of the three measurement tools ostensibly used to identify the Loch Ness monster, namely instruments developed by Van Hiel et al. (2006), Conway et al. (2018), and Costello et al. (2022). In some cases, we believe, these scales may measure liberal or left-leaning attitudes, but these attitudes have little or no connection to authoritarianism per se, as it has been conceptualized by philosophers and social scientists in terms of cognitive rigidity, social conformity, anti-democratic sentiment, obedience to authoritarian leaders, and prejudice against "deviant" groups in society (e.g., Adorno et al., 1950; Altemeyer, 1996, 1998; Brown, 1965; Duckitt et al., 2010; Dunwoody & Funke, 2016; Feldman et al., 2021; Hetherington & Weiler, 2009; Napier & Jost, 2008; Stone & Smith, 1993). As we will see, some accounts of LWA emphasize violent tendencies borne of rebelliousness (e.g., Costello et al., 2022), which has typically been understood as the opposite of authoritarianism (e.g., Kohn, 1972; Kreml, 1977). In other cases, scales appear to tap into genuinely authoritarian dispositions, but they have little or no connection to liberalism (e.g., Van Hiel et al., 2006). In strong contrast to the triumphalism of those who celebrate having caught the elusive Loch Ness monster (Conway et al., 2018; Costello et al., 2022), the current state of research instead reminds us of the infamous "surgeon's photograph," which surfaced in 1934, ostensibly providing visual proof of Nessie's existence. Later, however, the picture was revealed to have merely captured a piece of plastic affixed to a toy submarine (Lyons, 2000).

Research by Van Hiel and Colleagues (2006)

Alain Van Hiel and colleagues (2006) began by revisiting Altemeyer's (1996) efforts to develop an LWA scale that would mirror the tripartite conceptualization of RWA in terms of authoritarian aggression, authoritarian submission, and conventionalism. Altemeyer tried to recast each of these three themes to make them at least potentially attractive to leftists. Specifically, Altemeyer conceptualized LWA in terms of generalized aggression *against established authorities*, submission to authorities *dedicated to overthrowing the established authorities*, and conformity to norms enforced by the *leaders of a revolutionary movement*. It is noteworthy that none of these elements were likely to resonate with liberals (Feldman et al., 2021), although they might have resonated with revolutionary leftists (Alto et al., 2022). In any case, Altemeyer failed to identify a single left-wing authoritarian who scored 6 or above on a 9-point scale in several Canadian samples totaling 2554 respondents. This is what prompted Altemeyer (1996, p. 216) to invoke the Loch Ness monster: "an occasional shadow, but no monster?"

Van Hiel et al. (2006) picked up where Altemeyer (1996) left off, focusing on obedience to left-wing leaders and support for political violence. They selected and updated several of Altemeyer's LWA items. The result was an 8-item scale that dropped the concept of conventionalism altogether and homed in on two rather than three factors, namely (1) left-wing aggression (with sample items such as "I agree with the basic idea of communism of overthrowing the

Establishment—with or without violence—and giving its wealth to the poor" and "It would be wrong to solve our problems by acts of violence against the conservative Establishment" [reverse-scored]) and (2) left-wing submission (with sample items such as "A revolutionary movement is justified in demanding obedience and conformity of its members" and "A left-wing party is not justified in demanding too much conformity and obedience, even after a revolution" [reverse-scored]).

The researchers first administered this scale to two samples of Flemish voters in Belgium and obtained results that were very similar to what Altemeyer (1996) had observed in Canada. In Study 1, only 4% of the sample (eight people) scored (slightly) above the scale midpoint. In Study 2, only 3.4% (nine people) scored (again, slightly) above the midpoint. It is important to point out that in these two studies—and in the earlier studies by Altemeyer (1996)—LWA scores were positively rather than negatively correlated with RWA scores (with rs ranging from .11 to .22), raising serious questions about whether these items tapped into left-leaning (as opposed to right-leaning) sentiments at all.

Van Hiel et al. (2006) also contacted a small sample of political activists, comprised of 20 communists, 21 anarchists, 16 members of traditional (moderate) political parties, and 11 far-right (fascist, neo-Nazi) extremists in Belgium. Whereas none of the moderates or fascists scored above the midpoint on the LWA scale, 65% of the communists did (and 45% of them [nine people] scored between 4 and 5 [the maximum] on the scale). This suggests that something resembling LWA was observable in a very small minority of Europeans who identified as extreme activists. However, there is another finding which suggests that scores on Van Hiel et al.'s measure, at least in this highly unrepresentative sample, were driven more by leftism than by authoritarianism. In the sample of anarchists, 28.6% (six people) scored above the scale midpoint, although—as Van Hiel et al. pointed out—they were clearly anti-authoritarian in outlook. The authors wrote, "Anarchists . . . are expected to fight any regime as long as they consider it to be authoritarian, even if this regime could be classified as left-wing. They can therefore only be classified as 'left-wing aggressive' but not as left-wing authoritarians" (p. 774).

To pursue these matters further, we administered Van Hiel et al.'s (2006) LWA scale along with other measures to two independent samples, which were combined and then split on a random basis into two halves so that we could conduct both exploratory (n = 449) and confirmatory (n = 448) analyses.[1] One sample was recruited through Amazon's Mechanical Turk platform (N = 514). The gender composition of the sample was 46.1% women, 51.2% men, 0.4% other, and 1.9% declining to respond. The ethnic composition was 69.6% White, 14.4% Black, 7.9% Asian, 3.1% Native American, 5.1% Hispanic or Latino, 1.6% other, and 2.3% declining to respond. The mean age was 35.81 ($SD = 12.43$). The other sample consisted of 383 undergraduate students at New York University. The gender composition of the sample was 78.9% women, 20.4% men, 0.2% other, and 1.1% declining to respond. The ethnic composition of the sample was 33.5% White, 8.8% Black, 44.8% Asian, 1.1% Native American, 1.6% Arab or Middle Eastern, 14.7% Hispanic or Latino, 4.2% other, and 1.6% declining to respond. The mean age was 19.32 ($SD = 1.58$).

We observed that the two factors specified by Van Hiel et al. (2006), left-wing aggression and left-wing submission, were significantly intercorrelated at .59 in the exploratory sample (Sample 1) and .63 in the confirmatory sample (Sample 2). However, there were very few high scorers in absolute terms (see Table S1 in the Online Supplement at https://osf.io/y7rbq/). Only 9%–14% of respondents scored above the scale midpoint. Moreover, only 1% of respondents scored above 5 on a 7-point scale on either the total scale or the left-wing submission subscale. Only 3% scored above 5 out of 7 on the left-wing aggression subscale.

An even bigger problem is that scores on the Van Hiel-LWA scale and its two subscales failed to correlate with other political and psychological variables that one would expect if they were tapping into an orientation that was both liberal-leftist and authoritarian (i.e., dogmatic, rigid, and intolerant of ambiguity). Total LWA scores in Sample 1 were uncorrelated with political orientation (i.e., self-identified liberalism–conservatism), and in Sample 2 they were significantly and positively correlated with *conservatism*—rather than liberalism (see Table 10.1). In both samples, total "LWA" scores were significantly and positively correlated with RWA scores (with rs ranging from .19 to .35, $p < .001$) as well as the endorsement of authoritarian childrearing values (with rs ranging from .14 [$p = .003$] to .27 [$p < .001$]). Total LWA scores were also positively correlated with dogmatism ($.26 \leq r \leq .33, p < .001$) and intolerance of ambiguity ($.19 \leq r \leq .23, p < .001$) and negatively correlated with the need for order (rs = $-.12, .019 \leq p \leq .021$).

When we inspected individual items, we found in Sample 1 that only two of the eight items comprising the Van Hiel-LWA scale were significantly correlated with self-identified liberalism: "I agree with the basic idea of communism of overthrowing the Establishment—with or without violence—and giving its wealth to the poor" ($r = -.17, p < .001$) and "The conservative Establishment has so much power and is so unfair that we have to submit to the leaders and rules of a revolutionary movement to destroy them" ($r = -.10, p = .034$). In Sample 2, however, the former item was uncorrelated with

Problems with "Left-Wing Authoritarianism" 191

Table 10.1 Bivariate Correlations Between Scores on Van Hiel et al.'s (2006) LWA Scale and Subscales and Other Political and Psychological Measures

	Sample 1 (exploratory) $N = 449$			Sample 2 (confirmatory) $N = 448$		
	V-LWA (Total)	V-LWA (Agg)	V-LWA (Sub)	V-LWA (Total)	V-LWA (Agg)	V-LWA (Sub)
Political conservatism (symbolic ideology)	−.04	−.10*	.01	.14**	.06	.20***
Authoritarian childrearing values	.14*	.08	.18***	.27***	.17***	.31***
Dogmatism	.26***	.19***	.27***	.33***	.21***	.39***
Intolerance of ambiguity	.19***	.09	.25***	.23***	.11*	.30***
Need for order	−.12*	−.19***	−.02	−.12*	−.18***	−.03
Altemeyer-LWA	.77***	.63***	.75***	.78***	.68***	.75***
Conway-LWA	.34***	.33***	.27***	.17***	.20***	.10*
RWA	.19***	.07	.25***	.35***	.20**	.42***

Note. * $p < .05$. ** $p < .01$. *** $p < .001$. Agg = aggression; LWA = left-wing authoritarianism; RWA = right-wing authoritarianism; Sub = submission; V-LWA = Van Hiel-LWA.

liberalism–conservatism ($r = -.01, p = .823$), and the latter item was correlated with conservatism ($r = .11, p = .023$). None of the other items were significantly correlated with political orientation in Sample 1 (see Table S2a and b).

In Sample 2, liberals were more likely to endorse two of the con-trait items: "Even a revolutionary left-wing movement that fights against the totally unjust right-wing system does not have the right to tell its members how to think and act" ($r = -.18, p < .001$) and "Even though the conservative establishment who controls our country is repressive and unfair, society should only be reformed through nonviolent means") also correlates negatively with ideology ($r = -.13, p = .006$). That is, conservatives were more likely than liberals to disagree with these two reverse-coded items, and they were also more likely to endorse one of the pro-trait items: "A revolutionary movement is justified in demanding obedience and conformity of its members" ($r = .24, p < .001$). Thus, most of the Van Hiel-LWA items were unrelated to political orientation, and there was scant evidence that any of them were linked to self-identified liberalism. On the contrary, in some cases, they were linked to self-identified conservatism.

All of this suggests that Van Hiel et al.'s LWA scale is measuring authoritarianism but not leftism, and certainly not liberalism. It is true that scores on this measure correlated positively with other ostensibly LWA scales by Altemeyer (1996) and Conway et al. (2018), but this is probably because of general authoritarianism, not leftism, given that scores on the Van Hiel scale were positively correlated with RWA and, in one of our two samples, conservative self-identification. The same is true of Van Hiel et al.'s submission subscale, which was significantly correlated with the endorsement of authoritarian childrearing values and other authoritarian indicators, including RWA, except for the need for order. In Sample 1 scores on the submission subscale were uncorrelated with political orientation, and in Sample 2 they were correlated with conservative—not liberal—self-identification. The aggression subscale was correlated with liberal self-identification in Sample 1 but not Sample 2. In Sample 2 the aggression subscale was positively correlated with RWA ($r = .20$, $p < .001$) and other indicators of authoritarianism, except for the need for order. Our conclusion, based on these data, is that the Van Hiel-LWA scale may tap into certain authoritarian inclinations, but it does not tap into uniquely leftist concerns, and certainly not liberal attitudes in US samples.

Research by Conway and Colleagues (2018)

The admitted failure of Van Hiel and colleagues (2006) to identify left-wing authoritarians in the general population did not deter Conway and colleagues (2018) from trying again. However, it is very far from clear that they captured the Loch Ness monster, as they announced triumphantly. Conway et al.—following Duckitt et al. (2010) and Dunwoody and Funke (2016), among others—criticized Altemeyer (1998) for writing RWA items that confounded authoritarian inclinations with conservative-rightist content (p. 1051). But, by taking Altemeyer's scale as their starting point and then adding more content, Conway and colleagues made the problem worse. They intentionally injected liberal and leftist content into their LWA scale, and in some cases, they turned double-barreled items into triple-barreled items (see also Saunders et al., 2020).

Let us take a few examples. Altemeyer's (1998) RWA scale includes the following item: "Our country desperately needs a mighty leader who will do what has to be done to destroy the radical new ways and sinfulness that are ruining us." Conway and colleagues converted this to an LWA item as follows: "Our country desperately needs a mighty and liberal leader who will do what has to be done to destroy the radical traditional ways of doing things that are ruining us". There are at least two significant problems with the latter item, even in comparison with the former. First, the phrase *radical traditional* is oxymoronic: How could anyone be radical and, at the same time, traditional? Second, by inserting the word *liberal* Conway et al. injected blatantly political content, despite the fact that Altemeyer's original item made no reference to a "conservative" leader. It is hardly surprising that liberals would be more likely than conservatives to endorse the first barrel of this double-barreled item: "Our country desperately needs a mighty and liberal leader." Furthermore, eight of the 20 items on Conway et al.'s LWA scale make explicit mention of "Christians" or "Christian fundamentalists," and four others mention "God," "prayer," or "religion." A careful inspection of the Conway-LWA scale leads to the troubling conclusion that it may be nothing more than a referendum on how respondents feel about Christian fundamentalists.

Here is another, related conceptual problem. Altemeyer (1998) wrote the following RWA item: "It is always better to trust the judgment of the proper authorities in government and religion than to listen to the noisy rabble-rousers in our society who are trying to create doubt in people's minds." Conway et al. (2018) converted this item to the following: "It's always better to trust the judgment of the proper authorities in science with respect to issues like global warming and evolution than to listen to the noisy rabble-rousers in our society who are trying to create doubts in people's minds." Again, Conway and colleagues have deliberately injected specific attitudinal contents about global warming and evolution—two major issues on which liberals and conservatives (as groups) are well known to disagree. It is hardly surprising that liberals would be more likely than conservatives to trust scientists about issues of global warming and evolution, and it is far from clear that scientists are the kinds of "established authorities" that inspire mindless submission (see also Azevedo & Jost, 2021). Even worse, one could argue that this item is quadruple-barreled, insofar as it confounds (1) trust in science, (2) attitudes about global warming, (3) attitudes about evolution, and (4) rejection of "rabble-rousers" (who, in this context, are presumably taken to be skeptics about global warming and/or evolution).

We had serious doubts about what Conway et al.'s (2018) LWA scale was measuring, so we conducted our own factor analyses in R (Kabacoff, 2021; see R Foundation for Statistical Computing, 2020) using the two exploratory and confirmatory data sets described above. (Conway et al. treated the scale as unidimensional and in a footnote mentioned only that "exploratory factor analyses ... revealed similar structures across both the RWA and LWA scale", p. 1055). We initially obtained a four-factor solution, with each factor having eigenvalues greater than their simulated eigenvalues; we used the Kaiser-Guttman criterion and retained only the two factors with eigenvalues greater than 1. The ensuing exploratory factor analysis extracted two factors using ML extraction and oblimin rotation, and this solution accounted for 43% of the variance in item responses, $\chi^2 (151) = 617.10$, $p < .001$, demonstrating adequate simple structure with minimal cross-loadings between factors. Accordingly, we retained the two-factor solution for interpretation.

Inspection of the items revealed that the first factor captured a pro-trait orientation, that is, characteristics that Conway et al. (2018) associated with LWA, that is, the holding of liberal, progressive, and pro-science attitudes and opinions that were suspicious of religion and tradition. The second factor captured a con-trait orientation, that is, the rejection of the above attitudinal positions. It is quite common in psychometrics for pro-trait and con-trait orientations to load onto separate factors, but in this case the pro-trait and con-trait subscores were very weakly correlated in our exploratory sample ($r = -.14$, prior to reverse-scoring the con-trait items) and completely uncorrelated in our confirmatory sample ($r = .02$). Considering these results, we believe that the Conway-LWA scale should only be used and interpreted in terms of the two independent, possibly orthogonal factors (or subscales), which measure whether people like or dislike Christian fundamentalists (compared to being indifferent to them).

More respondents scored highly on the con-trait items (prior to reverse-scoring) than the pro-trait items, which means that more individuals in our studies reported liking than disliking Christian fundamentalists (see Table S3 in the Online Supplement). For the con-trait items, 50%–52% of the respondents scored above the scale midpoint, and 19%–20% of the sample strongly agreed with items such as this: "Christian Fundamentalists and others who have rebelled against the established sciences are no doubt every bit as good and virtuous as those who agree with the best scientific minds." For the pro-trait items, 38%–42% scored above the scale midpoint, but only 14%–16% averaged more than 5 on the 7-point scale. Thus, only 15% in the two samples strongly agreed with items such as this one: "It's always better to trust the judgment of the proper authorities in science with respect to issues like global warming and evolution than to listen to the noisy rabble-rousers in our society who are trying to create doubts in people's minds."

Correlations between scores on the two Conway-LWA subscales and other variables are shown in Table 10.2. The results show, quite clearly, that the people who endorsed the con-trait items (e.g., respondents who agreed with items like "Christian Fundamentalists should be praised for being brave enough to defy the current societal and legal norms") were, in fact, more rigid, dogmatic, and authoritarian than the people who endorsed the pro-trait items (e.g., "This country would work a lot better if certain groups of Christian troublemakers would just shut up and accept their group's proper place in society").[2] In both samples, endorsement of con-trait items was positively associated with dogmatism ($rs = .22–.24$), intolerance of ambiguity ($rs = .19–.28$),

Table 10.2 Bivariate Correlations Between Scores on Conway et al.'s (2018) LWA Scale and Subscales and Other Political and Psychological Measures

	Sample 1 (exploratory) N = 449			Sample 2 (confirmatory) N = 448		
	CN-LWA (Total)	F1 (Pro Trait)	F2 (Con Trait)	CN-LWA (total)	F1 (Pro Trait)	F2 (Con Trait)
Political conservatism (symbolic ideology)	–.49***	–.27***	.51***	–.40***	–.16**	.42***
Authoritarian child-rearing values	–.19***	.04	.35***	–.20***	.12*	.39***
Dogmatism	–.11*	.06	.22***	–.05	.17***	.24***
Intolerance of ambiguity	–.04	.10*	.19***	–.16**	.05	.28***
Need for order	–.09†	–.05	.08†	–.19***	–.12*	.16**
Altemeyer-LWA	.42***	.57***	–.07	.34***	.53***	.07
Van Hiel-LWA	.34***	.49***	–.03	.17***	.40***	.17***
RWA	–.34***	–.15*	.39***	–.32***	–.03	.44***

Note. †p < .10. *p < .05. **p < .01. ***p < .001. CN-LWA = Conway-LWA; LWA = left-wing authoritarianism, RWA = right-wing authoritarianism. The con-trait items are not reverse-scored in the columns marked F2, but they are reverse-scored when used in calculating total LWA scores.

authoritarian childrearing values (rs = .35–.39), and RWA scores (rs = .39–.44). It was also strongly correlated with self-identified political conservatism (rs = .42–.51; all correlations were statistically significant, p < .001). Total Conway-LWA scores were significantly and negatively correlated with intolerance of ambiguity, need for order, and authoritarian childrearing values in one or both of our samples.

What about people who endorsed the pro-trait items devised by Conway et al. (2018)? They were indeed fairly liberal, with correlations ranging from –.16 (p = .001) to –.27 (p < .001). They scored significantly lower on the RWA scale in the exploratory sample (r = –.15, p = .002) but not the confirmatory sample (r = –.03, p = .518). They also scored higher on the LWA scales developed by Altemeyer (1996) and Van Hiel et al. (2006), but this is probably because they endorsed leftist attitudinal content, not because they were especially authoritarian. The endorsement of pro-trait items was unrelated to authoritarian childrearing in Sample 1 (r = .04, p = .366) and positively correlated with it in Sample 2 (r = .12, p = .019). Those who endorsed the pro-trait items were also less likely to endorse authoritarian childrearing values than people who endorsed the con-trait items. In the confirmatory sample, for instance, the difference between .12 and .39 was highly significant, $Z = 4.34$, $p < .001$. Compared to those who endorsed the con-trait items, those who endorsed the pro-trait items were less tolerant of ambiguity in Sample 1 ($r = .10, p = .033$) but not in Sample 2 ($r = .05, p = .340$); they were lower on the need for order in one sample ($r = -.12, p = .021$) but not the other ($r = -.05, p = .296$). They were more dogmatic in one sample ($r = .17, p < .001$) but not the other ($r = .06, p = .236$).

Our conclusion is straightforward: The scale by Conway et al. (2018), who claimed to have found the Loch Ness monster, may capture liberal-leftist attitudes; but there is no evidence that it captures anything resembling authoritarianism. On the contrary, in our two samples, people who endorsed their anti-LWA items were more authoritarian, dogmatic, and intolerant of ambiguity than people who endorsed the pro-LWA items. This is precisely the opposite of Conway and colleagues' own substantive conclusion.

Research by Costello and Colleagues (2022)

The most ambitious attempt yet to capture LWA comes from Costello et al. (2022), whose favorite example is The Weathermen, a group of underground leftists who operated from 1969 to 1977 and protested aggressively against the Vietnam War and other policies of the American establishment. However, as Badaan and Jost (2020) noted, the parallels between The Weathermen and right-wing authoritarians are few and far between:

> In contrast to the hundreds killed by right-wing extremists in the US in recent years, the Weathermen largely targeted government property and would often warn people to leave the premises before their attacks. They are known to be responsible for only three deaths—and all of them were members of the group who died accidentally while making bombs. (p. 236)

On a single day, January 6, 2021, right-wing supporters of President Donald Trump staged an attack on the US Capitol building, leading to the eventual deaths of nine people, three times as many people as the Weathermen killed in 9 years of operation.

Costello et al. (2022) cite approvingly the research program by Conway et al. (2018), concluding that the latter "found extensive support from a large, multi-faceted construct validational investigation" and provided "strong evidence that elements of authoritarianism are present in ideologically left-wing US samples" (p. 138). As noted above, this is not at all what our investigation suggests. Instead, Conway and colleagues appear to have largely measured differences between people who support and those who reject the religious right (especially "Christian fundamentalists"). Our results show that it is the former—not the latter—group that exhibits more authoritarian characteristics.

Costello and colleagues (2022) developed an entirely new LWA scale to identify left-wing extremists (not liberals) who were "generally dogmatic, hostile toward the present hierarchy, prejudiced and punitive toward perceived enemies, disposed toward moral absolutism, and tolerant of political violence" (p. 139). After several iterations with a multitude of items, the researchers eventually arrived at a three-factor scale with the following subscales: (1) anti-hierarchical aggression (AHA), which includes items such as "When the tables are turned on the oppressors at the top of society, I will enjoy watching them suffer the violence that they have inflicted on so many others"; (2) anti-conventionalism (AC), which includes items such as "It is important that we destroy the West's nationalist, imperialist values"; and (3) top-down censorship (TDC), which includes items such as "I am in favor of allowing the government to shut down right-wing internet sites and blogs that promote nutty, hateful positions."

These items may tap into left-wing extremism and even aggression, but the first two factors, at least, have nothing to do with authoritarianism per se. On the contrary, the first factor would be more aptly characterized as rebelliousness, which at one time was recognized by social psychologists to be the opposite of authoritarianism (e.g., Kohn, 1972; Kreml, 1977). The first factor also includes items that seem sadistic—or perhaps diagnostic of psychopathy rather than any particular ideological commitment. The second factor appears to capture strong antipathy toward conservatives and right-wing political actors and support for progressive and radical social movements. It, too, seems to capture a spirit of rebelliousness rather than obedience to authority. The third factor does mention "authorities" such as the government and universities in at least a few of the items, and other items on this factor appear to measure support for censorship (vs. free speech). Other items on this factor may have something to do with "political correctness," but they have little or nothing to do with authoritarianism per se: "I should have the right not to be exposed to offensive views" and "Colleges and universities that permit speakers with intolerant views should be publicly condemned."

Many of the Costello-LWA items are very strongly worded, such as these two: "Most rich Wall Street executives deserve to be thrown in prison" and "The rich should be stripped of their belongings and status." Because of the extremity of these opinions, it is important to know how much of the general population actually endorses them. Only one of Costello et al.'s studies used a nationally representative sample (Study 6), so we focused on this study. We thank Thomas Costello for making this data set publicly available on the Open Science Framework (OSF) website, enabling us to conduct additional analyses.

One troubling observation we made upon conducting our own analyses is that the exclusion criteria used by Costello and colleagues (2022) resulted in the disproportionate removal of those Republican respondents who endorsed the most extreme statements. Costello et al. wrote in footnote 16 in their article that,

> We aired [sic] on the side of caution, such that participants who failed any one of our three attention checks were screened out. We adopted this strict approach to mitigate the possibility that our analyses of low base-rate outcomes, such as participation in political violence, were not distorted as a result of errant responding. (p. 158)

The first two attention check items were as follows: (1) "A 22-year-old boy is older than a 12-year-old boy" and (2) "Balls are round."[3] Responses were provided on a continuous scale ranging from 1 (*Strongly disagree*) to 7 (*Strongly agree*), but we have been unable to determine what cutoff point Costello and colleagues used. A third attention check item asked participants to "Write a sentence that you think has probably never been said before." According to Costello (personal communication), "If a participant left the answer blank, wrote gibberish, failed to produce an actual sentence, or wrote a sentence that was not at all unusual, that participant was excluded. This was done to identify both 'bots' and careless responding." Information about how the third attention check item was coded was not provided in the OSF materials, so we were unable to determine how it was used to screen participants.

The application of these exclusion criteria resulted in the removal of 26% of the total number of Republican respondents, compared with 14% of the Democratic respondents (see Table S4 in the Online Supplement). We worried that high rates of exclusion—and a partisan asymmetry in rates of exclusion—may have affected the substantive conclusions drawn by Costello and colleagues (2022). Therefore, we conducted additional analyses on their full sample (unscreened). When all Republican respondents were included in the analyses, we found that in many cases they endorsed the so-called LWA items as enthusiastically as Democratic respondents. In Table S5, for instance, we see that 2.9% of Republicans and 3.0% of Democrats strongly agreed that "Certain elements in our society must be made to pay for the violence of their ancestors" and that 3.3% of Republicans and 3.4% of Democrats strongly agreed that "Political violence can be constructive when it serves the cause of social justice." On two of the items, we found that in the unscreened sample Republicans were more likely than Democrats to endorse them. Whereas 2.6% of Democrats strongly agreed that "America would be much better off if all of the rich people were at the bottom of the social ladder," 3.3% of Republicans felt this way. Likewise, only 2.2% of Democrats strongly agreed that "Rich people should be forced to give up virtually all of their wealth," as compared with 4.1% of Republicans.

These findings call into question the assumption made by Costello et al. (2022) that respondents who agreed with their items were exclusively or overwhelmingly leftist. On many of the more strongly worded items, the differences between Democrats and Republicans were very small; and, in some cases, Republican respondents were as likely or even more likely to endorse them, in comparison with Democratic respondents. It also appears that for most of the items listed in Table S5 fewer than 5% of respondents—whether Democrats or Republicans—enthusiastically endorsed them.

For other of Costello et al.'s (2022) items, leftists did agree more strongly with them than rightists. In a sample of roughly 1000 respondents from their Study 6 data set, we observed strong negative correlations between scores on the AC subscale and social ($r = -.60$), economic ($r = -.60$), and political ($r = -.65$) conservatism. For the other two factors, the correlations with political orientation were quite a bit lower but still statistically significant ($p < .001$). Correlations between AHA subscale scores ranged from $-.27$ for social conservatism and $-.28$ for political conservatism to $-.36$ for economic conservatism. Correlations between the TDC subscale scores ranged from $-.10$ for social conservatism and $-.20$ for political conservatism to $-.30$ for economic conservatism. Unfortunately, it seems that there were no non-political measures of authoritarian dispositions (such as intolerance of ambiguity or childrearing values) administered in this study (although there were measures of support for political violence). This means that the correlations between political orientation and LWA scores could be attributable to the fact that the items contained an abundance of attitudinal referents that were politically loaded, such as *rich people*; *Wall Street executives*; *Republican politicians*; *far-left leaders*; *political conservatives*; *radical and progressive moral values*; *Bible camps*; *Fox News, right-wing talk radio*; *sexist, homophobic, or racist views*; and *neo-Nazis*. Given that very few respondents overall endorsed the most strongly worded items (see Table S5), it is quite plausible that people on the left simply expressed more liking for "far-left leaders" and "radical and progressive moral values" and more disliking of *rich people*; *Wall Street executives; Republican politicians; political conservatives; Bible camps; Fox news, right-wing talk radio; sexist, homophobic, or racist views;* and *neo-Nazis* compared to those on the right. This would hardly be surprising, and it is a far cry from demonstrating that the United States has a significant problem with left-wing extremism—let alone authoritarianism (rather than, say, rebelliousness)—that mirrors the problem on the right, which has been documented by, among others, the FBI, the Anti-Defamation League, the Southern Poverty Law Center, and researchers using the Profiles of Individual Radicalization in the United States and Global Terrorism databases (see Badaan & Jost, 2020; Haltiwanger, 2019; Jasko et al., 2022; Morlin, 2018).

Is the "Search" for Liberal-Leftist Authoritarianism Misguided?

We believe that recent attempts to document LWA—especially among self-identified liberals, as opposed to left-wing extremists—are deeply misguided. This is because, as Todosijević and Enyedi (2008) put it, "liberal orientation and center-left identification constitute the political counter-pole of authoritarianism" (p. 767). We have seen that—in their eagerness to paint a symmetrical picture of left and right—some scholars, including Costello et al. (2022), have greatly distorted the concept of authoritarianism, sometimes transforming it into the very opposite of authoritarianism, namely rebelliousness. Furthermore, the practice of "both-sideology," which—on our view—draws false equivalences between leftists and rightists, obscures many important ideological differences, including the fact that over a 70-year period (1948–2018) left-wingers in the United States had 68% lower odds of engaging in political violence in comparison with right-wingers, whose rates of political violence were equivalent to those of Islamist extremists (Jasko et al., 2022).

From our perspective, there is an even bigger, more fundamental problem with the entire research literature on LWA to date. The question of whether some subset of individuals, however small, on the liberal left can be found—after intensive searching—to display certain authoritarian traits is the wrong question altogether. A better question, it seems to us, is whether there is an "elective affinity" (or a mutual attraction) between liberal-leftist belief systems and authoritarian, that is, anti-democratic, psychological tendencies associated with cognitive rigidity, social conformity, obedience to authority, and prejudice against minority groups in society. We do know that such an affinity exists between conservative-rightist ideologies and these authoritarian characteristics (Jost, 2021; Nilsson & Jost, 2020). But is there a way in which faithful adherence to liberal-leftist ideology similarly reflects and perpetuates these same sorts of authoritarian responses? We think not. It makes more sense to conclude that liberal-leftists who embrace rigid, submissive, antidemocratic ways of thinking are betraying their ideology rather than embracing it more fervently (see also Jost et al., 2022).

Thus, it is certainly possible for liberal-Democratic voters in the United States to exhibit authoritarian tendencies. But what does this mean? Does it mean that their liberal-Democratic leanings are causally linked to their authoritarian inclinations? No, the opposite is probably closer to the truth: Their commitment to the ostensibly liberal principles of the Democratic Party presumably attenuates—rather than exacerbates—whatever authoritarian prejudices they may harbor. It follows from this line of thinking that more authoritarian Democratic voters would be at greater risk than less authoritarian Democratic voters of being swayed by conservative Republican political elites, to the extent that there is an elective affinity (or mutual attraction) between authoritarian dispositions and conservative-rightist (vs. liberal-leftist) ideology.[4]

A much more extreme example of this general phenomenon was observed by Erich Fromm (1980/1984) in a landmark study conducted in Germany in 1929.

> For many adherents of left-wing parties there was a far-reaching accord between personality and party programme. These people wanted freedom, equality and happiness for all; they hated war and sympathized with the oppressed. Their convictions and commitment were passionate and strong. Others showed a comparable attitude but their emotional commitment was weaker; their main emotional interests were concentrated on family, work, hobbies, or personal goals. They had never hesitated in their political support of left-wing parties, but the strength of their convictions was ultimately weaker. . . . Finally, there was a third type, whose political convictions—though strong enough—were not reliable. These people were filled with hate and anger against everyone who had money and who appeared to enjoy life. That part of the socialist platform which aimed at the overthrow of the propertied class strongly appealed to them. On the other hand, items such as freedom and equality had not the slightest attraction for them, since they willingly obeyed every powerful authority they admired; they liked to control others, in so far as they had the power to do so. Their unreliability finally came into the open at the point when a programme such as that of the National Socialists was offered to them. This programme not only corresponded with the feelings which had made the Socialist programme attractive but also appealed to

that side of their nature which Socialism had not satisfied or had unconsciously opposed. In such cases they were transformed from unreliable leftists into convinced National Socialists. (p. 43)

Thus, according to Fromm, some supporters of leftist parties (the "third type") did exhibit authoritarian characteristics, but this led them to abandon their leftist commitments as soon as RWA ascended in Germany.

It is also important to recall that although Fromm (1980/1984) noted that some left-wing voters exhibited authoritarian inclinations, he consistently observed ideological asymmetries in authoritarian tendencies, even when comparing left-wing extremists (such as communists and revolutionary socialists) to political conservatives and right-wing extremists (such as Nazis). As shown in Table 10.3, conservatives and Nazis were much more likely than communists and left socialists to oppose women's independence, favor punishment for abortion, and believe that corporal punishment was necessary for bringing up children. Rightists were also more likely than leftists to declare that Jews were responsible for inflation, "the individual has only himself to blame for his own fate," and that wars cannot be prevented. Thus, the empirical evidence that an elective affinity exists between authoritarianism and conservative, right-wing ideological preferences—and that no comparable affinity exists between authoritarianism and several strands of left-wing socialism—goes back nearly a century (see also Altemeyer, 1988).

Conclusion

When Jordan Peterson resigned his tenured faculty position at the University of Toronto in 2022, he cited several ideologically motivated complaints; one was that social psychology was "so corrupt that it denied the existence of left-wing authoritarianism for six decades after World War II" (Peterson, 2022). This, like many of his other conspiratorial complaints about supporters of diversity and inclusion, was false. On the contrary, social psychologists have searched again and again for LWA, with precious little to show for it, at least in North America and western Europe (e.g., Altemeyer, 1988, 1996; Conway et al., 2018; Costello et al., 2022; Van Hiel et al., 2006). As noted earlier in this chapter, when authoritarianism is measured in a non-political way—as in terms of childrearing values—there is overwhelming evidence of ideological asymmetry, even as far back as 1929 (see Fromm, 1980/1984). Authoritarianism is positively correlated with conservative, rightist political preferences—and negatively correlated with liberal, leftist preferences—not

Table 10.3 Percentage of Left-Wing and Right-Wing Voters Who Endorsed Authoritarianism Items in Erich Fromm's Study of German Public Opinion in 1929

Item	Left-wing parties			Right-wing parties	
	Communists	Left Socialists	Social Democrats	Conservatives	Nazis
Do you think it is right for women to go out to work? (Pct. answering "no")	23%	5%	24%	53%	65%
Do you think it is right for married women to go out to work? (Pct. answering "no")	51%	51%	71%	100%	89%
Do you like short hair in women? (Pct. answering "no")	3%	2%	8%	37%	29%
What do you think about punishment for abortion? (Pct. "for" it)	1%	0%	3%	26%	30%
Do you think one can bring up children entirely without corporal punishment? (Pct. answering "no")	15%	6%	19%	42%	39%
The individual has only himself to blame for his own fate. (Pct. answering "yes")	22%	14%	27%	34%	59%
Jews are responsible for inflation. (Pct. agreeing)	0%	0%	1%	8%	25%
Wars cannot be prevented. (Pct. agreeing)	3%	2%	3%	15%	47%

Note: "Conservatives" were characterized by Fromm (1980/1984) as *Bürgerliche*, which included supporters of "all organizations to the right of the Social Democrats, except for the National Socialists: the German People's Party, the [Catholic] Centre, the Swabian Peasants Party and others" (p. 74). Pct. = percentage.

only in the United States (Bizumic & Duckitt, 2018; Cizmar et al., 2014; Hetherington & Weiler, 2009; Stenner, 2005), the United Kingdom (Golec de Zavala et al., 2017; Peitz et al., 2018; Zmigrod et al., 2018), France (Jost, 2019; Mayer, 2011; Vasilopoulos & Lachat, 2017), and Germany (Clemens et al., 2020; Crepaz, 2020) but also in many other European and Latin American countries (e.g., see Nilsson & Jost, 2020).

Despite the enormity of the evidence, the impression persists that LWA is a serious, possibly monstrous social problem and that academics have been derelict in their duties when it comes to saying so (e.g., Eysenck, 1954/1999; Peterson, 2022; Satel, 2021; Shils, 1954). Recent interest in the topic is attributable to research programs in personality and social psychology by Conway et al. (2018) and Costello et al. (2022). Although these authors claim to have finally captured the Loch Ness monster, we conclude that they have been no more successful than Altemeyer (1996) or Van Hiel et al. (2006) in pinpointing a Western psychological syndrome of authoritarianism on the left that in any way parallels authoritarianism on the right. On the contrary, the analyses we have carried out thus far suggest that the LWA scale developed by Conway and colleagues is basically a referendum on the religious right in the United States and that, in fact, supporters of "Christian fundamentalists" exhibit more evidence of dogmatism, rigidity, and authoritarianism than their opponents do. This is precisely the opposite of what Conway et al. concluded.

Research by Costello et al. (2022) is also problematic in many ways. Some of their items may tap into extreme forms of rebelliousness, but this is not the same thing as authoritarianism, which—according to decades of theory and research in social science—involves submission as well as aggression and, more to the point, anti-democratic rather than egalitarian commitments. A more serious problem is that when highly dubious exclusion criteria are relaxed, Republicans are sometimes less likely, sometimes as likely, and sometimes more likely to endorse strongly worded LWA items compared to Democrats. Some of the items they endorse appear to capture antisocial, potentially violent tendencies rather than ideological commitment to any kind of leftist—let alone liberal—philosophy. These researchers, we think, have not proved the existence of the Loch Ness monster, although they may have stumbled upon the research equivalent of the "surgeon's photograph."

We conclude with a final observation, which is that the "hunt" for left-wing authoritarians in the United States is itself misguided, as noted above. No doubt one can find a smattering of left-wing extremists who are capable of very bad behavior, including violence. This hardly means that there is a serious social problem or a pervasive syndrome of "liberal" or left-wing authoritarianism that compares in any way to the support that former President

Donald Trump received from millions of Americans in not one but two presidential campaigns that stirred up anti-democratic sentiment and overt hostility directed at journalists, foreigners, immigrants, and various racial/ethnic minority groups (e.g., Choma & Hanoch, 2017; Crowson & Brandes, 2017; Godbole et al., 2022; Knuckey & Hassan, 2020; Ludeke et al., 2018; MacWilliams, 2016; Womick et al., 2019). It would be foolish for social scientists, of all people, to deny or overlook the fact that for decades in the United States right-wing extremists have committed far more hate crimes and other acts of political violence than left-wing extremists (Badaan & Jost, 2020; Haltiwanger, 2019; Jasko et al., 2022; Morlin, 2018).

To be clear, we are not suggesting that no one on the left could ever be considered authoritarian. In the course of human history, of course, there have been authoritarian movements and regimes aligned with the political left (e.g., Shils, 1954). Importantly, however, this is not something we have witnessed in the United States or Canada, which helps to explain why there are long-standing ideological asymmetries in these countries (Altemeyer, 1988). Furthermore, the knee-jerk assumption made by some supporters of the capitalist system that socialism appeals solely or primarily to people with authoritarian inclinations is unsupported by the facts. As a historical matter, Marx and Engels were in fact highly committed to democracy, equality, and freedom, despite their use of the controversial but widely misunderstood phrase "dictatorship of the proletariat" (e.g., Brenkert, 1983; Draper, 1962; Niemi, 2011). As Bertrand Russell (1938/2004) wrote, "Marx pointed out that there could be no real equalisation of power through politics alone, while economic power remained monarchical or oligarchic. It followed that economic power must be in the hands of the State, and the State must be democratic" (pp. 233–234). Thus, part of Marx's critique of capitalism was that it hindered the causes of democracy, equality, and freedom. Marxian socialism, like liberalism, is a fundamentally anti-authoritarian philosophy, even if it is undeniable that some historical actors have exploited Marxian ideology for totalitarian ends.

Nor are we claiming that everyone on the right should be considered authoritarian. As social scientists we are concerned with covariations or "elective affinities" between ideological and psychological preferences (Jost, 2021). The evidence summarized by Nilsson and Jost (2020)—and many other authors over the years (e.g., Adorno et al., 1950; Altemeyer, 1988, 1996; Brown, 1965; Hetherington & Weiler, 2009; Sidanius & Pratto, 2001; Stone & Smith, 1993)—leads to the inescapable conclusion that in Western societies there is a positive association between authoritarianism and right-wing conservatism and a negative association between authoritarianism and liberal-leftism. It follows that if Republicans in the United States were less conservative than they are now, they would also be less authoritarian. If Democrats were less liberal, on the other hand, they would be more authoritarian, on average. We need to distinguish, therefore, between the psychological characteristics exhibited by individuals and groups at any given point in time and the psychological characteristics they would exhibit if they were to hold belief systems that are different from the ones they are holding now.

Acknowledgments

We thank V. Badaan, Verónica Benet-Martínez, Stanley Feldman, Mark Hoffarth, and Felipe Vilanova for very helpful discussions of the issues addressed in this chapter. Some of this work was presented by the lead author at the 2020 meeting of the Society of Personality and Social Psychology in New Orleans. We are grateful for the feedback we received on that occasion. Finally, we thank Jonathan Baron and Chadly Stern for insightful feedback on an earlier draft of this chapter.

Notes

1. We thank Verónica Benet-Martínez for recommending this procedure.
2. There are many notable differences in the wording of these two items. The con-trait item in this case praises Christians for behaving bravely, whereas the pro-trait item mentions "Christian troublemakers" and suggests they should "shut up" and "accept their group's proper place in society." Given how extremely loaded the language is for pro-trait items, it is remarkable, if not extraordinary, that the endorsement of con-trait items was more strongly associated with rigidity, dogmatism, and authoritarianism than was the endorsement of pro-trait items. One possible interpretation of these findings is that in writing these items Conway et al. (2018) stacked the deck and—at least according to our analyses—lost the bet anyway before declaring victory.
3. These are peculiar attention check items for several reasons. For one thing, a 22-year-old male is not considered a "boy" at all but rather a "man." For another, American footballs are not round, although most other balls are, of course, round.
4. It also follows from our analysis that politicians on the left who exhibit authoritarian tendencies may pick up support from voters who might otherwise prefer rightist candidates. Consistent with this possibility, a large-scale survey of 18 Latin American countries found that whereas authoritarianism—measured in terms of parenting (or childrearing) attitudes—predicted support for RWA candidates across the board, it only predicted support for LWA candidates among right-wing voters (Cohen & Smith, 2016).

References

Adorno, T. W., Frenkel-Brunswik, E., Levinson, D. J., & Sanford, R. N. (1950). *The authoritarian personality*. Harper.
Altemeyer, B. (1988). *Enemies of freedom: Understanding right-wing-authoritarianism*. Jossey-Bass.
Altemeyer, B. (1996). *The authoritarian specter*. Harvard University Press.
Altemeyer, B. (1998). The other "authoritarian personality." In M. Zanna (Ed.), *Advances in experimental social psychology* (Vol. 30, pp. 47–92). Academic Press. https://doi.org/10.1016/S0065-2601(08)60382-2
Alto, A., Flores-Robles, G., Anderson, K., Wylie, J., Satter, L., & Gantman, A. P. (2022). "I put liberal but LOL": Investigating psychological differences between political leftists and liberals. PsyArXiv Preprints. https://doi.org/10.31234/osf.io/3qgep
Azevedo, F., & Jost, J. T. (2021). The ideological basis of antiscientific attitudes: Effects of authoritarianism, conservatism, religiosity, social dominance, and system justification. *Group Processes & Intergroup Relations*, 24(4), 518–549. https://doi.org/10.1177%2F1368430221990104
Badaan, V., & Jost, J. T. (2020). Conceptual, empirical, and practical problems with the claim that intolerance, prejudice, and discrimination are equivalent on the political left and right. *Current Opinion in Behavioral Sciences*, 34, 229–238. https://doi.org/10.1016/j.cobeha.2020.07.007Bizumic, B., & Duckitt, J. (2018). Investigating right wing authoritarianism with a very short authoritarianism scale. *Journal of Social and Political Psychology*, 6, 129–150. https://doi.org/10.5964/jspp.v6i1.835
Brenkert, G. G. (1983). *Marx's ethics of freedom*. Routledge.
Brown, R. (1965). The authoritarian personality and the organization of attitudes. In R. Brown (Ed.), *Social psychology* (pp. 477–546). Free Press. https://psycnet.apa.org/doi/10.4324/9780203505984-2
Choma, B. L., & Hanoch, Y. (2017). Cognitive ability and authoritarianism: Understanding support for Trump and Clinton. *Personality and Individual Differences*, 106, 287–291. https://doi.org/10.1016/j.paid.2016.10.054
Cizmar, A. M., Layman, G. C., McTague, J., Pearson-Merkowitz, S., & Spivey, M. (2014). Authoritarianism and American political behavior from 1952 to 2008. *Political Research Quarterly*, 67(1), 71–83. https://doi.org/10.1177%2F1065912913492019
Clemens, V., Decker, O., Plener, P. L., Witt, A., Sachser, C., Brähler, E., & Fegert, J. M. (2020). Authoritarianism and the transgenerational transmission of corporal punishment. *Child Abuse & Neglect*, 106, Article 104537. https://doi.org/10.1016/j.chiabu.2020.104537
Cohen, M. J., & Smith, A. E. (2016). Do authoritarians vote for authoritarians? Evidence from Latin America. *Research & Politics*, 3(4), Article 2053168016684066. https://doi.org/10.1177%2F2053168016684066
Conway, L. G., III, Houck, S. C., Gornick, L. J., & Repke, M. R. (2018). Finding the Loch Ness monster: Left-wing authoritarianism in the United States. *Political Psychology*, 39(5), 1049–1067. https://doi.org/10.1111/pops.12470
Conway, L. G., III, & McFarland, J. D. (2019). Do right-wing and left-wing authoritarianism predict election outcomes? Support for Obama and Trump across two United States presidential elections. *Personality and Individual Differences*, 138, 84–87. https://doi.org/10.1016/j.paid.2018.09.033
Conway, L. G., III, McFarland, J. D., Costello, T. H., & Lilienfeld, S. O. (2021). The curious case of left-wing authoritarianism: When authoritarian persons meet anti-authoritarian norms. *Journal of Theoretical Social Psychology*, 5(4), 423–442. https://doi.org/10.1002/jts5.108

Costello, T. H., Bowes, S. M., Stevens, S. T., Waldman, I. D., Tasimi, A., & Lilienfeld, S. O. (2022). Clarifying the structure and nature of left-wing authoritarianism. *Journal of Personality and Social Psychology, 122*(1), 135–170. https://psycnet.apa.org/doi/10.1037/pspp0000341

Crepaz, M. M. (2020). Coveting uniformity in a diverse world: The authoritarian roots of welfare chauvinism in postmigration crisis Germany. *Social Science Quarterly, 101*(4), 1255–1270. https://doi.org/10.1111/ssqu.12798

Crowson, H. M., & Brandes, J. A. (2017). Differentiating between Donald Trump and Hillary Clinton voters using facets of right-wing authoritarianism and social-dominance orientation: A brief report. *Psychological Reports, 120*(3), 364–373. https://doi.org/10.1177%2F0033294117697089

De Regt, S., Mortelmans, D., & Smits, T. (2011). Left-wing authoritarianism is not a myth, but a worrisome reality. Evidence from 13 eastern European countries. *Communist and Post-Communist Studies, 44*(4), 299–308. https://doi.org/10.1016/j.postcomstud.2011.10.006

Draper, H. (1962). Marx and the dictatorship of the proletariat. *New Politics, 1*, 91–104.

Duckitt, J., Bizumic, B., Krauss, S. W., & Heled, E. (2010). A tripartite approach to right-wing authoritarianism: The authoritarianism–conservatism–traditionalism model. *Political Psychology, 31*(5), 685–715. https://doi.org/10.1111/j.1467-9221.2010.00781.x

Dunwoody, P. T., & Funke, F. (2016). The aggression–submission–conventionalism scale: Testing a new three factor measure of authoritarianism. *Journal of Social and Political Psychology, 4*(2), 571–600. https://doi.org/10.5964/jspp.v4i2.168

Eysenck, H. J. (1981). Left-wing authoritarianism: Myth or reality? *Political Psychology, 3*(1/2), 234–238. https://doi.org/10.2307/3791293

Eysenck, H. J. (1999). *The psychology of politics*. Transaction. (Original work published 1954).Feldman, S., Mérola, V., & Dollman, J. (2021). The psychology of authoritarianism and support for illiberal policies and parties. In A. Sajó, R. Uitz, & S. Holmes (Eds.), *Routledge handbook of illiberalism* (pp. 635–654). Routledge.

Fromm, E. (1984). *The working class in Weimar Germany: A psychological and sociological study* (W. Bonss, Ed.; B. Weinberger, Trans.). Harvard University Press. (Original work published 1980).

Godbole, M. A., Flores-Robles, G., Malvar, N. A., & Valian, V. V. (2022). Who do you like? Who will you vote for? Political ideology and person perception in the 2020 US presidential election. *Analyses of Social Issues and Public Policy, 22*(1), 30–65.

Goldberg, J. (2009). *Liberal fascism: The secret history of the American left, from Mussolini to the politics of change*. Crown Forum.

Golec de Zavala, A., Guerra, R., & Simão, C. (2017). The relationship between the Brexit vote and individual predictors of prejudice: Collective narcissism, right wing authoritarianism, social dominance orientation. *Frontiers in Psychology, 8*, Article 2023. https://doi.org/10.3389/fpsyg.2017.02023

Haltiwanger, J. (2019). All of the extremist killings in the US in 2018 had links to right-wing extremism, according to new report. *Business Insider*. https://www.businessinsider.com.au/extremist-killings-links-right-wing-extremism-report-2019-1

Hetherington, M. J., & Weiler, J. D. (2009). *Authoritarianism and polarization in American politics*. Cambridge University Press.

Jasko, K., LaFree, G., Piazza, J., & Becker, M. H. (2022). A comparison of political violence by left-wing, right-wing, and Islamist extremists in the United States and the world. *Proceedings of the National Academy of Sciences of the United States of America, 119*(30), Article e2122593119.

Jost, J. T. (2019). Anger and authoritarianism mediate the effects of fear on support for the far right—What Vasilopoulos et al. (2019) really found. *Political Psychology, 40*(4), 705–711. https://doi.org/10.1111/pops.12567

Jost, J. T. (2021). *Left and right: The psychological significance of a political distinction*. Oxford University Press.

Jost, J. T., Gries, T., & Müller, V. (2022). Costs and benefits of a market-based model of ideological choice: Responding to consumers and critics. *Psychological Inquiry, 33*, 123–137.

Kabacoff, R. (2021). *factorAnalysis: Principal components and factor analysis* (Version 0.1.0) [Computer software]. R Foundation for Statistical Computing.

Knuckey, J., & Hassan, K. (2020). Authoritarianism and support for Trump in the 2016 presidential election. *The Social Science Journal, 59*(1), 47–60. https://doi.org/10.1016/j.soscij.2019.06.008

Kohn, P. M. (1972). The authoritarianism-rebellion scale: A balanced F scale with left-wing reversals. *Sociometry, 35*(1), 176–189. https://doi.org/10.2307/2786557

Kreml, W. P. (1977). *The anti-authoritarian personality*. Pergamon.

Ludeke, S. G., Klitgaard, C. N., & Vitriol, J. (2018). Comprehensively-measured authoritarianism does predict vote choice: The importance of authoritarianism's facets, ideological sorting, and the particular candidate. *Personality and Individual Differences, 123*, 209–216. https://doi.org/10.1016/j.paid.2017.11.019

Lyons, S. (2000, November). *Birth of a legend (The beast of Loch Ness* Part 3). Nova Online. https://www.pbs.org/wgbh/nova/lochness/legend3.html

MacWilliams, M. (2016, January 17). One weird trait that predicts whether you're a Trump supporter. *Politico*. http://www.politico.com/magazine/story/2016/01/donald-trump-2016-authoritarian-213533

Mayer, N. (2011). Why extremes don't meet: Le Pen and Besancenot voters in the 2007 French presidential election. *French Politics, Culture & Society, 29*(3), 101–120. https://doi.org/10.3167/fpcs.2011.290307

Morlin, B. (2018, September 12). *Study shows two-thirds of U.S. terrorism tied to right-wing extremists*. Southern Poverty Law Center. https://www.splcenter.org/hatewatch/2018/09/12/study-shows-two-thirds-us-terrorism-tied-right-wing-extremists

Napier, J., & Jost, J. (2008). The "antidemocratic personality" revisited: A cross-national investigation of working-class authoritarianism. *Journal of Social Issues, 64*(3), 595–617. https://doi.org/10.1111/j.1540-4560.2008.00579.x

Niemi, W. L. (2011). Karl Marx's sociological theory of democracy: Civil society and political rights. *The Social Science Journal, 48*(1), 39–51. https://doi.org/10.1016/j.soscij.2010.07.002

Nilsson, A., & Jost, J. T. (2020). The authoritarian–conservatism nexus. *Current Opinion in Behavioral Sciences, 34*, 148–154. https://doi.org/10.1016/j.cobeha.2020.03.003

Peitz, L., Dhont, K., & Seyd, B. (2018). The psychology of supranationalism: Its ideological correlates and implications for EU attitudes and post-Brexit preferences. *Political Psychology, 39*(6), 1305–1322. https://doi.org/10.1111/pops.12542

Peterson, J. (2022). *Jordan Peterson: Why I am no longer a tenured professor at the University of Toronto*. Retrieved from https://nationalpost.com/opinion/jordan-peterson-why-i-am-no-longer-a-tenured-professor-at-the-university-of-toronto.

R Foundation for Statistical Computing. (2020). *R: A language and environment for statistical computing* [Computer software]. https://www.R-project.org/

Rokeach, M. (1960). *The open and closed mind: Investigations into the nature of belief systems and personality systems*. Basic Books.

Russell, B. (2004). *Power: A new social analysis*. Routledge. (Original work published 1938)

Satel, S. (2021, September 25). The experts somehow overlooked authoritarians on the left. *The Atlantic*. https://www.theatlantic.com/ideas/archive/2021/09/psychological-dimensions-left-wing-authoritarianism/620185/

Saunders, B. A., Badaan, V., Hoffarth, M., & Jost, J. T. (2020, February 27–29). Spotting the Loch Ness monster, or smiling for the surgeon's photograph? A critique of Conway and colleagues' (2018) research on left-wing authoritarianism. In L. G. Conway III (Chair), *Is left-wing authoritarianism real? Evidence on both sides of the debate* [Symposium]. 21st Society for Personality and Social Psychology Annual Convention, New Orleans, LA, United States.

Shils, E. A. (1954). Authoritarianism: "Right" and "left." In R. Christie & M. Jahoda (Eds.), *Studies in the scope and method of "The Authoritarian Personality"* (pp. 24–49). Free Press.

Sidanius, J., & Pratto, F. (2001). *Social dominance. An intergroup theory of social hierarchy and oppression.* Cambridge University Press.

Stenner, K. (2005). *The authoritarian dynamic.* Cambridge University Press. https://doi.org/10.1017/CBO9780511614712

Stone, W. F., & Smith, L. D. (1993). Authoritarianism: Left and right. In W. F. Stone, G. Lederer, & R. Christie (Eds.), *Strength and weakness: The authoritarian personality today* (pp. 144–156). Springer.

Todosijević, B., & Enyedi, Z. (2008). Authoritarianism without dominant ideology: Political manifestations of authoritarian attitudes in Hungary. *Political Psychology, 29*(5), 767–787. https://doi.org/10.1111/j.1467-9221.2008.00663.x

Van Hiel, A., Duriez, B., & Kossowska, M. (2006). The presence of left-wing authoritarianism in western Europe and its relationship with conservative ideology. *Political Psychology, 27*(5), 769–793. https://doi.org/10.1111/j.1467-9221.2006.00532.x

Vasilopoulos, P., & Lachat, R. (2018). Authoritarianism and political choice in France. *Acta Politica, 53*(4), 612–634. https://dx.doi.org/10.1057/s41269-017-0066-9

Womick, J., Rothmund, T., Azevedo, F., King, L. A., & Jost, J. T. (2019). Group-based dominance and authoritarian aggression predict support for Donald Trump in the 2016 US presidential election. *Social Psychological and Personality Science, 10*(5), 643–652. https://doi.org/10.1177%2F1948550618778290

Zmigrod, L., Rentfrow, P. J., & Robbins, T. W. (2018). Cognitive underpinnings of nationalistic ideology in the context of Brexit. *Proceedings of the National Academy of Sciences of the United States of America, 115*(19), E4532–E4540. https://doi.org/10.1073/pnas.1708960115

11
New Evidence on an Enduring Question

The Role of Political Ideology and Extremism in Dogmatic Thinking

Chadly Stern and Benjamin C. Ruisch

For nearly a century, researchers have debated how people across the political spectrum differ in their psychological profiles (e.g., Adorno et al., 1950; Baron & Jost, 2019; Ditto et al., 2019). In other words, are there particular constellations of psychological traits that correlate with—or perhaps even drive—particular sets of political beliefs? Among the most enduring and hotly contested questions concerns how a person's political beliefs correspond to their degree of dogmatic thinking. In particular, past and contemporary debates have focused on whether the conservatism of a person's political beliefs (i.e., the "direction" of their ideology, from conservative/right to liberal/left) or the extremity of their beliefs (from moderate to extreme) are linked to dogmatic thinking styles. These questions continue to be the subject of much research within psychology, political science, and related fields. To date, however, there has been little theoretical integration across findings, and the debate about whether and how political beliefs relate to dogmatism has largely reached an impasse. Here, we review contemporary research that speaks to how political conservatism and extremity relate to dogmatism. To help advance this long-standing debate, we organize our review to highlight when conservatism versus extremity might be more likely to relate to dogmatic thinking.

Dogmatism, Political Conservatism, and Extremism

Rokeach (1954) originally defined dogmatism as "(a) a relatively closed cognitive organization of beliefs and disbeliefs about reality, (b) organized around a central set of beliefs about absolute authority which, in turn, (c) provides a framework for patterns of intolerance and qualified tolerance towards others" (p. 195). Rokeach's attempt to comprehensively capture the construct of dogmatism was laudable. However, his theorizing included various constructs that were empirically and conceptually distinguished from dogmatism over time (e.g., authoritarianism; Vacchiano et al., 1969), and some researchers viewed his purportedly content-free measure of dogmatism as tacitly possessing ideological content (Parrott & Brown, 1972). Subsequent definitions and measurements have become more refined as researchers continued to examine the origins and consequences of dogmatic thinking.

Drawing from more recent work, we define dogmatism as a tendency to hold one's beliefs and principles as objectively correct, without consideration of the evidence or the opinions of others (adapted from Oxford Languages, 2021). This definition is consistent with other theoretical accounts in the literature (e.g., Schulz et al., 2020; Toner et al., 2013; Zmigrod, 2022), as well as with modern measures that capture a more general and truly content-free tendency toward dogmatic thinking, including Altemeyer's (2002) Dogmatism Scale (e.g., "If you are 'open-minded' about the most important things in life, you will probably reach the wrong conclusions") and measures of dogmatic intolerance (e.g., "How I feel about issues is the truth"; van Prooijen & Krouwel, 2017).

As with dogmatism, conceptualizations of political ideology have been refined over time. Currently, many scholars conceptualize political ideology as a single dimension ranging from liberal/left to conservative/right (Jost et al., 2009; Stern, 2022). Conservatives and those on the right are motivated to preserve tradition and hierarchical social order, which often leads them to defend the "status quo" or current state of affairs. In contrast, liberals and those on the left are motivated to support novel changes to society and promote a more equal social system, which often leads them to challenge the current state of affairs (Jost et al., 2009; Stern, 2022).

Two prominent models have attempted to explain the relation between political ideology and dogmatic thought. First, the *rigidity of the right* model argues that more conservative (vs. liberal) individuals tend to possess a distinct constellation of goals, motivations, and cognitive processing styles focused on achieving certainty and closure. To the degree that these motivations prompt dogmatic thinking styles, conservatism is expected to relate to greater dogmatism (Jost et al., 2003a, 2018). The second prominent perspective is the *rigidity of the extremes* model, which proposes that people with more extreme political beliefs display greater dogmatic thinking than those with more moderate views, regardless of the content of the ideology (Greenberg & Jonas, 2003; van Prooijen & Krouwel, 2017; Zmigrod, 2022). In other words, this model argues that both extreme liberals and extreme conservatives express greater dogmatism than individuals who hold more moderate beliefs (e.g., centrists and those who are liberal- or conservative-leaning).

Although these models have often been pitted against one another (e.g., Greenberg & Jonas, 2003; Jost et al., 2003b), they are not inherently incompatible. Rather, there are at least three ways in which the apparent conflict between these models can be reconciled. First, it is possible that one model is simply "right" and one is "wrong," in the sense that one explains the actual relation between political beliefs and dogmatism while the other does not. Second, both conservatism and extremity could independently relate to dogmatism, such that conservatives are more dogmatic than liberals while, simultaneously, extremists are more dogmatic than moderates. Third, it is possible that each model is correct under certain conditions, such that in some situations political conservatism is more closely associated with dogmatism, while in others extremity is more relevant. In the current review, we assess the relative likelihood of these three different possibilities.

A large body of research has amassed over the last 70+ years that relates to the debate between the rigidity of the right and rigidity of the extremes models. The intensity and longevity of this debate are perhaps rooted in the wide-ranging implications of these questions for understanding political cognition and behavior. Uncovering systematic differences in dogmatism between individuals of differing ideologies would have implications for effective messaging, persuasion, communication, and, ultimately, bridging the gap between individuals of opposing ideologies.

Research examining the association between political beliefs and dogmatic thinking has observed conflicting patterns of results that suggest that both the rigidity of the right and rigidity of the extremes models may currently be incomplete. Specifically, some scholars have documented an effect of conservatism but not extremity (Toner et al., 2013), while others have observed effects of extremity but not conservatism (van Prooijen & Krouwel, 2017). Still others have found that both conservatism and extremity are related to greater dogmatism (Harris & Van Bavel, 2021). Thus far, however, there is no compelling theoretical framework that accounts for these conflicting findings. Despite decades of debate, research has yet to clarify whether—or, perhaps, under what conditions—the rigidity of the right and rigidity of the extremes models might be more or less correct.

Dogmatic Thinking in Political and Non-political Domains

In the present chapter, we aim to shed new light on the classic debate regarding the relation between political beliefs and dogmatism through reviewing and integrating recent evidence concerning when dogmatic thinking is (and is not) related to both political conservatism and ideological extremism. Drawing from current evidence, we suggest a possible means of reconciling the mixed findings of past work. We argue that the degree to which a domain activates an individual's political beliefs and identity may be a critical factor in determining whether political conservatism or ideological extremity will be more closely linked to dogmatism.

We propose that in *ideologically neutral* contexts—that is, in situations where judgments are perceived as being unrelated to political identities—political conservatism will be most closely related to dogmatism. We derive this prediction by integrating several lines of past work. First, epistemic motivations to achieve cognitive closure, structure, and certainty in everyday life play a key role in human decision-making processes and dogmatic thinking (Kruglanski, 2013; Mayseless & Kruglanski, 1987). Such epistemic motivations are likely to be privileged in one's goal hierarchy unless overridden by countervailing goals (Kruglanski, 2013; Mayseless & Kruglanski, 1987). Further, political conservatism is associated with stronger motivations to achieve closure and certainty (Jost et al., 2003a, 2018). In light of these findings, we speculate that conservatism is most readily associated with greater dogmatism in non-political or ideologically neutral contexts.

When political identities are activated, however, the defense of one's closely held beliefs about the political world might take priority over epistemic goals about reaching closure (Huddy, 2001; Van Bavel & Pereira, 2018). As a result, ideological extremity may be more likely to predict dogmatism in political domains. For example, liberals and conservatives appear motivated to defend their political views to a comparable magnitude (Brandt & Crawford, 2020). Similarly, needs for certainty appear to be unrelated to motivated reasoning about political topics (Guay & Johnston, 2022). Insofar as ideological extremity reflects a commitment to one's political beliefs, we anticipate that extremity—among both liberals and conservatives—will predict greater dogmatism in domains where political beliefs are salient, particularly when judgments are viewed as affirming or communicating one's political identity.

In this review we have taken four important steps to best advance the long-standing debate about dogmatism. First, based on recent critiques regarding the use of self-report measures to assess ideological differences (e.g., possible content overlap between "political" and "non-political" measures, ideological differences in self-presentation strategies; Kahan, 2012; Malka et al., 2017; Van Hiel et al., 2016), we avoid self-report measures of dogmatism in favor of more indirect and behavioral indicators of dogmatic thinking—in particular, cognitive rigidity and judgment confidence. Second, we focus specifically on political ideology rather than related constructs such as authoritarianism, partisanship, nationalism, and religiosity, to ensure that the reviewed findings speak most directly to the conservatism–extremity debate. (We note, however, that these related constructs may be associated with dogmatism as well; Zmigrod, 2020.) Third, we focus on contemporary and emerging research to capitalize on methodological advances and circumvent commonly criticized weaknesses of some older research (e.g., small sample sizes). Fourth, we separately examine the evidence for dogmatic thinking in both non-political and political domains to test the potential validity of our proposal that the importance of political conservatism and ideological extremity may depend on the relevance of one's political identity to the judgment domain at hand. In so doing, we aim to advance the classic debate regarding how both conservatism and ideological extremity relate to dogmatic thinking.

Cognitive Rigidity

In earlier research, few studies used behavioral tasks to assess cognitive rigidity. For example, Van Hiel et al. (2010) identified only three studies examining the association between conservatism and rigidity on behavioral tasks. More recently, however, there has been a sharp increase in research using behavioral tasks that directly gauge cognitive rigidity. To our knowledge, there has not yet been a review of this more recent work in relation to the debate between the rigidity of the right and rigidity of the extremes models.

Cognitive Rigidity in Non-political Domains

Amodio and colleagues (2007) conducted one of the first modern studies examining whether conservatism would be associated with cognitive rigidity on a non-political behavioral task. In the study, participants completed a non-political "go/no-go" task in which they were instructed to enter a "go" response (press a key on a keyboard) when presented with one stimulus (a letter of the alphabet) and to withhold from responding when presented with a different stimulus (a different letter). Eighty percent of trials required a go response, meaning that correctly withholding a response on no-go trials required updating a dominant response pattern. Conservatism was associated with lower accuracy on trials that necessitated withholding a response, suggesting that more conservative participants exhibited less flexibility in updating the habitual response.

In recent work, Zmigrod et al. (2018) assessed cognitive flexibility using two tasks: the Wisconsin Card Sorting Test, which measures whether people update in response to novel task rules and reward contingencies, and the Remote Association Test, which captures the degree to which people generate conceptual associations among words. Success on both of these tasks is viewed as reflecting greater cognitive flexibility. The authors observed that conservatism was associated with worse performance on both tasks, providing additional evidence that greater conservatism may be linked to lower cognitive flexibility.

Importantly, Amodio et al. (2007) proposed that ideological differences in cognitive flexibility would not lead to better performance on all behavioral tasks among liberals. Rather, they speculated that conservatism would be associated with enhanced performance on tasks requiring a more rigid or fixed response style. Recent findings support this idea. In a study by Buechner et al. (2021), participants were presented with a 10 × 20 number grid and asked to count the frequency with which an even number came directly after an odd number in a row. Participants were asked to only focus on rows that possessed a label from a specific category (e.g., *animals*), and each row in the grid was labeled with examples from a category (e.g., *horse*). Participants then completed the task two times. The second time they completed the task they were told to focus either on rows with the same category examples as in the first trial (e.g., staying with *animals*) or to use new category examples (e.g., switching from *animals* to *countries*). Conservatism was associated with greater accuracy when focusing on the same category across trials (a rigid behavioral style) but was associated with less accuracy when participants were required to update the category on which they focused (a flexible behavior style).

Greater cognitive rigidity among more conservative individuals also manifests in stronger reliance on intuitive thought processes, which consists of using automatic responses to form judgments. This process contrasts with analytic thought, which occurs when people reflect on and subsequently override their initial responses (Pennycook et al., 2014). For example, on average, conservatism is linked to greater intuitive responses on the Cognitive Reflection Test (CRT; Jost et al., 2018). The CRT includes questions in which intuitive judgment results in an incorrect answer and reflective or analytic thought is needed to achieve the correct response. For instance, the question "In a lake, there is a patch of lily pads. Every day, the patch doubles in size. If it takes 48 days for the patch to cover the entire lake, how long would it take for the patch to cover half of the lake?" has an intuitive response of 24 days, but the correct response achieved through analytic reasoning is 47 days.

Most previous research examining the relation between political beliefs and rigidity has drawn from theoretical models to generate predictions and select appropriate methodology for testing those predictions. Diverging from this style, Zmigrod et al. (2021) used a data-driven approach to model variation in ideological differences across cognitive tasks. Specifically, they had participants complete a battery of cognitive tasks that were compiled in previous research for purposes other than examining ideology (e.g., analyzing self-regulation). Thus, the specific tasks chosen were not influenced by the researchers' beliefs about which tasks might support different predictions. Consistent with the previously reviewed findings, the authors observed that conservatism was associated with "reduced strategic information processing," which indexed lower flexibility in working memory capacity and planning. Interestingly, Zmigrod and colleagues also found that conservatism was associated with greater caution in perceptual decision-making tasks, which reflected the amount of information that people acquired before providing a final response. The authors speculated that conservatives' stronger desire for certainty may have prompted this greater caution.

There is little evidence, however, for an association between ideological extremity and cognitive flexibility on non-political behavioral tasks. Few published papers report such associations, and those that do provide limited or mixed support for such a connection. Buechner et al. (2021) found that extremity was not related to cognitive flexibility across a variety of behavioral tasks (e.g., the task requiring rigid or flexible styles described earlier). At apparent odds with Buechner and colleagues' findings, Zmigrod et al. (2020) observed a consistent quadratic (but not linear) relation between strength of partisanship (i.e., the degree to which people felt identity fusion with the Republican relative to the Democratic Party) and rigidity on several behavioral tasks, suggesting that the strength with which one identifies with their preferred political party may be associated with greater rigidity. It is worth considering, however, that there may be an important distinction between partisanship strength and political ideology: Political ideology reflects the content of people's beliefs (e.g., how they believe society should be structured), whereas partisanship strength captures group identification processes (Iyengar et al., 2019; Van Bavel & Pereira, 2018). Thus, while Zmigrod et al.'s (2020) findings indicate that people who express strong commitment to a political party display greater cognitive rigidity (see also Lammers et al., 2017), they do not necessarily speak to the debate about how political beliefs are related to dogmatism. Nevertheless, research should continue to explore this possibility in more systematic ways.

Cognitive Rigidity in Political Domains

The work reviewed above demonstrates that in non-political domains, political ideology—and not political extremity—appears to be the best predictor of cognitive rigidity. However, in politically relevant domains, rigidity and closed-mindedness appear to emerge regardless of the content of people's political beliefs. For example, in one study, Frimer et al. (2017) informed participants that they had been entered into a drawing where they could receive a bonus payment ($10) and that they would subsequently be presented with statements that challenge their views on same-sex marriage. Participants were also given the choice of reading statements that support their views on same-sex marriage, but the possible drawing prize would be reduced (to $7). A majority (63%) of participants opted to view statements supporting their views despite the reduced financial outcome on the drawing, and the rate of choosing this outcome did not significantly differ between people holding liberal and conservative views. Relatedly, Ditto et al. (2019) conducted a meta-analysis of 51 studies examining whether people were more likely to evaluate information in a more positive manner when it supports (vs. challenges) their political beliefs. They found that liberals and conservatives displayed this bias at a comparable magnitude.

Some findings also indicate that rigidity in political domains is stronger among people with more extreme political views. For example, Zwicker et al. (2020) observed that people with more extreme political views self-reported more stability in their political opinions (e.g., scoring lower on items such as "My opinions about political issues have changed in the last few years"), but there was not a consistent effect of conservatism on stability. Further, they also found that extremists displayed greater objective stability in their political ideology over the course of approximately 6 weeks. These findings suggest that the extremity of one's political views might be a key factor for understanding rigidity in political domains. Intriguingly, however, Frimer et al. (2017) also noted that the extremity of people's political views did not significantly predict whether they chose to see attitude-consistent information about same-sex marriage, suggesting that there may be further nuance remaining to identify in the relation between extremity and rigidity in the political domain.

Cognitive Rigidity Summary

The degree to which a task possesses politically relevant content appears to impact whether political conservatism or ideological extremity more closely corresponds to greater cognitive rigidity. On non-political tasks, cognitive rigidity is more pronounced among politically conservative (vs. liberal) individuals. Conversely, there is little evidence to suggest that flexibility on these types of politically neutral tasks varies based on the extremity of a person's political ideology. In contrast, rigidity on highly charged political topics appears to emerge at a similar magnitude across the political spectrum and in many instances seems to most readily manifest among people with more extreme (vs. moderate) political views.

Confidence

Confidence refers to the degree to which people believe that their judgments, decisions, beliefs, and attitudes are objectively correct (Dunning, 2012; Wagner et al., 2012). Thinking that one's beliefs and attitudes are accurate is an indicator of dogmatic thinking (Goldsmith & Goldsmith, 1980) and has been broadly linked to a range of important psychological outcomes, including goal pursuit (Higgins, 2019), persuasion (Briñol & Petty, 2022), and confirmation bias (Rollwage et al., 2020). Thus, determining whether and how political beliefs may systematically relate to confidence stands as a critical question. In this section, we review findings concerning the degree to which conservatism and ideological extremity relate to confidence.

Confidence in Non-political Domains

Several lines of work have examined the relation between political ideology and confidence in non-political domains. On the whole, this work tends to suggest that political conservatism—and not ideological extremity—is associated with greater confidence. For example, we (Ruisch & Stern, 2021) systematically examined the degree to which conservatism and ideological extremity were associated with confidence on various non-political tasks. In one study participants viewed images showing constellations of dots that varied in number. Participants entered their judgment of how many dots they believed appeared on the screen and then indicated confidence in their judgment. Overall, conservatism was associated with greater judgment confidence, and this relationship remained when adjusting for accuracy on the task. Thus, conservatives were not simply more confident because of ideological differences in accuracy.

We observed a similar relationship between conservatism and confidence in several additional studies, which examined both memory recall (e.g., determining what color was missing from an array of color squares) and judgments made in the moment (e.g., distance estimates to visible landmarks). Point estimates for the conservatism–confidence association and extremity–confidence association across studies are shown in Figure 11.1. A within-paper meta-analysis indicated that the average conservatism–confidence association was positive and moderate in magnitude (β = .20) both at zero-order and when adjusting for extremity. In contrast, there was no positive association between extremity and confidence. After adjusting for conservatism, the average extremity–confidence association was β = −.0003, and the average zero-order association was negative (β = −.06), such that extremists exhibited lower confidence than moderates.

Examining the psychological processes underlying these liberal–conservative confidence differences, we found that these effects appear to stem from differences in how liberals and conservatives deliberate and make decisions. Specifically, we found that conservatives (vs. liberals) exhibited a lower motivation to deliberate, which manifested as a tendency to consider a smaller range of possible response options before making a final judgment. These differences in deliberation statistically accounted for part of the relation between conservatism and confidence.

Related research converges on the conclusion that conservatism might also be linked to unjustified confidence on non-political tasks. Rollwage et al. (2018) assessed confidence in visual perception judgments (which of two patches contained a greater number of flickering dots). The findings indicated that conservatism was associated with a bias toward overconfidence in judgments—in other words, their confidence surpassed what would be expected based on the objective accuracy of their judgments.

Interestingly, some research provides evidence that appears to diverge from the idea that conservatives are more confident on non-political tasks. For example, Newman and Sargent (2021) examined the degree to which people held ambivalent (i.e., a mix of positive and negative) attitudes toward a range of non-political topics (e.g., ice cream, movies, storms). The authors assessed attitudinal ambivalence in three ways: (1) a five-item measure capturing subjective ratings of how "mixed" people's feelings and beliefs were about an issue, (2) a single item from this measure gauging whether people's feelings about an issue were on "one side" or "mixed," and (3) an "objective" ambivalence score calculated with the formula (positive feelings + negative feelings)/2 − |positive feelings − negative feelings|. They observed that, overall, greater conservatism was significantly linked to higher levels of attitudinal ambivalence on the subjective assessments and marginally associated with higher ambivalence on the objective measure.

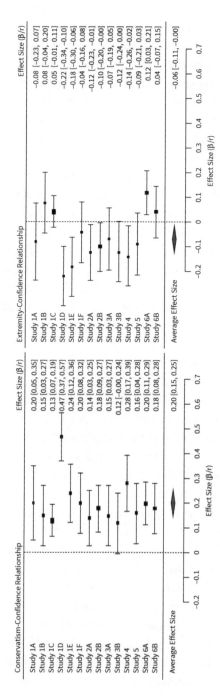

Figure 11.1 Individual point estimates and meta-analytic effect size between conservatism and confidence (left panel) and between extremity and confidence (right panel) across studies in Ruisch and Stern (2021). (Reproduced from Ruisch, B. C., & Stern, C. [2021]. The confident conservative: Ideological differences in judgment and decision-making confidence. *Journal of Experimental Psychology: General, 150*, 527–544. https://doi.org/10.1037/xge0000898.)

These findings could be interpreted as suggesting that conservatism was associated with lower attitude confidence. One possible explanation for the divergent pattern of results may be that the previously reviewed studies by Ruisch and Stern (2021) and Rollwage et al. (2018) used tasks that were novel or less likely to be frequently encountered in daily life. In contrast, Newman and Sargent (2021) examined attitudes toward objects and issues that people were likely to have frequently considered, meaning that people had been able to form their attitudes over long periods of time. People who report a stronger motivation to deliberate express greater confidence in attitudes toward non-novel topics (DeMarree et al., 2020). Thus, one speculative possibility is that liberals—who report a stronger dispositional motivation to engage in deliberative thought (e.g., Stern & Axt, 2021)—may simply be more likely than conservatives to continually reflect on their attitudes over time, and therefore eventually come to form greater certainty in these attitudes. Another possibility to explain the different patterns of findings is that confidence and ambivalence represent distinct constructs (Connor & Sparks, 2002). A person could be confident that they have both positive and negative feelings toward a topic or could feel positively toward a topic while also being uncertain about that judgment. Future research could test these possibilities.

Some findings have also been interpreted as suggesting that extremists may be more confident on certain non-political tasks. Brandt et al. (2015) found that people with more extreme (vs. moderate) political views were less likely to rely on experimenter-provided values when making estimates in an anchoring task. Although the authors describe this effect as reflecting greater confidence among the extremes, they also report several findings that seem to challenge this interpretation. First, the authors observed that attitudinal extremity was marginally associated with lower certainty in answers to the experimenter-generated anchoring items. Second, lesser reliance on an experimentally generated anchor is likely to capture reactance to external influence, rather than confidence. Specifically, the authors note that "the effects may have been driven by extremists being more likely than moderates to reject outside information rather than by extremists overvaluing their own opinions more than moderates" (p. 200). Third, greater reliance on self-generated anchors and certainty of answers derived from self-generated anchors—more direct assessments of confidence—were unrelated to extremity. Thus, these findings do not appear to support an association between extremity and confidence per se but may instead reflect other processes—for example, that people with more extreme (vs. moderate) views are more reactive on non-political tasks.

Confidence in Political Domains

Several studies have captured confidence in political domains using relatively indirect measures. For example, participants in one study (Toner et al., 2013) reported their attitudes toward nine contentious political topics (e.g., abortion, affirmative action) and the degree to which they believed that those attitudes were more correct than those that others hold (i.e., "belief superiority"). The authors found a quadratic relation between political ideology and political belief superiority, such that people with more extreme (vs. moderate) beliefs expressed greater superiority in their beliefs. Conversely, there was no consistent relation between conservatism and belief superiority. Subsequent research has consistently replicated the association between extremity of political views and greater political belief superiority (Brandt et al., 2015; Harris & Van Bavel, 2021; Schulz et al., 2020).

Similarly, some research suggests that people who hold more extreme political views are also more confident in their comprehension of issues than is justifiable (Fernbach et al., 2013). In other words, they might be overconfident, in the sense that they overestimate how objectively accurate their judgments and decisions are. For example, in one study, van Prooijen et al. (2018) asked Dutch participants whether they believed that statements about the 2016 EU refugee crisis were true or false (e.g., "In the first two months of 2016, 4318 people sought asylum in the Netherlands") and how certain they were in their answers. The authors observed that people who held more extreme (vs. moderate) political beliefs reported greater certainty in their beliefs—even after accounting for objective factual knowledge about the crisis, indicating that stronger certainty among the extremes was not attributable to superior knowledge. Conversely, no association was observed between conservatism and certainty in these political judgments.

Relatedly, Costello and Bowes (2023) examined how political ideology was associated with *absolute certainty* of one's political beliefs, which constitutes views that people hold absent of any uncertainty. The authors argued that absolute certainty "reflects a category error" and "is equally irrational for all beliefs" (footnote 2). Participants indicated how certain they were that their political beliefs were correct on a 0%–100% scale, and individuals who reported 100% were coded as having absolute certainty about their views. The findings indicated a quadratic relation between political ideology and absolutely certainty, such that there was a higher probability of reporting absolute certainty in one's political views among people who held more extreme (vs. moderate) beliefs. Conservatism was not associated with the likelihood of holding absolute certainty about political beliefs.

Confidence Summary

The reviewed findings suggest that both conservatism and extremity may relate to confidence but that these relations are context-dependent. In particular, the presence of politically relevant content in a task appears to shape whether political conservatism or extremity most closely corresponds to confidence. Conservatism is linked to greater judgment confidence on tasks that are devoid of political content (e.g., estimating numbers of dots), although there is some initial evidence suggesting that the relation between conservatism and stronger confidence might reverse for frequently considered non-political topics toward which people have formed attitudes over time. Conversely, the evidence regarding whether extremity relates to confidence on non-political tasks is less clear. On contentiously debated political topics, however, extremity—but not conservatism—corresponds to greater confidence, manifesting as a greater perceived superiority of one's views and greater (unjustified) certainty that those views are correct.

General Summary and Future Directions

In this chapter we reviewed recent studies examining the role of political conservatism and ideological extremity in dogmatic thinking. This recent work, which overcomes many of the critiques levied at older research on the subject (e.g., small sample sizes, tacitly political content in measures of dogmatism) appears to provide a relatively consistent picture of how political beliefs relate to dogmatism. We partially confirmed classic perspectives, finding that those on the political right (vs. left) often do exhibit more dogmatic traits. Importantly, however, we also identified certain circumstances under which the extremity of a person's ideology (i.e., how strongly liberal or conservative they are) might be an equally (or perhaps even more) potent predictor of dogmatism.

The diversity of approaches that recent research has employed allowed us to provide a preliminary examination of whether the existence of political content in a judgment domain propels ideological extremity to be a stronger driver of dogmatism, whereas the absence of political content results in conservatism playing a more impactful role. Consistent with our proposed ideas, the preponderance of current evidence suggests that the rigidity of the right model might best explain how people's political beliefs predict dogmatic thinking on non-political tasks, whereas dogmatism in political domains might better be accounted for by the rigidity of the extremes perspective.

Despite these supportive initial findings, however, further research is needed to fully elucidate the nature of the relation between political beliefs and dogmatism. In particular, researchers may wish to take a more systematic approach to testing our predictions regarding the influence of political content. That is, although the current literature appears to provide initial support for our predictions, the political and non-political tasks reviewed in this chapter differed in a number of ways that make direct comparison difficult. Ideally, future work would hold the type of task as constant as possible, while manipulating the presence versus absence of political content (e.g., using a fixed set of stimuli and randomizing whether those stimuli are said to hold political relevance).

Similarly, future work may wish to disentangle whether the greater dogmatism exhibited by extremists in political domains is motivational in nature (e.g., extremists feeling more compelled than moderates to affirm their political identities) or whether it stems from other processes (e.g., extremists having more frequently rehearsed their political judgments). To test this question, researchers might employ tools such as self-affirmation manipulations to assuage identity-related motivations and examine whether this undercuts extremists' greater political dogmatism. Examining the processes underlying these effects will also contribute to a better understanding of precisely what type of political content is necessary to elicit greater dogmatism among ideological extremists.

Other remaining questions include the degree to which the effects reviewed above are specific to certain dimensions of political ideology (e.g., social vs. economic conservatism) versus applying to liberalism–conservatism writ large. For example, past work suggests that greater reliance on intuitive thought is more closely related to social than economic conservatism (Talhelm, 2018; Talhelm et al., 2015; Yilmaz & Saribay, 2017; Yilmaz et al., 2020). Similarly, Zmigrod et al. (2020) found that social conservatism was more consistently associated with rigid thinking styles than was economic conservatism. Further consideration of whether and when political ideology is better modeled in a multidimensional manner, and the implications of this conceptualization for understanding dogmatic thinking, could be generative for future research.

Concluding Remarks

In this brief review, we provided a concise overview of some of the latest research on the long-standing question of how political conservatism and ideological extremity relate to dogmatism. This work has bridged numerous areas of psychology—for example, judgment and decision-making, attitudes, and cognitive psychology—and has incorporated an array of methodological tools and paradigms to provide novel insight into this long-intransigent debate. Despite the variety of approaches, this work appears to present a relatively consistent pattern of results. In short, both the rigidity of the right and rigidity of the extremes models hold some truth—although the predictive power of each model appears to differ as a function of the specific conditions of the judgment at hand. In non-political domains, conservatism appears to be associated with greater dogmatism: Conservatives exhibit greater cognitive rigidity and judgment confidence than do their more liberal counterparts. However, in the political domain, ideological extremity appears to be the more potent predictor of dogmatism: More extreme individuals show greater rigidity of thought and confidence in their political judgments and attitudes than moderates. To be sure, many questions remain, and there is certain to be additional nuance to this general political-versus-non-political divide that future research will need to elucidate. Nevertheless, our hope and intention are that this proposed framework may take us one step closer to settling this debate that has held fast for the last 70+ years.

References

Adorno, T. W., Frenkel-Brunswik, E., Levinson, D. J., & Sanford, R. N. (1950). *The authoritarian personality*. Harper.

Altemeyer, B. (2002). Dogmatic behavior among students: Testing a new measure of dogmatism. *The Journal of Social Psychology, 142*, 713–721. https://doi.org/10.1080/00224540209603931

Amodio, D. M., Jost, J. T., Master, S. L., & Yee, C. M. (2007). Neurocognitive correlates of liberalism and conservatism. *Nature Neuroscience, 10*(10), 1246–1247. https://doi.org/10.1038/nn1979

Baron, J., & Jost, J. T. (2019). False equivalence: Are liberals and conservatives in the United States equally biased? *Perspectives on Psychological Science, 14*(2), 292–303. https://doi.org/10.1177/1745691618788876

Brandt, M. J., & Crawford, J. T. (2020). Worldview conflict and prejudice. In B. Gawronski (Ed.), *Advances in experimental social psychology* (Vol. 61, pp. 1–66). Academic Press. https://doi.org/10.1016/bs.aesp.2019.09.002

Brandt, M. J., Evans, A. M., & Crawford, J. T. (2015). The unthinking or confident extremist? Political extremists are more likely than moderates to reject experimenter-generated anchors. *Psychological Science, 26*(2), 189–202. https://doi.org/10.1177/0956797614559730

Briñol, P., & Petty, R. E. (2022). Self-validation theory: An integrative framework for understanding when thoughts become consequential. *Psychological Review, 129*(2), 340–367. https://doi.org/10.1037/rev0000340

Buechner, B. M., Clarkson, J. J., Otto, A. S., Hirt, E. R., & Ho, M. C. (2021). Political ideology and executive functioning: The effect of conservatism and liberalism on cognitive flexibility and working memory performance. *Social Psychological and PersonalityScience, 12*(2), 237–247. https://doi.org/10.1177/1948550620913187

Conner, M., & Sparks, P. (2002). Ambivalence and attitudes. *European Review of Social Psychology, 12*(1), 37–70. https://doi.org/10.1080/14792772143000012

Costello, T. H., & Bowes, S. M. (2023). Absolute certainty and political ideology: A systematic test of curvilinearity. *Social Psychological and Personality Science, 14*(1), 93–102. https://doi.org/10.31234/osf.io/fegzt

DeMarree, K. G., Petty, R. E., Briñol, P., & Xia, J. (2020). Documenting individual differences in the propensity to hold attitudes with certainty. *Journal of Personality and Social Psychology, 119*, 1239–1265. https://doi.org/10.1037/pspa0000241

Ditto, P. H., Liu, B. S., Clark, C. J., Wojcik, S. P., Chen, E. E., Grady, R. H., Celniker, J. B., & Zinger, J. F. (2019). At least bias is bipartisan: A meta-analytic comparison of partisan bias in liberals and conservatives. *Perspectives on Psychological Science, 14*(2), 273–291. https://doi.org/10.1177/1745691617746796

Dunning, D. (2012). Confidence considered: Assessing the quality of decisions and performance. In K. Demarree & P. Brinol (Eds.), *Social metacognition* (pp. 63–80). Psychology Press.

Fernbach, P. M., Rogers, T., Fox, C. R., & Sloman, S. A. (2013). Political extremism is supported by an illusion of understanding. *Psychological Science, 24*(6), 939–946. https://doi.org/10.1177/0956797612464058

Frimer, J. A., Skitka, L. J., & Motyl, M. (2017). Liberals and conservatives are similarly motivated to avoid exposure to one another's opinions. *Journal of Experimental Social Psychology, 72*, 1–12. https://doi.org/10.1016/j.jesp.2017.04.003

Goldsmith, E. B., & Goldsmith, R. E. (1980). Dogmatism and confidence as related factors in evaluation of new products. *Psychological Reports, 47*, 1068–1070. https://doi.org/10.2466/pr0.1980.47.3f.1068

Greenberg, J., & Jonas, E. (2003). Psychological motives and political orientation—The left, the right, and the rigid: Comment on Jost et al. (2003). *Psychological Bulletin, 129*(3), 376–382. https://doi.org/10.1037/0033-2909.129.3.376

Guay, B., & Johnston, C. D. (2022). Ideological asymmetries and the determinants of politically motivated reasoning. *American Journal of Political Science, 66*(2), 285–301. https://doi.org/10.1111/ajps.12624

Harris, E. A., & Van Bavel, J. J. (2021). Preregistered replication of "Feeling superior is a bipartisan issue: Extremity (not direction) of political views predicts perceived belief superiority". *Psychological Science, 32*(3), 451–458. https://doi.org/10.1177/0956797620968792

Higgins, E. T. (2019). What reigns supreme: Value, control, or truth? *Motivation Science, 5*(3), 185–201. https://doi.org/10.1037/mot0000150

Huddy, L. (2001). From social to political identity: A critical examination of social identity theory. *Political Psychology, 22*(1), 127–156. https://doi.org/10.1111/0162-895X.00230

Iyengar, S., Lelkes, Y., Levendusky, M., Malhotra, N., & Westwood, S. J. (2019). The origins and consequences of affective polarization in the United States. *Annual Review of Political Science, 22*, 129–146. https://doi.org/10.1146/annurev-polisci-051117-073034

Jost, J. T., Federico, C. M., & Napier, J. L. (2009). Political ideology: Its structure, functions, and elective affinities. *Annual Review of Psychology, 60*, 307–337. https://doi.org/10.1146/annurev.psych.60.110707.163600

Jost, J. T., Glaser, J., Kruglanski, A. W., & Sulloway, F. J. (2003a). Political conservatism as motivated social cognition. *Psychological Bulletin, 129*(3), 339–375. https://doi.org/10.1037/0033-2909.129.3.339

Jost, J. T., Glaser, J., Kruglanski, A. W., & Sulloway, F. J. (2003b). Exceptions that prove the rule—Using a theory of motivated social cognition to account for ideological incongruities and political anomalies: Reply to Greenberg and Jonas (2003). *Psychological Bulletin, 129*(3), 383–393. https://doi.org/10.1037/0033-2909.129.3.383

Jost, J. T., Sterling, J., & Stern, C. (2018). Getting closure on conservatism, or the politics of epistemic and existential motivation. In C. Kopetz & A. Fishbach (Eds.), *The motivation-cognition interface, from the lab to the real world: A festschrift in honor of Arie W. Kruglanski* (Vol. 1, pp. 56–87). Routledge. https://doi.org/10.4324/9781315171388-4

Kahan, D. M. (2012). Ideology, motivated reasoning, and cognitive reflection: An experimental study. *Judgment and Decision Making, 8*, 407–424.

Kruglanski, A. W. (2013). *Lay epistemics and human knowledge: Cognitive and motivational bases.* Springer Science & Business Media.

Lammers, J., Koch, A., Conway, P., & Brandt, M. J. (2017). The political domain appears simpler to the politically extreme than to political moderates. *Social Psychological and Personality Science, 8*(6), 612–622. https://doi.org/10.1177/1948550616678456

Malka, A., Lelkes, Y., & Holzer, N. (2017). Rethinking the rigidity of the right model: Three suboptimal methodological practices and their implications. In J. T. Crawford & L. Jussim (Eds.), *Frontiers of social psychology: Politics of social psychology* (pp. 116–135). Psychology Press. https://doi.org/10.4324/9781315112619-8

Mayseless, O., & Kruglanski, A. W. (1987). What makes you so sure? Effects of epistemic motivations on judgmental confidence. *Organizational Behavior and Human Decision Processes, 39*(2), 162–183. https://doi.org/10.1016/0749-5978(87)90036-7

Newman, L. S., & Sargent, R. H. (2021). Liberals report lower levels of attitudinal ambivalence than conservatives. *Social Psychological and Personality Science, 12*(5), 780–788. https://doi.org/10.1177/1948550620939798

Oxford Languages (2021). Dogmatism. https://languages.oup.com/google-dictionary-en/

Parrott, G., & Brown, L. (1972). Political bias in the Rokeach Dogmatism Scale. *Psychological Reports, 30*(3), 805–806. https://doi.org/10.2466/pr0.1972.30.3.805

Pennycook, G., Cheyne, J. A., Barr, N., Koehler, D. J., & Fugelsang, J. A. (2014). The role of analytic thinking in moral judgements and values. *Thinking & Reasoning, 20*(2), 188–214. https://doi.org/10.1080/13546783.2013.865000

Rokeach, M. (1954). The nature and meaning of dogmatism. *Psychological Review, 61*(3), 194–204. https://doi.org/10.1037/h0060752

Rollwage, M., Dolan, R. J., & Fleming, S. M. (2018). Metacognitive failure as a feature of those holding radical beliefs. *Current Biology, 28*(24), 4014–4021. https://doi.org/10.1016/j.cub.2018.10.053

Rollwage, M., Loosen, A., Hauser, T. U., Moran, R., Dolan, R. J., & Fleming, S. M. (2020). Confidence drives a neural confirmation bias. *Nature Communications, 11*(1), Article 2634. https://doi.org/10.1038/s41467-020-16278-6

Ruisch, B. C., & Stern, C. (2021). The confident conservative: Ideological differences in judgment and decision-making confidence. *Journal of Experimental Psychology: General, 150*, 527–544. https://doi.org/10.1037/xge0000898

Schulz, L., Rollwage, M., Dolan, R. J., & Fleming, S. M. (2020). Dogmatism manifests in lowered information search under uncertainty. *Proceedings of the National Academy of Sciences of the United States of America, 117*(49), 31527–31534. https://doi.org/10.1073/pnas.2009641117

Stern, C. (2022). Political ideology and social categorization. In B. Gawronski (Ed.), *Advances in experimental social psychology* (Vol. 65, pp. 167–233). Academic Press. https://doi.org/10.1016/bs.aesp.2021.11.003

Stern, C., & Axt, J. R. (2021). Ideological differences in race and gender stereotyping. *Social Cognition, 39*, 259–294. https://doi.org/10.1521/soco.2021.39.2.259

Talhelm, T. (2018). Hong Kong liberals are WEIRD: Analytic thought increases support for liberal policies. *Personality and Social Psychology Bulletin, 44*(5), 717–728. https://doi.org/10.1177/0146167217746151

Talhelm, T., Haidt, J., Oishi, S., Zhang, X., Miao, F. F., & Chen, S. (2015). Liberals think more analytically (more "WEIRD") than conservatives. *Personality and Social Psychology Bulletin*, *41*(2), 250–267. https://doi.org/10.1177/0146167214563672

Toner, K., Leary, M. R., Asher, M. W., & Jongman-Sereno, K. P. (2013). Feeling superior is a bipartisan issue: Extremity (not direction) of political views predicts perceived belief superiority. *Psychological Science*, *24*(12), 2454–2462. https://doi.org/10.1177/0956797613494848

Vacchiano, R. B., Strauss, P. S., & Hochman, L. (1969). The open and closed mind: A review of dogmatism. *Psychological Bulletin*, *71*(4), 261–273.

Van Bavel, J. J., & Pereira, A. (2018). The partisan brain: An identity-based model of political belief. *Trends in Cognitive Sciences*, *22*(3), 213–224. https://doi.org/10.1016/j.tics.2018.01.004

Van Hiel, A., Onraet, E., Crowson, H. M., & Roets, A. (2016). The relationship between right-wing attitudes and cognitive style: A comparison of self-report and behavioural measures of rigidity and intolerance of ambiguity. *European Journal of Personality*, *30*(6), 523–531. https://doi.org/10.1002/per.2082

Van Hiel, A., Onraet, E., & De Pauw, S. (2010). The relationship between social-cultural attitudes and behavioral measures of cognitive style: A meta-analytic integration of studies. *Journal of Personality*, *78*(6), 1765–1800. https://doi.org/10.1111/j.1467-6494.2010.00669.x

van Prooijen, J. W., & Krouwel, A. P. (2017). Extreme political beliefs predict dogmatic intolerance. *Social Psychological and Personality Science*, *8*(3), 292–300. https://doi.org/10.1177/1948550616671403

van Prooijen, J. W., Krouwel, A. P., & Emmer, J. (2018). Ideological responses to the EU refugee crisis: The left, the right, and the extremes. *Social Psychological and Personality Science*, *9*(2), 143–150. https://doi.org/10.1177/1948550617731501

Wagner, B. C., Briñol, P., & Petty, R. E. (2012). Dimensions of metacognitive judgment: Implications for attitude change. In P. Briñol & K. DeMarree (Eds.), *Social metacognition* (pp. 43–61). Psychology Press.

Yilmaz, O., & Saribay, S. A. (2017). The relationship between cognitive style and political orientation depends on the measures used. *Judgment and Decision Making*, *12*, 140–147.

Yilmaz, O., Saribay, S. A., & Iyer, R. (2020). Are neo-liberals more intuitive? Undetected libertarians confound the relation between analytic cognitive style and economic conservatism. *Current Psychology*, *39*(1), 25–32. https://doi.org/10.1007/s12144-019-0130-x

Zmigrod, L. (2020). The role of cognitive rigidity in political ideologies: Theory, evidence, and future directions. *Current Opinion in Behavioral Sciences*, *34*, 34–39. https://doi.org/10.1016/j.cobeha.2019.10.016

Zmigrod, L. (2022). A psychology of ideology: Unpacking the psychological structure of ideological thinking. *Perspectives on Psychological Science*, *17*(4), 1072–1092. https://doi.org/10.1177/17456916211044140

Zmigrod, L., Eisenberg, I. W., Bissett, P. G., Robbins, T. W., & Poldrack, R. A. (2021). The cognitive and perceptual correlates of ideological attitudes: A data-driven approach. *Philosophical Transactions of the Royal Society B*, *376*(1822), Article 20200424. https://doi.org/10.1098/rstb.2020.0424

Zmigrod, L., Rentfrow, P. J., & Robbins, T. W. (2018). Cognitive underpinnings of nationalistic ideology in the context of Brexit. *Proceedings of the National Academy of Sciences of the United States of America*, *115*(19), E4532–E4540. https://doi.org/10.1073/pnas.1708960115

Zmigrod, L., Rentfrow, P. J., & Robbins, T. W. (2020). The partisan mind: Is extreme political partisanship related to cognitive inflexibility? *Journal of Experimental Psychology: General*, *149*, 407–418. https://doi.org/10.1037/xge0000661

Zwicker, M. V., van Prooijen, J. W., & Krouwel, A. P. (2020). Persistent beliefs: Political extremism predicts ideological stability over time. *Group Processes & Intergroup Relations*, *23*(8), 1137–1149. https://doi.org/10.1177/1368430220917753

VI
DOGMATISM AND OPEN-MINDEDNESS

The Interplay of Affect, Motivation, and Cognition

12
Open-Mindedness and Dogmatism in a Darwinian World

The Roles of Affective Appraisals over Time and Circumstance

George E. Marcus[1]

Introduction

One of the oldest clichés is that it is the winners who write history. Enlightenment proponents reversed the normative status of tradition (stability) and of progress (directed changes). Prior to the Enlightenment, tradition in various guises and cultural practices, in various locales, and in various historical periods was valued and protected by institutional devices, typically hierarchical forms of rule in most cultures, in family, in clans, and in nation-states (Sidanius & Pratto, 2004). Enlightenment thinkers promised a new world of ever-improving circumstances, diminishing poverty, ever-widening integration, increasing peace, diminishing violence, and democratic rule (Kant, 1970; Smith, 1986). To accomplish this program of inevitable progress they recommended adopting new patterns of thought and action, notably elevating individual autonomy of thought and action as well as democracy.

The consideration of dogmatism and open-mindedness is generally treated as a central fulcrum to mark the transition from the pre- to the post-Enlightenment.[2] In the pre-Enlightenment period those defending the old order treat what is now labeled *dogmatism* as righteous support of the proper order, defining that orientation as proper obedience, fidelity, loyalty, steadfastness, and faith (Maistre, 1977). From this standpoint *open-mindedness* is cast as gullibility leading to undependability. In the pre-Enlightenment period, *openness* is understood as frivolous indulgence of flights of fancy that leads people astray, thereby weakening the bonds that sustain the social order.

The terms *dogmatism* and *open-mindedness* are deeply enmeshed in the larger, heavily normative dispute between the two warring sides.[3] As such, dogmatism and open-mindedness are deeply normative. Moreover, they have been assigned qualities at a very grandiose and abstract level, descriptions that suit the requirements of the political over the scientific. However, enhancing the science of human decision-making recommends setting aside the normative assigned roles: dogmatism as villain and open-mindedness as virtue. I begin by viewing dogmatism and open-mindedness through the lens of environmental fitness. The result of this exploration yields new understandings of the mechanisms that sustain the social order.

Reframing in Terms of Environmental Fitness

All forms of life confront a profound challenge. To survive, a species must achieve evolutionary fitness. Sharks represent one approach. Whales represent another. Both species share the same environment, the seas, and both have endured. But they both face an existential challenge. The environment they seek to exploit is knowable only as to the past and present. What the environment will become on the morrow is unknown. All species, including humans, lack foresight.

Sharks evolved by relying on one strategy. Whales evolved via a second strategy. The shark strategy is to presume the environment tomorrow is and will continue to be familiar. They evolved the specific capabilities to successfully exploit that specific environmental niche. That route, find a successful way and reproduce that way from generation to generation, has served the species well as shark species have persisted for hundreds of millions of years. But that route has an obvious flaw. The demise of dinosaurs exemplifies that flaw. When a massive asteroid crashed into the earth, dinosaurs found themselves no longer in their familiar environment. All their accumulated array of skills and capabilities were no longer able to sustain them, except for the dinosaur species that have since evolved as birds.

Whales evolved through a different strategy. Evolving as a social species, via sexual reproduction, they added diversity and the ability to rely on fluid cultural learning. Whales live in bonded groups called pods. Impressive is their capacity to communicate within and from one family group (pod) to other pods and over considerable distances (Xanthopoulos, 2021). How that adds to their endurance as a species can be seen in recent research on sperm whales and their response to predation by New England whalers.

New England whalers hunted whales to obtain their oil. American whalers first hunted in the Atlantic. They then rounded Cape Horn, thereby reaching the Pacific, and began hunting the southern sperm whales. These whale pods confronted a new threat. Sperm whales had learned to deal with predation by orcas by forming defense circles, extending their powerful flukes to beat off their attackers. But this defensive strategy was not just ineffective against whalers; it proved especially deadly. Sperm whales facing each other, staying in a fixed place, left them easy targets for the harpoons of the whalers.

In the first hunting season in the southern Pacific, sperm whales that survived the attacks communicated to other distant pods of this new predator. They used their intelligence to develop and then share new tactics to other pods of whales. As a result, in the subsequent hunting seasons in these Pacific waters, the whalers found far less success than in that first year (Whitehead et al., 2021).

The human species evolved by taking advantage of both strategies. And those strategies are each tied to the cultural practices specific to time and place. The flexibility to develop different cultural collectives, each differently evolving over time and space, added to the diverse array of possible living formulations. Dogmatism is the shark strategy: Find what works, and build that deeply into the fabric of being a shark. Open-mindedness is the whale strategy: Find what works, but rely on the ability to come to new understandings and then consider new solutions. This ability to detach from learned practices is especially valuable when there are new problems.[4] The first option is achieved by relying on evolved capabilities, enshrined in the species' DNA, and by the cultural practices embedded in habituated patterns of thought and action (Aristotle, 1985; Bargh & Chartrand, 1999; James, 1890).

The second option is also reliance on heritable capabilities and cultural practices, such as those recommended by the Enlightenment project (e.g., the modern university). In the case of the human species, sexual reproduction generates diversity in many factors as humans go from generation to generation.[5] Diversity is an insurance policy against risk. Who knows when we might need people taller or shorter, more devoted or more imaginative? If we live in a changing world, then it is best to have some who are perhaps ill-suited to the current environment but who might be better suited to the next. And that diversity allows different iterations to test their viability, for reality will reward some and punish others.[6] The Enlightenment project is built on the premise of fostering free exploration for all so that newer and more successful modes of thought and action can be discovered and distributed widely (Kant, 1970).

Cooperation adds adaptive strengths to communities (Axelrod, 1983). But, to that, the human species adds a considerable flexibility in the variants of cultures, producing many different cultural communities. That in turn generates a problem. Any system of cooperation requires "buy-in"" to the many diverse norms that sustain the deft coordination (Goffman, 1971). Moreover, the knowledge of the norms that ensure successful collaboration, whether they be among those of equal status or among those unequal, are highly complex, as Goffman details. They are embedded in procedural memory, hence not consciously accessible, but only crudely through observation of their main features (Van Zomeren et al., 2018). Varieties of reward of proper behavior and punishment against improper behavior are monitored by "intuitive" processing, which occurs very early, faster, and more accurately than the later available conscious awareness (Albrechtsen et al., 2009). Effective social cooperation requires that many aspects of thought and action need to be learned, mastered, and properly and deftly executed by those who reside in any given community, large or small. Humans are oriented to closely monitor others to thereby enable facile collective agency (Chartrand & Bargh, 1999). Much of this is done well before conscious awareness (Hoffman, 2019).

As to the choice between the two strategies, experience shows that each route is fallible. Neither is always superior to the other. Each has led to profound disasters. For some societies, the reliance on tradition led to their demise (Diamond, 2005). And some who tried a new imagined future found it produced horrific outcomes (Kiernan, 2008; Snyder, 2010).

MacKuen and colleagues (1992, p. 597) contrast two different forms of intelligence: "Consider two caricatures: peasant and banker. The peasant judges [based on] ... personal experience.... The banker, in contrast, is indifferent about the past except as it portends the future." Much like sharks, peasants know their terrain, the particulars of it, the seasons, and the recurring circumstances their farms face, such as periods of drought, how long they last, how often they occur, whether there is a risk of hail, how to judge the quality of seeds, and much more. For example, what will be this season's likely harvest and what will it bring in the market, as well as the price of things needed to sustain family and farm? And yet more, what are the neighbors like, the vendors, the local government officials, and so on?

This is rich, detailed knowledge, even if incomplete and on occasion erroneous. Peasant farms can and do founder on the unexpected: an unknown plant disease; an infestation that does not yield to any known intervention; someone upstream diverting the water needed for their farm, as in the novels by Marcel Pagnol, *Jean de Florette* and *Manon of the Springs* (Pagnol, 1988); or the appearance of larger and richer competitors or new, more productive methods of farming that peasants, hewing to tradition, are unlikely to adopt.

The banker is making a different bet and depends on different skills. Bankers are on the lookout for new projects, perhaps a housing development, a new warehouse, or a new medical practice. But that calculation is necessarily mindful of the uncertainty of the moment as the return lies in the future. Bankers expressly bet on the possibility of a new project being the better choice. This formulation describes the decision makers as stable orientations—one is either a peasant or a banker.

But there is a second aspect to this dual orientation, banker or peasant. All of us can compare the actual present to our expectations for the present. And that comparison can guide us to lean toward peasant or banker. If we are in a seemingly familiar environment, then we can better rely on all we have learned to swiftly and deftly display the vast inventory of habituated behaviors and thoughts, both individual and social. Human brains have the capacity to recognize and act on sensory input very fast, well before the mind's partial and most often impotent grasp (Rolls, 2013).[7] But if we face a novel, uncertain environment, then we need to suppress reliance on that inventory of habits so that we can come to a new understanding, create or select a better option untainted by extant loyalties.

Renewed attention to how humans execute collaboration in the many mundane and consequential acts they undertake has implications for how we have understood threat. Rather than threats being of a single sort, identified by heightened fear, threats have some measure of two quite different facets. One facet of threat is the novel, the unexpected; and such departures from the familiar are identified by fear (Gray, 1987). The other facet of threat is the sundry efforts internal and external to disrupt the normal mutual collaboration that sustains social comity. And that sort of threat is identified by heightened anger (Marcus et al., 2019). Keeping people in a community safe requires two very different mechanisms, one that manages threats that are predominantly novel and one that manages threats to the sundry norms that enable smooth execution of collaborative acts.

The human capacity to shift from the peasant stance to the banker stance has been demonstrated in political science (Marcus, 1988; Marcus & MacKuen, 1993) and in psychology (Chaiken & Trope, 1999). The peasant and banker archetypes capture the default "intuitive" and the "deliberative" departure from that default intuitive, respectively. Within a political context, the former state of mind is often labeled *motivated reasoning* or *resolute partisanship*, whereas the latter can be labeled *motivated deliberation* or *reflective deliberation*. Motivated reasoning or resolute partisanship is associated with dogmatism and involves reliance upon proven habits of thought and action. Motivated or reflective deliberation is associated with open-mindedness, an inhibition of familiar habits accompanied by exploration of the novel and careful selection of the best course of thought and action (MacKuen et al., 2010).

Unsurprising in light of the politicized history of these terms, one being the good and the other being the bad, it has been common to treat these two judgment orientations, dogmatism and open-mindedness, as mutually exclusive. That is, one is engaged in either one or the other, either as a function of personality disposition or as driven by the circumstance of the moment. By expressly measuring them we can treat that habit of construction as a testable proposition. And, as I shall show, these two orientations are not polar opposites. Rather, they are two different, unrelated orientations, with each being usefully available in some, but not all, circumstances. And that has ramifications for how we understand ourselves and democratic regimes and their superiority to authoritarian regimes.

Data and Measures

In the late spring of 2010, I and my colleagues Michael B. MacKuen and W. Russell Neuman conducted a number of large-scale survey experiments.[8] The data obtained are intended to be representative of American adults collected online using KN standard methodology (now GfK Custom Research). One of the survey experiments includes 1545 participants representing a broad cross section of American adults. Given the nature of survey measurement error and individual differences in both personality and other background factors, we took advantage of the enhanced statistical power of a large N study. The experimental survey included three stories about terrorism. After reading one of these stories, participants completed self-report measures that assessed their dogmatic and open-minded reactions to the issues described in the story. In addition, participants completed measures of their affective appraisals of the story as well as measures of more chronic individual difference characteristics.

Terrorism Stories

Participants were randomly assigned to read one of three different stories about terrorism. Each focused on a specific aspect of terrorism in the context of the US experience.[9] The diverse stories ensure that we have a diverse array of situational conditions represented in the data. One story focused on the success of US government agencies in keeping US ports safe. Another focused on the various efforts of al-Qaeda and Osama bin Laden, its leader, to attack the United States. The third focused on the FBI's inability to identify how many domestic terror cells there might be and where they might be. In sum, participants were exposed to diverse and heterogenous circumstances and generated their understanding of each of three different strategic considerations. These strategic considerations involved the following: how substantial are the available resources, and how responsive is the environment to reward-seeking (levels of enthusiasm); how uncertain and novel is the environment depicted in the story (levels of fear); and how consequential are the norm violations that are present in the story (levels of anger).

Measures of Dogmatism and Open-Mindedness

After reading a randomly assigned story, participants completed eight items that assessed their dogmatic and open-minded orientations. The four dogmatism items assessed devotion to strict reliance on a given course of action and disinterest in exploring other possibilities or differing voices. Specifically, four items that assess "resolute partisanship" were used to tap dogmatic reactions (e.g., "These issues and events provide no room for compromise").[10] The four open-mindedness items assessed interest in exploring diverse viewpoints and interest in deliberating about the best course of action. Specifically, four items that assess "reflective deliberation" were used to tap open-minded reactions (e.g., "These sorts of issues and events have two sides and I want to look at both of them").[11] These items were used to create two scales: *Dogmatism (Resolute Partisanship)* and *Open-Mindedness (Reflective Deliberation)*. These served as dependent measures in the main analyses reported in this chapter.

Individual Difference Measures (Chronic Predictors)

One purpose of this research was to examine whether chronic individual difference characteristics determine the participants' level of dogmatism and open-mindedness. Thus, the survey also included a large battery of 44 items that assess the Big Five personality traits (John, 1990; McCrae & John, 1992). These items assessed five personality dimensions: extraversion versus introversion, neuroticism versus emotional stability, agreeableness versus individual autonomy, conscientiousness versus task flexibility, and openness to experience versus steadfast focus. We included three other stable dispositions that also warrant consideration, the first two of which are political dispositions: partisan identification, in the United States as Republican and Democrat (Converse & Markus, 1979); ideological identification, left, in the United States liberal, or right, in the United States conservative (Fleury & Lewis-Beck, 1993); and, need for cognition, given that the banker orientation demands comfort, perhaps even an affinity for thoughtful consideration (Cacioppo & Petty, 1982). These dispositions are stable, largely unchanging over a life course; and their influence in the political realm remains stable as well (Conley, 1984; McCrae & Costa, 2003).

Affective Appraisals (Contemporary Predictors)

In an important paper, Stanley Feldman and Karen Stenner (1997) found that a stable disposition, authoritarianism, was greatly enhanced in its influence on judgments when people confront threatening circumstances. This recommends assessing the contemporary understandings people have of the circumstantial moment. These understandings are likely to influence both dogmatism and open-mindedness. Moreover, dispositions and contemporary understandings of the circumstantial moment may have interactive effects on dogmatism and open-mindedness.

Previous research has shown that three affective evaluations are continuously assessing any given story, event, individual, or group (Neuman et al., 2018). To secure a full understanding of how people assess the moment, I rely on the Theory of Affective Intelligence's "Affect Appraisal Battery," which incorporates validated measures of those three affective evaluations: fear, anger, and enthusiasm (Marcus et al., 2017). Thus, we can assess the impact of stable dispositions, eight in all; contemporary understandings, three affective state appraisals in all; and the possibility of interactions between "trait" and "state," following the route that Feldman and Stenner identified. Studies based solely on trait influences may prove problematic as the analysis is likely underspecified, being inattentive to state influences.

Taken together the data have some strengths and some important weaknesses. The sample is diverse and large. The measures of the three affective appraisals and of the personality dispositions rely on validated measures and on multiple items to define each disposition. The scales exploring dogmatism (resolute partisanship) and open-mindedness (reflective deliberation) each use multiple items and have been previously validated (Marcus et al., 2017). The multiple stimulus stories offer a rich stimulus array. But this is only one study and hence suffers the risk of being a black swan. Moreover, the study focus, terrorism, is itself but one topic, one among a vast array of political, social, and economic topics that engage people. Finally, while the included dispositions are well chosen and well measured, there are other important dispositions not available in these data.

Empirical Analyses

The results are organized into three parts. The first section explores what can be learned from the distributions of *Resolute Partisanship (Dogmatism)* and of *Reflective Deliberation (Open-Mindedness)*. Do these scales anchor two opposing orientations such that one end anchors the most dogmatic and the other end is marked by the most open-minded? The second section examines the extent to which these two orientations are driven by stable personality and political dispositions and contemporaneous affective appraisals. The third section considers the extent to which the contemporaneous and the dispositional interweave in either a complementary or antagonistic fashion. In each section, the overarching question is "Can the results be understood as enhancing or impinging on evolutionary fitness?"[12]

Resolute Partisanship and Reflective Deliberation

A common focus of late is "affective polarization" (Druckman & Levendusky, 2019). The speculation is that the antagonism between contending views of the public good, both large and small, is fueled by emotion: *affective polarization*. To the extent that conflicts become increasingly fraught, so the story goes, the political middle shrivels as affective polarization drives people to the extremes. Further, political elites will use emotion to mobilize and bind their political supporters (Fine & Hunt, 2021). And given the importance of the 9/11 attack on the American public, this suggests that Resolute Partisanship (dogmatism) would be skewed to the high end of the scale. Similarly, when focused on terrorism, we might expect that few would be drawn to Reflective Deliberation (open-mindedness) as deliberating over various ways to best deal with terrorists would not be a popular stance.

In fact, these two measures were found to be clearly normally distributed (not skewed). Moreover, the measures of dogmatism (Resolute Partisanship) and open-mindedness (Reflective Deliberation) are uncorrelated, $r = -.15$, $n = 1544$, a result replicated in other studies (Marcus, 2021). The normal distribution of these two orientations and their apposite connection do not support the common view that these orientations are contending opponents. It would seem that people can avail themselves, at any given time, of either stance (MacKuen et al., 2010).

That everyone can take advantage of either orientation, sometimes dogmatic and sometimes open-minded, supports a functional view of affective appraisals. That interpretation is supported to the extent that we find that people move to adopt the orientation that best suits the circumstances they face (see Chapter 7 in this volume). Moving to greater reliance on and defense of extant habits of thought and action when the norms that enable collaborative agency are being violated is a functional dynamic that sustains the community. Being willing to abandon normally sustaining patterns of thought and action and the norms that enable cooperative engagement with others is similarly an apt response when the circumstances are novel and uncertain.

Predicting Resolute Partisanship and Reflective Deliberation: Effects of Contemporaneous Affective Appraisals and Dispositions

What can we say about what moves people to stronger reliance on Resolute Partisanship (dogmatism) and what moves people to turn to stronger reliance on Reflective Deliberation (open-mindedness)? Given that the two orientations are unrelated, it would be inappropriate to treat them as opposite anchors of a single dimension. Thus, separate analyses were performed to predict each of these two orientations.

The analyses proceed in two steps. First, I explore the direct effects of affective appraisals: What are the effects of fear, anger, and enthusiasm? Then I add the eight dispositions: the two political dispositions, partisan and ideological identification, and the six personality dispositions, the "Big Five" and need for cognition. Table 12.1 shows the results obtained when predicting Resolute Partisanship (dogmatism). The most notable point in comparing the two columns is what changes in the coefficients for the three affective appraisals when the eight dispositions are added to the analysis.

Table 12.1 shows that two affective appraisals—enthusiasm, modestly, and anger, more vigorously—are linked to people taking a more assertive stance on partisan resolve (dogmatism). Among the stable dispositions, three of the eight modestly impact partisan resolve. Republicans, and those who self-identify as conservative, modestly favor a more robust position on Resolute Partisanship (dogmatism). The same is true for conscientiousness. Of these five influences, anger's impact has double the influence of any of the other consequential influences.

It is worth remarking that heightened fear has no influence. This null result for fear is but the latest in a string of published results that suggest that the common attribution of fear as the core driver of steadfast loyalty to traditions and conventional authority is wrong largely because of inattention to anger (Vasilopoulos et al., 2019; Vasilopoulou & Wagner, 2017). Anger's role as the

Table 12.1 Predicting Resolute Partisanship (Dogmatism)

	Predictors: contemporary affective appraisals	Predictors: contemporary affective appraisals and dispositions
Affective appraisals		
Fear (anxiety)	−.04 (.02)	−.05 (.02)
Anger (aversion)	.22** (.02)	.20** (.02)
Enthusiasm	.10** (.02)	.08** (.02)
Dispositions		
Partisan identity—Democrat high		−.08** (.02)
Ideological identity—liberal high		−.07** (.02)
Extraversion		.03 (.02)
Agreeableness		−.07 (.03)
Conscientiousness		.10** (.03)
Neuroticism		.02 (.02)
Openness to experience		.00 (.03)
Need for cognition		−.05 (.03)
**p < .01	Adjusted R^2 = .08	Adjusted R^2 = .14

defender of the norms suggests that people rely on anger, not fear, to support the traditions of social practices on which they rely (Marcus, 2021; Marcus et al., 1995, 2019).

As to enthusiasm and anger, it should also be noted that environmental fitness is a reasonable interpretation of their influences. After all, the general view is that Resolute Partisanship (dogmatism) is the default stance. It makes sense that it is the default because familiar practices enable sociability and generally benefit individuals and their community. Additionally, anger strengthens communities, by identifying breaches in the norms that sustain cooperative behaviors and then mobilizing the angry to defend against those who threaten the social foundations of that community. Importantly, as I noted above, in modern societies even more so than in traditional societies, there are multiple arrays of conflicting and competing communities, each with a different array of norms on which they are reliant.

Columns 1 and 2 of Table 12.2 present that same analysis as in Table 12.1 but for the second judgment orientation, the more open-minded stance of Reflective Deliberation. Many of the patterns displayed in Table 12.1 are revealed here as well. The addition of dispositions to the analyses does not alter

Table 12.2 Predicting Reflective Deliberation (Open-Mindedness)

	Predictors: contemporary affective appraisals	Predictors: contemporary appraisals and dispositions	Predictors: contemporary appraisals, dispositions, and interactions
Affective appraisals			
Fear (anxiety)	.13** (.02)	.11** (.02)	.38** (.08)
Anger (aversion)	−.13** (.02)	−.09** (.02)	−.09** (.02)
Enthusiasm	.07** (.02)	.07** (.02)	.07** (.02)
Dispositions			
Partisan identity— Democrat high		.07** (.02)	.04** (.02)
Ideological identity— liberal high		.15** (.02)	.15** (.02)
Extraversion		.01 (.02)	.01 (.02)
Agreeableness		.15** (.03)	.33** (.06)
Conscientiousness		.03 (.03)	.04 (.03)
Neuroticism		.10** (.02)	.10** (.02)
Openness to experience		.07 (.03)	.08 (.03)
Need for cognition		.05 (.03)	.05 (.02)
Interactions			
Agreeableness by fear			−.35** (.10)
**$p < .01$	Adjusted $R^2 = .03$	Adjusted $R^2 = .15$	Adjusted $R^2 = .16$

the coefficients of the three affective appraisals. Again, political dispositions are consequential, though more so for ideological identification than for partisan identification. Democrats and liberals are more likely to endorse Reflective Deliberation (open-mindedness), while Republicans and conservatives are contrary.

Each of the affective appraisals is consequential. Having a positive sense of one's available resources and the ability to accomplish a positive outcome (i.e., heightened enthusiasm) is related to elevated endorsement of Reflective Deliberation (open-mindedness). However, it is the two "negative" appraisals that are doing more of the work. Heightened fear, favoring greater open-mindedness, and heightened anger, inhibiting, each affirm expectations. Novelty, identified by heightened fear, stimulates open-mindedness, whereas understanding the moment as a familiar challenge to valued norms, identified by heightened anger, stimulates a dogmatic closure to open considerations.

Of the personality dispositions, agreeableness and neuroticism are each consequential. Given that the social demands of Reflective Deliberation (open-mindedness) are high, working in an unfamiliar context with individuals who are also perhaps strangers, such collaborative ventures place a premium on those who have the resourcefulness to work in such conditions. Agreeableness provides social skills that empower working with others, especially when in newly constructed groupings. Thus, the more agreeable are better suited to function in novel circumstances.

A long-standing view of the neuroticism factor of personality has held it to be a general emotionality sensitivity. Neuroticism might be better understood as a more narrowly focused disposition. Rather than applying across all emotions, neuroticism is more precisely focused on conditions of uncertainty and novelty. High neuroticism is perhaps better understood as the "canary in the mine." Those high on neuroticism are more sensitive to novelty and the unexpected. Those low on neuroticism are better able to resist distractions.

In sum, people are stimulated to abandon confident faith in the sundry routines that direct their lives for a more open consideration of change by heightened fear and by heightened enthusiasm. They are also more likely to do so if they are liberal, high on agreeableness and high on neuroticism. They are less likely to do so if they understand the circumstances as a familiar challenge, identified and then driven by heightened anger.

Predicting Dogmatism and Open-Mindedness: Interactions Between Contemporaneous Affective Appraisals and Dispositions

Two published papers early on identified the ability of contemporary circumstances to fundamentally alter reliance on otherwise stable dispositions. Marcus and MacKuen (1993) provided corroboration of Jeffrey Gray's (1987) research showing that increased fear inhibits reliance on otherwise powerful habituated choices (see also Brader, 2006; Valentino et al., 2009). Feldman and Stenner (1997) find that the authoritarian disposition stays rather dormant until the contemporary circumstances are perceived as threatening. Thus, one contemporary appraisal can reduce otherwise influential dispositions. But others can increase the influence of otherwise modestly consequential dispositions.

To identify which of all possible interactions would merit attention, I relied on the MFPIGEN Stata module (Royston, 2012). That module identifies significant interactions using fractional polynomials. The initial examination of the MFPIGEN run for Resolute Partisanship (dogmatism), using a more relaxed probability test standard of $p < .05$, identifies six plausible interactions.

However, when rerunning the regression with those six plausible interactions along with the three affective appraisals and the eight dispositions, none reach the $p < .01$ (or the $p < .05$) level for rejecting the null hypothesis. Thus, in these data, there is no evidence of significant interactions when predicting Resolute Partisanship (dogmatism). When predicting dogmatism, this suggests that all are reliant on anger to swiftly identify breaches in the salient norms (Marcus, 2002; Valentino et al., 2011).

Running the same analysis for Reflective Deliberation (open-mindedness) finds one consequential interaction (see Column 3, Table 12.2). There is one robust interaction, $t = 3.47$, $p < .001$, that between fear and agreeableness, shown in Figure 12.1. This interaction fits well within the environmental fitness perspective. Those high in agreeableness are high in Reflective Deliberation (open-mindedness) across the full range of fear. On the other hand, it is those low in agreeableness who are strongly influenced by increasing levels of fear. Low agreeable types who are less fearful are not disposed to Reflective Deliberation (open-mindedness). However, as fear increases, the low agreeable types become more open-minded. As shown in the third column of Table 12.1, fear and agreeableness produce very potent direct effects. But the interaction shows that fear can motivate even those most disagreeable types.

When the agreeableness × fear interaction is entered in full regression analysis, two of the direct effects show substantial changes in their coefficients (Column 3, Table 12.2). First, the fear appraisal more than triples, from .11 to .38, and second, agreeableness more than doubles, from .15 to .33. Thus,

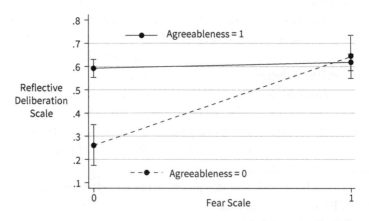

Figure 12.1 Reflective deliberation interaction—agreeableness and fear. CI = confidence interval.

these two factors, one a contemporaneous understanding of degree of novelty–uncertainty and one a stable and enduring disposition, have very robust impacts in shifting people to adopt a more open-minded stance. Finally, as with resolute partisanship, neither political disposition shows interactions with the contemporaneous affective appraisals, a result that is contrary to the claimed left–right emotionality bias.

The overall pattern shows people availing themselves of two available judgment orientations, a robust reliance on extant convictions, habits of thought, and action as well as open-minded reconsideration. Which is made manifest is controlled by a combination of contemporaneous affective appraisals and by a number of political and personality dispositions. These are largely independently influential, at least with respect to the dispositions available for empirical analysis in this study. There are some obvious dispositions one would wish to explore, among them authoritarianism (Feldman et al., 2022), social dominance orientation (Pratto et al., 1994), conservatism as to gender norms (Valentino et al., 2018), and system justification (Jost et al., 2004).

Conclusions

The central argument of this chapter is that dogmatism and open-mindedness are not mutually antagonistic worldviews. Rather, they are each available to all humans. Which becomes manifest is a function of both political and personality dispositions and contemporaneous understandings of whatever is being faced. Moreover, this duality serves to address a fundamental challenge that all variants of life face, the lack of foresight and the changes, gradual to instantaneous, and threats, familiar and novel, that lurk unseeable ahead.

The best available criterion as to when to remain steadfast and when to depart for seemingly better possibilities is a simple comparison of the nature of the moment and our expectations for that moment. That comparison is executed continuously and rapidly (Gray, 1987). It occurs so rapidly that well before the availability of conscious awareness humans have no introspective access to that process (Hoffman, 2019).

It has long been understood that the capacity to embed practices is essential to humans (Aristotle, 1985; James, 1890, Chapter 4). This capability is displayed everywhere in everyday life and in all manner of complexities. Thus, dogmatism is a part of all human lives and necessarily so. But all humans have the ability, though not to equal measure, to set aside reliance on their habits for new possibilities.

That facile availability, to shift from closed to open and back again, enables us to adjust to circumstances. We can adopt comfortable reliance on the familiar habits of thought and action in familiar circumstances, and we can put all those habits aside for open learning and deliberation on what are the best means for securing a better outcome in novel circumstances. Only democratic regimes reinforce that dual capability both by preparing their publics with proper civic education and by securing the rule of law. Authoritarian regimes with their punitive destruction of civil society, demands of servile compliance by the public, and putting obsequiousness as the principal hiring standard, generates a society fragile, rigid, undermined by systemic corruption, and thereby unable to adapt to the world as it reveals itself.

Can we live in a world and survive without knowing whether the world is safely familiar or not? And can we live with others, some we know and most we do not, without knowing whether their actions will be consistent with the specific rich array of norms pertinent to that moment? The questions argue for obvious answers. Some advance the universal value of open-mindedness as an essential feature of modern life (Benhabib, 1996; Young, 2010). Others argue for the ability to remain steadfast as essential for successful political achievement (Rosenblum, 2008; Shapiro, 2016). We all have to live in circumstances wherein each of these positions is better suited to the demands of the moment. However, the knowledge of which of those routes is best is only available in retrospect, a stance not available when choices have to be made.

Notes

1. Address Correspondence to George E. Marcus, gmarcus@williams.edu
2. This discussion is clearly a gross oversimplification of a complex and regionally varied topic (Israel, 2011). With the invention of democracy in Athens the contested discussion of the merits of hierarchical authority as against democratic practices had begun millennia before the 17th and 18th centuries (Ober, 2008, 2013). It is worth noting that those who proclaim the public's incompetence (Bernstein, 2021; Rosenberg, 2017) do not offer a parallel assessment of elite competence. I have little doubt such a comparison would display far more ample evidence of elite incompetence than of public incompetence (with far greater consequences as elites have greater heft on those consequences).
3. However, it should be noted that by and large the product of the Enlightenment vision has largely been highly successful as a more peaceful and fecund world, with a great increase in human population and decrease in the proportion thereof living in poverty (Easterbrook, 2021), the results being observed and endorsed by much of the world's population (Inglehart, 2018).
4. For a fuller account of these strategies, see Marcus (2002, 2013, 2021).
5. People vary in their physical features and personality from their parents but not in the number of eyes, nostrils, senses, and many other factors.

6. Some social species have their social structures so rigidly encased in their DNA that they have the benefit of the one social structure they inherit generation to generation, but only that one structure is possible. They gain the strength of the collective, but that strength precludes exploration within or outside of that structure (insect species are the obvious example).
7. The consensus is that conscious awareness becomes available 500 milliseconds after the brain receives sensory and soma sensory signals, while preconscious processes generate understandings and initiate actions at or before 200 milliseconds (Marcus, 2012, Chapters 4–5)
8. For a full presentation of the experiment's results, see Marcus (2021).
9. See https://www.researchgate.net/publication/346215432_Target_Story_Stimulipdf for complete stories.
10. The three additional *Resolute Partisanship (Dogmatism)* items were "I am certain that my point of view on these issues and events is the right one," "In dealing with these sorts of issues and events listening to everyone is going to get us entangled and produce endless debate," and "We just can't afford to take each and every minority view on these issues and events into account."
11. The three additional *Reflective Deliberation (Open-Mindedness)* items were "These sorts of issues and events should be resolved so that everybody's needs are met," "To solve these sorts of issues and events everyone's concerns should be heard," and "These sorts of issues and events are best resolved by listening to everyone's concerns."
12. The present chapter summarizes and presents analyses that specifically focus on the underpinnings of dogmatic (resolute partisanship) and open-minded (reflective deliberation) reactions and, as such, differs from previous treatments and presentations of these data.

References

Albrechtsen, J. S., Meissner, C. A., & Susa, K. J. (2009). Can intuition improve deception detection performance? *Journal of Experimental Social Psychology*, 45(4), 1052–1055. https://doi.org/10.1016/j.jesp.2009.05.017

Aristotle. (1985). *Nicomachean ethics* (P. Wheelwright, Trans.). Odyssey Press.

Axelrod, R. (1983). *The evolution of cooperation*. Harvard University Press.

Bargh, J. A., & Chartrand, T. L. (1999). The unbearable automaticity of being. *American Psychologist*, 54(7), 462–479. https://doi.org/10.1037/0003-066X.54.7.462

Benhabib, S. (1996). Toward a deliberative model of democratic legitimacy. In S. Benhabib (Ed.), *Democracy and difference: Contesting the boundaries of the political* (pp. 67–94). Princeton University Press. https://doi.org/10.1515/9780691234168-005

Bernstein, W. J. (2021). *The delusions of crowds: Why people go mad in groups*. Atlantic Monthly Press.

Brader, T. (2006). *Campaigning for hearts and minds: How emotional appeals in political ads work*. University of Chicago Press. https://doi.org/10.7208/chicago/9780226788302.001.0001

Cacioppo, J. T., & Petty, R. E. (1982). The need for cognition. *Journal of Personality and Social Psychology*, 42(1), 116–131. https://doi.org/10.1037/0022-3514.42.1.116

Chaiken, S., & Trope, Y. (Eds.). (1999). *Dual process models in social psychology*. Guilford Press.

Chartrand, T. L., & Bargh, J. A. (1999). The chameleon effect: The perception–behavior link and social interaction. *Journal of Personality and Social Psychology, 76*(6), 893–910. https://doi.org/10.1037/0022-3514.76.6.893

Conley, J. J. (1984). Longitudinal consistency of adult personality: Self-reported psychological characteristics across 45 years. *Journal of Personality and Social Psychology, 47*(6), 1325–1333. https://doi.org/10.1037/0022-3514.47.6.1325

Converse, P. E., & Markus, G. B. (1979). Plus ça change . . . : New CPS election study panel. *American Political Science Review, 73*, 32–49. https://doi.org/10.2307/1954729

Diamond, J. M. (2005). *Collapse: How societies choose to fail or succeed*. Viking.

Druckman, J. N., & Levendusky, M. S. (2019). What do we measure when we measure affective polarization? *Public Opinion Quarterly, 83*(1), 114–122. https://doi.org/10.1093/poq/nfz003

Easterbrook, G. (2021). *The blue age: How the US Navy created global prosperity—and why we're in danger of losing it*. Public Affairs.

Feldman, S., Mérola, V., & Dollman, J. (2022). The psychology of authoritarianism and support for illiberal policies and parties. In A. Sajó, R. Uitz, & S. Holmes (Eds.), *Routledge handbook of illiberalism* (pp. 635–654). Taylor Francis. https://doi.org/10.4324/9780367260569-46

Feldman, S., & Stenner, K. (1997). Perceived threat and authoritarianism. *Political Psychology, 18*(4), 741–770. https://doi.org/10.1111/0162-895X.00077

Fine, J. A., & Hunt, M. F. (2021). Negativity and elite message diffusion on social media. *Political Behavior*. Advance online publication. https://doi.org/10.1007/s11109-021-09740-8

Fleury, C. J., & Lewis-Beck, M. S. (1993). Anchoring the French voter: Ideology versus party. *Journal of Politics, 55*(4), 1100–1109. https://doi.org/10.2307/2131950

Goffman, E. (1971). *Relations in public*. Basic Books.

Gray, J. A. (1987). *The psychology of fear and stress* (2nd ed.). Cambridge University Press.

Hoffman, D. D. (2019). *The case against reality*. Allen Lane.

Inglehart, R. (2018). *Cultural evolution: People's motivations are changing, and reshaping the world*. Cambridge University Press. https://doi.org/10.1017/9781108613880

Israel, J. I. (2011). *Democratic enlightenment: Philosophy, revolution, and human rights 1750–1790*. Oxford University Press.

James, W. (1890). *The principles of psychology, Vol. 1*. Henry Holt and Co. https://doi.org/10.1037/10538-000

John, O. P. (1990). The "Big Five" factor taxonomy: Dimensions of personality in the natural language and in questionnaires. In L. A. Pervin (Ed.), *Handbook of personality theory and research* (pp. 66–100). Guilford Press.

Jost, J. T., Banaji, M. R., & Nosek, B. A. (2004). A decade of system justification theory: Accumulated evidence of conscious and unconscious bolstering of the status quo. *Political Psychology, 25*(6), 881–919. https://doi.org/10.1111/j.1467-9221.2004.00402.x

Kant, I. (1970). An answer to the question:"'What is enlightenment?" In *Kant: Political writings* (H. Reiss, Ed.; H. B. Nisbet, Trans.; pp. 54–60). Cambridge University Press.

Kiernan, B. (2008). *The Pol Pot regime: Race, power, and genocide in Cambodia under the Khmer Rouge, 1975–79* (3rd ed.). Yale University Press.

MacKuen, M. B., Wolak, J., Keele, L., & Marcus, G. E. (2010). Civic engagements: Resolute partisanship or reflective deliberation. *American Journal of Political Science, 54*(2), 440–458. https://doi.org/10.1111/j.1540-5907.2010.00440.x

Maistre, J. M. (1977). *Essay on the generative principle of political constitutions*. Scholars' Facsimiles & Reprints.

Marcus, G. E. (1988). The structure of emotional response: 1984 presidential candidates. *American Political Science Review, 82*(3), 735–761. https://doi.org/10.2307/1962488

Marcus, G. E. (2002). *The sentimental citizen: Emotion in democratic politics*. Pennsylvania State University Press.

Marcus, G. E. (2012). *Political psychology: Neuroscience, genetics and politics*. Oxford University Press.
Marcus, G. E. (2013). The theory of affective intelligence and liberal politics. In N. Demertzis (Ed.), *Emotions in politics: The affect dimension in political tension* (pp. 17–38). Palgrave Macmillan. https://doi.org/10.1057/9781137025661_2
Marcus, G. E. (2021). The rise of populism: The politics of justice, anger, and grievance. In J. Forgas, B. Crano, & K. Fiedler (Eds.), *The psychology of populism* (pp. 81–104). Routledge.
Marcus, G. E., & MacKuen, M. B. (1993). Anxiety, enthusiasm and the vote: The emotional underpinnings of learning and involvement during presidential campaigns. *American Political Science Review, 87*(3), 688–701. https://doi.org/10.2307/2938743
Marcus, G. E., Neuman, W. R., & MacKuen, M. B. (2017). Measuring emotional response: Comparing alternative approaches to measurement. *Political Science Research and Methods, 5*(4), 733–754. https://doi.org/10.1017/psrm.2015.65
Marcus, G. E., Sullivan, J. L., Theiss-Morse, E., & Wood, S. L. (1995). *With malice toward some: How people make civil liberties judgments*. Cambridge University Press. https://doi.org/10.1017/CBO9781139174046
Marcus, G. E., Valentino, N. A., Vasilopoulos, P., & Foucault, M. (2019). Applying the theory of affective intelligence to support for authoritarian policies and parties. *Advances in Political Psychology, 40*(S1), 109–139. https://doi.org/10.1111/pops.12571
McCrae, R. R., & Costa, P. T. (2003). *Personality in adulthood: A five-factor theory perspective* (2nd ed.). Guilford Press. https://doi.org/10.4324/9780203428412
McCrae, R. R., & John, O. P. (1992). An introduction to the five-factor model and its applications. *Journal of Personality, 60*, 175–215. https://doi.org/10.1111/j.1467-6494.1992.tb00970.x
Neuman, W. R., Marcus, G. E., & MacKuen, M. B. (2018). Hardwired for news: Affective intelligence and political attention. *Journal of Broadcasting & Electronic Media, 62*(4), 614–635. https://doi.org/10.1080/08838151.2018.1523169
Ober, J. (2008). *Democracy and knowledge: Innovation and learning in classical Athens*. Princeton University Press. https://doi.org/10.1515/9781400828807
Ober, J. (2013). Democracy's wisdom: An Aristotelian middle way for collective judgment. *American Political Science Review, 107*(1), 104–122. https://doi.org/10.1017/S0003055412000627
Pagnol, M. (1988). *Jean de Florette and Manon of the springs: Two novels*. Macmillan.
Pratto, F., Sidanius, J., Stallworth, L. M., & Malle, B. F. (1994). Social dominance orientation: A personality variable predicting social and political attitudes. *Journal of Personality and Social Psychology, 67*(4), 741–763. https://doi.org/10.1037/0022-3514.67.4.741
Rolls, E. T. (2013). *Emotion and decision-making explained*. Oxford University Press. https://doi.org/10.1093/acprof:oso/9780199659890.001.0001
Rosenberg, S. (2017). Unfit for democracy? Irrational, rationalizing, and biologically predisposed citizens. *Critical Review, 29*(3), 362–387. https://doi.org/10.1080/08913811.2017.1410982
Rosenblum, N. L. (2008). *On the side of the angels: An appreciation of parties and partisanship*. Princeton University Press.
Royston, P. (2012). *MFPIGEN: Stata module for modelling and displaying interactions between continuous predictors* [Statistical Software Components S457439]. Department of Economics, Boston College.
Shapiro, I. (2016). Against impartiality. *Journal of Politics, 78*(2), 467–480. https://doi.org/10.1086/684477
Sidanius, J., & Pratto, F. (2004). Social dominance theory: A new synthesis. In J. T. Jost & J. Sidanius (Eds.), *Political psychology: Key readings* (pp. 315–332). Psychology Press. https://doi.org/10.4324/9780203505984-18

Smith, A. (1986). *The wealth of nations*. Viking.
Snyder, T. (2010). *Bloodlands: Europe between Hitler and Stalin*. Basic Books.
Valentino, N. A., Banks, A. J., Hutchings, V. L., & Davis, A. K. (2009). Selective exposure in the internet age: The interaction between anxiety and information utility. *Political Psychology*, *30*(4), 591–613. https://doi.org/10.1111/j.1467-9221.2009.00716.x
Valentino, N. A., Brader, T., Groenendyk, E. W., Gregorowicz, K., & Hutchings, V. L. (2011). Election night's alright for fighting: The role of emotions in political participation. *Journal of Politics*, *73*(1), 156–170. https://doi.org/10.1017/S0022381610000939
Valentino, N. A., Wayne, C., & Oceno, M. (2018). Mobilizing sexism: The interaction of emotion and gender attitudes in the 2016 US presidential election. *Public Opinion Quarterly*, *82*(S1), 213–235. https://doi.org/10.1093/poq/nfy003
Van Zomeren, M., Kutlaca, M., & Turner-Zwinkels, F. M. (2018). Integrating who "we" are with what "we" (will not) stand for: A further extension of the social identity model of collective action. *European Review of Social Psychology*, *29*(1), 122–166. https://doi.org/10.1080/10463283.2018.1479347
Vasilopoulos, P., Marcus, G. E., Valentino, N. A., & Foucault, M. (2019). Fear, anger, and voting for the far right: Evidence from the November 13, 2015 Paris terror attacks. *Political Psychology*, *40*(4), 679–696. https://doi.org/10.1111/pops.12513
Vasilopoulou, S., & Wagner, M. (2017). Fear, anger and enthusiasm about the European Union: Effects of emotional reactions on public preferences towards European integration. *European Union Politics*, *18*(3), 382–405. https://doi.org/10.1177/1465116517698048
Whitehead, H., Smith, T. D., & Rendell, L. (2021). Adaptation of sperm whales to open-boat whalers: Rapid social learning on a large scale? *Biology Letters*, *17*, Article 20210030. https://doi.org/10.1098/rsbl.2021.0030
Xanthopoulos, D. (Director). (2021). *Fathom* [Documentary film]. Apple TV+. https://tv.apple.com/us/movie/fathom/umc.cmc.5dba56sgwst50iuh5h9uqpdsq
Young, I. M. (2010). *Responsibility for justice*. Oxford University Press.

13
Feeling Open- or Closed-Minded

The Role of Affective Feelings in the Closing or Opening of the Mind

Akila Raoul and Jeffrey R. Huntsinger

The idea that some affective states open minds and others close minds is central to many classic and contemporary models of the opened and closed mind (e.g., Adorno et al., 1950/2019; Freud, 1925/1963; Rokeach, 1963). Specific affective states (e.g., anxiety) are thought to trigger a closing of the mind, and others (e.g., happiness) are thought to trigger an opening of the mind. In what follows, we provide a review of the role of affective states in classic and contemporary models of open-minded cognition, all of which propose the idea that they have dedicated and direct effects on open-minded cognition. We then present a new approach, called the *affect-as-cognitive-feedback account*, which proposes a flexible rather than fixed effect of affect on open-minded cognition. We present some evidence for this flexible effect of affect on open-minded cognition before closing with larger implications for the role of affect in the context of political polarization, as well as ideas for future research.

Classic Approaches to the Open and Closed Mind

Open-minded cognition is defined as a bipolar continuum that ranges from open-mindedness to closed-mindedness. When people think in an open-minded way, they are more inclined to consider a wide range of perspectives, attitudes, and beliefs, some of which might even contradict their own opinions. In contrast, closed-minded thinking is dogmatic and results in people processing information in ways that confirm their preexisting attitudes (Price et al., 2015). The concept of dogmatism was studied alongside the theory of authoritarianism, which has been linked to conservatism, a preference for strict laws, and support for punitive social control (Duckitt, 2009). Several factors can influence whether someone thinks open- or closed-mindedly, one of which is a person's affective state.

Research examining the affective antecedents of open-mindedness can be traced back to research on the authoritarian personality (Adorno et al., 1950/2019). Following World War II, researchers scrambled to understand the Nazis' rise to power in Germany and, more generally, under what conditions fascism arises. The authoritarian personality is an extreme form of right-wing conservatism and was originally defined by nine elements: conventionalism, submission to authority, aggression toward those who differ in mindset, anti-intraception, superstition and stereotypy, power and toughness, destructiveness and cynicism, projectivity, and a preoccupation with sex and violence (Adorno et al., 1950/2019).

Right-wing authoritarianism was further characterized by excessive concerns with upholding social norms, submission to authority figures in one's society, and heightened aggression against those who challenge these social norms and disobey authority figures (Altemeyer & Altemeyer, 1981). The concept has been extensively studied in the political domain and has been linked to prejudice and discrimination. Right-wing authoritarianism has been found to predict support for the restriction of civil liberties, especially when faced with a threat of terrorism (Cohrs et al., 2005), increased ingroup favoritism (Duckitt & Sibley, 2010), and an increased reliance on traditional gender roles (Peterson & Zurbriggen, 2010).

A key defining characteristic of the authoritarian personality is cognitive rigidity or dogmatism, which is a mental state in which an individual shows an inability to yield to views that oppose their own and adapt to newly presented information. In contrast, someone who is cognitively flexible is better able to adapt to change and consider alternative viewpoints. Research has found that increased perceptions of threat can lead to greater rigidity (Pally, 1955), and there are many ways in which affect can influence threat perception. Additionally, this cognitive rigidity leaves no room for ambiguity and causes people to find any uncertainty to be greatly unpleasant.

Much of the early research on authoritarianism was inspired by Freudian psychoanalytic perspectives that were popular at the time. According to Freud's psychoanalytic perspective, emotional ambivalence plays a central role in the development of personality structure in children (Freud, 1925/1963). Researchers of authoritarianism took this idea and added the notion that early parent–child interactions cause the emergence of individual differences in ability to tolerate such emotional ambivalence and that such differences have implications for authoritarianism, cognitive rigidity, and dogmatism (Frenkel-Brunswik, 1949).

According to this view, individuals develop an intolerance to ambiguity as a result of emotional ambivalence stemming from feelings of hostility toward their parents that arise from an overly strict parenting style (Frenkel-Brunswik, 1949). Ambiguity was believed to lead to uncertainty and anxiety. Thus, for those who are intolerant of ambiguity, ambiguity was an aversive or threatening state that causes people to seek out certainty as a method to reduce such feelings. The theory suggested that this intolerance to ambiguity could result in people relying on easy and familiar information, such as stereotypes and prejudicial beliefs. In this way, anxiety was theorized to result in closed-minded thinking as a way to reduce such feelings because it "satisfies the need to know" (Rokeach, 1960).

Contemporary Approaches to the Open and Closed Mind

These early perspectives served as important precursors for contemporary theories that focus on the role of uncertainty and anxiety as triggers of closed-mindedness (Jost et al., 2003). Cognitive closure is an epistemic motivation that is believed to be triggered by threat and uncertainty and has been experimentally induced through means such as increased time pressure (Kruglanski & Freund, 1983). Having a need for closure is characterized by desiring order and structure, experiencing emotional discomfort from ambiguity, being impatient during decision-making, possessing a desire for predictability, and processing in a closed-minded fashion. This closed-mindedness results from a reliance on easily accessible information that quickly reduces feelings of anxiety and threat that arise from ambiguity about a situation, and individuals tend to mentally freeze on this information, making it difficult for them to consider alternative viewpoints. This need for closure has been found to increase stereotyping, the reliance on primacy effects when forming impressions (Kruglanski & Freund, 1983; Webster & Kruglanski, 1994), and resistance to persuasive methods (Kruglanski et al., 1993). While the need for closure is linked to closed-mindedness, it also has important implications for an increased endorsement of inequality (Jost et al., 2003).

Another theory linked to the opening and closing of the mind is *terror management theory* (Greenberg et al., 1986, 1990), which identifies the existential anxiety that arises from thoughts about one's mortality as an antecedent to closed-minded thinking. This theory suggests that the awareness of one's mortality and a desire for self-preservation cause one to become paralyzed by death anxiety. In cases of heightened mortality salience, people become highly motivated to reduce the resulting anxiety. This desire to cope with the heightened anxiety often leads to an increased defense of one's personal views and decreased tolerance of opposing views, or closed-mindedness (Jost et al., 2003). Research shows that when mortality is salient, individuals are less tolerant of those with opposing cultural worldviews, dissimilar others, and members of out-groups (Greenberg et al., 1990). Mortality salience, or death anxiety, has also been linked to a cultural closed-mindedness in which people are reluctant to learn about cultures other than their own (Agroskin et al., 2016).

The approaches discussed so far all suggest that negative affective states like fear and anxiety, which are related to ambiguity, uncertainty, and threat, may close the mind. Other approaches suggest that positive emotions may instead open the mind. According to the *broaden-and-build theory* (Fredrickson, 2001, 2004), positive emotions broaden the mind, and negative emotions narrow the mind. Positive emotions such as joy trigger creativity, playfulness, and open-mindedness, leading one to desire exploration and absorb new information. This broadening of the mind is believed to be adaptive through the building of long-lasting intellectual, social, and physical resources. Negative emotions such as anxiety trigger a narrowed mindset, which can be adaptive in threatening situations because a narrowed mindset promotes quick thinking and responses. Positive emotions, on the other hand, widen the range of thoughts and actions that come to mind, leading to a diverse array of choices (Fredrickson, 2004).

The classic and contemporary approaches to the open and closed mind we just reviewed maintain that an open or closed mind emerges as a direct consequence of affect. Unlike these approaches, the *affect-as-information account* (Schwarz & Clore, 1983, 1996) proposes that the information that affect provides is key to such effects, not the affect itself. And the information from affect depends on what the affect appears to be about.

According to this account, affective feelings are conscious information about unconscious appraisals of situations. The earliest conceptualizations of the affect-as-information account pertained exclusively to affective influences on judgment (Schwarz & Clore, 1983), proposing that affective feelings served as input to evaluative judgments. The model was later expanded to account for differences in thinking (i.e., cognitive processing). Consistent with functional theories of emotion that propose that affective feelings serve a signaling function that adaptively guides thinking and behavior (e.g., Frijda, 1986), later versions of the account asserted that affective feelings can serve to direct our thinking by providing information about the environment (Clore et al., 2001; Schwarz, 1990). According to this view, negative affective feelings indicate the presence of a problem, and therefore trigger more careful, detailed, and bottom-up processing in an attempt to solve the problem. Positive affective feelings, by contrast, signal a safe and benign environment, one that does not require such careful processing, and therefore trigger a reliance on heuristic, top-down processing that have served one well in the past.

Often, closed minds are associated with rigid or narrow-minded thinking (Rokeach, 1960). Research on attentional and perceptual focus has shown that negative affective feelings lead to a narrowing of attention and perception, leading to a focus on the trees to the neglect of the forest (Gasper & Clore, 2002). In this research, participants were placed in a positive, negative, or neutral mood. They then completed a measure of global and local perceptual focus (see Gasper & Clore, 2002, Figure 2). The results showed that participants in negative moods focused narrowly, whereas those in positive moods focused more broadly during the task. Other research showing that such broadening and narrowing occur during encoding of information suggests that positive and negative affect may fundamentally adjust the scope of visual attention (Rowe et al., 2007). The broadening effect of positive affective feelings can also be seen in a tendency of happy people to have a wider array of thoughts and actions come to mind (Fredrickson, 2004). The opposite appears to be the case for negative affective feelings, which seem to narrow the thoughts and actions that come to mind.

An open mind is often understood to be a mind that is open to entertaining new ideas, in other words a creative mind (Rokeach, 1960). Research on creativity has shown that positive affective feelings lead to greater creativity and formation of more inclusive categories (e.g., Isen, 1987; Isen & Daubman, 1984). Compared to neutral moods, happy moods lead individuals to include non-prototypical exemplars in common categories and to engage in more creative problem-solving. Thus, positive affective feelings lead individuals to perceive relatedness among diverse stimuli. Other work has shown that positive affective feelings allow individuals to be better able to think of ideas for how objects may serve different purposes (e.g., grinding up a brick to create makeup).

The experience of positive affect also makes people more open-minded toward those who are different from them. Research shows that happy moods promote greater empathy and perspective-taking toward people with dissimilar cultural perspectives (Nelson, 2009). A similar effect can be seen at the group level. In this research (Dovidio et al., 1995), happy moods, as compared to neutral moods, promoted a more inclusive representation of groups such that group boundaries were blurred between groups, leading to a sense of "we," not us versus them.

The experience of awe seems to open the mind (Keltner & Haidt, 2003). Awe has two features. The first is vastness, which involves the experience of something larger than the self or the experience of something outside our ordinary, everyday experience. The second involves accommodation, which involves assimilating this new experience into existing beliefs and mental structures. The beauty of nature and having an intellectual epiphany often elicit strong feelings of awe. Research on awe finds that it promotes humility and increases feelings of uncertainty that in turn lead individuals to show less conviction in their ideological positions, reduced political polarization, and more openness to interacting with ideological opponents (Stancato & Keltner, 2021). Other research has shown that individuals prone to experience awe and those induced to feel awe in the laboratory tend to be lower in need for cognitive closure (Shiota et al., 2007). In this way, then, awe leads to a more open mind.

The emotion disgust appears to close the mind. Individual differences in disgust sensitivity are negatively correlated with openness to experience (Olatunji et al., 2008). Induced disgust seems to make individuals more prone to prefer structure and avoid uncertainty (Donato & Miceli, 2019). Disgusted individuals also make harsher moral judgments, reflecting a tendency to see the world in black and white (Schnall et al., 2008). It has also been argued that emotionally driven intuitions drive moral judgments. Feelings of disgust are believed to cause people to rely on their initial intuitions when faced with moral questions, such as having sex with one's sibling or a dead chicken; and they will stick with these intuitions even when faced with rational alternative viewpoints (Haidt, 2001).

A similar association between affective feelings and closed-mindedness can be seen in research on emotional disorders and certain phobias. In this research, participants' responses on a clinical measure of anxiety were positively associated with responses on a measure of authoritarian defense and negatively associated with responses on a measure of tolerance of ambiguity (Pilisuk, 1963). Such results are consistent with modern anxiety disorder models that place intolerance of uncertainty as a core component of the experience of clinically significant anxiety, such as generalized anxiety disorder (Carleton, 2012). Similar results are found for contamination-related obsessive-compulsive disorder, which involves feelings of disgust (Olatunji et al., 2007). Here, research finds that individuals with obsessive-compulsive disorder show greater intolerance of uncertainty than individuals without this disorder (Tolin et al., 2003).

An Affect-as-Cognitive-Feedback Account

Classic and contemporary approaches to the open and closed mind would all seem to suggest that particular affective feelings directly trigger an open mind or a closed mind. Positive affective feelings (e.g., joy and contentment) cause the mind to open, whereas negative affective feelings (e.g., fear and anxiety) cause the mind to close. We now turn to an approach that suggests that the influence of affective feelings on the closing and opening of the mind may be far more flexible than previously realized.

The affect-as-cognitive-feedback account (Huntsinger et al., 2014) builds on the affect-as-information model and represents a more malleable variation of the earlier processing model. Rather than only providing information about the nature of the situation, the affect-as-cognitive-feedback account asserts that the information that affect conveys is considerably more general and less constrained than originally thought. According to this view, the influence of positive and negative affect on thinking is like that of reward and punishment in that they are not dedicated to any one cognitive outcome but tend to reinforce or deter whatever cognitive responses are associated with them. Thus, affective feelings provide feedback about the value of cognitively accessible ways of thinking, including temporarily and chronically accessible tendencies to be open- or closed-minded.

Positive affect may lead people to view accessible ways of thinking (i.e., open- or closed-mindedness) as effective or appropriate ways of acting in the world. Negative affect should have just the opposite effect. Positive affect, in effect, serves as a green light that prompts the use of accessible ways of thinking, and negative affect serves as a red light that blocks the use of such ways of thinking.

According to the affect-as-cognitive-feedback account, then, the influence of affective feelings on open- and closed-minded thinking should be flexible. Because affective feelings simply provide feedback about accessible styles of cognition, their impact on open- and closed-minded thinking should depend on what ways of thinking happen to be accessible at the moment (see Figure 13.1).

If the impact of affect on cognition is highly malleable, as suggested by the affect-as-cognitive-feedback account, why then did past research find what appeared to be a dedicated link between the two? This apparent contradiction can be resolved by recognizing that there is remarkable similarity in the kinds of thought processes that are cognitively accessible for most people most of the time and in most situations. Indeed, because certain thought processes are common or default processes, this account predicts the previous pattern of influences of affect on cognition discovered in past research described earlier. Global and heuristic thinking are both highly dominant cognitive styles for most people most of the time (Bruner, 1957; Kimchi, 1992; Köhler, 1929; Navon, 1977, 1981; Pomerantz et al., 1977; Reicher, 1969). Therefore, rather

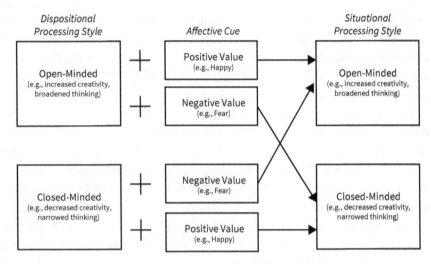

Figure 13.1 Affect-as-cognitive-feedback hypothesis in the context of open-mindedness.

than directly triggering one or another style of processes, positive and negative affect may have simply conferred positive and negative value on these highly accessible ways of approaching incoming information. Because past research did not manipulate the particular cognitive context experienced by participants, there was no opportunity to observe anything but what appeared to be a dedicated link between affect and cognition. To test the account, then, one must manipulate the current cognitive context to reveal flexibility in the influence of affect on cognition. In sum, although our account provides a more flexible view of the relationship between affect and cognition than other classical and contemporary theories, it does not necessarily suggest that previous research findings were incorrect.

Research consistent with this view includes recent work showing a flexible influence of affective feelings on the breadth of attention (Huntsinger, 2012; Huntsinger et al., 2010). In this work (Huntsinger, 2012), tendencies to focus narrowly or broadly were induced via a modified version of the Navon task in which participants are asked to respond primarily to the global or local features of a compound stimulus. Next, participants experienced the mood manipulation in which happy or sad moods were induced by asking participants to recall happy or sad life events. Finally, participants completed a measure of attentional scope, in this case a traditional flanker task in which participants are asked to respond to the identity of a central letter while ignoring irrelevant flanking letters. On some trials the flanking letters are compatible (HHHHH), and on other trials the flanking letters are incompatible (SSHSS) with the central letter. A broadened scope of attention results in more processing of irrelevant flanking letters and therefore a slowed reaction time on the task compared to a narrow scope of attention. The results showed that when tendencies to focus broadly were induced, happy participants showed a broadened attention, whereas sad participants showed a narrowed attention. The opposite occurred when tendencies to focus narrowly were induced. Now, happy participants showed a narrowed attention, whereas sad participants showed a broadened attention.

Similar flexibility can be seen in research on creative thinking (Huntsinger & Ray, 2016). In this research, participants were primed to think globally or locally using the Navon task described above. Next, participants were put in happy or sad moods by reading happy or sad stories and then completed several different measures of creative cognition. In one study they were asked to come up with creative uses for a brick (Study 1), in another they completed the remote associates test and other insight problems (Study 2), and in a final study they completed a breadth of categorization task (Study 3). In each study, when primed to think globally, happy participants generated more creative responses on each outcome than sad participants. However, when primed to think locally, happy participants generated fewer creative responses on each outcome than sad participants.

Other work shows that affective feelings modify whether people follow their chronic tendencies to be open- or closed-minded. The idea here is that positive affective feelings will green-light such tendencies, and negative affective feelings will stop-light them. Consistent with this idea is work on dispositional differences in need for cognitive closure that varied the affective feelings of participants (Kossowska & Bar-Tal, 2013). In a first study, participants' dispositional levels of need for closure were measured, and happy and sad moods were induced via an emotional writing task. Following this, participants completed an impression formation task. In this task, participants read some initial information that indicated that the person was friendly or unfriendly. They were then given the opportunity to read more about this person. Some of this information was consistent with their first impression, and some was inconsistent with their first impression. The results showed that happy participants high in need for cognitive closure selected less information inconsistent with their first impression than those low in need for cognitive closure. No such differences were found for sad participants. A similar result was found in a second study that measured tendencies to recall schema-consistent or schema-inconsistent information.

Affect and Political Polarization

Many politically charged topics elicit strong emotional reactions that then influence the polarization of political beliefs and behaviors. One theory that explores the impact affect can have on political beliefs and behaviors is the *affective intelligence theory* (AIT; Marcus, 2000; Marcus & MacKuen, 1996). The AIT attempts to explain why individuals might reject their existing loyalties to political candidates, parties, and policies or alternatively why they might strengthen these loyalties. The theory focuses on the relationship between emotional reactions, specifically anger and anxiety, and the extent to which people seek out more or less political information. Politicians often suggest that fear and anxiety lead to more political polarization, especially during times of high threat (e.g., following a terrorist attack; Bush, 2001). Similarly, political scientists propose that threat increases authoritarianism that then causes people to rely heavily on their strongly held political dispositions (Feldman & Stenner, 1997). However, the AIT proposes that this strengthening of one's preexisting beliefs is instead activated by anger, rather than fear and anxiety. According to the theory, the affective appraisal associated with an emotion determines political polarization. For example, the experience of anger is associated with an appraisal that the situation reflects a normative violation and greater feelings of certainty, which increases reliance on partisan political beliefs. By contrast, fear and anxiety are associated with appraisals of uncertainty, which decreases reliance on partisan political beliefs. In sum, the theory suggests that anger acts to defend oneself against threats to one's predispositions (e.g., through selective information exposure), while anxiety leads people to abandon these predispositions and instead seek out better alternative solutions to address the threat that might not necessarily align with their preexisting beliefs (Marcus et al., 2019).

Research and findings inspired by the AIT are compatible with the affect-as-cognitive-feedback account, though the proposed mechanisms differ somewhat. From our view, because anxiety is associated with uncertainty, it confers negative value on dominant or usual ways of thinking (e.g., strongly held political dispositions), leading anxious individuals to abandon these ways of thinking. Thus, anxiety should lessen political polarization and lead to more open-minded and unbiased information-seeking. Because anger is associated with feelings of certainty and having the moral high ground, it confers positive value on dominant or usual ways of thinking, leading angry individuals to embrace these ways of thinking. Thus, anger should enhance political polarization and lead to less open-minded and more biased information-seeking. This influence of anger and anxiety on political polarization is consistent with other research that found that anxiety increases the quantity and quality of information-seeking, while anger decreases the quantity and quality of information-seeking (Eastin & Guinsler, 2006; Parker & Isbell, 2010; Valentino et al., 2008). These findings all suggest that anxiety motivates people to learn in the face of uncertainty. This in turn can create more informed and less biased voters and ultimately decrease political polarization. Anger motivates people to stick with their preexisting political beliefs. This in turn can create less informed and more biased voters and ultimately increase political polarization.

Future Research on Affect and the Open and Closed Mind

The affect-as-cognitive-feedback account suggests the importance of taking into consideration mental contexts when trying to understand how affect can influence the opening and closing of the mind. Future research could explore the antecedents of open-minded cognition by attempting to understand how general open-minded cognition as well as situation-specific open-mindedness can change depending on an individual's current and accessible mental state.

In the context of open-minded cognition, the affect-as-cognitive-feedback account would imply that individuals who are predisposed to be more open-minded would engage in more open-minded thinking when in a positive mood but would engage in more close-minded thinking in a negative mood. By contrast, people who are naturally more closed-minded would continue being closed-minded while in a positive mood and would be more open-minded while in a negative mood. A similar pattern should emerge for manipulated open- and closed-mindedness. Thus, the influence of affective states on open-minded thinking is determined by the particular cognitive context in which it is experienced (see Figure 13.1). Future studies could manipulate open- and closed-mindedness before inducing positive or negative emotions and then measure outcomes relevant to open-mindedness to explore these ideas.

Coda

Affective states play a key role in opening and closing the mind. Early research emphasized psychodynamic principles in explaining the influence of affective states on closed-mindedness, with affective states such as emotional ambivalence, threat, and uncertainty playing a central role. Later theories abandoned Freudian principles and broadened their focus to positive emotions, such as joy, in opening the mind. A common theme across all theories was that particular affective states triggered an open or closed mind. However, new theory (i.e., the affect-as-cognitive-feedback account; Huntsinger et al., 2014) and research suggests that such a simple conclusion may need revision. This research shows that whether affective states open or close the mind depends on the particular cognitive context in which they are experienced, such that both positive and negative affects may either open the mind or close it. This theory, among others, has important implications for the role affect plays in political polarization and people's openness to engage in unbiased information-seeking.

References

Adorno, T., Frenkel-Brenswik, E., Levinson, D. J., & Sanford, R. N. (2019). *The authoritarian personality*. Verso Books. (Original work published 1950)

Agroskin, D., Jonas, E., Klackl, J., & Prentice, M. (2016). Inhibition underlies the effect of high need for closure on cultural closed-mindedness under mortality salience. *Frontiers in Psychology, 7*, Article 1583. https://doi.org/10.3389/fpsyg.2016.01583

Altemeyer, R. A., & Altemeyer, B. (1981). *Right-wing authoritarianism*. University of Manitoba Press.

Bruner, J. S. (1957). On perceptual readiness. *Psychological Review, 64*(2), 123–152. https://psycnet.apa.org/doi/10.1037/h0043805

Bush, G. W. (2001, September 11). *Statement by the president in his address to the nation*. The White House. https://georgewbush-whitehouse.archives.gov/news/releases/2001/09/20010911-16.html

Carleton, R. N. (2012). The intolerance of uncertainty construct in the context of anxiety disorders: Theoretical and practical perspectives. *Expert Review of Neurotherapeutics, 12*(8), 937–947. https://doi.org/10.1586/ern.12.82

Clore, G. L., Wyer, R. S., Jr., Dienes, B., Gasper, K., Gohm, C., & Isbell, L. (2001). Affective feelings as feedback: Some cognitive consequences. In L. L. Martin & G. L. Clore (Eds.), *Theories of mood and cognition: A user's guidebook* (pp. 27–62). Lawrence Erlbaum Associates.

Cohrs, J. C., Kielmann, S., Maes, J., & Moschner, B. (2005). Effects of right-wing authoritarianism and threat from terrorism on restriction of civil liberties. *Analyses of Social Issues and Public Policy, 5*(1), 263–276. https://doi.org/10.1111/j.1530-2415.2005.00071.x

Donato, C., & Miceli, G. (2020). The effect of disgust on preference for structure: Evidence for a double-sided response. *Journal of Consumer Behaviour, 19*(1), 68–79. https://doi.org/10.1002/cb.1795

Dovidio, J. F., Gaertner, S. L., Isen, A. M., & Lowrance, R. (1995). Group representations and intergroup bias: Positive affect, similarity, and group size. *Personality and Social Psychology Bulletin, 21*(8), 856–865. https://doi.org/10.1177%2F0146167295218009

Duckitt, J. (2009). Authoritarianism and dogmatism. In M. R. Leary & R. H. Hoyle (Eds.), *Handbook of individual differences in social behavior* (pp. 298–317). Guilford Press.

Duckitt, J., & Sibley, C. G. (2010). Personality, ideology, prejudice, and politics: A dual-process motivational model. *Journal of Personality*, 78(6), 1861–1894. https://doi.org/10.1111/j.1467-6494.2010.00672.x

Eastin, M. S., & Guinsler, N. M. (2006). Worried and wired: Effects of health anxiety on information-seeking and health care utilization behaviors. *CyberPsychology & Behavior*, 9(4), 494–498. https://doi.org/10.1089/cpb.2006.9.494

Feldman, S., & Stenner, K. (1997). Perceived threat and authoritarianism. *Political Psychology*, 18(4), 741–770. https://doi.org/10.1111/0162-895X.00077

Fredrickson, B. L. (2001). The role of positive emotions in positive psychology: The broaden-and-build theory of positive emotions. *American Psychologist*, 56(3), 218–226. https://psycnet.apa.org/doi/10.1037/0003-066X.56.3.218

Fredrickson, B. L. (2004). The broaden-and-build theory of positive emotions. *Philosophical Transactions of the Royal Society of London. Series B: Biological Sciences*, 359(1449), 1367–1377. https://doi.org/10.1098/rstb.2004.1512

Frenkel-Brunswik, E. (1949). Intolerance of ambiguity as an emotional and perceptual personality variable. *Journal of Personality*, 18, 108–143. https://psycnet.apa.org/doi/10.1111/j.1467-6494.1949.tb01236.x

Freud, S. (1963). *An autobiographical study*. W. W. Norton & Company. (Original work published 1925)

Frijda, N. H. (1986). *The emotions*. Cambridge University Press.

Gasper, K., & Clore, G. L. (2002). Attending to the big picture: Mood and global versus local processing of visual information. *Psychological Science*, 13(1), 34–40. https://doi.org/10.1111%2F1467-9280.00406

Greenberg, J., Pyszczynski, T., & Solomon, S. (1986). The causes and consequences of a need for self-esteem: A terror management theory. In R. F. Baumeister (Ed.), *Public self and private self* (pp. 189–212). Springer-Verlag. https://doi.org/10.1007/978-1-4613-9564-5_10

Greenberg, J., Pyszczynski, T., Solomon, S., Rosenblatt, A., Veeder, M., Kirkland, S., & Lyon, D. (1990). Evidence for terror management theory II: The effects of mortality salience on reactions to those who threaten or bolster the cultural worldview. *Journal of Personality and Social Psychology*, 58(2), 308–318. https://psycnet.apa.org/doi/10.1037/0022-3514.58.2.308

Haidt, J. (2001). The emotional dog and its rational tail: A social intuitionist approach to moral judgment. *Psychological Review*, 108(4), 814–834. https://psycnet.apa.org/doi/10.1037/0033-295X.108.4.814

Huntsinger, J. R. (2012). Does positive affect broaden and negative affect narrow attentional scope? A new answer to an old question. *Journal of Experimental Psychology: General*, 141, 595–600. https://psycnet.apa.org/doi/10.1037/a0027709

Huntsinger, J. R., Clore, G. L., & Bar-Anan, Y. (2010) Mood and global–local focus: Priming a local focus reverses the link between mood and global–local processing. *Emotion*, 10, 722–726. https://psycnet.apa.org/doi/10.1037/a0019356

Huntsinger, J. R., Isbell, L. M., & Clore, G. L. (2014). The affective control of thought: Malleable, not fixed. *Psychological Review*, 121(4), 600–618. https://psycnet.apa.org/doi/10.1037/a0037669

Huntsinger, J. R., & Ray, C. (2016). A flexible influence of affective feelings on creative and analytic performance. *Emotion*, 16(6), 826–837. https://psycnet.apa.org/doi/10.1037/emo0000188

Isen, A. M. (1987). Positive affect, cognitive processes, and social behavior. In L. Berkowitz (Ed.), *Advances in experimental social psychology* (Vol. 20, pp. 203–253). Academic Press.

Isen, A. M., & Daubman, K. A. (1984). The influence of affect on categorization. *Journal of Personality and Social Psychology*, *47*(6), 1206–1217. https://psycnet.apa.org/doi/10.1037/0022-3514.47.6.1206

Jost, J. T., Glaser, J., Kruglanski, A. W., & Sulloway, F. J. (2003). Political conservatism as motivated social cognition. *Psychological Bulletin*, *129*(3), 339–375. https://psycnet.apa.org/doi/10.1037/0033-2909.129.3.339

Keltner, D., & Haidt, J. (2003). Approaching awe, a moral, spiritual, and aesthetic emotion. *Cognition and Emotion*, *17*(2), 297–314. https://doi.org/10.1080/02699930302297

Kimchi, R. (1992). Primacy of wholistic processing and global/local paradigm: A critical review. *Psychological Bulletin*, *112*(1), 24–38. https://psycnet.apa.org/doi/10.1037/0033-2909.112.1.24

Köhler, W. (1929). An old pseudoproblem. *Naturwissenschaften*, *17*, 395–401.

Kossowska, M., & Bar-Tal, Y. (2013). Positive mood boosts the expression of a dispositional need for closure. *Cognition & Emotion*, *27*(7), 1181–1201. https://doi.org/10.1080/02699931.2013.778817

Kruglanski, A. W., & Freund, T. (1983). The freezing and unfreezing of lay-inferences: Effects on impressional primacy, ethnic stereotyping, and numerical anchoring. *Journal of Experimental Social Psychology*, *19*(5), 448–468. https://doi.org/10.1016/0022-1031(83)90022-7

Kruglanski, A. W., Webster, D. M., & Klem, A. (1993). Motivated resistance and openness to persuasion in the presence or absence of prior information. *Journal of Personality and Social Psychology*, *65*(5), 861–876. https://psycnet.apa.org/doi/10.1037/0022-3514.65.5.861

Marcus, G. E. (2000). Emotions in politics. *Annual Review of Political Science*, *3*(1), 221–250. https://doi.org/10.1146/annurev.polisci.3.1.221

Marcus, G. E., & MacKuen, M. (1996). *Measuring mood in the 1995 NES Pilot Study*. National Election Studies Board.

Marcus, G. E., Valentino, N. A., Vasilopoulos, P., & Foucault, M. (2019). Applying the theory of affective intelligence to support for authoritarian policies and parties. *Political Psychology*, *40*, 109–139. https://doi.org/10.1111/pops.12571

Navon, D. (1977). Forest before trees: The precedence of global features in visual perception. *Cognitive Psychology*, *9*(3), 353–383. https://doi.org/10.1016/0010-0285(77)90012-3

Navon, D. (1981). The forest revisited: More on global precedence. *Psychological Research*, *43*(1), 1–32. https://doi.org/10.1007/BF00309635

Nelson, D. W. (2009). Feeling good and open-minded: The impact of positive affect on cross cultural empathic responding. *The Journal of Positive Psychology*, *4*(1), 53–63. https://doi.org/10.1080/17439760802357859

Olatunji, B. O., Haidt, J., McKay, D., & David, B. (2008). Core, animal reminder, and contamination disgust: Three kinds of disgust with distinct personality, behavioral, physiological, and clinical correlates. *Journal of Research in Personality*, *42*(5), 1243–1259. https://doi.org/10.1016/j.jrp.2008.03.009

Olatunji, B. O., Lohr, J. M., Sawchuk, C. N., & Tolin, D. F. (2007). Multimodal assessment of disgust in contamination-related obsessive-compulsive disorder. *Behaviour Research and Therapy*, *45*(2), 263–276. https://doi.org/10.1016/j.brat.2006.03.004

Pally, S. (1955). Cognitive rigidity as a function of threat. *Journal of Personality*, *23*, 346–355. https://psycnet.apa.org/doi/10.1111/j.1467-6494.1955.tb01161.x

Parker, M. T., & Isbell, L. M. (2010). How I vote depends on how I feel: The differential impact of anger and fear on political information processing. *Psychological Science*, *21*(4), 548–550. https://doi.org/10.1177%2F0956797610364006

Peterson, B. E., & Zurbriggen, E. L. (2010). Gender, sexuality, and the authoritarian personality. *Journal of Personality*, *78*(6), 1801–1826. https://doi.org/10.1111/j.1467-6494.2010.00670.x

Pilisuk, M. (1963). Anxiety, self-acceptance, and open-mindedness. *Journal of Clinical Psychology, 19*(4), 387–391. https://doi.org/10.1002/1097-4679(196310)19:4%3C387::AID-JCLP2270190402%3E3.0.CO;2-D

Pomerantz, J. R., Sager, L. C., & Stoever, R. J. (1977). Perception of wholes and of their component parts: Some configural superiority effects. *Journal of Experimental Psychology: Human Perception and Performance, 3*(3), 422–435. https://psycnet.apa.org/doi/10.1037/0096-1523.3.3.422

Price, E., Ottati, V., Wilson, C., & Kim, S. (2015). Open-minded cognition. *Personality and Social Psychology Bulletin, 41*(11), 1488–1504. https://doi.org/10.1177%2F0146167215600528

Reicher, G. M. (1969). Perceptual recognition as a function of meaningfulness of stimulus material. *Journal of Experimental Psychology, 81*(2), 275–280. https://psycnet.apa.org/doi/10.1037/h0027768

Rokeach, M. (1960). *The open and closed mind: Investigations into the nature of belief systems and personality systems*. Basic Books.

Rokeach, M. (1963). The double agreement phenomenon: Three hypotheses. *Psychological Review, 70*(4), 304–309. https://psycnet.apa.org/doi/10.1037/h0045483

Rowe, G., Hirsh, J. B., & Anderson, A. K. (2007). Positive affect increases the breadth of attentional selection. *Proceedings of the National Academy of Sciences of the United States of America, 104*(1), 383–388. https://doi.org/10.1073/pnas.0605198104

Schnall, S., Haidt, J., Clore, G. L., & Jordan, A. H. (2008). Disgust as embodied moral judgment. *Personality and Social Psychology Bulletin, 34*(8), 1096–1109. https://doi.org/10.1177%2F0146167208317771

Schwarz, N. (1990). Feelings as information: Informational and motivational functions of affective states. In E. T. Higgins & R. M. Sorrentino (Eds.), *Handbook of motivation and cognition: Foundations of social behavior* (Vol. 2, pp. 527–561). Guilford Press.

Schwarz, N., & Clore, G. L. (1983). Mood, misattribution, and judgments of well-being: informative and directive functions of affective states. *Journal of Personality and Social Psychology, 45*(3), 513–523. https://psycnet.apa.org/doi/10.1037/0022-3514.45.3.513

Schwarz, N., & Clore, G. L. (1996). Feelings and phenomenal experiences. In E. T. Higgins & A. Kruglanski (Eds.), *Social psychology: A handbook of basci principles* (pp. 385–407). Guilford Press.

Shiota, M. N., Keltner, D., & Mossman, A. (2007). The nature of awe: Elicitors, appraisals, and effects on self-concept. *Cognition and Emotion, 21*(5), 944–963. https://doi.org/10.1080/02699930600923668

Stancato, D. M., & Keltner, D. (2021). Awe, ideological conviction, and perceptions of ideological opponents. *Emotion, 21*(1), 61–72. https://psycnet.apa.org/doi/10.1037/emo0000665

Tolin, D. F., Abramowitz, J. S., Brigidi, B. D., & Foa, E. B. (2003). Intolerance of uncertainty in obsessive-compulsive disorder. *Journal of Anxiety Disorders, 17*(2), 233–242. https://doi.org/10.1016/S0887-6185(02)00182-2

Valentino, N. A., Hutchings, V. L., Banks, A. J., & Davis, A. K. (2008). Is a worried citizen a good citizen? Emotions, political information seeking, and learning via the internet. *Political Psychology, 29*(2), 247–273. https://doi.org/10.1111/j.1467-9221.2008.00625.x

Webster, D. M., & Kruglanski, A. W. (1994). Individual differences in need for cognitive closure. *Journal of Personality and Social Psychology, 67*(6), 1049–1062. https://psycnet.apa.org/doi/10.1037/0022-3514.67.6.1049

14
Terror Management, Dogmatism, and Open-Mindedness

Dylan E. Horner, Alex Sielaff, Sheldon Solomon, and Jeff Greenberg

> the problem of life is how to grow out of fetishism, of idol worship, and continually broaden and expand one's horizons, allegiances, the quality of his preoccupations. This means that the person's main task is to put his self-esteem as firmly as possible under his own control; he has to try to get individual and durable ways to earn self-esteem. It means, too, that he has to free himself from a slavery to things that are close at hand.
> —**Ernest Becker (1971, *The Birth and Death of Meaning*, p. 191)**

Harboring well-defined conceptions of the world and embracing clear delineations of "good" and "bad" derived from such worldviews enables people to feel a sense of order and meaning in their lives. For instance, gravitating toward political leaders who focus on the greatness of one's in-group and espouse efforts to heroically triumph over perceived evil bolsters people's perception that they play a significant role in something great and enduring. However, at present, sharp in-group–out-group distinctions are producing a polarized political environment that provokes dogmatic engagement with one's own particular worldview, as well as intergroup animus that blocks compromise and progress toward common social goals (see Chapter 2 in this volume). And these consequences too often foster discrimination, violence, stunted personal growth, and stalled socioeconomic progress. When others threaten one's perspectives and allegiances (e.g., by criticizing one's beliefs or simply holding allegiances different from their own), individuals may respond with hostility and disdain, accompanied by fervent demonstrations that their perspective is "right." Indeed, history is riddled with examples of how rigid worldviews promote dogmatic thinking that can lead to deleterious outcomes for those with different political, social, ethnic, and religious identities, prompting the main character in James Joyce's *Ulysses* (1922/2012, p. 34) to famously declare that "History is a nightmare from which I am trying to awake." Modern examples would include the Soviet Union, Nazi Germany, fascist Italy under Mussolini, and communist China.[1]

Yet, from a terror management theory (TMT) perspective (Greenberg et al., 1986, 2014), such rigid and clear conceptions of reality help people mitigate the potential anxiety inherent in the awareness of mortality. By embracing and defending dogmatic worldviews and upholding a sense of value within them, people can perceive their lives as enduring and meaningful, rather than finite and purposeless. Research shows that rigid worldviews can serve to manage death-related anxieties and concerns. However, research has also shown that existential terror can be assuaged by upholding values such as tolerance and open-mindedness, resulting in more prosocial and benevolent outcomes. The present chapter highlights this large body of empirical work demonstrating how death awareness motivates a host of rigid and closed-minded attitudes and beliefs, and it reviews a number of factors that can prevent these outcomes and instead promote open-mindedness and tolerance.

Terror Management Theory (TMT)

> What does it mean to be a self-conscious animal? The idea is ludicrous. . . . It means to know that one is food for worms. This is the terror: to have emerged from nothing, to have a name, consciousness of self, deep inner feelings, an excruciating inner yearning for life and self-expression—and with all this yet to die.
> —Ernest Becker (1973, *The Denial of Death*, p. 87)

From early childhood to the end of life, psychological security depends on one's ability to cope with the awareness of vulnerability and mortality, an awareness that conflicts with the evolutionary desire for continued life. Indeed, a substantial proportion of human activity is geared toward avoiding or postponing death and is evident in areas such as healthcare, politics, economics, military actions, environmentalism, and social justice efforts. Nevertheless, humans recognize that death is inevitable and can happen unexpectedly at any time. As such, there is a potential for existential anxiety or terror at any given moment.

Terror Management Theory (TMT; Greenberg et al., 1986) is based largely on cultural anthropologist Ernest Becker's (1971, 1973) interdisciplinary account of the motivational underpinnings of human behavior. Following

Darwin, Becker and TMT assume that humans share with all forms of life a biological predisposition toward survival and reproduction. We are, however, unique in our predilection for abstract symbolic thought. One component of such cognitive complexity is explicit self-awareness, or consciousness. Humans are so smart that they realize that they exist, and this engenders both awe and dread. Knowing that we are alive is often a source of awe, joy, and spontaneous exuberance. Conversely, knowing that we are alive can be dreadful in that it makes us poignantly and profoundly aware that, like all living things, our lives are of finite duration; we are perpetually vulnerable to obliteration at any time for reasons that cannot always be anticipated or forestalled, and we are embodied entities who are no more consequential or enduring than carrots or cockroaches. Such realizations engender potentially debilitating existential terror that could undermine effective instrumental behavior and reproductive fitness. Humans manage this potential terror by maintaining faith in their *cultural worldviews* and striving for a sense of personal value (i.e., self-esteem) within their worldviews.

According to TMT, cultural worldviews offer conceptions of reality that imbue life with order, stability, purpose, and meaning. Worldviews address basic questions about life and death and provide standards for valued behavior. When people live up to these standards, they gain a sense of personal value and enduring significance and feel qualified for their worldview-prescribed form of literal or symbolic immortality. That is, they feel that they will transcend death literally (e.g., through reincarnation or an afterlife) and/or symbolically (e.g., having achievements that will have a lasting impact, being remembered, or being part of a great nation). For example, most religions promise some form of literal immortality through an immortal soul or an afterlife, and devotees who live up to the standards of their religion can feel that they are on the path to obtaining their worldview-prescribed form of eternal life (e.g., repenting for one's sins and going to heaven in Christianity). Cultures also provide routes to symbolic immortality to those with personal accomplishments or contributions to ongoing social, political, scientific, and artistic endeavors that have some enduring impact (e.g., soldiers dedicating their lives to glorify their country, musicians creating songs that are remembered for generations, or people simply showing kindness and leaving a lasting impression on those around them). By maintaining close relationships with others, people's worldviews and accomplishments are validated, and their sense of legacy can be bolstered through offspring or extended social groups.

Thus, by maintaining faith in cultural worldviews, striving for self-esteem, and maintaining close relationships, people are afforded a sense of psychological security that enables them to manage the potential for existential anxiety inherent in the awareness of mortality. Having a sense of personal value within a cultural system of meaning allows people to see life as lasting and meaningful rather than finite and purposeless; having a sense of literal and/or symbolic transcendence helps people to feel like they will continue on in some way after death and overcome the cognizance "that one is food for worms" (Becker, 1973).

Empirical Evidence for TMT

Since the 1990s, research conducted in over 20 countries around the world has investigated the terror management function of self-esteem, cultural worldviews, and close relationships (for reviews, see Routledge & Vess, 2019). Much of this work has been guided by three central hypotheses: the mortality salience (MS) hypothesis, the anxiety-buffer hypothesis, and the death-thought accessibility (DTA) hypothesis (for a review, see Schimel et al., 2019).

First, the *MS hypothesis* states that if psychological structures (e.g., self-esteem, worldviews, and close relationships) serve to mitigate death-related anxieties, then making mortality salient should motivate people to defend and affirm these structures.[1] Indeed, MS motivates people to fortify their bases of meaning and value, for example, by denigrating and harming those with different beliefs (e.g., McGregor et al., 1998), striving for self-esteem in worldview-relevant domains (e.g., Zestcott et al., 2016), and expressing greater motivation to maintain close relationships and have children (e.g., Cox & Arndt, 2012; Fritsche et al., 2007). For a meta-analytic review of MS effects, see Burke et al. (2010).

TMT posits a dual-process model of defense, such that death awareness motivates qualitatively different defensive responses depending on whether or not death thought is in focal attention (Pyszczynski et al., 1999). Specifically, when death thought is in focal attention, *proximal defenses* are instigated, problem-solving strategies aimed at minimizing the perceived or actual threat of death (e.g., increased safety checks or health-oriented behavior, denying one's vulnerability, suppressing death-related thoughts) in order to push the problem of death from current conscious awareness. However, death thoughts removed from focal attention remain cognitively accessible, and this heightened accessibility of death thought instigates *distal defenses* (i.e., worldview defense, self-esteem striving, and commitment to close relationships).

Second, the *anxiety-buffer hypothesis* states that if psychological structures serve to protect people from death awareness and existential anxiety, then bolstering or affirming these structures should reduce death-related anxiety and mitigate defensive responses to MS. Indeed, dispositionally high or experimentally bolstered self-esteem reduces self-reported anxiety and physiological arousal in response to threat and mitigates defensive reactions typically elicited by MS inductions (e.g., Greenberg, Solomon, et al., 1992). Affirming one's worldviews and sense of meaning also diminishes MS effects (e.g., Schmeichel & Martens, 2005).

Finally, the *DTA hypothesis* states that if certain psychological structures serve to buffer against death awareness, then undermining these structures should increase the accessibility of death-related cognition. Research has found that threats to people's self-esteem, worldviews, and close relationships increase DTA. For example, Christian fundamentalists confronted with logical inconsistencies in the Bible (Friedman & Rholes, 2007), Americans asked to ponder undesired aspects of themselves (Ogilvie et al., 2008), and Israelis asked to think about disruptions in their current romantic relationship (Florian et al., 2002) showed increased DTA. Moreover, conditions that increase DTA are the same conditions that lead to worldview defense, self-esteem striving, and commitment to close relationships (for review, see Hayes et al., 2010).

Terror Management in Everyday Life

Intimations of mortality appear in myriad ways in people's day-to-day lives: illness or death of loved ones, natural disasters, acts of terrorism, political insurrections, economic instability, environmental perturbations, and worldwide pandemics. Indeed, studies have established that such real-world reminders of mortality have the same effects as a typical MS induction. For example, people report greater support for and perceived importance of worldview-relevant values when surveyed near a funeral home compared to several blocks away (Jonas et al., 2002; Pyszczynski et al., 1996). Moreover, scenes of destruction (Vail, Arndt, Motyl, & Pyszczynski, 2012) and news of terrorism (Das et al., 2009) can increase DTA and worldview defense. Contemplating death-related policy concerns (e.g., war, gun control) can also increase worldview defense (Vail et al., 2020), and experiencing the death of close others is associated with greater in-group favoritism and stronger valuing of important identities (e.g., Chatard et al., 2010; Lifshin et al., 2017). Together, these findings suggest that close proximity to real-world reminders of death stimulates strivings for value and meaning.

Terror Management and Dogmatism

In a cultural milieu of varied and alternative attitudes and beliefs, people often encounter others who hold different worldviews than their own, both between and within cultures. This undermines the validity of one's own worldview, as the presence of different others who seem to be functioning well with a very different set of beliefs and values calls into question the truth of one's own beliefs. Thus, alternative worldviews, in addition to real-world reminders of mortality and the ever-present awareness of death, pose threats to people's psychological security. To manage the potential for death-related anxiety inherent in these threats, people often become more dogmatic, closed-minded, and intolerant toward others and ideas that differ from their own. By doing so, people can uphold the veracity of the security-providing worldviews that they rely on to manage existential terror.

Politics and Nationalism

A large body of research has shown that people respond to death reminders by derogating those with different political and nationalistic beliefs, showing more favorable reactions toward similar others, and supporting leaders and policies that espouse rigid worldviews that offer clear delineations of what is "good" and "bad," focusing on the greatness of the in-group and the need to heroically triumph over perceived evil (for a review, see Pyszczynski, 2013). For example, American participants reminded of mortality (vs. various aversive control topics) show increased denigration of those who are critical of the United States but greater positive evaluations of those who express favorable views of the United States (e.g., Greenberg et al., 1990). In other words, MS leads people to hold negative attitudes toward worldview-threatening others, which likely engenders further dogmatic thinking when faced with people holding different beliefs.

Additionally, MS increases support for hostility and actual aggression toward those with different attitudes and beliefs. For instance, Pyszczynski et al. (2006) demonstrated that MS increases support for the use of extreme military tactics against perceived "enemy" nations. Specifically, MS increased Americans' support for pre-emptive use of nuclear and chemical weapons against Iran, Syria, and North Korea; and MS increased Iranians' support for martyrdom attacks against Americans, as well as their willingness to become martyrs themselves. Similarly, MS increases willingness to self-sacrifice for one's country (i.e., British participants' willingness to self-sacrifice for

England; Routledge & Arndt, 2008) and increases aggression toward those with opposing political orientations (i.e., greater allocation of hot sauce to someone with a strong dislike for spicy food if they challenged participants' political views; McGregor et al., 1998). Notably, these forms of defense in response to death reminders alleviate typical MS-induced DTA (e.g., Arndt et al., 1997), suggesting that derogating and aggressing against those with alternative political and nationalistic beliefs serve a terror management function to assuage death awareness.

In addition to amplifying hostility and aggression toward those with divergent political and nationalistic beliefs, MS increases support for charismatic leaders who espouse simple and rigid worldviews that bolster people's sense of being part of something great. For example, following the terrorist attacks on the World Trade Center and Pentagon on September 11, 2001, Landau et al. (2004) found, prior to the 2004 US presidential election, that MS led American participants to express greater support for then-president George W. Bush and his counterterrorism policies. President Bush's appeal likely came from his patriotic and steadfast rhetoric, in which he stated that the United States was a "mighty giant" and that his administration would "rid the world of evil-doers" (Purdum, 2001). In a similar vein, Cohen et al. (2004) found that MS increased support for a charismatic leader (who made statements such as "You are not just an ordinary citizen, you are part of a special state and a special nation") compared to task-oriented and relationship-oriented leaders (see also Kosloff et al., 2010). Moreover, prior to the 2016 US presidential election, Cohen et al. (2017) demonstrated that MS increased support for Donald Trump over Hillary Clinton; this heightened support for Trump in response to MS can likely be attributed to his charismatic and bold promise to "Make America Great Again" (Campbell, 2015). Consistent with this explanation, in a national sample obtained in 2017, Hinckley (2021) found that while White authoritarians were more likely to view Trump as a strong leader relative to non-authoritarians, so were non-authoritarians (regardless of political affiliation) in areas of the country with higher mortality rates. Together, these findings illustrate that death awareness motivates people to support leaders who boldly proclaim the moral superiority and strength of their worldview, leading to closed-mindedness and dogmatism.

Religion

People also cling rigidly to their religious worldviews, defending them in the wake of death awareness and alternative beliefs. For example, Greenberg et al. (1990) asked Christian participants to evaluate the intelligence and likability of other presumed participants who were depicted as either Christian or Jewish. In response to MS (compared to a control condition), Christians had more favorable evaluations of the presumed in-group member (Christian target) and more negative evaluations of the presumed out-group member (Jewish target). Similarly, Vail et al. (2019) found that MS increased support for anti-Islamic attitudes among Americans.

People also become more entrenched in their own religious beliefs and opposed to different perspectives in response to intimations of mortality. Research by Vail, Arndt, and Abdollahi (2012) showed that MS increased Christian participants' self-reported religiosity and belief in God/Jesus, as well as increased their denial of Allah; conversely, MS increased Iranian Muslim participants' religiosity and belief in Allah and their denial of God/Jesus. Moreover, Vess et al. (2009) demonstrated that MS led religious fundamentalists to become more supportive of prayer as an effective treatment for illness and to report a greater likelihood for faith-based medical refusals, even when integrating faith and medicine was presented as a possibility. Death awareness thus appears to lead people to evaluate alternative religious beliefs more harshly and become more invested in their own beliefs; this closed-mindedness helps people maintain the psychological security afforded to them by their own religious convictions.

Distancing from those who do not share the same religious beliefs serves to reinforce one's faith in the validity of one's own worldview. Indeed, having knowledge of the desecration of opposing religious symbols prevents typical MS-induced DTA (Cohen et al., 2013). Moreover, a study conducted by Hayes et al. (2008) showed that American Christians who were exposed to an article about the Christian holy city of Nazareth being overcome by Muslims showed greater DTA, but not if they were also exposed to a report indicating that a plane full of Muslims had been killed in a crash on their way to Nazareth. These results indicate that rigid and unwavering religious beliefs help to allay existential concerns, and that the annihilation of alternative religious symbols and devotees bolsters the protection afforded by one's convictions.

Structure and Stereotypes

In addition to rigidity in political and religious domains, death awareness motivates people to cling to orderly and structured views of the world more generally. By maintaining the sense that one's environment is orderly and predictable, people can minimize ambiguity and feel a sense of stability and consistency which helps maintain faith in their worldviews. For example, studies have shown that individuals who are predisposed to seek structure are motivated by death awareness to view their personal characteristics as more coherent and clearly defined, as well as show greater preferences for causal and just-world interpretations of social events (Landau, Greenberg, Sullivan, et al., 2009; Landau et al., 2004). Maintaining such structured views of the world helps to allay death-related anxieties and concerns; indeed, Routledge et al. (2013) showed that MS increases death anxiety among those low, but not high, in personal need for structure.

Such preference for clear and rigid delineations of people's social worlds is also evidenced in research showing that MS motivates greater preferences for stereotypes. For instance, Schimel et al. (1999) demonstrated that MS motivated participants to report a greater preference for individuals behaving in stereotype-consistent ways (e.g., more favorable evaluations of a female aspiring to be a fashion writer vs. a sports writer). Interestingly, stereotypic thinking in response to death awareness has also been found in people's own performance; Landau, Greenberg, and Rothschild (2009) showed that MS improved performance on academic test items when they incidentally affirmed prevailing stereotypes and impaired performance if excelling would violate stereotypical norms.

The Bright Side: Terror Management, Tolerance, and Open-Mindedness

The literature reviewed above demonstrates how existential anxiety motivates a host of dogmatic, rigid, and closed-minded attitudes and behaviors. Indeed, many presentations of TMT and much of its empirical literature have focused on these rigid and often aggressive defensives geared toward defending people's cultural worldviews and sources of value. Such focus is aligned with Ernest Becker's (1971, 1973) general orientation, as well as trends in social psychological research, both having largely focused on understanding harmful social phenomena like prejudice and discrimination. However, these deleterious outcomes are not inevitable in the face of death awareness, and research has revealed factors that reduce these defensive responses and some that may even contribute to open-mindedness. In other words, there is a "bright side" to terror management, such that existential anxiety can fuel motivation toward openness and more socially constructive outcomes (for a review, see Vail, Juhl, et al., 2012).

Preventing Rigid and Closed-Minded Defenses

Research has identified moderators of MS effects on hostile and rigid worldview defense. For example, political orientation plays an important role in determining the outcomes of worldview defense (Greenberg & Jonas, 2003). Research by Greenberg, Simon, et al. (1992) showed that MS motivated politically conservative participants to report more favorable evaluations of a politically similar target and harsher evaluations of a politically dissimilar target, a finding consistent with typical MS effects (e.g., Greenberg et al., 1990); however, among politically liberal participants, MS instead led to more favorable evaluations of a politically dissimilar target, suggesting that MS led liberal participants to uphold the value of tolerance and open-mindedness typically observed in politically liberal worldviews. Similar findings have also been found concerning right-wing authoritarianism (RWA); MS motivates more negative evaluations of immigrants among those high in RWA but more positive evaluations among those low in RWA (Weise et al., 2012). Thus, MS motivates people to defend important dimensions of their cultural worldview; in many cases, these important dimensions can promote greater tolerance and open-mindedness, as well as acceptance for dissimilar others.

In addition, more inclusive and prosocial orientations foster more socially constructive reactions to MS. For example, an emphasis on shared human experiences can help motivate more tolerance in the face of death. Motyl et al. (2011) found that when American participants were primed with shared human experiences (e.g., viewing images of people from other cultures engaging in common human activities), MS motivated greater tolerance of immigrants, lower anti-Arab prejudices, and increased support for international peace-making rather than hostility. In a similar vein, Pyszczynski et al. (2012) showed that by broadening the inclusiveness of one's in-group (i.e., by focusing on the collective global threat of climate change), MS motivated heightened support for international peace-making among Americans and greater support for peaceful coexistence with Israeli Jews (amidst the 2009 Israeli military incursion into Gaza) among Palestinian citizens of Israel who reported high perceptions of common humanity. Such findings illustrate that focusing on a commonly shared cause and expanding one's perceived in-group can help people manage death-related concerns in more socially constructive ways.

Finally, research has found that people with more intrinsic (vs. extrinsic) worldview orientations manage death-related anxieties and concerns in a less defensive fashion. In other words, people who are more intrinsically oriented to their worldview (characterized by deep internalization of beliefs, motivation based on authentic and autonomous functioning) compared to those who are more extrinsically oriented (characterized by instrumental motivations, motivation based on external contingencies) respond to death awareness in less deleterious ways. For example, Jonas and Fischer (2006) showed that stronger intrinsic religiosity mitigates typical MS-induced DTA, and German participants with high intrinsic religiosity who had the opportunity to affirm their religious beliefs did not show heightened worldview defense in response to mortality reminders. Other work has found that MS motivates worldview defense among those who base their sense of value on extrinsic and contingent sources of worth but not among those with more intrinsic esteem orientations (Williams et al., 2010), and Vail et al. (2020) showed that autonomous orientations mitigate MS-induced worldview defense. Such intrinsic orientations and internal bases of self-worth have been described elsewhere as supporting a particularly durable buffer against death awareness (e.g., Pyszczynski et al., 2003). As such, these findings suggest that people with more intrinsic orientations toward important personal values and goals may be able to manage death awareness more effectively and, as a result, engage in their social worlds with less defensiveness and more open-mindedness.

Defending Prosocial and Benevolent Values

In addition to various individual and contextual factors that can diminish MS-induced defensiveness and potentially lead to greater tolerance and open-mindedness, cultural emphasis on particular values is especially important. Given that cultures imbue life with purpose and meaning and that people strive to live up to their worldview-prescribed standards of worth, when cultural standards emphasize prosocial values, death awareness motivates people to uphold these values in both their attitudes and behaviors.

Indeed, when prosocial dimensions of one's worldview are made salient, death awareness motivates people to uphold and defend these values. For example, when values of pacifism, benevolence, and tolerance are made salient, MS leads participants to report more favorable evaluations of dissimilar and worldview-threatening others (e.g., Greenberg, Simon, et al., 1992; Jonas et al., 2008). Moreover, MS can increase actual helping-related behaviors toward those in need when the cultural value of helping is made salient (Gailliot et al., 2008), and making salient the importance of tolerance mitigates MS-induced prejudice (Vail et al., 2019). Finally, Routledge and Arndt (2009) showed that MS increased religious and nationalistic worldview exploration when participants were informed that creativity was culturally valued or given the opportunity to actually express creativity in a design task. Together, these findings illustrate how death awareness can motivate people to uphold prosocial values, and they highlight the importance of cultural valuing for tolerance, flexibility, and open-mindedness.

Directions for Future Research

People manage the awareness of death by upholding and defending their bases of psychological security, and the research we have reviewed demonstrates that although the awareness of mortality can lead to a host of closed-minded and dogmatic outcomes, it can also motivate more prosocial and open-minded orientations. Understanding the conditions under which death awareness can motivate more socially constructive and less deleterious defenses is important and a valuable avenue for future research.

For instance, when focused on a shared cause and a more expansive in-group, death awareness can motivate more socially constructive outcomes. As such, future research could identify ways to expand people's perceived in-group and effectively bolster the importance of collective efforts. Some research has found that death awareness motivates more openness and exploration among bicultural individuals with high identity hybridity (greater integration and blending of one's different cultures; Zhang et al., 2014), as well as bolstering intentions for socially mindful behavior (e.g., intentions for mask-wearing and social distancing during the COVID-19 pandemic) when people are primed with collectivism (Courtney et al., 2022). Following such lines of work, future studies could investigate how people might manage death-related anxieties in ways that promote greater appreciation for diversity and common humanity, as well as how these values could be integrated into existing cultural systems.

Additionally, future research could address how certain sociopolitical climates might impact the effect of death awareness on dogmatic and closed-minded outcomes. For instance, a classic finding from the TMT literature—that MS leads Americans to report greater denigration of people who are critical of the United States (e.g., Greenberg et al., 1994)—did not replicate in a multi-lab replication effort consisting of studies conducted across 21 labs run 22 years later (Klein et al., 2019). Although some have interpreted this null finding as evidence against MS effects, this work (conducted shortly after Donald Trump won the 2016 US presidential election) utilized an anti–United States essay focused on the United States being unfair to lower–socioeconomic status people and members of minority groups. As described above, MS effects depend on the values and norms currently salient for the individual and what values and attitudes the person embraces. At the time of data collection, it is likely that many, if not most, Americans probably agreed with the arguments made in this "anti–United States" essay and therefore did not consistently engage in denigration as a form of worldview defense, the way the American sample did in the early 1990s. In fact, the last author of this chapter was consulted by Klein et al. (2019) and advised the researchers against using the anti–United States essay developed in the early 1990s during the Bush administration because it would not be discrepant from most Americans' worldviews soon after Donald Trump was elected president, which is precisely when the research was conducted.

Importantly, a reanalysis of the Klein et al. (2019) data revealed that an MS effect along the lines of what was found in the early 1990s was evident when the researchers followed the procedures advised by TMT experts among White American participants (Chatard et al., 2020). Moreover, a *p*-curve analysis of more than 800 MS studies conducted by Chen et al. (2022) showed evidential value of the MS hypothesis, suggesting that there is indeed a reliable MS effect in the literature. Such findings converge with prior meta-analytic reviews showing MS effects across a variety of domains (e.g., Burke et al., 2010). Thus, worldview defense in response to MS may take different shapes depending on individual differences, sociopolitical climates, and proximity to contemporary events, so future research should aim to further identify how such idiosyncratic, historical, and sociopolitical factors can lead to either dogmatic or open-minded engagements with the world.

Moreover, although those who dispositionally seek structure respond to death awareness with greater preference for orderly and well-defined views of the world, those low in this proclivity for structure are motivated by death awareness toward creativity and openness to non-traditional ideas (Landau et al., 2004; Routledge & Juhl, 2012). Future research could explore ways to promote structure while simultaneously encompassing prosocial values and openness to constructive change, allowing people with varying proclivities for seeking structure to defend against death awareness in ways that support more undogmatic attitudes toward other people and social issues.

Finally, future research could focus on ways to promote more intrinsic and autonomous orientations toward people's worldviews as self-determined orientations appear to mitigate MS-induced defensiveness (e.g., Williams et al., 2010). Some work has found that conscious death thought can lead to derogation of extrinsic goals (Kosloff & Greenberg, 2009), and those who have had near-death experiences or work in environments in which they are frequently exposed to death show a decreased interest in extrinsic pursuits and report a heightened focus on helping others (e.g., DeArmond, 2013; Noyes et al., 2009). It is also possible that mystical-type experiences, when occasioned in supportive and intentional contexts, may be able to shift people toward more intrinsically oriented values (Sielaff, 2021). Thus, one route for future work could be to further understand the processes underlying these shifts in dealing with death awareness and testing how explicit and deliberate considerations of death could be effectively applied more broadly (e.g., through training or death education programs) to help people manage their death-related anxieties and concerns in open-minded and prosocial ways.

Note

1. Researchers typically make mortality salient by having people respond to two open-ended questions: "Please briefly describe the emotions that the thought of your own death arouses in you" and "Jot down, as specifically as you can, what you think will happen to you physically as you die and once you are physically dead." Other manipulations of mortality salience include viewing graphic depictions of death, being interviewed in front of a funeral home, or completing fear-of-death questionnaires, among other inductions (for review, see Cox et al., 2019).

References

Arndt, J., Greenberg, J., Solomon, S., Pyszczynski, T., & Simon, L. (1997). Suppression, accessibility of death-related thoughts, and cultural worldview defense: Exploring the psychodynamics of terror management. *Journal of Personality and Social Psychology, 73*(1), 5–18.

Becker, E. (1971). *The birth and death of meaning* (2nd ed.). Free Press.

Becker, E. (1973). *The denial of death*. Free Press.

Burke, B. L., Martens, A., & Faucher, E. H. (2010). Two decades of terror management theory: A meta-analysis of mortality salience research. *Personality and Social Psychology Review, 14*(2), 155–195. https://doi.org/10.1177/1088868309352321

Campbell, C. (2015, May 12). Donald Trump trademarked a Ronald Reagan slogan and would like to stop other Republicans from using it. *Business Insider*. https://www.businessinsider.com/donald-trump-trademarked-make-america-great-again-2015-5

Chatard, A., Arndt, J., & Pyszczynski, T. (2010). Loss shapes political views? Terror management, political ideology, and the death of close others. *Basic and Applied Social Psychology, 32*(1), 2–7. https://doi.org/10.1080/01973530903539713

Chatard, A., Hirschberger, G., & Pyszczynski, T. (2020). *A word of caution about Many Labs 4: If you fail to follow your preregistered plan, you may fail to find a real effect*. PsyArXiv Preprints. https://psyarxiv.com/ejubn

Chen, L., Benjamin, R., Lai, A., & Heine, S. J. (2022). *Managing the terror of publication bias: A comprehensive p-curve analysis of the terror management theory literature*. PsyArXiv Preprints. https://psyarxiv.com/kuhy6

Cohen, F., Soenke, M., Solomon, S., & Greenberg, J. (2013). Evidence for a role of death thought in American attitudes toward symbols of Islam. *Journal of Experimental Social Psychology, 49*(2), 189–194. https://doi.org/10.1016/j.jesp.2012.09.006

Cohen, F., Solomon, S., & Kaplin, D. (2017). You're hired! Mortality salience increases Americans' support for Donald Trump. *Analyses of Social Issues and Public Policy, 17*(1), 339–357. https://doi.org/10.1111/asap.12143

Cohen, F., Solomon, S., Maxfield, M., Pyszczynski, T., & Greenberg, J. (2004). Fatal attraction: The effects of mortality salience on evaluations of charismatic, task-oriented, and relationship-oriented leaders. *Psychological Science, 15*(12), 846–851. https://doi.org/10.1111/j.0956-7976.2004.00765.x

Courtney, E. P., Felig, R. N., & Goldenberg, J. L. (2022). Together we can slow the spread of COVID-19: The interactive effects of priming collectivism and mortality salience on virus-related health behaviour intentions. *British Journal of Social Psychology, 61*, 410–431. https://doi.org/10.1111/bjso.12487

Cox, C. R., & Arndt, J. (2012). How sweet it is to be loved by you: The role of perceived regard in the terror management of close relationships. *Journal of Personality and Social Psychology, 102*(3), 616–632. http://dx.doi.org/10.1037/a0025947

Cox, C. R., Darrell, A., & Arrowood, R. B. (2019). The method behind the science: A guide to conducting terror management theory research. In C. Routledge & M. Vess (Eds.), *Handbook of terror management* (pp. 85–132). Elsevier Academic Press.

Das, E., Bushman, B. J., Bezemer, M. D., Kerkhof, P., & Vermeulen, I. E. (2009). How terrorism news reports increase prejudice against outgroups: A terror management account. *Journal of Experimental Social Psychology, 45*(3), 453–459. http://dx.doi.org/10.1016/j.jesp.2008.12.001

DeArmond, I. M. (2013). The psychological experience of hospice workers during encounters with death. *OMEGA—Journal of Death and Dying, 66*(4), 281–299. https://doi.org/10.2190/OM.66.4.a

Florian, V., Mikulincer, M., & Hirschberger, G. (2002). The anxiety-buffering function of close relationships: Evidence that relationship commitment acts as a terror management mechanism. *Journal of Personality and Social Psychology, 82*(4), 527–542. https://doi.org/10.1037/0022-3514.82.4.527

Friedman, M., & Rholes, W. S. (2007). Successfully challenging fundamentalist beliefs results in increased death awareness. *Journal of Experimental Social Psychology, 43*(5), 794–801. https://doi.org/10.1016/j.jesp.2006.07.008

Fritsche, I., Jonas, E., Fischer, P., Koranyi, N., Berger, N., & Fleischmann, B. (2007). Mortality salience and the desire for offspring. *Journal of Experimental Social Psychology, 43*(5), 753–762. https://doi.org/10.1016/j.jesp.2006.10.003

Gailliot, M. T., Stillman, T. F., Schmeichel, B. J., Maner, J. K., & Plant, E. A. (2008). Mortality salience increases adherence to salient norms and values. *Personality and Social Psychology Bulletin, 34*(7), 993–1003. https://doi.org/10.1177/0146167208316791

Greenberg, J., & Jonas, E. (2003). Psychological motives and political orientation—The left, the right, and the rigid: Comment on Jost et al. (2003). *Psychological Bulletin, 129*(3), 376–382. https://doi.org/10.1037/0033-2909.129.3.376

Greenberg, J., Pyszczynski, T., & Solomon, S. (1986). The causes and consequences of a need for self-esteem: A terror management theory. In R. F. Baumeister (Ed.), *Public self and private self* (pp. 189–212). Springer.

Greenberg, J., Pyszczynski, T., Solomon, S., Rosenblatt, A., Veeder, M., Kirkland, S., & Lyon, D. (1990). Evidence for terror management theory II: The effects of mortality salience on reactions to those who threaten or bolster the cultural worldview. *Journal of Personality and Social Psychology, 58*(2), 308–318.

Greenberg, J., Pyszczynski, T., Solomon, S., Simon, L., & Breus, M. (1994). Role of consciousness and accessibility of death-related thoughts in mortality salience effects. *Journal of Personality and Social Psychology, 67*(4), 627–637. http://dx.doi.org/10.1037/0022-3514.67.4.627

Greenberg, J., Simon, L., Pyszczynski, T., Solomon, S., & Chatel, D. (1992). Terror management and tolerance: Does mortality salience always intensify negative reactions to others who threaten one's worldview? *Journal of Personality and Social Psychology, 63*(2), 212–220.

Greenberg, J., Solomon, S., Pyszczynski, T., Rosenblatt, A., Burling, J., Lyon, D., Simon, L., & Pinel, E. (1992). Why do people need self-esteem? Converging evidence that self-esteem serves an anxiety-buffering function. *Journal of Personality and Social Psychology, 63*(6), 913–922.

Greenberg, J., Vail, K., & Pyszczynski, T. (2014). Terror management theory and research: How the desire for death transcendence drives our strivings for meaning and significance. In A. J. Elliot (Ed.), *Advances in motivation science* (pp. 85–134). Elsevier Academic Press.

Hayes, J., Schimel, J., Arndt, J., & Faucher, E. H. (2010). A theoretical and empirical review of the death-thought accessibility concept in terror management research. *Psychological Bulletin, 136*(5), 699–739. http://dx.doi.org/10.1037/a0020524

Hayes, J., Schimel, J., & Williams, T. J. (2008). Fighting death with death: The buffering effects of learning that worldview violators have died. *Psychological Science, 19*(5), 501–507. https://doi.org/10.1111/j.1467-9280.2008.02115.x

Hinckley, R. A. (2021). Local existential threat, authoritarianism, and support for right-wing populism. *The Social Science Journal*. Advance online publication. https://doi.org/10.1080/03623319.2020.1859816

Jonas, E., & Fischer, P. (2006). Terror management and religion: Evidence that intrinsic religiousness mitigates worldview defense following mortality salience. *Journal of Personality and Social Psychology, 91*(3), 553–567. http://dx.doi.org/10.1037/0022-3514.91.3.553

Jonas, E., Martens, A., Kayser, D. N., Fritsche, I., Sullivan, D., & Greenberg, J. (2008). Focus theory of normative conduct and terror-management theory: The interactive impact of mortality salience and norm salience on social judgment. *Journal of Personality and Social Psychology, 95*(6), 1239–1251. https://doi.org/10.1037/a0013593

Jonas, E., Schimel, J., Greenberg, J., & Pyszczynski, T. (2002). The Scrooge effect: Evidence that mortality salience increases prosocial attitudes and behavior. *Personality and Social Psychology Bulletin, 28*(10), 1342–1353. https://doi.org/10.1177/014616702236834

Joyce, J. (2012). *Ulysses*. Dover Publications. (Original work published 1922)

Klein, R. A., Cook, C. L., Ebersole, C., & Ratliff, K. A. (2019). *Many Labs 4: Failure to replicate mortality salience effect with and without original author involvement.* PsyArXiv Preprints. https://psyarxiv.com/vef2c

Kosloff, S., & Greenberg, J. (2009). Pearls in the desert: Death reminders provoke immediate derogation of extrinsic goals, but delayed inflation. *Journal of Experimental Social Psychology, 45*(1), 197–203. http://dx.doi.org/10.1016/j.jesp.2008.08.022

Kosloff, S., Greenberg, J., Weise, D., & Solomon, S. (2010). The effects of mortality salience on political preferences: The roles of charisma and political orientation. *Journal of Experimental Social Psychology, 46*(1), 139–145. https://doi.org/10.1016/j.jesp.2009.09.002

Landau, M. J., Greenberg, J., & Rothschild, Z. K. (2009). Motivated cultural worldview adherence and culturally loaded test performance. *Personality and Social Psychology Bulletin, 35*, 442–453. https://doi.org/10.1177/0146167208329630

Landau, M. J., Greenberg, J., Sullivan, D., Routledge, C., & Arndt, J. (2009). The protective identity: Evidence that mortality salience heightens the clarity and coherence of the self-concept. *Journal of Experimental Social Psychology, 45*(4), 796–807. https://doi.org/10.1016/j.jesp.2009.05.013

Landau, M. J., Johns, M., Greenberg, J., Pyszczynski, T., Martens, A., Goldenberg, J. L., & Solomon, S. (2004). A function of form: Terror management and structuring the social world. *Journal of Personality and Social Psychology, 87*(2), 190–210. http://dx.doi.org/10.1037/0022-3514.87.2.190

Lifshin, U., Helm, P. J., Greenberg, J., Soenke, M., Ashish, D., & Sullivan, D. (2017). Managing the death of close others: Evidence of higher valuing of ingroup identity in young adults who have experienced the death of a close other. *Self and Identity, 16*(5), 580–606. https://doi.org/10.1080/15298868.2017.1294106

McGregor, H. A., Lieberman, J. D., Greenberg, J., Solomon, S., Arndt, J., Simon, L., & Pyszczynski, T. (1998). Terror management and aggression: Evidence that mortality salience motivates aggression against worldview-threatening others. *Journal of Personality and Social Psychology, 74*(3), 590–605.

Motyl, M., Hart, J., Pyszczynski, T., Weise, D., Maxfield, M., & Siedel, A. (2011). Subtle priming of shared human experiences eliminates threat-induced negativity toward Arabs, immigrants, and peace-making. *Journal of Experimental Social Psychology, 47*, 1179–1184. https://doi.org/10.1016/j.jesp.2011.04.010

Noyes, R., Fenwick, P., Holden, J. M., & Christian, S. R. (2009). Aftereffects of pleasurable Western adult near-death experiences. In J. M. Holden, B. Greyson, & D. James (Eds.), *The handbook of near-death experiences: Thirty years of investigation* (pp. 41–62). Praeger/ABC-CLIO.

Ogilvie, D. M., Cohen, F., & Solomon, S. (2008). The undesired self: Deadly connotations. *Journal of Research in Personality, 42*(3), 564–576. https://doi.org/10.1016/j.jrp.2007.07.012

Purdum, T. S. (2001, September 17). After the attacks: The White House; Bush warns of a wrathful, shadowy and inventive war. *The New York Times.* https://www.nytimes.com/2001/09/17/us/after-attacks-white-house-bush-warns-wrathful-shadowy-inventive-war.html

Pyszczynski, T. (2013). Terror management of fear, hate, political conflict, and political violence: A review. *TPM-Testing, Psychometrics, Methodology Kin Applied Psychology, 20*(4), 313–326.

Pyszczynski, T., Abdollahi, A., Solomon, S., Greenberg, J., Cohen, F., & Weise, D. (2006). Mortality salience, martyrdom, and military might: The great Satan versus the axis of evil. *Personality and Social Psychology Bulletin, 32*(4), 525–537. https://doi.org/10.1177/0146167205282157

Pyszczynski, T., Greenberg, J., & Goldenberg, J. L. (2003). Freedom versus fear: On the defense, growth, and expansion of the self. In M. R. Leary & J. P. Tangney (Eds.), *Handbook of self and identity* (pp. 314–343). Guilford Press.

Pyszczynski, T., Greenberg, J., & Solomon, S. (1999). A dual-process model of defense against conscious and unconscious death-related thoughts: An extension of terror management theory. *Psychological Review, 106*(4), 835–845. http://dx.doi.org/10.1037/0033-295X.106.4.835

Pyszczynski, T., Motyl, M., Vail, K. E., Hirschberger, G., Arndt, J., & Kesebir, P. (2012). Drawing attention to global climate change decreases support for war. *Peace and Conflict: Journal of Peace Psychology, 18*(4), 354–368. http://dx.doi.org/10.1037/a0030328

Pyszczynski, T., Wicklund, R. A., Floresku, S., Koch, H., Gauch, G., Solomon, S., & Greenberg, J. (1996). Whistling in the dark: Exaggerated consensus estimates in response to incidental reminders of mortality. *Psychological Science, 7*(6), 332–336. https://doi.org/10.1111%2Fj.1467-9280.1996.tb00384.x

Routledge, C., & Arndt, J. (2008). Self-sacrifice as self-defence: Mortality salience increases efforts to affirm a symbolic immortal self at the expense of the physical self. *European Journal of Social Psychology, 38*, 531–541. https://doi.org/10.1002/ejsp.442

Routledge, C. D., & Arndt, J. (2009). Creative terror management: Creativity as a facilitator of cultural exploration after mortality salience. *Personality and Social Psychology Bulletin, 35*(4), 493–505. https://doi.org/10.1177/0146167208329629

Routledge, C., & Juhl, J. (2012). The creative spark of death: The effects of mortality salience and personal need for structure on creativity. *Motivation and Emotion, 36,* 478–482. https://doi.org/10.1007/s11031-011-9274-1

Routledge, C., Juhl, J., & Vess, M. (2013). Mortality salience increases death-anxiety for individuals low in personal need for structure. *Motivation and Emotion, 37,* 303–307. https://doi.org/10.1007/s11031-012-9313-6

Routledge, C., & Vess, M. (2019). *Handbook of terror management.* Elsevier Academic Press.

Schimel, J., Hayes, J., & Sharp, M. (2019). A consideration of three critical hypotheses. In C. Routledge & M. Vess (Eds.), *Handbook of terror management* (pp. 1–30). Elsevier Academic Press.

Schimel, J., Simon, L., Greenberg, J., Pyszczynski, T., Solomon, S., Waxmonsky, J., & Arndt, J. (1999). Stereotypes and terror management: Evidence that mortality salience enhances stereotypic thinking and preferences. *Journal of Personality and Social Psychology, 77*(5), 905–926. http://dx.doi.org/10.1037/0022-3514.77.5.905

Schmeichel, B. J., & Martens, A. (2005). Self-affirmation and mortality salience: Affirming values reduces worldview defense and death-thought accessibility. *Personality and Social Psychology Bulletin, 31*(5), 658–667. https://doi.org/10.1177/0146167204271567

Sielaff, A. (2021). *Investigating the potential for mystical-type experiences and related phenomena to shift existential perspectives* [Unpublished master's thesis]. University of Arizona.

Vail, K. E., Arndt, J., & Abdollahi, A. (2012). Exploring the existential function of religion and supernatural agent beliefs among Christians, Muslims, atheists, and agnostics. *Personality and Social Psychology Bulletin, 38*(10), 1288–1300. https://doi.org/10.1177%2F0146167212449361

Vail, K. E., Arndt, J., Motyl, M., & Pyszczynski, T. (2012). The aftermath of destruction: Images of destroyed buildings increase support for war, dogmatism, and death thought accessibility. *Journal of Experimental Social Psychology, 48*(5), 1069–1081. https://doi.org/10.1016/j.jesp.2012.05.004

Vail, K. E., Conti, J. P., Goad, A. N., & Horner, D. E. (2020). Existential threat fuels worldview defense, but not after priming autonomy orientation. *Basic and Applied Social Psychology, 42*(3), 150–166. https://doi.org/10.1080/01973533.2020.1726747

Vail, K. E., Courtney, E., & Arndt, J. (2019). The influence of existential threat and tolerance salience on anti-Islamic attitudes in American politics. *Political Psychology, 40*(5), 1143–1162. https://doi.org/10.1111/pops.12579

Vail, K. E., Juhl, J., Arndt, J., Vess, M., Routledge, C., & Rutjens, B. T. (2012). When death is good for life: Considering the positive trajectories of terror management. *Personality and Social Psychology Review, 16*(4), 303–329. https://doi.org/10.1177/1088868312440046

Vess, M., Arndt, J., Cox, C. R., Routledge, C., & Goldenberg, J. L. (2009). Exploring the existential function of religion: The effect of religious fundamentalism and mortality salience on faith-based medical refusals. *Journal of Personality and Social Psychology, 97*(2), 334–350. https://doi.org/10.1037/a0015545

Weise, D. R., Arciszewski, T., Verlhiac, J.-F., Pyszczynski, T., & Greenberg, J. (2012). Terror management and attitudes toward immigrants: Differential effects of mortality salience for low and high right-wing authoritarians. *European Psychologist, 17*(1), 63–72. https://doi.org/10.1027/1016-9040/a000056

Williams, T., Schimel, J., & Martens, A. (2010). The moderating role of extrinsic contingency focus on reactions to threat. *European Journal of Social Psychology, 40*(2), 300–320. https://doi.org/10.1002/ejsp.624

Zestcott, C. A., Lifshin, U., Helm, P., & Greenberg, J. (2016). He dies, he scores: Evidence that reminders of death motivate improved performance in basketball. *Journal of Sport & Exercise Psychology, 38*, 470–480. https://doi.org/10.1123/jsep.2016-0025

Zhang, R., Schimel, J., & Faucher, E. H. (2014). Bicultural terror management: Identity hybridity moderates the effect of mortality salience on biculturals' familiarity versus novelty seeking tendency. *Self and Identity, 13*(6), 714–739. https://doi.org/10.1080/15298868.2014.932835

Index

For the benefit of digital users, indexed terms that span two pages (e.g., 52–53) may, on occasion, appear on only one of those pages.

Tables and figures are indicated by *t* and *f* following the page number

abortion, polarization on, 41
acquiescence, three-factor confirmatory factor analysis model, 128, 129–32, 131*t*
actively open-minded thinking (AOT), 6–7, 12
   cognitive liberalism, 169–73
   conceptualization of, 13, 179
   cultural and individual determinants, 174–78
   cultural diversity, 172
   development of thinking standards, 172–73
   dual-process theory and cognitive reflection, 165–66
   formal approach to thinking, 163–65
   individual differences in cognitive style, 165–69
   introduction to, 162–69
   measures of, 167–69
   myside bias, 167–68
   myside bias items, 168–69
   overconfidence items, 169
   political correlates of, 169–71
   reflection/impulsivity (R/I), 166–67
   term, 162
activism, selective information-sharing, 52
Adorno, T. W., 185–86
affect
   future research on, 263
   open-mindedness and dogmatism, 13–15
   political polarization and, 262–63
   term, 13–14
affect-as-cognitive-feedback, 14–15
   account, 253, 258–61, 263–64
   affect-as-information model, 259
   attention and, 260–61
   hypothesis in context of open-mindedness, 260*f*
   impact of affect on cognition, 259–60
   Navon task and, 260–61
affect as information, 14–15
affect-as-information account, open and closed mind, 256–57
affective appraisals, contemporaneous, 242–45
affective feelings, closed-mindedness, 258
affective intelligence theory (AIT), political beliefs and behaviors, 262–63
affective polarization, 19–20, 26, 241
   evidence of, 21–33
   partisan and racial cues, 27
   partisan identity, 33–34
   persuadability, 34–35
affective states, 263–64
African Americans
   policing of, 41
   voting for Democratic candidates, 45
al-Qaeda, 238–39
Altemeyer, Bob, 185–86
   Dogmatism Scale, 212
   DOG Scale, 105
   left-wing authoritarianism (LWA) items, 188–89, 191–92, 191*t*
   RWA scale, 192–93
Amazon's Mechanical Turk platform, 189–90
American National Election Study (ANES), 20
   feeling thermometer data, 23
   feeling thermometer question, 21–7, 22*f*
   identification question, 35n.1
   individual-level variability in polarization, 28–33
   racial inequality and social services in 1992, 45
American Psychological Association, PsycInfo database, 103–4

288 Index

amount of elaboration, 7–8
ANES. *See* American National Election Study (ANES)
Anti-Defamation League, 199–200
anxiety-buffer hypothesis, terror management theory (TMT), 271–72
anxiety trigger, negative emotions, 256
AOT. *See* actively open-minded thinking (AOT)
Atlantic, The (magazine), 187
attitude(s)
    certainty, 63
    conceptualizing strength of a person's, 82
    confidence, 11
    extremity, 63
    individual differences in confidence, 69
    intergroup, 47–49
    political, 49–50
    strength of, 10, 11
    variables as sources of openness, 62–63
attitude confidence, individual differences in, 69
attitude polarization, sociological and psychological factors, 42, 43f, 53
authoritarian childrearing
    Conway et al's LWA scale and subscales, 194–96, 195t
    Van Hiel et al's LWA scale and subscales, 190, 191t
authoritarian personality, defining characteristic of, 254
Authoritarian Personality, The (Adorno et al), 185–86
authoritarian syndrome
    characteristics of, 186
    conservatism and, 186
    definition, 186
authoritarianism, 14, 179
    distortion of concept of, 200
    left- vs. right-, 204–6
    left-wing, 187, 202–5
    measure of, 186
    variable, 68
    See also left-wing authoritarianism (LWA); right-wing authoritarianism (RWA)
awe, experience of, 257–58

Baehr, Jason, 90–91
banker archetype
    form of intelligence, 236–37
    motivated deliberation, 237

Becker, Ernest, 268, 269–70, 276
belief(s)
    intellectual humility and change in, 88–90
    intellectual humility, open-mindedness, and strength of, 90–95
    perceptions of expertise, 92–93
    religious, spiritual, and moral convictions, 91–92
    superiority, 10
    uncertainty and, 81
    word, 91–92
"benevolent leader" syndrome, 26
benevolent values, defending, 278–79
biased elaboration, 9–10
biased information selection, 9
biased motive, individual differences in openness as, 69–70
Biden, Joseph, 4
Big 5 dimensions, attitude change, 67
big data, social distance and, 24–25
Big Five personality traits, 239–40, 242
bin Laden, Osama, 238–39
British Election Survey, 170
broaden-and-build theory, positive and negative emotions, 256
Bush, George W., 274

campaign messaging
    persuasion paradigm, 34–35
    rhetoric and, 34
Canada, right-wing authoritarianism in, 186
capitalism, Marx's critique of, 205
Carnegie Endowment for International Peace, 4
childhood socialization, 26
Christian(s), terror management and dogmatism, 274–75
Christian fundamentalists, Conway et al's LWA scale, 192–93, 194–95, 196–97
climate change, proposed policy, 104
climate crisis, nuclear energy, 103–4
Clinton, Hillary, 46–47, 187, 274
closed-minded, 59–60, 124
closed-minded cognition, 124
    dogmatic cognition and, 6, 124
    group contexts, 145
closed-minded defenses, preventing, 277–78
closed-minded thought, manifestations of, 9–10
closed-mindedness
    influence of affective states, 263–64

intellectual humility as opposite of, 84
rigid or narrow-minded thinking, 257
value of conviction and, 82–83
coefficient of variation, 29
cognitive biases, awareness of, 96–97
cognitive liberalism, 162–63, 176
   correlations of AOT, 169–71
   cultural and individual
      determinants, 174–78
   DivineCT (divine command and religion items), 174, 175, 177*f*
   general trait of, 169
   liberal (political liberalism), 174, 175–76, 177*f*
   method of study, 174–76
   Relig (religion), 174, 175, 177*f*
   Uscale (utilitarianism), 174, 175, 177*f*
cognitive reflection, dual-process theory and, 165–66
Cognitive Reflection Task (CRT), 216
Cognitive Reflection Test (CRT), 166
   correlations of, 172
   reflection/impulsivity (R/I), 166–67
cognitive rigidity, 215–18
   in non-political domains, 215–17
   in political domains, 218
   summary, 218–19
cognitive style, 6
Common Core learning, 113
communism, 186
communists, authoritarianism in Fromm's study, 202, 203*t*
Comprehensive Intellectual Humility Scale, 85*t*, 91–92
confidence, 10, 164–65, 219
   absolute certainty, 223
   attitude strength and, 11
   conservatism-, relationship, 221*f*, 222
   extremity-, relationship, 221*f*, 222
   in non-political domains, 219–22
   openness to change, 69
   in political domains, 223
   summary, 224
confirmation bias, people holding convictions, 83, 94
confirmatory factor analysis (CFA), 128
   situation-specific open-minded cognition (SOMC) and situation-specific open-minded normative perception (SNORM) items, 131*t*
Confucius, 172–73

congeniality hypothesis, 9
conservatism, 190
   authoritarianism and, 205–6
   cognitive rigidity and, 215
   confidence-, relationship, 221*f*, 222
   liberalism-, 225
   political, and extremism, 211–13
   political, and ideological extremity, 225–26
   social, 170, 178
   See also political conservatism
conservatives, authoritarianism items in Fromm's study, 202, 203*t*
conspiracy theories
   media and, 46–47
   selective judgment, 51–52
conventionalism, concept of, 188–89
convicted civility 93–94
conviction(s), 11, 97–98
   definition, 82
   interplay of intellectual humility, open-mindedness, and, 95–97
   open-mindedness and, 81
   religious, spiritual, and moral, 91–92
   value of, and closed-mindedness, 82–83
Conway et al research
   on Christian fundamentalists, 192–93, 194–95, 196–97
   left-wing authoritarianism (LWA), 192–96
   LWA items, 191–92, 191*t*
   LWA scale and sub scales for political and psychological measures, 194–95, 195*t*
cooperation, goal/expectation of hypothesis of, 146
core beliefs, 94
core values, 44
corrective dual-process theory, 166
cosmopolitanism, 170, 178
Costello, Thomas, C 197–98
   anti-conventionalism (AC), 197, 199–200
   anti-hierarchical aggression (AHA), 197, 199–200
   left-wing authoritarianism (LWA) research with colleagues, 196–200
   LWA scale items, 197–200
   top-down censorship (TDC), 197, 199–200
counterarguing, 9–10
COVID-19 pandemic, 64, 279
   vaccination against, 41, 103–4
creativity, open mind, 257
cultural diversity, cognitive liberalism, 172

Cultural Humility Scale, Adapted, 85t
culture wars, 41, 179
curiosity, individual differences, 69

Dalai Lama, 4
death anxiety, closed-mindedness, 255–56
death awareness, 279–81
death-thought accessibility (DTA)
  terror management and dogmatism, 275
  terror management theory, 271, 272
democracy, invention of, 248n.2
Democrat(s)
  advocates for open-mindedness, 151–52, 154–55
  American National Election Study (ANES), 35n.1
  dating and marriage, 25
  education policy, 149
  feeling thermometer data, 21, 22f
  identifying, 19, 21
  in- vs. out-party attitude differences (1964–2020), 30t
  liberal ideology affiliation of, 41–42
  liberal leanings of, 201
  liberal voters in, 201
  liberalism and authoritarianism, 205–6
  open-mindedness of party members, 150
  partisan favoritism, 27
  partisan identification, 239–40
  responses in Costello et al. items, 198–99
  resumés and labor market, 27–28
  selective exposure, 50
  social distance, 24
  "thermometer" questions about, 28–29
developmental thesis, 44
Dickens, Charles, 81
dictator game, partisan bias, 26–27
differential openness, 59–60
direction, search and inference, 164
directional bias in elaboration, 7–8
disgust emotion, closing the mind, 258
dissemination, 9
divine command theory, 170
dogmatic cognition, 6, 59–60, 124
dogmatic majority hypothesis, 152–54, 155–56
dogmatism, 5–8, 15, 179
  affect, open-mindedness and, 13–15
  affective appraisals, 240
  authoritarianism and, 253

Conway et al's LWA scale and subscales, 194–96, 195t
  data and measures of, 238–40
  definition of, 5–6, 211–12
  direction for future research, 279–81
  empirical analyses, 241–47
  individual difference measures, 239–40
  intellectual humility as opposite of, 84
  label, 233
  motivational and normative determinants of, 11–13
  open-mindedness and, 4
  political and non-political domains, 213–15
  political beliefs and, 224–25
  political conservatism and extremism, 211–13
  political conservatism and ideological extremity, 225–26
  politics and nationalism, 273–74
  predicting, 245–47
  predicting resolute partisanship, 243t
  religion, 274–75
  resolute partisanship, 239
  shark strategy, 235
  structure and stereotypes, 275–76
  term, 233–34
  terror management and, 273–76
  terror management theory, 14
  Van Hiel et al's LWA scale and subscales, 190, 191t
  variable, 68
  worldviews of open-mindedness and, 247–48
Dogmatism (DOG) Scale, Altemeyer, 105, 212
doubt, 72
dual-process theory, cognitive reflection and, 165–66

echo chambers, 41, 102
education
  core values, 44
  developmental thesis, 44
  direction of influence, 176–77
  policy of political groups, 149
  political ideology, 44
  segregation, 43–44
  socialization thesis, 44
elaboration likelihood model (ELM), 61, 66, 72
elective affinity, 186

authoritarian attitudes, 186
mutual attraction, 200–1
emotions
openness and, 67
variables affecting openness, 66
Enlightenment, 233, 235, 248n.3
environmental fitness
human species, 235–36
sharks, 234
whales, 234–35
epistemic motivation, 12
ethnicity
affective polarization, 27
segregation, 45
experience, direction of influence, 176–77
experimental design, selective exposure, 50
expertise
perceptions of, 92–93
self-perception of, 93
extremism
dogmatism, political conservatism and, 211–13
political conservatism and, 225–26
Eysenck, Hans, 185–86

fake news, susceptibility to, 170
fascism, 185–86
FBI, 199–200, 238–39
feeling of rightness, 166
feeling thermometer
individual differences in in- vs. out-party attitude differences (1964-2020), 30t
survey measures, 21–23
Feldman, Stanley, 240
filter bubbles, 102
flexible merit standard model, open-mindedness, 145–46
Foundation for Critical Thinking, 4
Fox News, partisan commentary, 33–34
Francis (Pope), 4
Frenkel-Brunswik, Else, 185–86
Fromm, Erich
landmark study in, 201–2
left- and right-wing voters on authoritarianism items of, 203t
fundamentalism, religious, 178

gay issues, tenability of, 129, 130t
General Intellectual Humility Scale, 105–6, 111
General Open-Minded Cognition (GOMC)

effect of, and tenability on SOMC, 139t
focus on directional bias, 124–26
incremental person and situation effects, 138–40
method, 138–40
overview, 127–28
SOMC and, 140
tenability and, for various scenarios, 138–40, 139t
trait open-mindedness, 126
general scenarios
materials and procedure, 134
tenability effects on SOMC mediated by SNORM, 134, 135t
General Social Survey, 41
German Public Opinion, Fromm's study, 201–2, 203t
Global Terrorism, 199–200
Goldberg, Jonah, 187
GOMC. See General Open-Minded Cognition (GOMC)
Google, political polarization and, 41
Google Trends, 41
group context
closed-minded cognition, 145
cooperation hypothesis, 146
in-group favoritism, 148
in-group–out-group hypothesis, 146–50
in-group vs. out-group members, 144
majority-minority status and open-minded cognition, 152–54
open-minded cognition, 145
open-mindedness and, 145
variable group norm hypothesis, 150–52
group decision-making, racial diversity on, 147
group polarization
group phenomenon, 144–45
producing closed-mindedness, 145

heuristic-systematic model (HSM), 61
human decision-making, science of, 233–34
human species
comparing peasant and banker, 236–37
diversity, 235
dogmatism and open-mindedness of, 233–34, 237–38, 247–48
environmental fitness of, 235–36
intelligence categories, 236
humility, individual differences, 69
Hurricane Katrina, 126, 129

identity strength, 20
ideological diversity, 147
ideological identity, group members, 147
ideology
  media and, 46–47
  sociological and structural processes, 42–47
immigration
  media and, 48
  polarization on, 41
implicit ambivalence, 63
Implicit Association Test (IAT), Party, 24
implicit bias, party affiliation, 27
individual differences in openness
  as biased motive, 69–70
  as objective motive, 69
individualism, 186
inference, 164
information processing, in-groups and out-groups, 147–49
information-seeking, links between intellectual humility and, 87–88
information sharing, selective, 52
in-group favoritism
  norm of, 148
  open-minded cognition, 148–49, 150
in-group-out-group hypothesis, group context, 146–50, 154
intellectual humility, 8, 97–98, 102–3
  benefits of, 97
  change in beliefs or opinions, 88–90
  conceptual features with open-mindedness and dogmatism, 105f
  conceptualizations of open-mindedness in measurement of, 85t
  construct, 103–7
  contributors to variability in specific, 109–14
  correlations of general and specific, by domains, topics, and tissues, 112t
  defining features of, 104
  definition of, 83–84, 85t
  as individual difference, 107
  interplay of open-mindedness, conviction and, 95–97
  links between information-seeking and, 87–88
  links between open-mindedness and, 87
  open-mindedness and, 81
  open-mindedness and strength of beliefs, 90–95

  opposite of dogmatism, 84
  opposite to closed-mindedness, 84
  as potential target of intervention, 114–16
  real-time interpersonal interactions, 89–90
  relation to open-mindedness, 83–90
  research in belief revision, 89
  specific, 107–9
Intellectual Humility Scale, 85t
Intellectual Humility subscale, Situated Wise Reasoning Scale, 85t
intergenerational transmission, polarized attitudes, 26
intergroup interactions, prisoner's dilemma games, 148
intergroup sensitivity effect, 148–49
International Baccalaureate, 4
internet censorship, general open-minded cognition and tenability, 138–40, 139t
internet restriction scenario, 138–40, 139t
  tenability of, 130t
intervention, intellectual humility as potential target of, 114–16
intolerance, identity strength and, 20
intolerance of ambiguity, 254–55
  Conway et al's LWA scale and subscales, 194–96, 195t
  Van Hiel et al's LWA scale and subscales, 190, 191t

Jean de Florette (Pagnol), 236
John Templeton Foundation, 103–4
journalism, partisan commentary of sources, 33–34
joy trigger, positive emotions, 256

K-12 curriculum, 111–13

labor market, resumés and partisanship, 27–28
Latinx households, campaign materials for, 45
left socialists, authoritarianism items in Fromm's study, 202, 203t
left-wing authoritarianism (LWA), 187–88
  correlations between scores on Conway-LWA subscales, 194–95, 195t
  correlations between scores on Van Hiel et al's-LWA subscales, 190, 191t
  Fromm landmark study, 201–2, 203t
  Loch Ness monster and, 186, 187–88, 196, 204

research by Conway and colleagues, 192–96
research by Costello and colleagues, 196–200
research by Van Hiel and colleagues, 188–92
on search for liberal-leftist, 200–2
Lerch, Christie, 162
Levinson, Daniel, 185–86
liberal-leftism, authoritarianism and, 205–6
Lincoln, Abraham, 123–24, 140–41
LWA. *See* left-wing authoritarianism (LWA)

MacKuen, Michael B., 238
majority-minority status, open-minded cognition and, 152–54
Manon of the Springs (Pagnol), 236
Marcia, James, 82–83
marijuana, legalization of, 111–13
marriage, partisanship and, 25
Marx, Karl, 205
media
  ideology and, 46–47
  political attitudes and, 49–50
  prejudices and stereotypes of American population, 48
  segregation and, 53
meta-beliefs, 106
metacognition, 173
metacognitive confidence, 10
metacognitive processes, impact of openness on, 62
MFPIGEN Stata module, 245–46
moral convictions, 11, 91–92
mortality salience (MS), 14
  closed-mindedness, 255–56
  effect of values and norms, 279–80
  future research, 279–81
  manipulations of, 281n.1
  prosocial and benevolent values, 278–79
  stereotypes, 276
  structure, 275–76
  tolerance and open-mindedness, 277–78
mortality salience (MS) hypothesis, 280
  terror management theory, 271
motivated deliberation, banker archetype, 237
motivated reasoning, peasant archetype, 237
MSNBC, partisan commentary of, 33–34

Multidimensional Intellectual Humility Scale, 85*t*
Muslims, terror management and dogmatism, 275
myside bias, 164
  belief overkill, 168
  direct measure of, 167
  indications of, 171
  items, 168–69
  polarization, 168
  predecisional distortion, 167
  probability distortion, 168
  selective exposure, 168

National Council for Social Studies, 4
nationalism, terror management and dogmatism, 273–74
Nazis, 185–86
  authoritarianism items in Fromm's study, 202, 203*t*
  rise to power in Germany, 254
need for closure
  individual differences, 69
  stereotyping, 255
need for cognition (NC) scale
  individual differences, 69
  openness, 64–65
need for order
  Conway et al's LWA scale and subscales, 194–96, 195*t*
  Van Hiel et al's LWA scale and subscales, 190, 191*t*
need to evaluate (NE) scale, 70
negative affect, 14–15
negative emotions, 256
Neuman, W. Russell, 238
neuroticism, 245
neutrality, 164
New York University, 189–90
non-political domains
  cognitive rigidity in, 215–17
  confidence in, 219–22
non-political thinking, dogmatism, 213–15
nuclear energy, climate crisis, 103–4

Obama, Barack, 46–47, 51
objective motive, individual differences in openness as, 69
online content
  automated personalization, 102
  consumption of, 102

online dating sites, 25
open and closed mind, future research on, 263
open-minded cognition, 124–26
  definition, 6–7, 253
  group contexts, 145
  majority-minority status and, 152–54
  term, 59–60
open-minded thought, manifestations of, 9–10
open-mindedness, 5–8, 15, 97–98, 233
  affect, and dogmatism, 13–15
  affective appraisals, 240
  conceptualizations of, 8
  conceptualizations of, in measurement of intellectual humility, 85t
  convictions and, 81
  correlational links between intellectual humility and, 87
  data and measures of, 238–40
  definition of, 124
  Democrat and Republican party members, 150–52
  dogmatism and, 4
  empirical analyses, 241–47
  flexible merit standard model, 145–46
  individual difference measures, 239–40
  individual differences, 124
  intellectual humility and, 81
  intellectual humility and its relation to, 83–90
  intellectual humility and strength of beliefs, 90–95
  interplay of intellectual humility, conviction and, 95–97
  motivational and normative determinants of, 11–13
  predicting, 245–47
  predicting reflective deliberation, 244t
  reflective deliberation, 239, 246f
  term, 59–60, 233–34
  terror management, tolerance and, 276–79
  value of, 83
  whale strategy, 235
  worldviews of dogmatism and, 247–48
openness, 7
  appraisal, 60
  attitude variables a sources of, 62–63
  Big 5 dimensions, 67
  considering persuasive information, 60
  definition of, 59–60
  elaboration likelihood model (ELM), 61, 66, 72
  future directions in, 71–73
  heuristic-systematic model (HSM), 61
  impact on meta-cognitive processes, 62
  impact on primary cognition, 61
  importance of signaling others, 60
  individual differences in, as biased motive, 69–70
  individual differences in, as objective motive, 69
  individual differences in general, 68–69
  individual differences in openness to experience, 69
  meaning of, 70–71
  moral basis interacting with message sidedness, 65f
  person variables as sources of, 67–70
  situational variables as sources of, 63–67
  term, 59
  treating as outcome, 60
Open Science Framework (OSF), 128, 197–98
opinions, intellectual humility and change in, 88–90
optimal thinking, general theory of, 162–63
out-group bias, 27
overconfidence, 10, 11, 101
  error, 165
  indications of, 171
  items, 169
overplacement, 101
overprecision, 101

Pagnol, Marcel, 236
parent-child correspondence, polarization, 26
parenting style, intolerance to ambiguity, 254–55
parochialism, 170, 178
partisan affect, survey measures of, 21–23, 22f
partisan beliefs, media and, 46–47
partisan bias, behavioral evidence of, 26–28
partisan favoritism, evidence of, 27
partisan identity, 20
  affective polarization and, 33–34
  thermometer differences, 33, 34f
partisan polarization, defining, 19
partisan selective exposure, 9
partisanship
  affective polarization, 27

driver of affective polarization, 31–33
  marriage, 25
  online dating and, 24–25
Party Implicit Association Test (IAT), 24
party members, open-mindedness of, 150–52
party polarization, regression model, 31, 32t, 33t
patriotism, 186
peasant archetype
  form of intelligence, 236–37
  motivated reasoning, 237
Pentagon, terrorist attack, 274
perceptions of openness, 65–66
person-situation incremental validity, scale validation and, 127
person variables, sources of openness, 67–70
Personal Attitude Stability Scale (PASS), 68
persuadability, 34–35
persuasion
  key process of, 72
  openness and, 70–71
  openness of person as recipient of, 72
persuasion bad, 70–71
persuasion good, 70–71
persuasion paradigm, 34–35
persuasive message, openness, 64–65
Peterson, Jordan, 202–4
Pew Research Center, 25
polarization, 5–8, 15
  affective, 19–20
  ANES time series identifying individual-level variability, 28–33
  definition of, 5, 19
  evidence of affective, 21–33
  intergenerational transmission of attitudes, 26
  open-mindedness, dogmatism, and, 4–5
  parent-child correspondence on, 26
  partisan, 19
  political ideology and, 41–42
  predictor variables of, 29
  regression analysis of, 31, 32t
polarized attitudes, sociological and psychological factors, 42, 43f
political conservatism
  Conway et al's LWA scale and subscales, 194–96, 195t
  dogmatism, and extremism, 211–13
  Van Hiel et al's LWA scale and subscales, 190, 191t
  See also conservatism

political dispositions, contemporaneous, 242–45
political domains
  cognitive rigidity, 218
  confidence in, 223
political ideology, 15
  absolute certainty, 223
  cognitive rigidity in, 218
  conceptualizations of, 212
  dogmatism and, 224–25
  education and, 44
  liberalism-conservatism, 225
  open-mindedness and, 4–5
  polarization and, 41–42
  race and ethnicity in, 45
political polarization
  affect and, 262–63
  cultural wars and, 41
  Google and, 41
  political attitudes and, 49–50
  term, 3–4
political scenarios
  materials and procedure, 134
  tenability effects on SOMC mediated by SNORM, 134, 136t
political thinking, dogmatism, 213–15
political tolerance, 20
politics, terror management and dogmatism, 273–74
Portrait Values Questionnaire, 105–6
positive affect, experience of, 257
positive emotions, 256
predecisional distortion, 167
prejudice, intergroup attitudes, 47–49
primary cognition, impact on openness on, 61
prisoner's dilemma games, interindividual interactions in, 148
Profiles of Individual Radicalization in the United States, 199–200
prosocial values, defending, 278–79
proximal defenses, terror management theory, 271
psychological processes, 43–44
  intergroup attitudes, 47–49
  political attitudes, 49–50
  selective exposure, 47–50
  selective judgment, 50–52
  selective sharing, 52
Puerto Rico, on becoming a US state, 155–56

race
  segregation, 45
  selective media exposure, 48
Race Implicit Association Test (IAT), 24
racial diversity, group decision-making, 147
racial stereotypes, intergroup attitudes, 47–48
radical traditional, phrase, 192–93
receptiveness, term, 59
reciprocity, social influence principle of, 63–64
reflective deliberation
  agreeableness and fear interaction, 246–47, 246f
  banker archetype, 237
  open-mindedness, 240, 241, 249n.11
  open-minded reactions, 239
  predicting, 242–45, 244t
  resolute partisanship and, 241–42
relative standard deviation (RSD), 29
  in- vs. out-party attitude differences, 30t, 31
religion, terror management and dogmatism, 274–75
religious convictions, 91–92
religious scenarios
  materials and procedure, 134
  tenability effects on SOMC mediated by SNORM, 134, 137t
Remote Association Test, 216
Republican(s)
  advocates for open-mindedness, 151–52, 154–55
  American National Election Study (ANES), 35n.1
  conservatism and authoritarianism, 205–6
  conservative voters, 201
  dating and marriage, 25
  education policy, 149
  feeling thermometer data, 21, 22f
  identifying, 19, 21
  in- vs. out-party attitude differences (1964–2020), 30t
  open-mindedness of party members, 150
  partisan favoritism, 27
  partisan identification, 239–40
  responses in Costello et al. items, 198–99
  resumés and labor market, 27–28
  selective exposure, 50
  social distance, 24
  "thermometer" questions about, 28–29
resistance, term, 11–12, 59
resistance to persuasion, 9–10, 11–12
resolute partisanship
  dogmatic reactions, 239
  dogmatism, 240, 241, 249n.10
  peasant archetype, 237
  predicting, 242–45, 243t
  reflective deliberation and, 241–42
right-wing authoritarianism (RWA), 186
  characterization of, 254
  Christian fundamentalists, 204
  mortality salience and, 277
  voters on authoritarianism items of Fromm's study, 203t
  See also left-wing authoritarianism (LWA)
right-wing authoritarians, The Weathermen and, 196
right-wing conservatism, authoritarianism and, 205–6
right-wing extremism, 185–86
rigidity of the extremes, model, 212
rigidity of the right, model, 212
Rokeach Dogmatism Scale, 105
Roosevelt, Theodore, 187
Russell, Bertrand, 205

Sanford, R. Nevitt, 185–86
search and seizure scenario
  general open-minded cognition and tenability, 138–40, 139t
  tenability of, 130t
search-inference framework, 164
segregation, 43–45, 53
  ideology, 41–42
  media and, 46–47
  race and ethnicity, 45
  selective information-processing, 53
  socioeconomic status and education, 43–44
selective exposure
  intergroup attitudes, 47–49
  political attitudes, 49–50
selective judgment, 9, 50–52
selective sharing, information, 9, 52
self-perception, expertise, 93
self-reflection, facilitating openness, 66
self-validation theory (SVT), 62
Shils, Edward, 185–86

situation-specific open-minded cognition (SOMC), 124, 140–41
　factorial and discriminant validation of, 128–32
　general scenarios, 135t
　General Open-Minded Cognition (GOMC) and, 139t, 140
　incremental person and situation effects, 138–40
　normative beliefs and intention, 126–27
　open-mindedness, 13
　political scenarios, 136t
　religious scenarios, 137t
　scale validation and incremental person-situation effect, 127
　situational scenarios, 130t
　tenability effect on, 134, 135t, 136t, 137t
　theoretical model, 125f
　three-factor confirmatory factor analysis model, 131t
situation-specific open-minded normative perception (SNORM), 140–41
　general scenarios, 135t, 139t
　incremental person and situation effects, 138–40
　political scenarios, 136t, 139t
　religious scenarios, 137t, 139t
　tenability effect on, 134, 135t, 136t, 137t
　three-factor confirmatory factor analysis model, 131t
situational variables, as sources of openness, 63–67
SNORM. See situation-specific open-minded normative perception (SNORM)
social cognitive theory, 49
social conservatism, 170, 178
social democrats, authoritarianism items in Fromm's study, 202, 203t
social distance, indicators of, 24–25
social identity, 49
social identity theory, 19, 48
　group memberships, 146–47
socialization, childhood, 26
socialization thesis, 44
socioeconomic status, segregation, 43–44
Socrates, 172–73
SOMC. See situation-specific open-minded cognition (SOMC)
sorting, term, 20
Southern Poverty Law Center, 199–200

specific intellectual humility, 107–9
　contributors to variability in, 109–14
　domain/topic/issue, 108–9, 110, 111–13, 112t
　model in conceptual form, 110
　people's beliefs about position, 108
Specific Intellectual Humility Scale, 85t, 113
spiritual convictions, 91–92
spiritual insight scenario
　general open-minded cognition and tenability, 138–40, 139t
　tenability of, 129, 130t
Stanovich, Keith, 162
State-Trait Intellectual Humility Scale, 85t
Stenner, Karen, 240
strength of attitudes, as sources of openness, 62–63
subjective norm (SNORM), 124
　open-mindedness, 13
　overview, 127–28
　theoretical model, 125f

tenability
　general scenarios, 135t
　political scenarios, 136t
　religious scenarios, 137t
　situational scenarios and, 130t
terrorism stories, 238–39
terrorist attacks
　Pentagon, 274
　World Trade Center, 274
terror management
　bright side to, 276–79
　direction for future research, 279–81
　dogmatism and, 273–76
　in everyday life, 272
　politics and nationalism, 273–74
　religion, 274–75
　structure and stereotypes, 275–76
　tolerance and open-mindedness, 276–79
terror management theory (TMT), 269–72
　anxiety-buffer hypothesis, 271–72
　death-thought accessibility (DTA) hypothesis, 271, 272
　dogmatism, 14
　empirical evidence for, 271–72
　opening and closing of mind, 255–56
　proximal defenses, 271
Theory of Affective Intelligence, 240

thinking
   development of standards, 172–73
   evidence, 163
   formal approach to, 163–65
   goals, 163
   possibilities, 163
Thinking and Deciding (Lerch), 162
thought, direction of influence, 176–77
Toplak, Maggie, 162
troubled confusion, identity, 96
Trump, Donald, 35, 46–47, 196, 204–5, 274, 279–80
trust game, partisan bias, 26–27

uncertainty, beliefs and, 81
United States
   authoritarianism in, 186, 187
   left-wing authoritarianism in, 187
   partisan identification, 239–40
University of Toronto, 202–4
Upbringing, direction of influence, 176–77
US Capitol building, January 6, 2021 attack on, 196
US Supreme Court, majority and minority written opinions, 153
utilitarian moral reasoning, 170

vaccination, COVID-19, 103–4, 108–9
Van Hiel, Alain
   left-wing authoritarianism (LWA) research, 188–92
   sample of political activists, 189
   scores on LWA scale and subscales for political and psychological measures, 190, 191*t*
variable group norm hypothesis, group context, 150–52
Vietnam War, 196

Weathermen, The, underground leftists, 196
West, Richard, 162
Wilson, Woodrow, 187
Wisconsin Card Sorting Test, 216
World Trade Center, 274
World War II, 202–4, 254
worldview, intrinsic (versus extrinsic), 277–78